ONE

PRESENTS

モブサイコ100

MOB PSYCHO

100

VOLUME 1

DARK HORSE MANGA

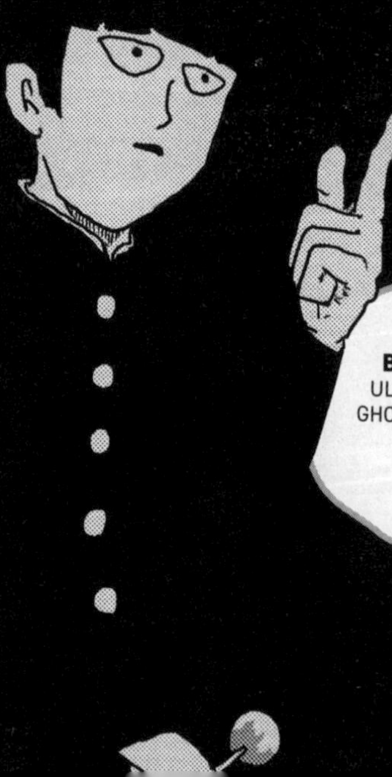

MOB PSYCHO 100 VOLUME 1
Translated by
KUMAR SIVASUBRAMANIAN
Lettering and Retouch by
JOHN CLARK
Edited by
CARL GUSTAV HORN

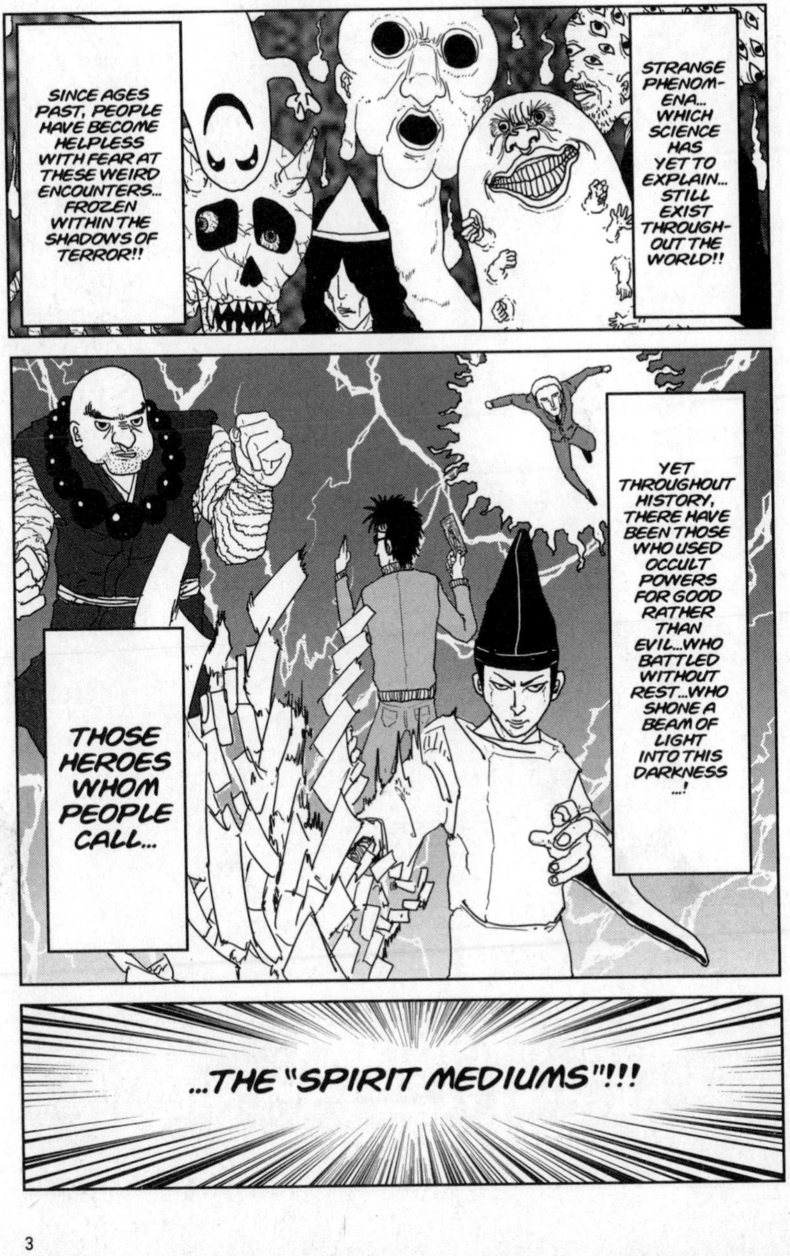
STRANGE PHENOMENA... WHICH SCIENCE HAS YET TO EXPLAIN... STILL EXIST THROUGHOUT THE WORLD!!
SINCE AGES PAST, PEOPLE HAVE BECOME HELPLESS WITH FEAR AT THESE WEIRD ENCOUNTERS... FROZEN WITHIN THE SHADOWS OF TERROR!!
YET THROUGHOUT HISTORY, THERE HAVE BEEN THOSE WHO USED OCCULT POWERS FOR GOOD RATHER THAN EVIL...WHO BATTLED WITHOUT REST...WHO SHONE A BEAM OF LIGHT INTO THIS DARKNESS...!
THOSE HEROES WHOM PEOPLE CALL...
...THE "SPIRIT MEDIUMS"!!!

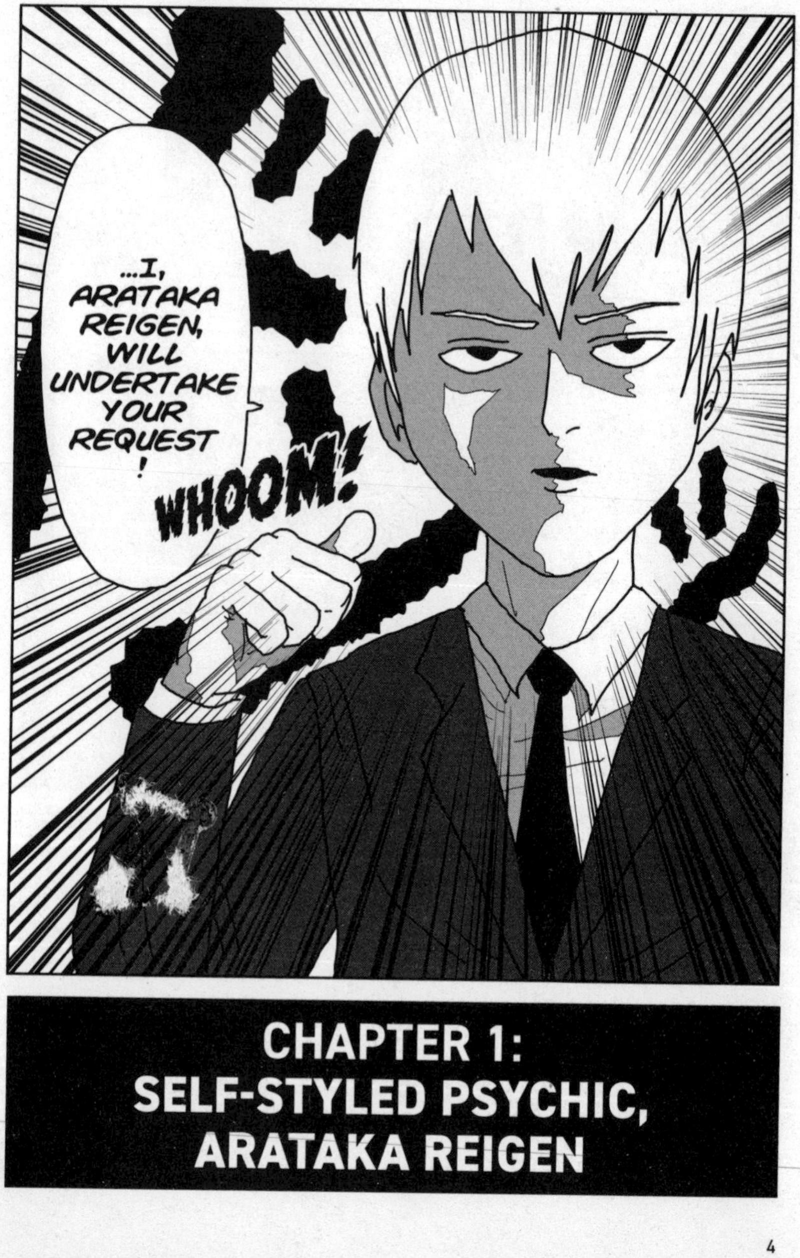
...I, ARATAKA REIGEN, WILL UNDERTAKE YOUR REQUEST!
WHOOM!

CHAPTER 1: SELF-STYLED PSYCHIC, ARATAKA REIGEN

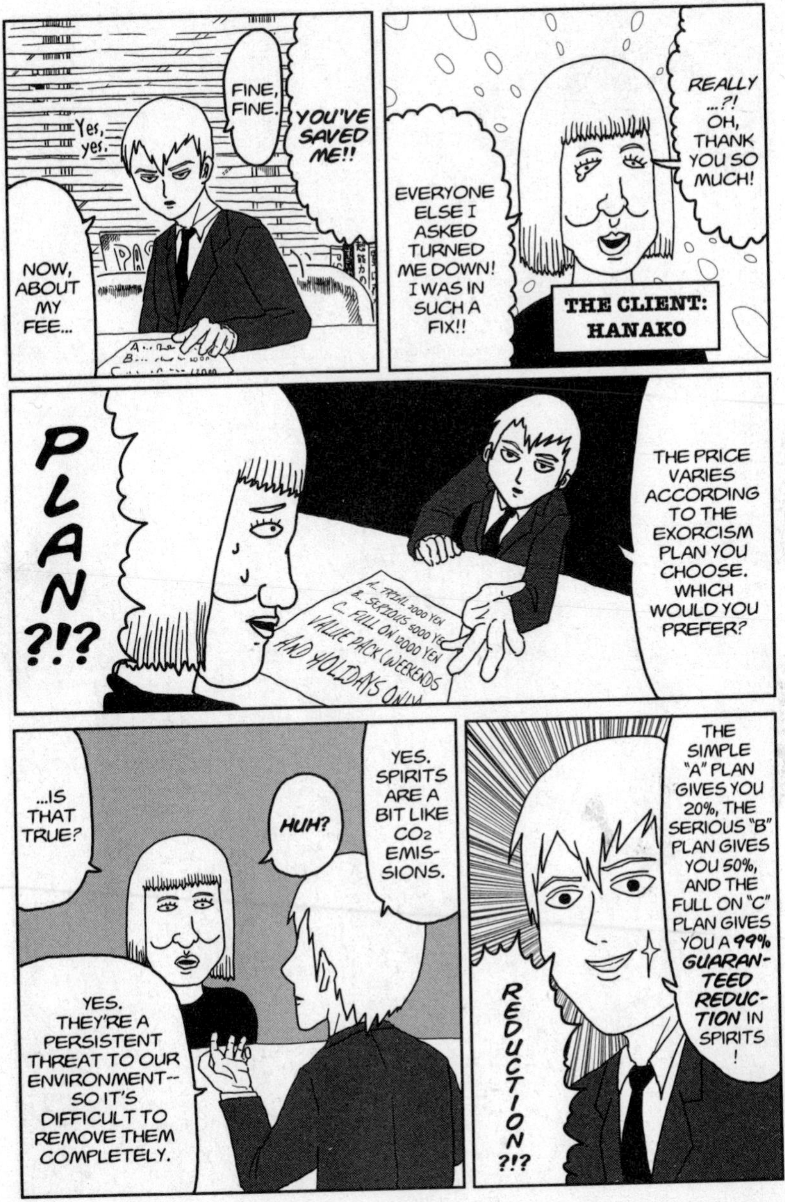
REALLY ...?! OH, THANK YOU SO MUCH!
EVERYONE ELSE I ASKED TURNED ME DOWN! I WAS IN SUCH A FIX!!
THE CLIENT: HANAKO
YOU'VE SAVED ME!!
FINE, FINE.
Yes, yes.
NOW, ABOUT MY FEE...
THE PRICE VARIES ACCORDING TO THE EXORCISM PLAN YOU CHOOSE. WHICH WOULD YOU PREFER?
A. TRIAL 2000 YEN
B. SERIOUS 5000 YEN
C. FULL ON 12000 YEN
VALUE PACK (WEEKENDS AND HOLIDAYS ONLY
PLAN?!?
THE SIMPLE "A" PLAN GIVES YOU 20%, THE SERIOUS "B" PLAN GIVES YOU 50%, AND THE FULL ON "C" PLAN GIVES YOU A 99% GUARANTEED REDUCTION IN SPIRITS!
REDUCTION?!?
YES. SPIRITS ARE A BIT LIKE CO_2 EMISSIONS.
HUH?
...IS THAT TRUE?
YES. THEY'RE A PERSISTENT THREAT TO OUR ENVIRONMENT-- SO IT'S DIFFICULT TO REMOVE THEM COMPLETELY.

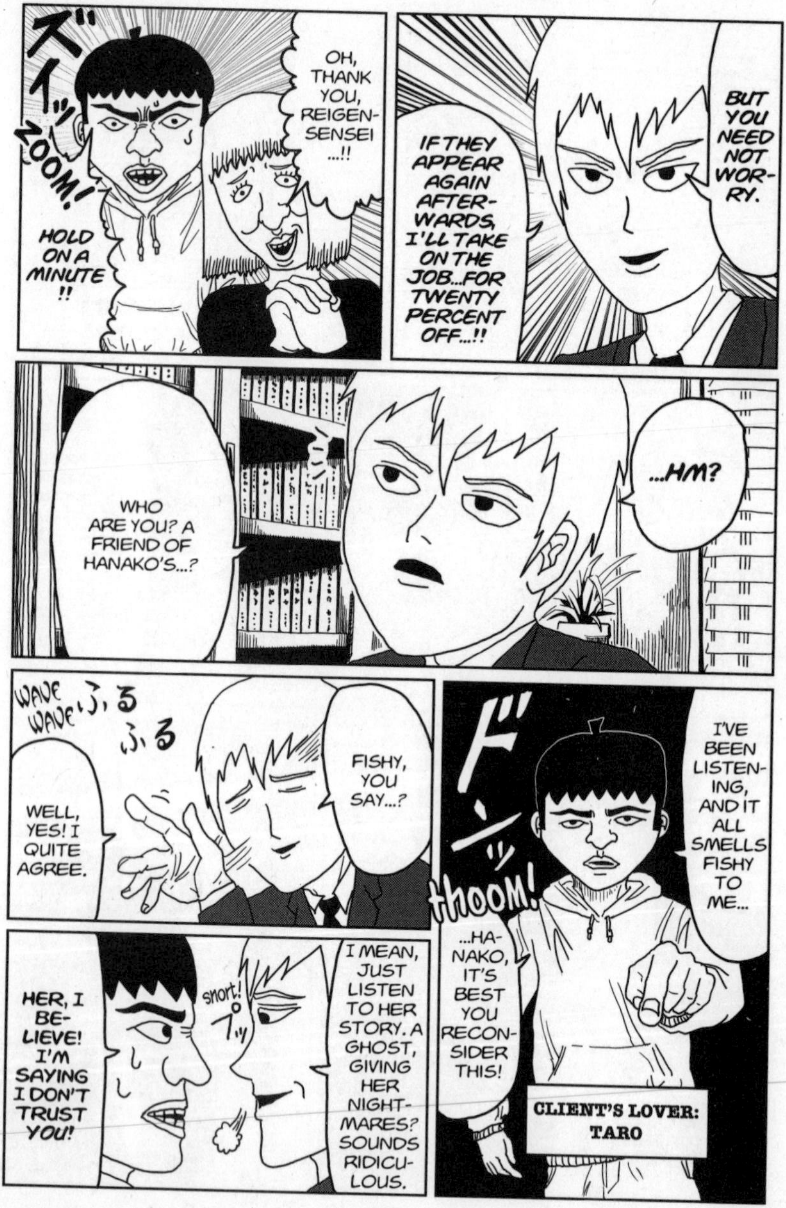
BUT YOU NEED NOT WORRY.
IF THEY APPEAR AGAIN AFTERWARDS, I'LL TAKE ON THE JOB...FOR TWENTY PERCENT OFF...!!
OH, THANK YOU, REIGEN-SENSEI ...!!
ズイッ
ZOOM!
HOLD ON A MINUTE !!
...HM?
WHO ARE YOU? A FRIEND OF HANAKO'S...?
ドンッ
thoom!
I'VE BEEN LISTENING, AND IT ALL SMELLS FISHY TO ME...
...HANAKO, IT'S BEST YOU RECONSIDER THIS!
CLIENT'S LOVER: TARO
FISHY, YOU SAY...?
ふるふる
WAVE WAVE
WELL, YES! I QUITE AGREE.
I MEAN, JUST LISTEN TO HER STORY. A GHOST, GIVING HER NIGHTMARES? SOUNDS RIDICULOUS.
プッ
snort!
HER, I BELIEVE! I'M SAYING I DON'T TRUST YOU!

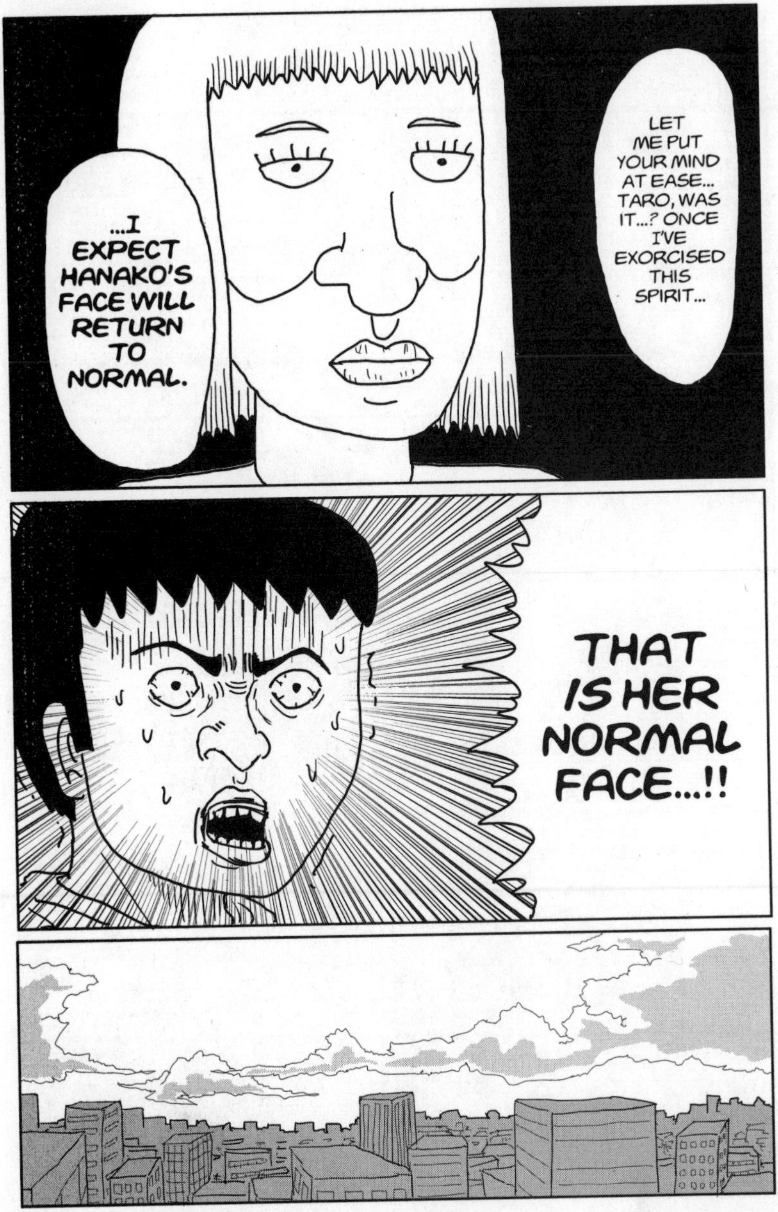
LET ME PUT YOUR MIND AT EASE... TARO, WAS IT...? ONCE I'VE EXORCISED THIS SPIRIT...
...I EXPECT HANAKO'S FACE WILL RETURN TO NORMAL.
THAT IS HER NORMAL FACE...!!

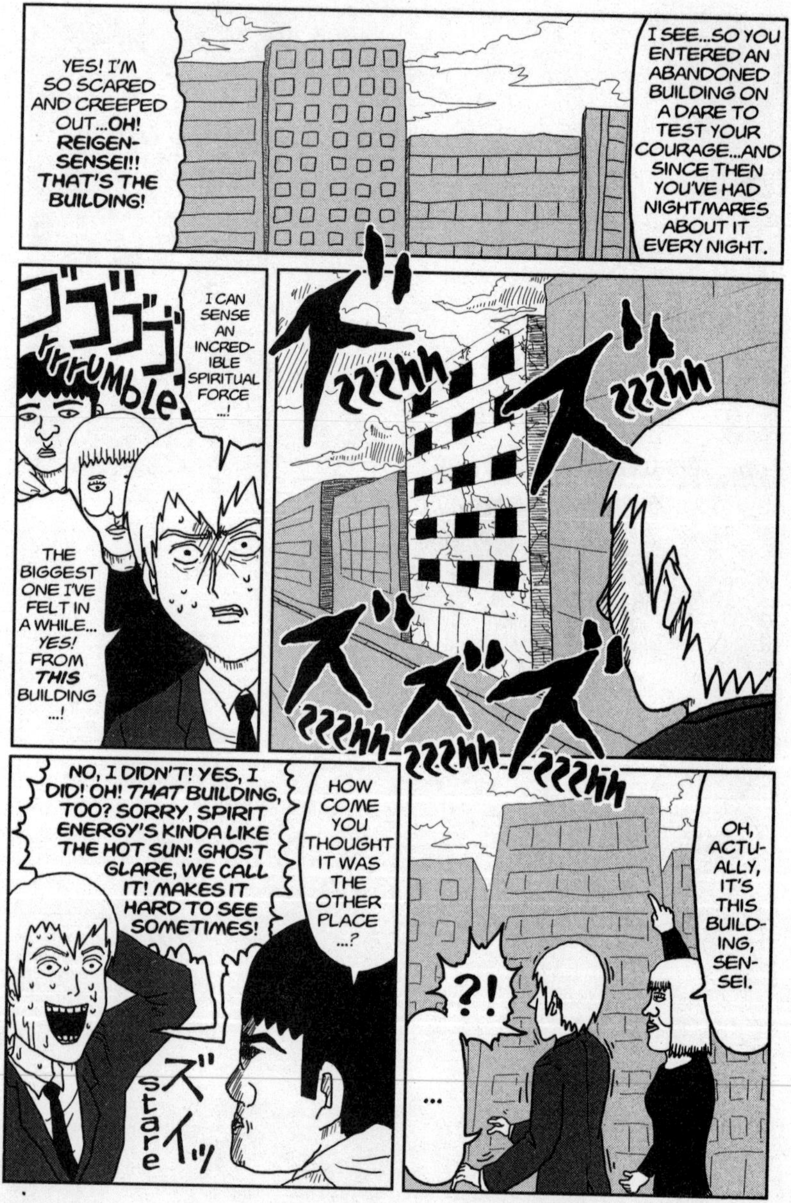

I SEE...SO YOU ENTERED AN ABANDONED BUILDING ON A DARE TO TEST YOUR COURAGE...AND SINCE THEN YOU'VE HAD NIGHTMARES ABOUT IT EVERY NIGHT.
YES! I'M SO SCARED AND CREEPED OUT...OH! REIGEN-SENSEI!! THAT'S THE BUILDING!
ズ
zzzzhn
ズ
zzzzhn
ズズズ
zzzzhn
zzzzhn
zzzzhn
I CAN SENSE AN INCREDIBLE SPIRITUAL FORCE ...!
ゴゴゴ
rrrumble
THE BIGGEST ONE I'VE FELT IN A WHILE... YES! FROM THIS BUILDING ...!
OH, ACTUALLY, IT'S THIS BUILDING, SENSEI.
?!
...
HOW COME YOU THOUGHT IT WAS THE OTHER PLACE ...?
NO, I DIDN'T! YES, I DID! OH! THAT BUILDING, TOO? SORRY, SPIRIT ENERGY'S KINDA LIKE THE HOT SUN! GHOST GLARE, WE CALL IT! MAKES IT HARD TO SEE SOMETIMES!
ズイッ
stare

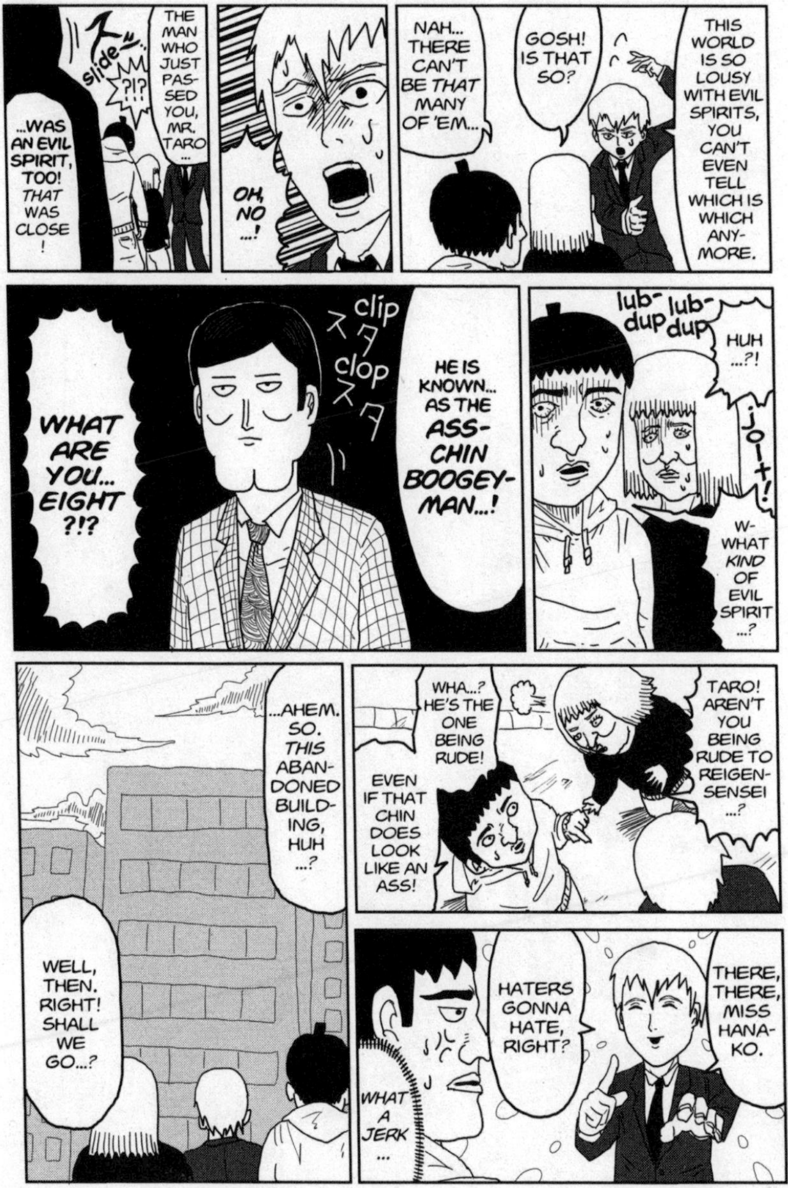
THIS WORLD IS SO LOUSY WITH EVIL SPIRITS, YOU CAN'T EVEN TELL WHICH IS WHICH ANYMORE.
GOSH! IS THAT SO?
NAH... THERE CAN'T BE *THAT* MANY OF 'EM...
OH, NO ...!
THE MAN WHO JUST PASSED YOU, MR. TARO...
slide
?!?
...WAS AN EVIL SPIRIT, TOO! *THAT WAS CLOSE!*
lub-dup lub-dup
HUH ...?!
jolt!
W-WHAT *KIND* OF EVIL SPIRIT ...?
HE IS KNOWN... AS THE **ASS-CHIN BOOGEYMAN...!**
clip スタ clop スタ
WHAT ARE YOU... EIGHT ?!?
TARO! AREN'T YOU BEING RUDE TO REIGEN-SENSEI ...?
WHA...? HE'S THE ONE BEING RUDE!
EVEN IF THAT CHIN DOES LOOK LIKE AN ASS!
THERE, THERE, MISS HANAKO.
HATERS GONNA HATE, RIGHT?
WHAT A JERK ...
...AHEM. SO. *THIS* ABANDONED BUILDING, HUH ...?
WELL, THEN. RIGHT! SHALL WE GO...?

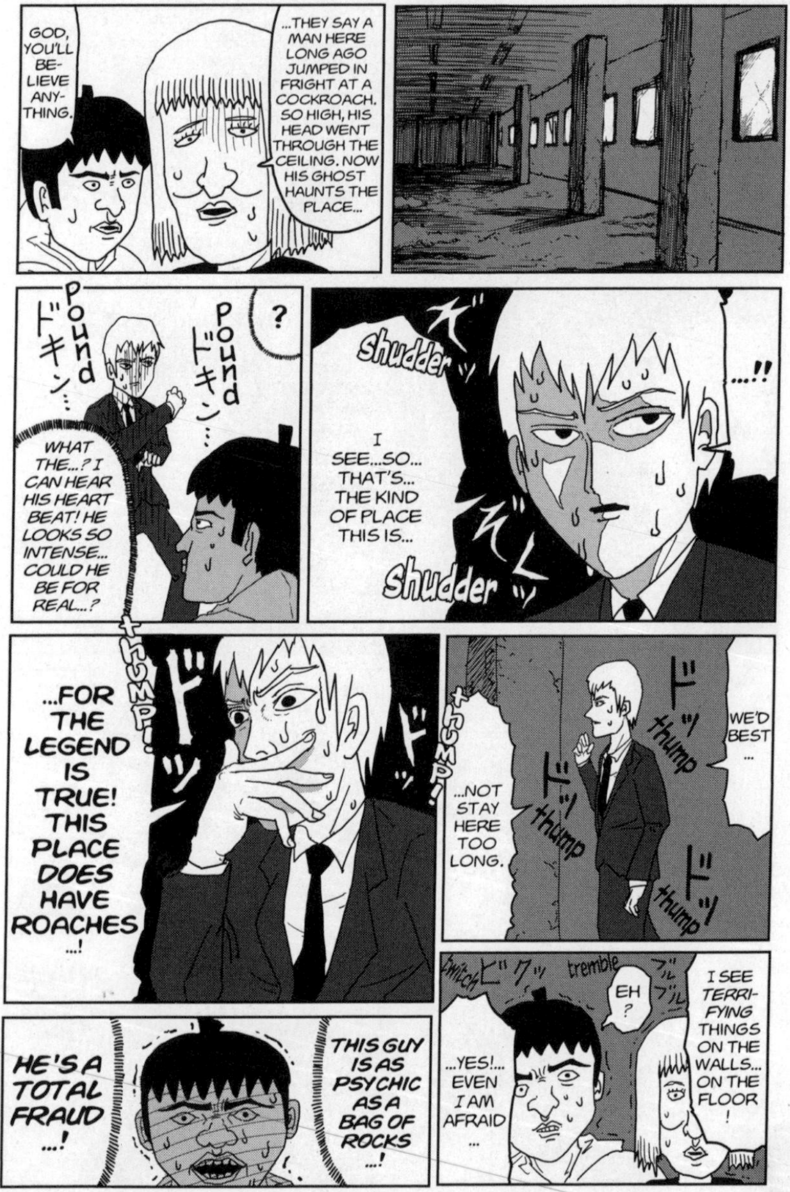
...THEY SAY A MAN HERE LONG AGO JUMPED IN FRIGHT AT A COCKROACH. SO HIGH, HIS HEAD WENT THROUGH THE CEILING. NOW HIS GHOST HAUNTS THE PLACE...
GOD, YOU'LL BE-LIEVE ANY-THING.
shudder ゾッ
...!!
I SEE...SO... THAT'S... THE KIND OF PLACE THIS IS...
shudder ぞわっ
?
Pound ドキン
Pound ドキン…
WHAT THE...? I CAN HEAR HIS HEART BEAT! HE LOOKS SO INTENSE... COULD HE BE FOR REAL...?
WE'D BEST...
...NOT STAY HERE TOO LONG.
thump ドッ
thump ドッ
thump ドッ
thump!
thump!
ドッ
ドッ
...FOR THE LEGEND IS TRUE! THIS PLACE DOES HAVE ROACHES...!
twitch ビクッ
tremble ブルブル
I SEE TERRI-FYING THINGS ON THE WALLS... ON THE FLOOR!
EH?
...YES!... EVEN I AM AFRAID...
THIS GUY IS AS PSYCHIC AS A BAG OF ROCKS...!
HE'S A TOTAL FRAUD...!

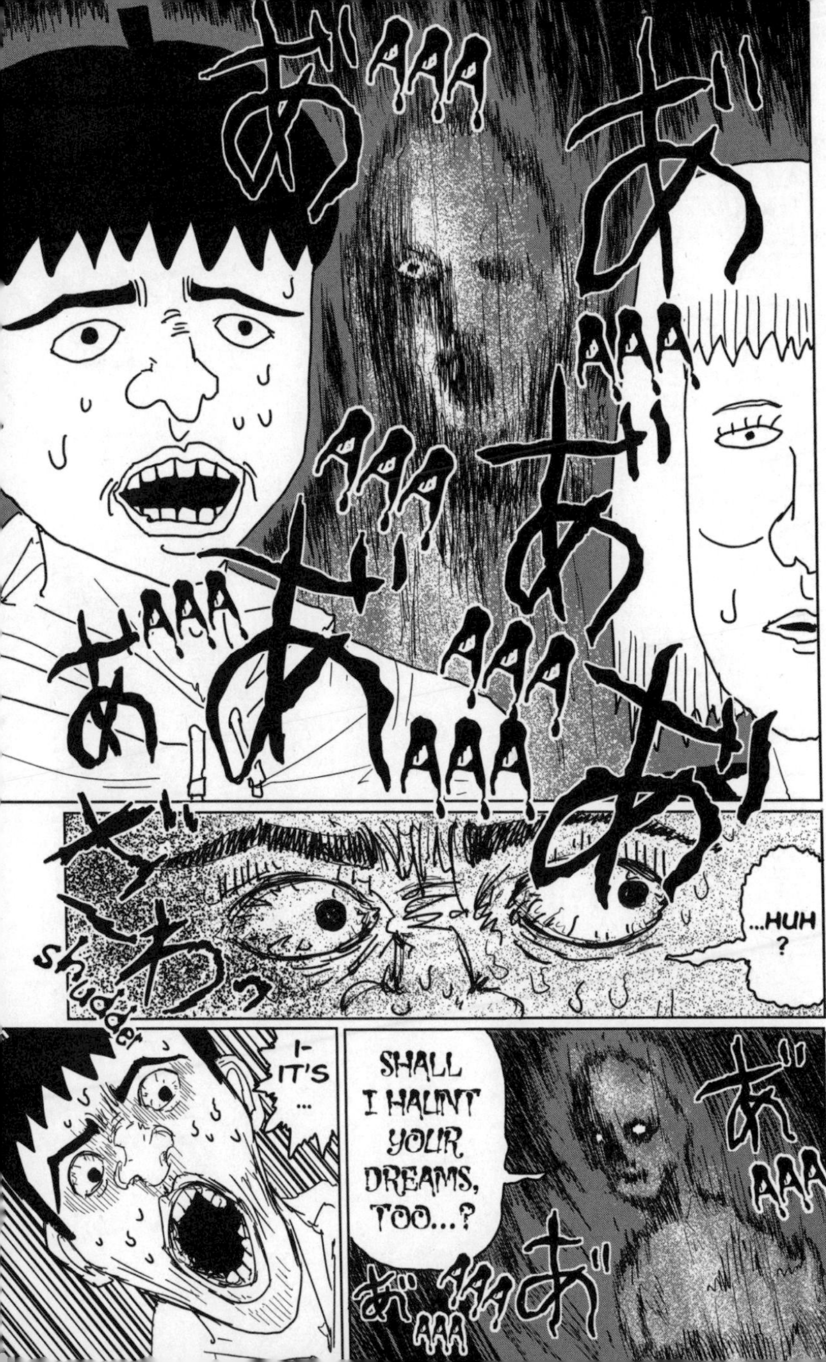
あ゛AAA
あ゛AAA
あ゛AAA
あ゛AAA
あ゛AAA AAA
あ゛
...HUH ?
ざわっ
shudder
あ゛AAA
SHALL I HAUNT YOUR DREAMS, TOO...?
あ゛AAA あ゛AAA
I- IT'S ...

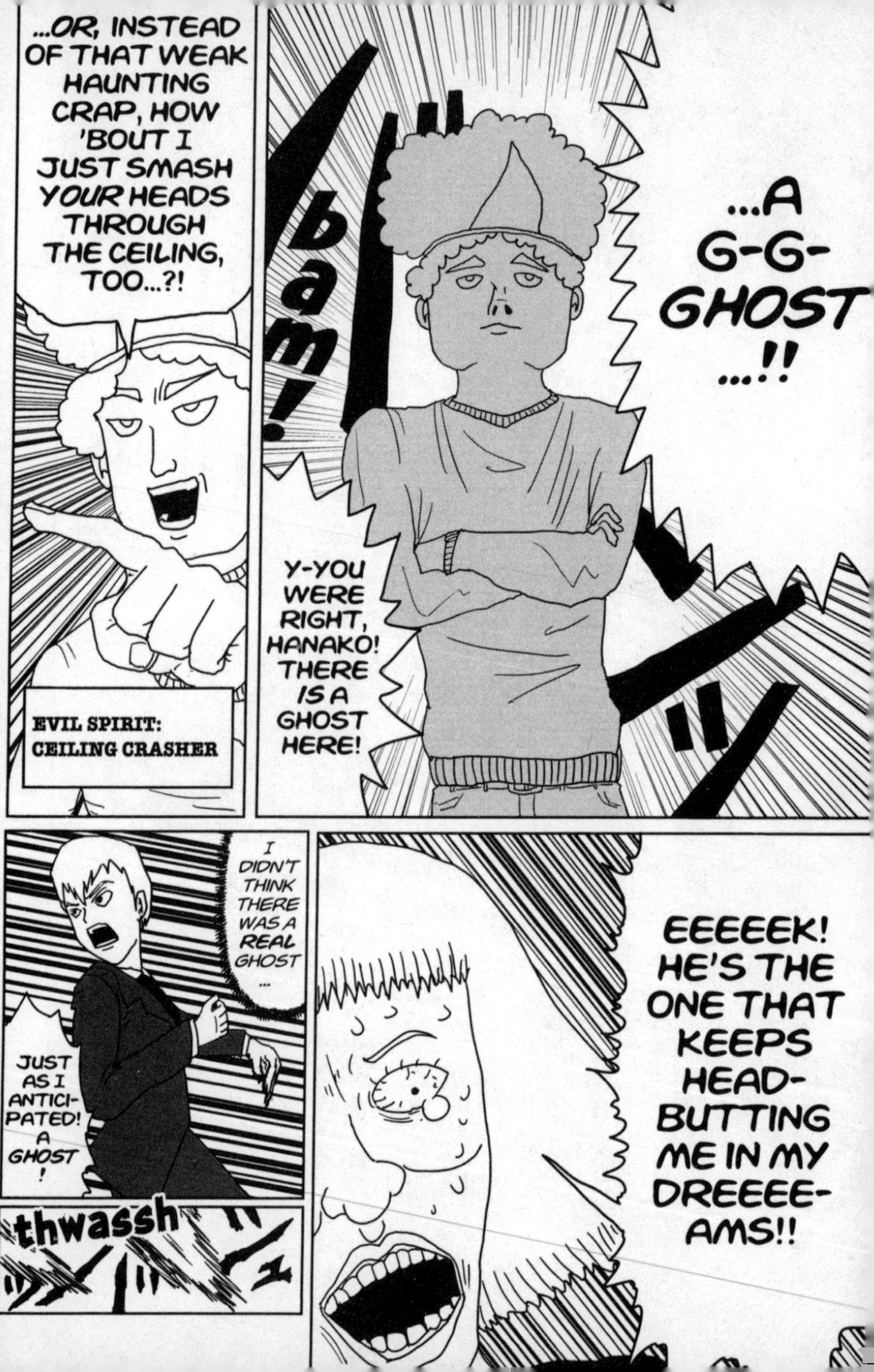

...A G-G-GHOST ...!!
bam!
Y-YOU WERE RIGHT, HANAKO! THERE IS A GHOST HERE!
...OR, INSTEAD OF THAT WEAK HAUNTING CRAP, HOW 'BOUT I JUST SMASH YOUR HEADS THROUGH THE CEILING, TOO...?!
EVIL SPIRIT: CEILING CRASHER
EEEEEK! HE'S THE ONE THAT KEEPS HEAD-BUTTING ME IN MY DREEEEE-AMS!!
I DIDN'T THINK THERE WAS A REAL GHOST ...
JUST AS I ANTICI-PATED! A GHOST !
thwassh

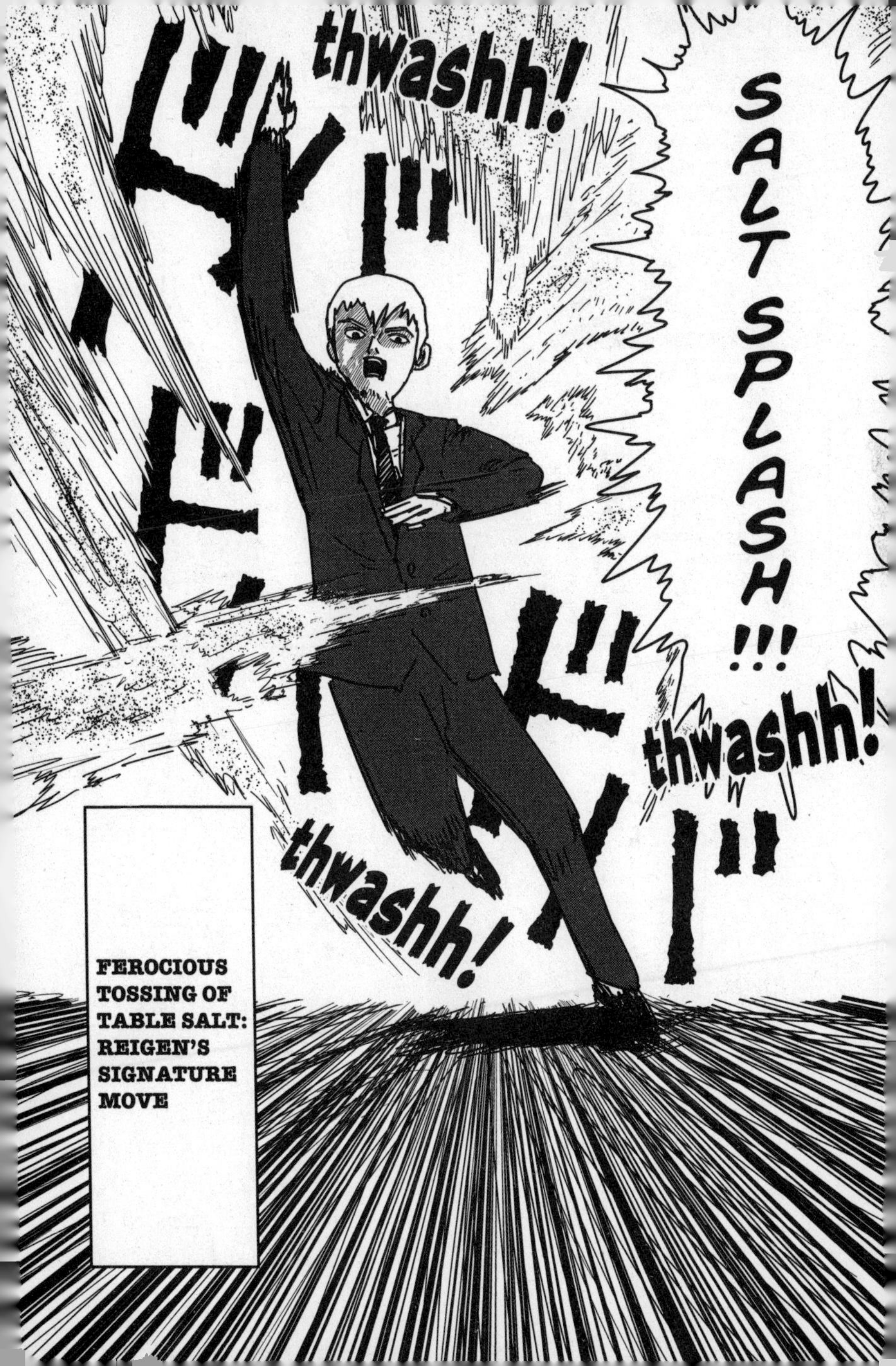
SALT SPLASH!!!
thwashh!
thwashh!
thwashh!
FEROCIOUS TOSSING OF TABLE SALT: REIGEN'S SIGNATURE MOVE

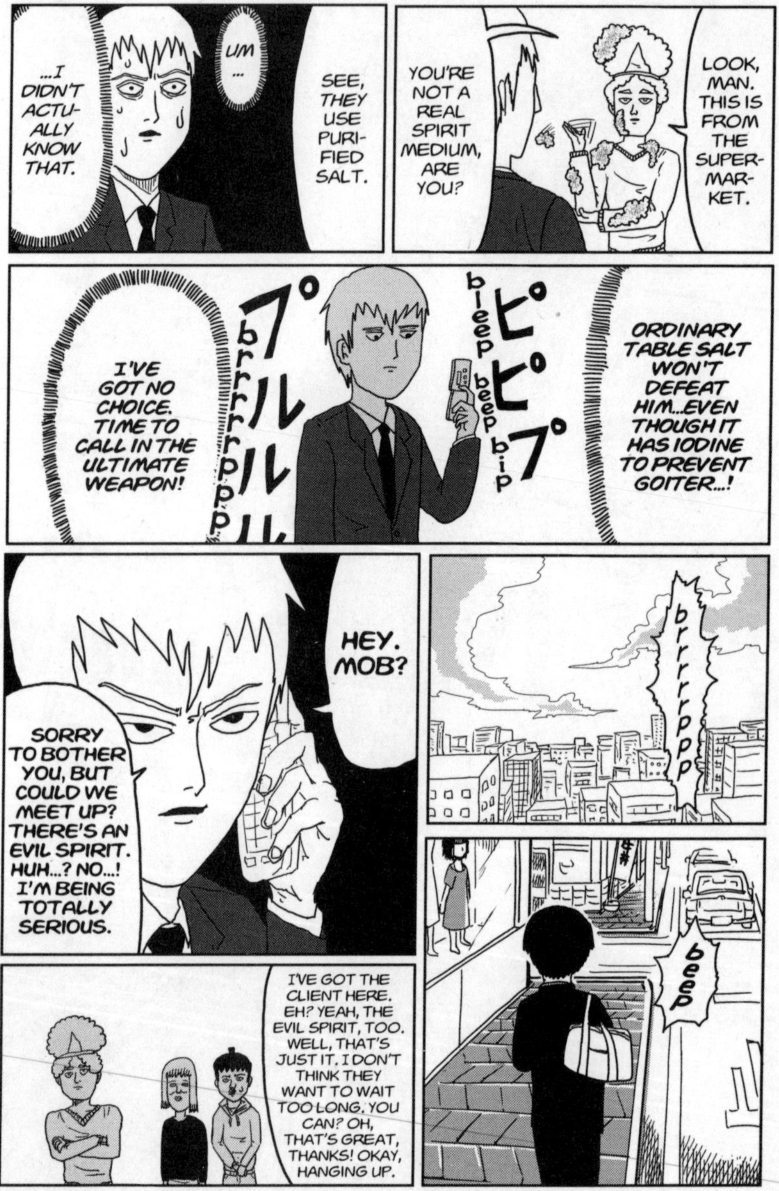
LOOK, MAN. THIS IS FROM THE SUPER-MAR-KET.
YOU'RE NOT A REAL SPIRIT MEDIUM, ARE YOU?
SEE, THEY USE PURI-FIED SALT.
UM ...
...I DIDN'T ACTU-ALLY KNOW THAT.
ORDINARY TABLE SALT WON'T DEFEAT HIM...EVEN THOUGH IT HAS IODINE TO PREVENT GOITER...!
ピピプ
bleep beep bip
プルルル
brrrrrppp
I'VE GOT NO CHOICE. TIME TO CALL IN THE ULTIMATE WEAPON!
brrrrrppp
beep
HEY. MOB?
SORRY TO BOTHER YOU, BUT COULD WE MEET UP? THERE'S AN EVIL SPIRIT. HUH...? NO...! I'M BEING TOTALLY SERIOUS.
I'VE GOT THE CLIENT HERE. EH? YEAH, THE EVIL SPIRIT, TOO. WELL, THAT'S JUST IT. I DON'T THINK THEY WANT TO WAIT TOO LONG. YOU CAN? OH, THAT'S GREAT, THANKS! OKAY, HANGING UP.

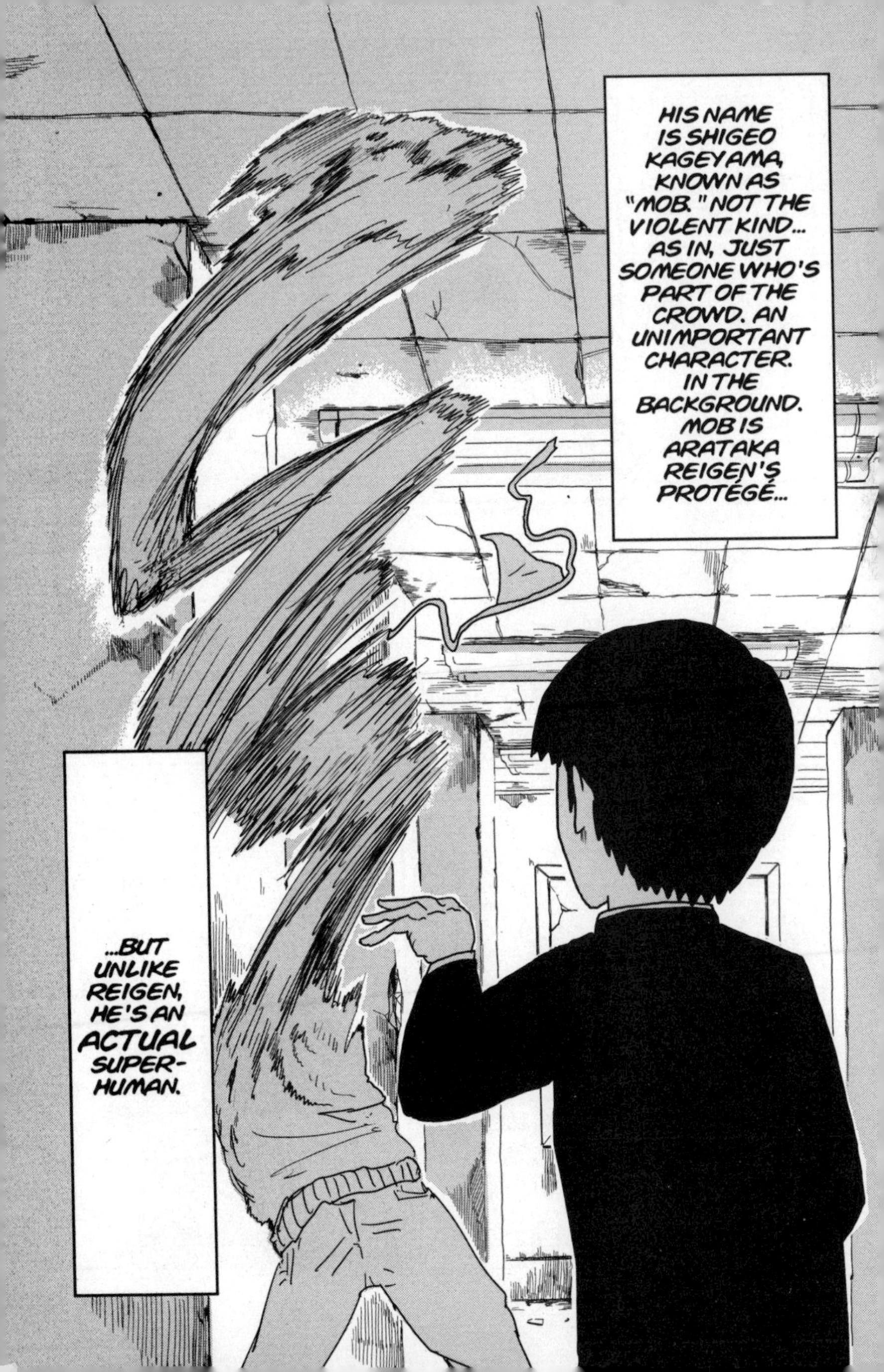
HIS NAME IS SHIGEO KAGEYAMA, KNOWN AS "MOB." NOT THE VIOLENT KIND... AS IN, JUST SOMEONE WHO'S PART OF THE CROWD. AN UNIMPORTANT CHARACTER. IN THE BACKGROUND. MOB IS ARATAKA REIGEN'S PROTÉGÉ...
...BUT UNLIKE REIGEN, HE'S AN ACTUAL SUPER-HUMAN.

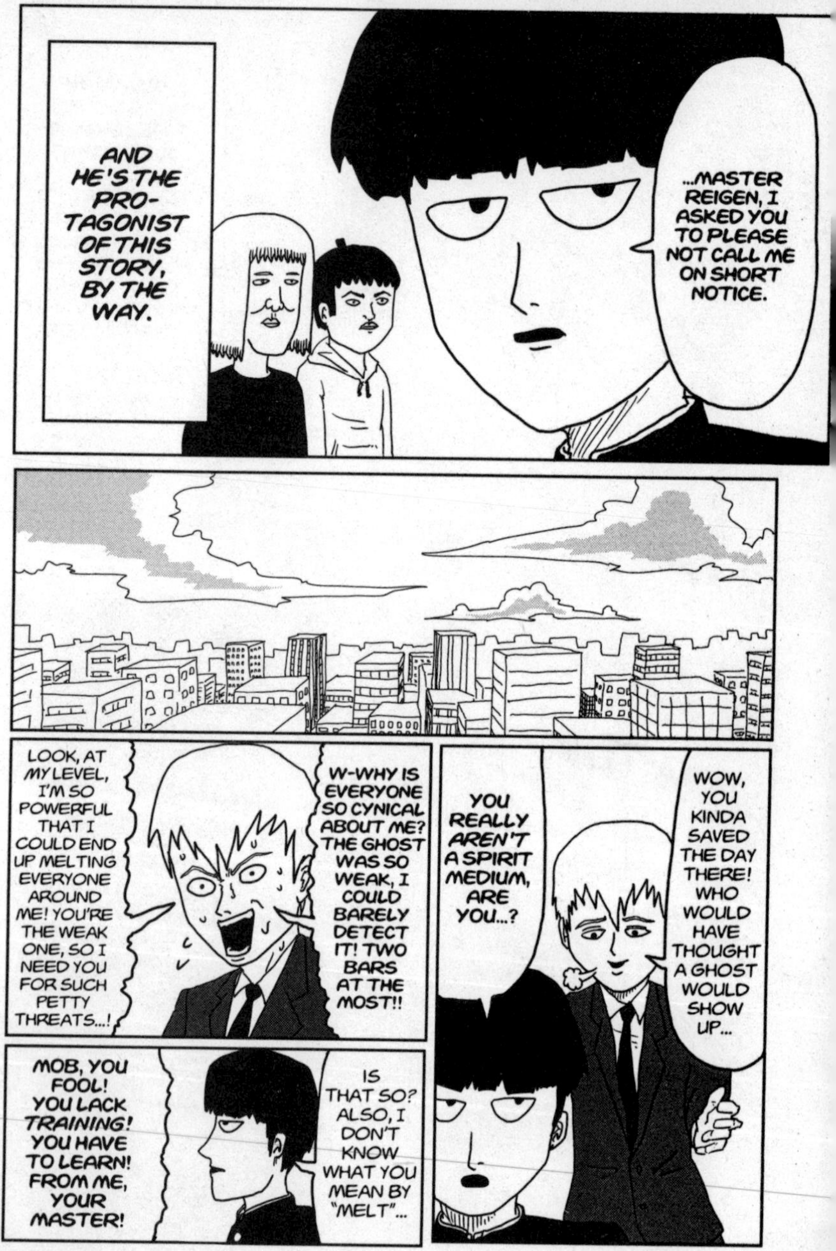
...MASTER REIGEN, I ASKED YOU TO PLEASE NOT CALL ME ON SHORT NOTICE.
AND HE'S THE PRO-TAGONIST OF THIS STORY, BY THE WAY.
WOW, YOU KINDA SAVED THE DAY THERE! WHO WOULD HAVE THOUGHT A GHOST WOULD SHOW UP...
YOU REALLY AREN'T A SPIRIT MEDIUM, ARE YOU...?
W-WHY IS EVERYONE SO CYNICAL ABOUT ME? THE GHOST WAS SO WEAK, I COULD BARELY DETECT IT! TWO BARS AT THE MOST!!
LOOK, AT MY LEVEL, I'M SO POWERFUL THAT I COULD END UP MELTING EVERYONE AROUND ME! YOU'RE THE WEAK ONE, SO I NEED YOU FOR SUCH PETTY THREATS...!
IS THAT SO? ALSO, I DON'T KNOW WHAT YOU MEAN BY "MELT"...
MOB, YOU FOOL! YOU LACK TRAINING! YOU HAVE TO LEARN! FROM ME, YOUR MASTER!

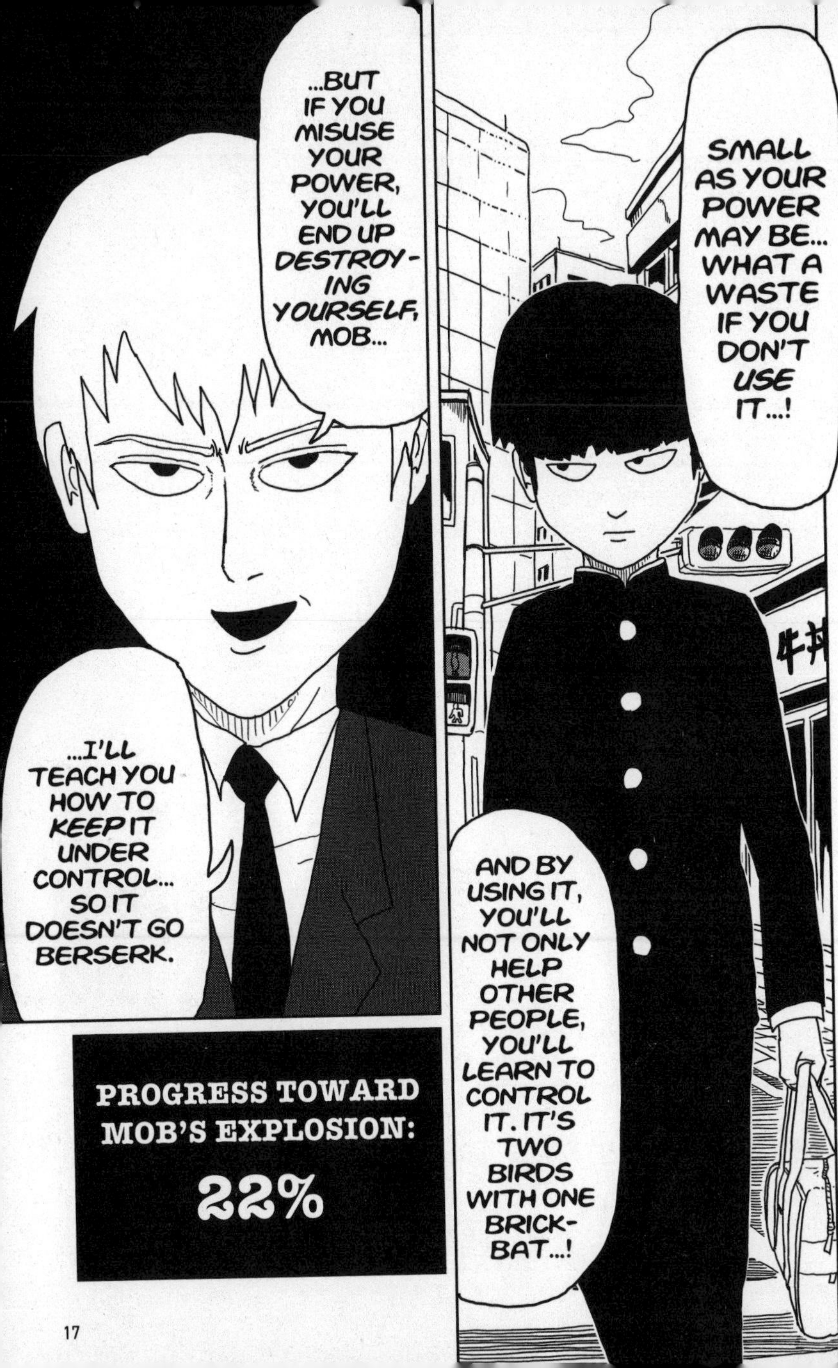
SMALL AS YOUR POWER MAY BE... WHAT A WASTE IF YOU DON'T *USE* IT...!
AND BY USING IT, YOU'LL NOT ONLY HELP OTHER PEOPLE, YOU'LL LEARN TO CONTROL IT. IT'S TWO BIRDS WITH ONE BRICK-BAT...!
...BUT IF YOU MISUSE YOUR POWER, YOU'LL END UP DESTROYING YOURSELF, MOB...
...I'LL TEACH YOU HOW TO *KEEP* IT UNDER CONTROL... SO IT DOESN'T GO BERSERK.
PROGRESS TOWARD MOB'S EXPLOSION:
22%

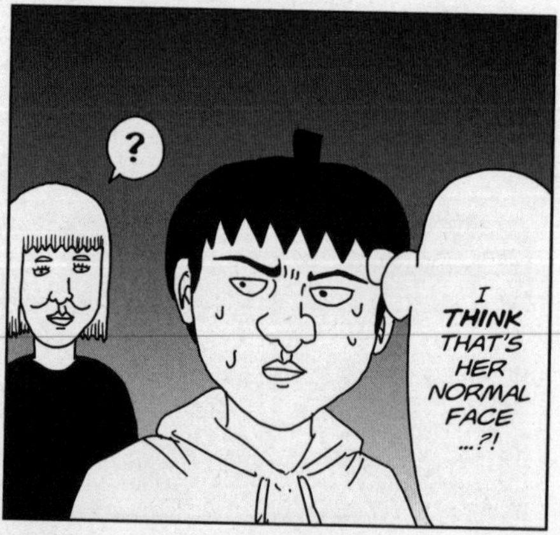
?
I THINK THAT'S HER NORMAL FACE ...?!

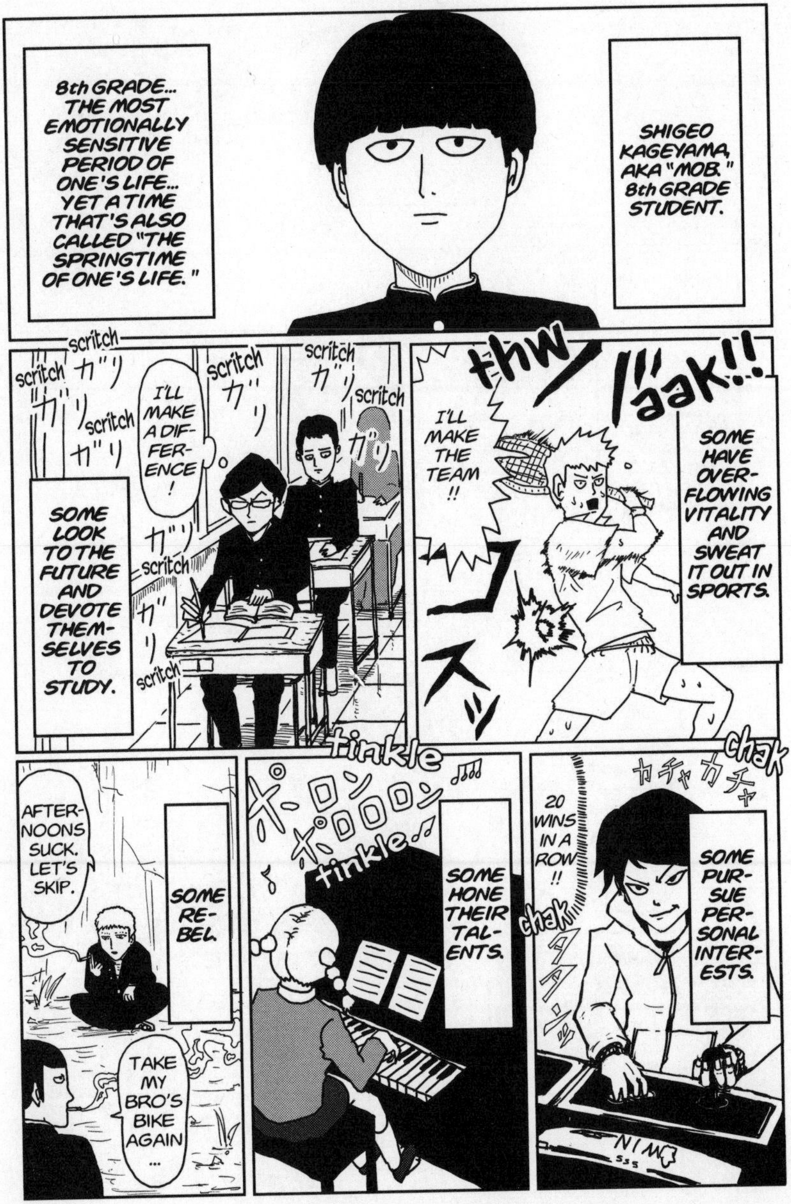
SHIGEO KAGEYAMA, AKA "MOB." 8th GRADE STUDENT.
8th GRADE... THE MOST EMOTIONALLY SENSITIVE PERIOD OF ONE'S LIFE... YET A TIME THAT'S ALSO CALLED "THE SPRINGTIME OF ONE'S LIFE."
thwaak!!
SOME HAVE OVER-FLOWING VITALITY AND SWEAT IT OUT IN SPORTS.
I'LL MAKE THE TEAM!!
scritch
scritch
scritch
scritch
I'LL MAKE A DIF-FER-ENCE!
SOME LOOK TO THE FUTURE AND DEVOTE THEM-SELVES TO STUDY.
scritch
scritch
chak
20 WINS IN A ROW!!
SOME PUR-SUE PER-SONAL INTER-ESTS.
chak
WIN
tinkle
tinkle
SOME HONE THEIR TAL-ENTS.
AFTER-NOONS SUCK. LET'S SKIP.
SOME RE-BEL.
TAKE MY BRO'S BIKE AGAIN...

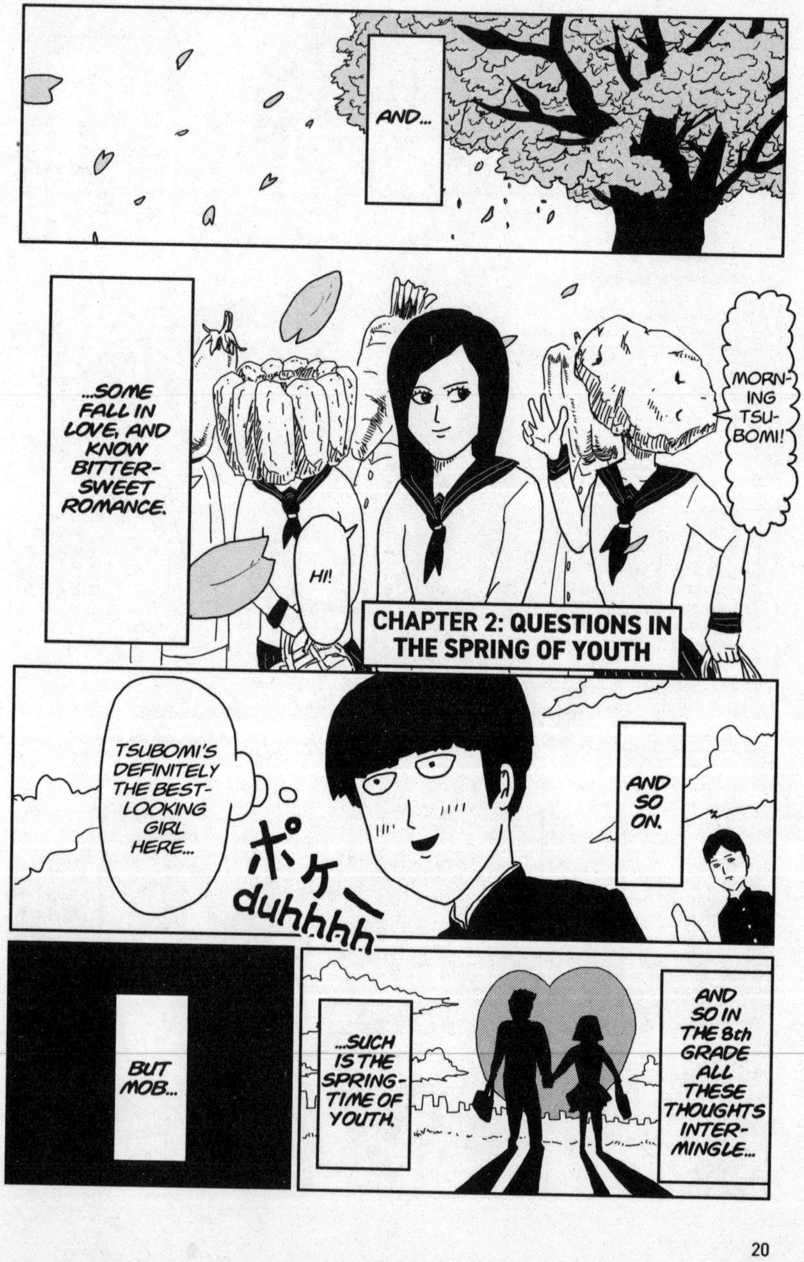
AND...
MORNING TSUBOMI!
...SOME FALL IN LOVE, AND KNOW BITTERSWEET ROMANCE.
HI!
CHAPTER 2: QUESTIONS IN THE SPRING OF YOUTH
AND SO ON.
TSUBOMI'S DEFINITELY THE BEST-LOOKING GIRL HERE...
ポケー
duhhhh
AND SO IN THE 8th GRADE ALL THESE THOUGHTS INTERMINGLE...
...SUCH IS THE SPRINGTIME OF YOUTH.
BUT MOB...

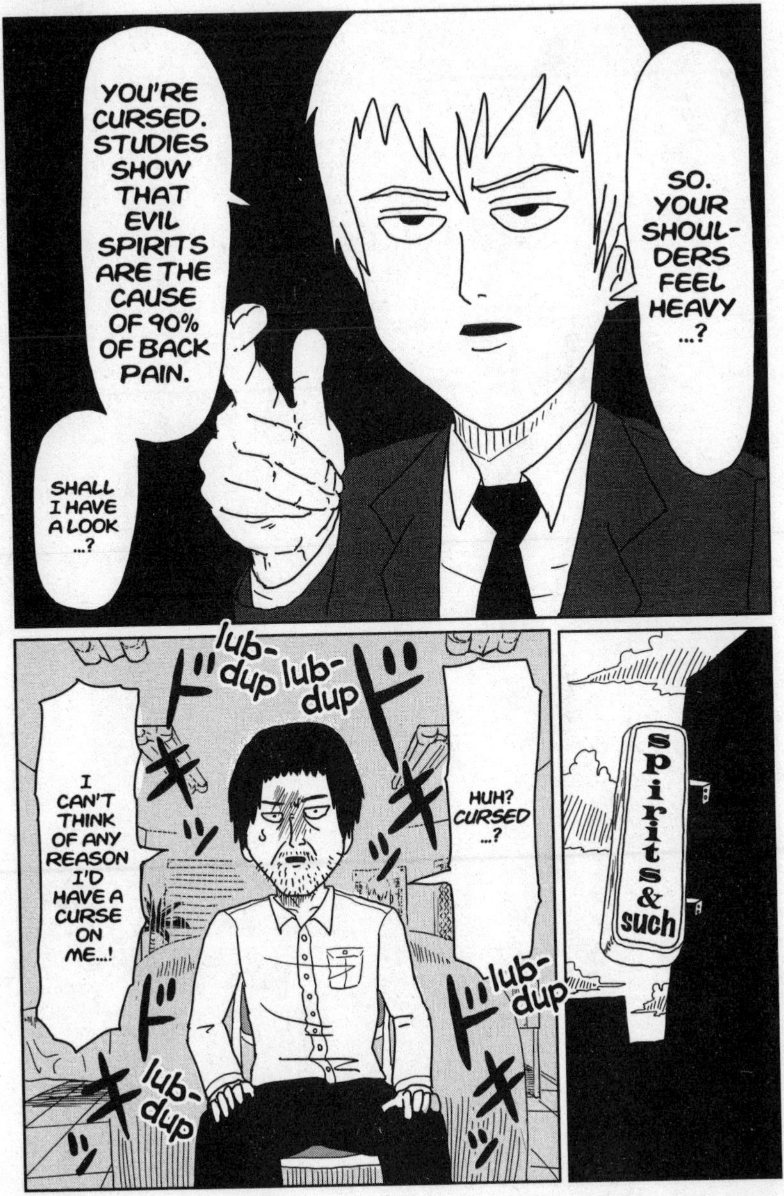
SO. YOUR SHOUL-DERS FEEL HEAVY ...?
YOU'RE CURSED. STUDIES SHOW THAT EVIL SPIRITS ARE THE CAUSE OF 90% OF BACK PAIN.
SHALL I HAVE A LOOK ...?
spirits & such
ドキッ
lub-dup lub-dup
HUH? CURSED ...?
I CAN'T THINK OF ANY REASON I'D HAVE A CURSE ON ME...!
lub-dup
lub-dup

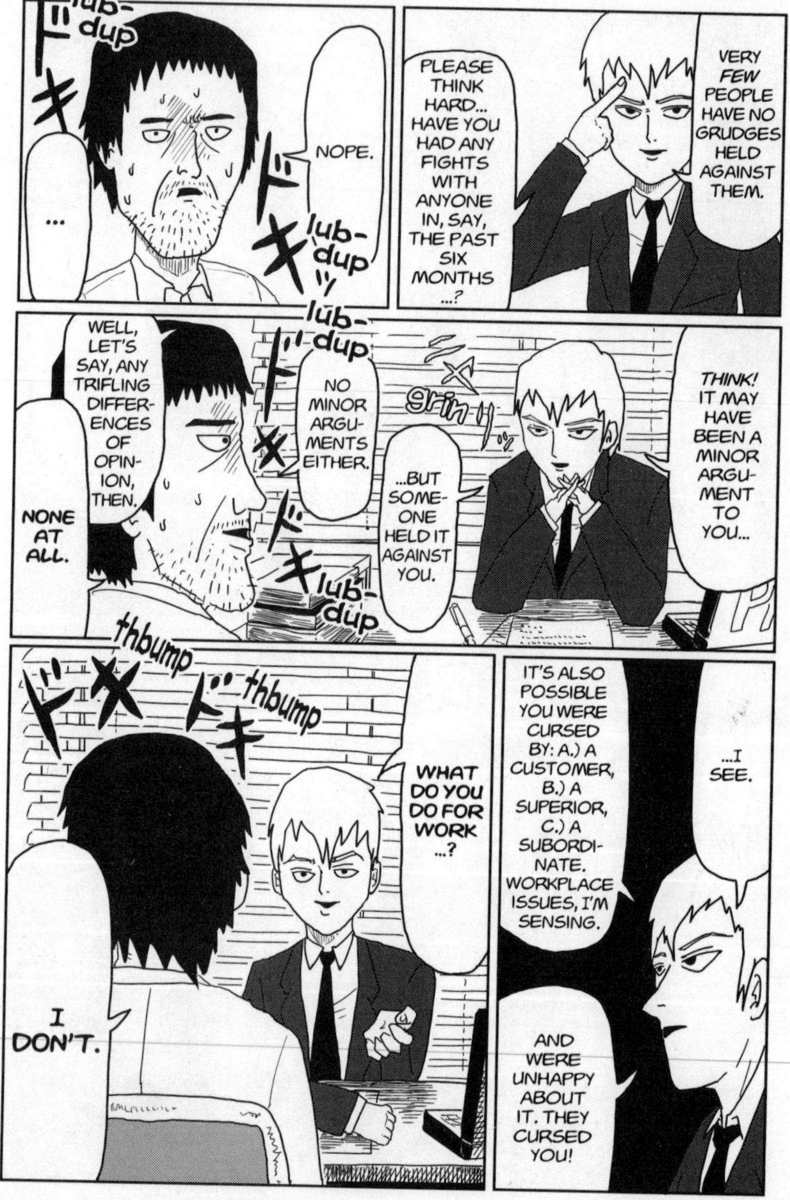
VERY FEW PEOPLE HAVE NO GRUDGES HELD AGAINST THEM.
PLEASE THINK HARD... HAVE YOU HAD ANY FIGHTS WITH ANYONE IN, SAY, THE PAST SIX MONTHS ...?
lub-dup
NOPE.
lub-dup
...
lub-dup
THINK! IT MAY HAVE BEEN A MINOR ARGUMENT TO YOU...
grin
...BUT SOMEONE HELD IT AGAINST YOU.
lub-dup
NO MINOR ARGUMENTS EITHER.
WELL, LET'S SAY, ANY TRIFLING DIFFERENCES OF OPINION, THEN.
NONE AT ALL.
IT'S ALSO POSSIBLE YOU WERE CURSED BY: A.) A CUSTOMER, B.) A SUPERIOR, C.) A SUBORDINATE. WORKPLACE ISSUES, I'M SENSING.
...I SEE.
AND WERE UNHAPPY ABOUT IT. THEY CURSED YOU!
thbump
thbump
WHAT DO YOU DO FOR WORK ...?
I DON'T.

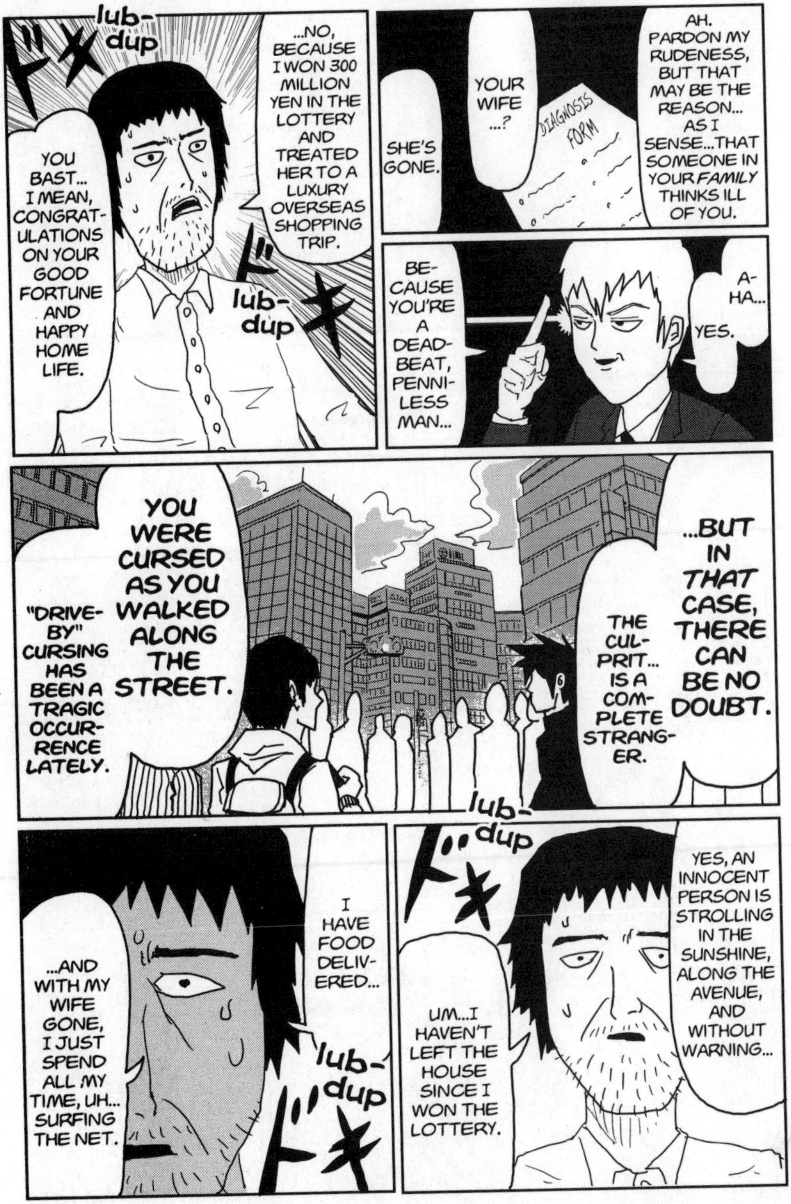
AH. PARDON MY RUDENESS, BUT THAT MAY BE THE REASON... AS I SENSE...THAT SOMEONE IN YOUR *FAMILY* THINKS ILL OF YOU.
YOUR WIFE ...?
SHE'S GONE.
A-HA...
YES.
BE-CAUSE YOU'RE A DEAD-BEAT, PENNI-LESS MAN...
lub-dup
...NO, BECAUSE I WON 300 MILLION YEN IN THE LOTTERY AND TREATED HER TO A LUXURY OVERSEAS SHOPPING TRIP.
YOU BAST... I MEAN, CONGRAT-ULATIONS ON YOUR GOOD FORTUNE AND HAPPY HOME LIFE.
lub-dup
...BUT IN *THAT* CASE, THERE CAN BE NO DOUBT.
THE CUL-PRIT... IS A COM-PLETE STRANG-ER.
YOU WERE CURSED AS YOU WALKED ALONG THE STREET.
"DRIVE-BY" CURSING HAS BEEN A TRAGIC OCCUR-RENCE LATELY.
lub-dup
YES, AN INNOCENT PERSON IS STROLLING IN THE SUNSHINE, ALONG THE AVENUE, AND WITHOUT WARNING...
UM...I HAVEN'T LEFT THE HOUSE SINCE I WON THE LOTTERY.
I HAVE FOOD DELIV-ERED...
...AND WITH MY WIFE GONE, I JUST SPEND ALL MY TIME, UH... SURFING THE NET.
lub-dup

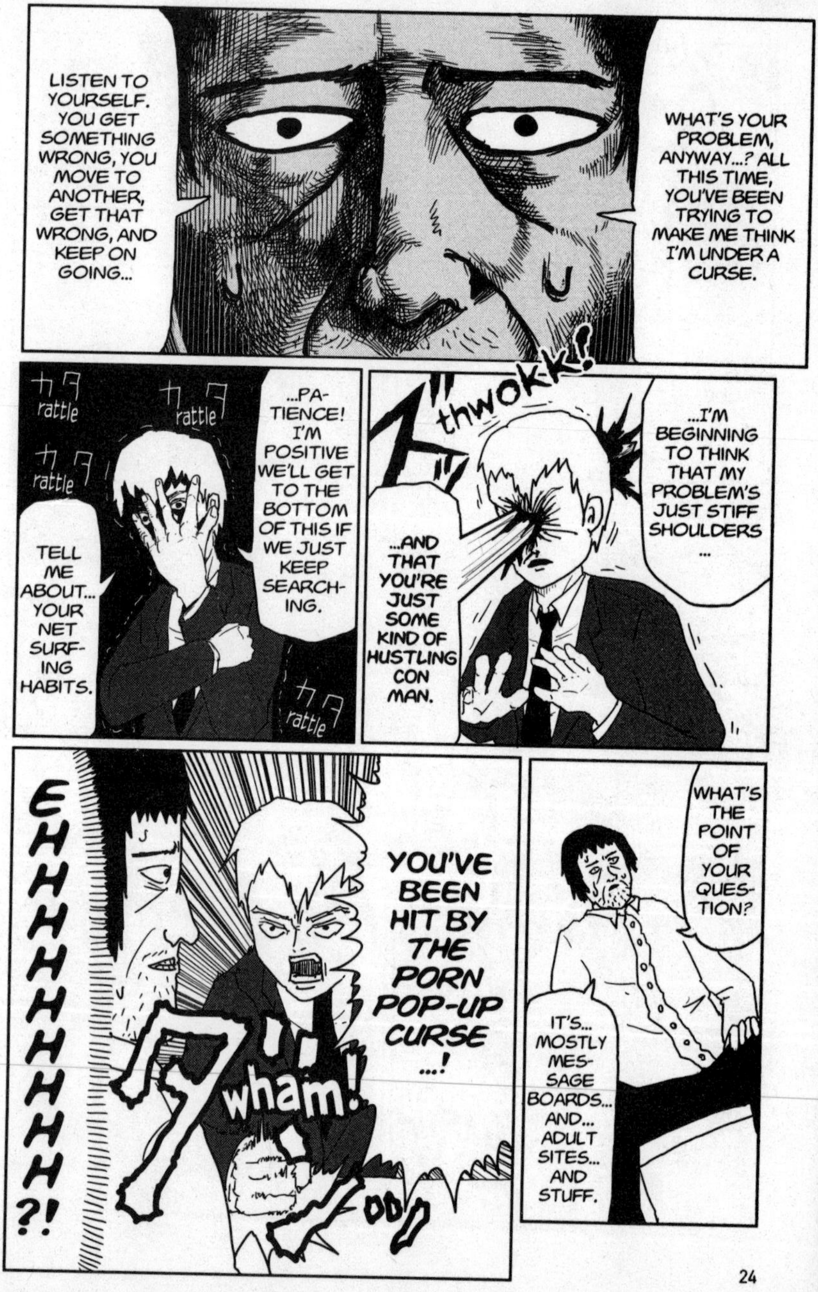

WHAT'S YOUR PROBLEM, ANYWAY...? ALL THIS TIME, YOU'VE BEEN TRYING TO MAKE ME THINK I'M UNDER A CURSE.
LISTEN TO YOURSELF. YOU GET SOMETHING WRONG, YOU MOVE TO ANOTHER, GET THAT WRONG, AND KEEP ON GOING...
thwokk!
...I'M BEGINNING TO THINK THAT MY PROBLEM'S JUST STIFF SHOULDERS...
...AND THAT YOU'RE JUST SOME KIND OF HUSTLING CON MAN.
カタ rattle
カタ rattle
カタ rattle
...PA-TIENCE! I'M POSITIVE WE'LL GET TO THE BOTTOM OF THIS IF WE JUST KEEP SEARCH-ING.
TELL ME ABOUT... YOUR NET SURF-ING HABITS.
カタ rattle
WHAT'S THE POINT OF YOUR QUES-TION?
IT'S... MOSTLY MES-SAGE BOARDS... AND... ADULT SITES... AND STUFF.
YOU'VE BEEN HIT BY THE PORN POP-UP CURSE...!
wham!
EHHHHHHHHHHH?!

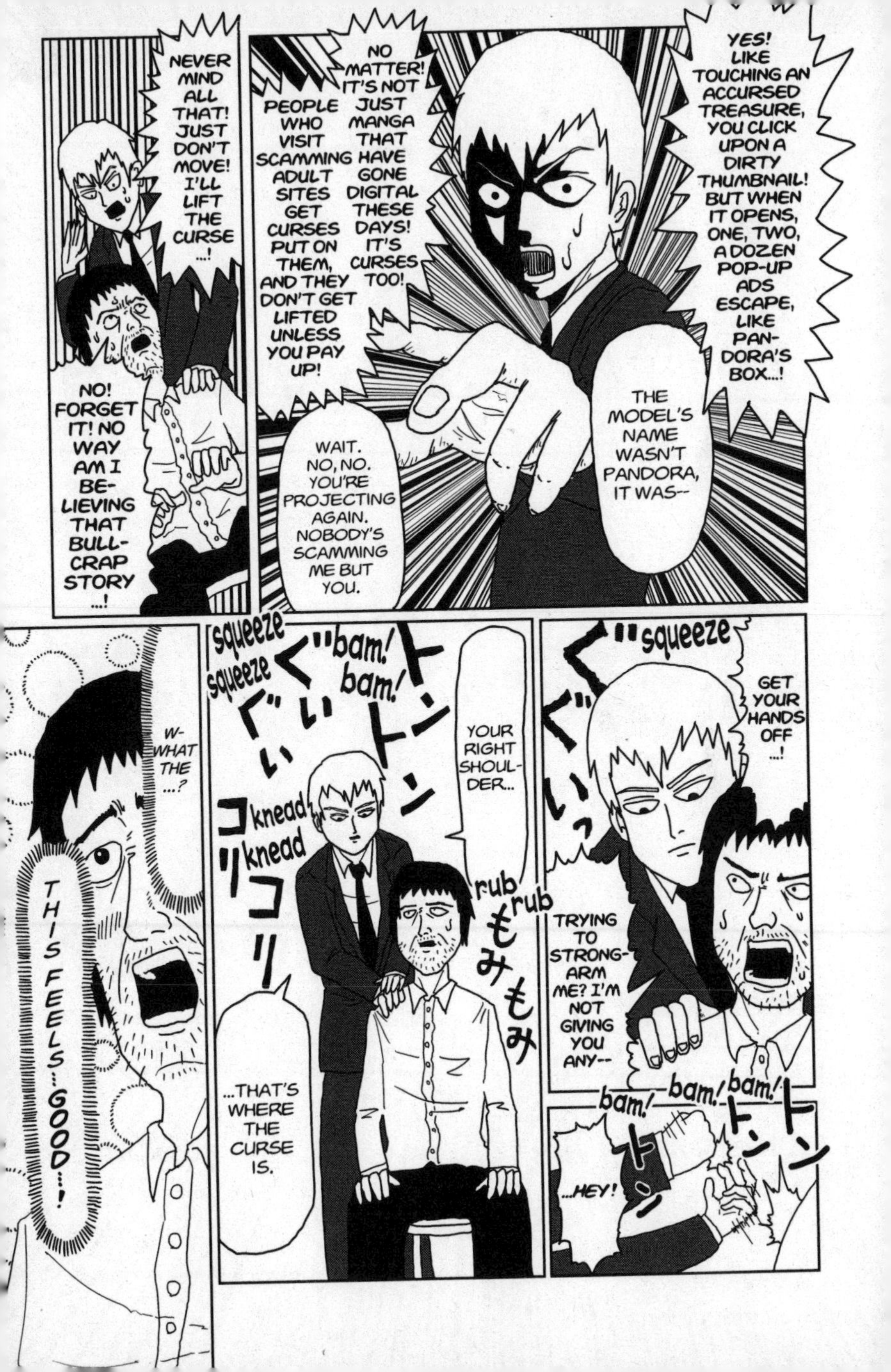
YES! LIKE TOUCHING AN ACCURSED TREASURE, YOU CLICK UPON A DIRTY THUMBNAIL! BUT WHEN IT OPENS, ONE, TWO, A DOZEN POP-UP ADS ESCAPE, LIKE PAN-DORA'S BOX...!
THE MODEL'S NAME WASN'T PANDORA, IT WAS--
NO MATTER! IT'S NOT JUST MANGA THAT HAVE GONE DIGITAL THESE DAYS! IT'S CURSES TOO!
PEOPLE WHO VISIT SCAMMING ADULT SITES GET CURSES PUT ON THEM, AND THEY DON'T GET LIFTED UNLESS YOU PAY UP!
WAIT. NO, NO. YOU'RE PROJECTING AGAIN. NOBODY'S SCAMMING ME BUT YOU.
NEVER MIND ALL THAT! JUST DON'T MOVE! I'LL LIFT THE CURSE ...!
NO! FORGET IT! NO WAY AM I BE-LIEVING THAT BULL-CRAP STORY ...!
squeeze
ぐいぐいっ
GET YOUR HANDS OFF ...!
TRYING TO STRONG-ARM ME? I'M NOT GIVING YOU ANY--
bam! bam! bam!
トントン
...HEY!
squeeze squeeze
ぐいぐい
bam! bam!
トントン
YOUR RIGHT SHOULDER...
knead knead
コリコリ
rub rub
もみもみ
...THAT'S WHERE THE CURSE IS.
W-WHAT THE ...?
THIS FEELS...GOOD...!

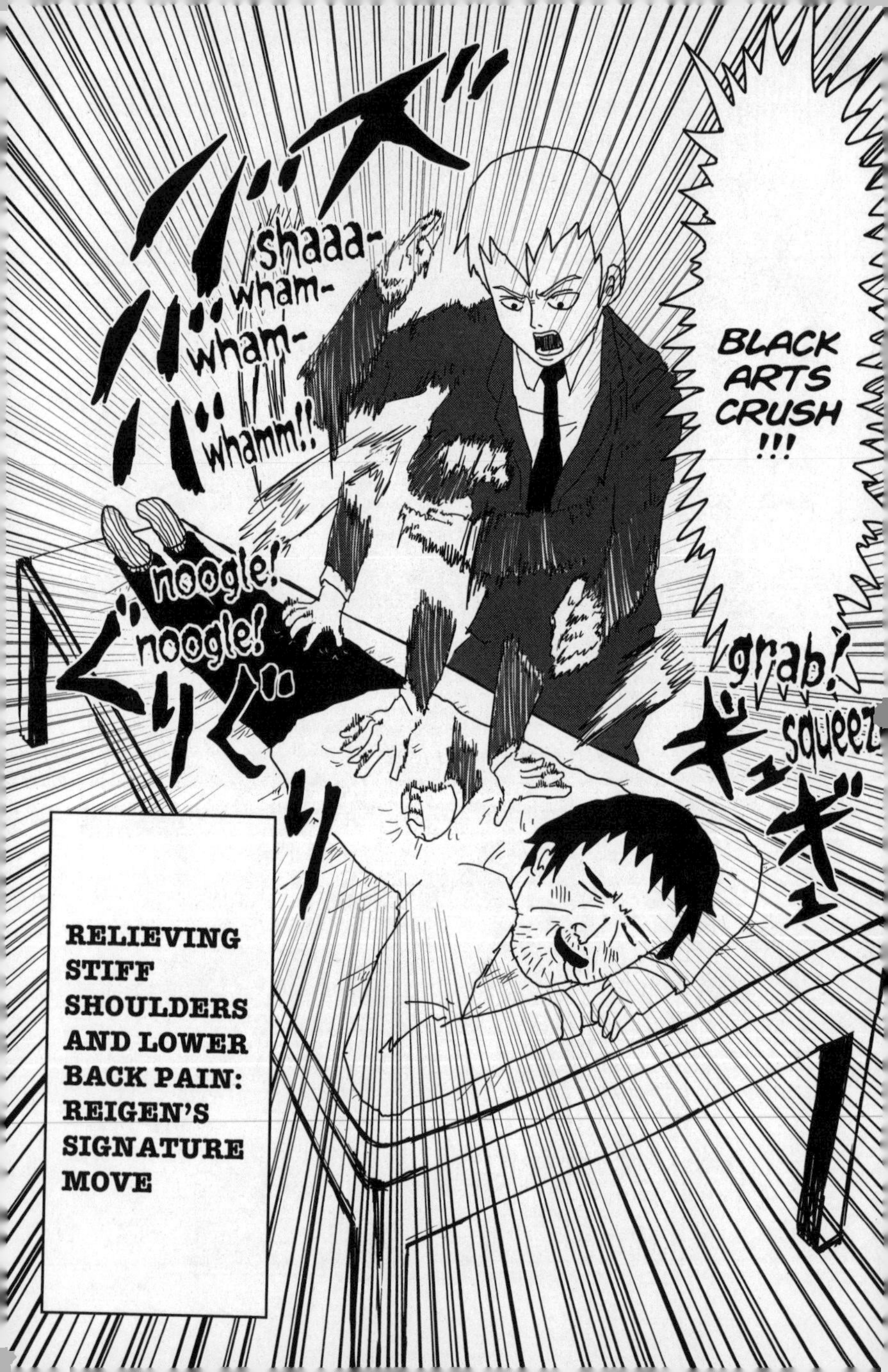

BLACK ARTS CRUSH!!!
shaaa-
wham-
wham-
whamm!!
grab!
squeez
noogle!
noogle!
RELIEVING STIFF SHOULDERS AND LOWER BACK PAIN: REIGEN'S SIGNATURE MOVE

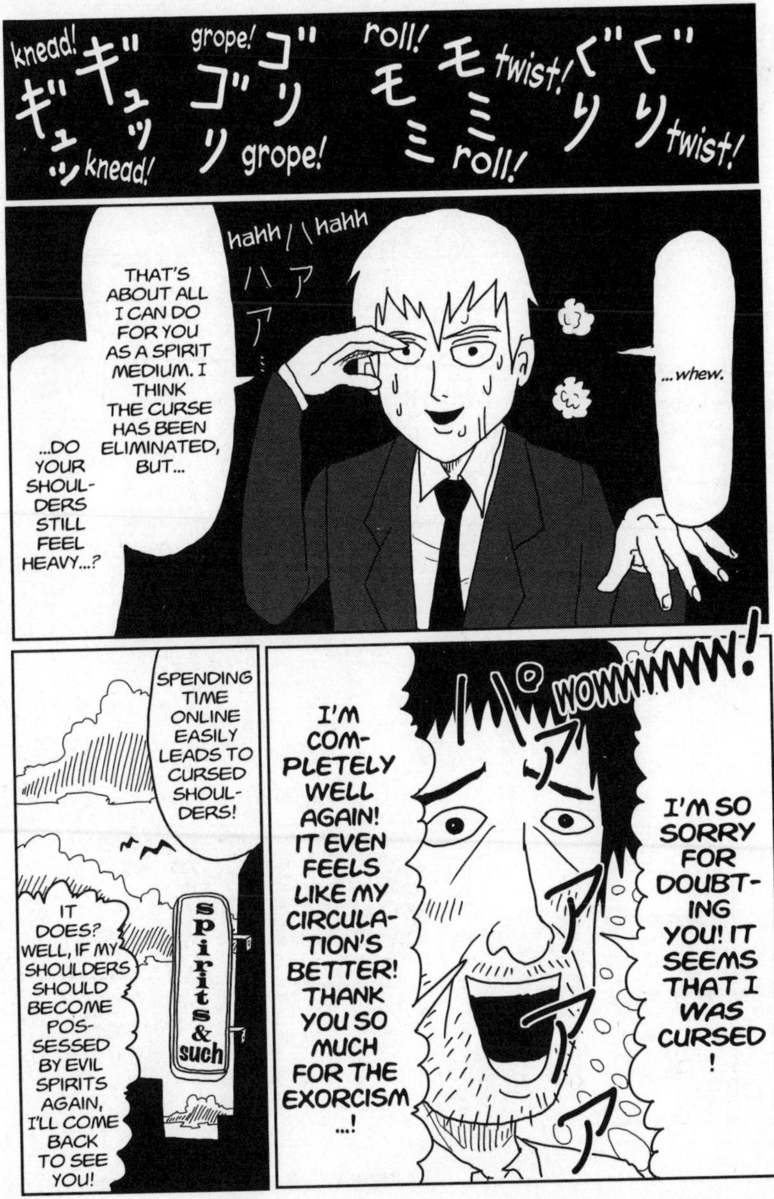
ぐり ぐり twist! twist!
モミ モミ roll! roll!
ゴリ ゴリ grope! grope!
ギュッ ギュッ knead! knead!
...whew.
hahh/\hahh
ハァ ハァ
THAT'S ABOUT ALL I CAN DO FOR YOU AS A SPIRIT MEDIUM. I THINK THE CURSE HAS BEEN ELIMINATED, BUT...
...DO YOUR SHOULDERS STILL FEEL HEAVY...?
パァァァ WOWWWWW!
I'M SO SORRY FOR DOUBTING YOU! IT SEEMS THAT I WAS CURSED!
I'M COMPLETELY WELL AGAIN! IT EVEN FEELS LIKE MY CIRCULATION'S BETTER! THANK YOU SO MUCH FOR THE EXORCISM...!
SPENDING TIME ONLINE EASILY LEADS TO CURSED SHOULDERS!
IT DOES? WELL, IF MY SHOULDERS SHOULD BECOME POSSESSED BY EVIL SPIRITS AGAIN, I'LL COME BACK TO SEE YOU!
spirits & such

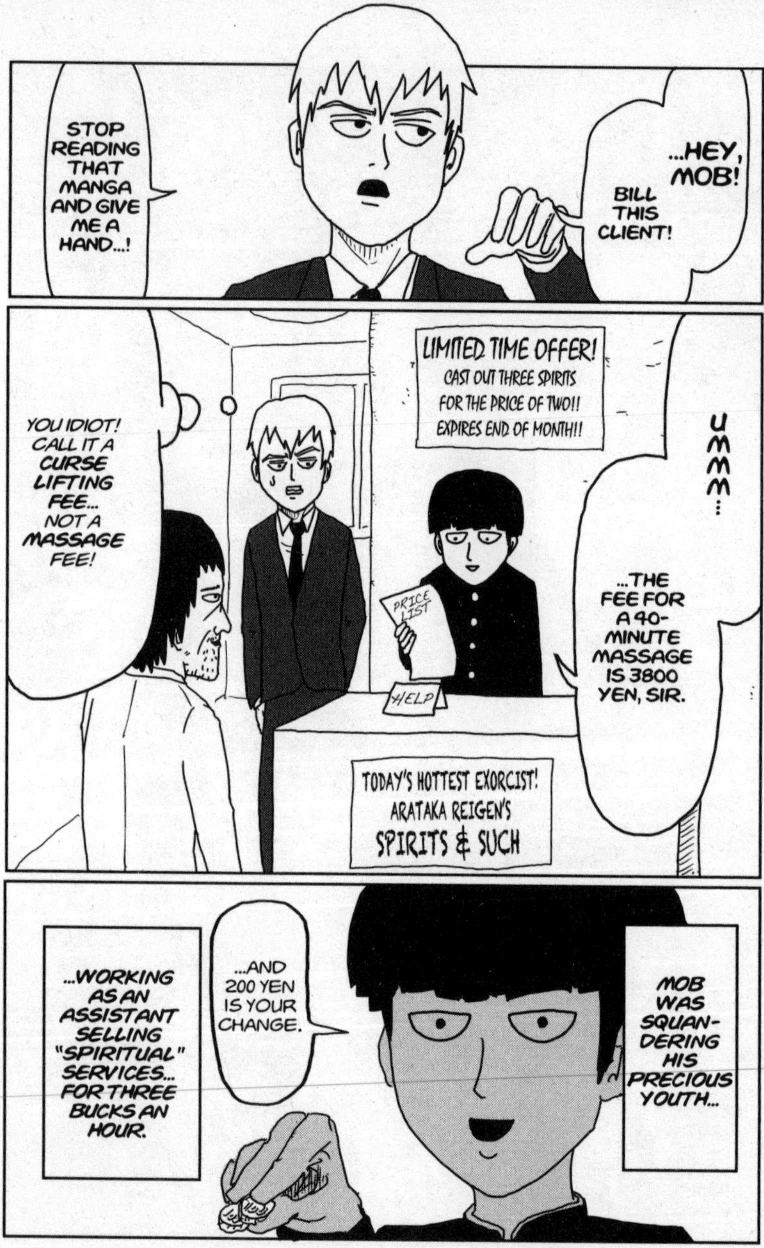
...HEY, MOB!
BILL THIS CLIENT!
STOP READING THAT MANGA AND GIVE ME A HAND...!
UMMM...
...THE FEE FOR A 40-MINUTE MASSAGE IS 3800 YEN, SIR.
LIMITED TIME OFFER! CAST OUT THREE SPIRITS FOR THE PRICE OF TWO!! EXPIRES END OF MONTH!!
PRICE LIST
HELP
TODAY'S HOTTEST EXORCIST! ARATAKA REIGEN'S SPIRITS & SUCH
YOU IDIOT! CALL IT A CURSE LIFTING FEE... NOT A MASSAGE FEE!
MOB WAS SQUANDERING HIS PRECIOUS YOUTH...
...AND 200 YEN IS YOUR CHANGE.
...WORKING AS AN ASSISTANT SELLING "SPIRITUAL" SERVICES... FOR THREE BUCKS AN HOUR.

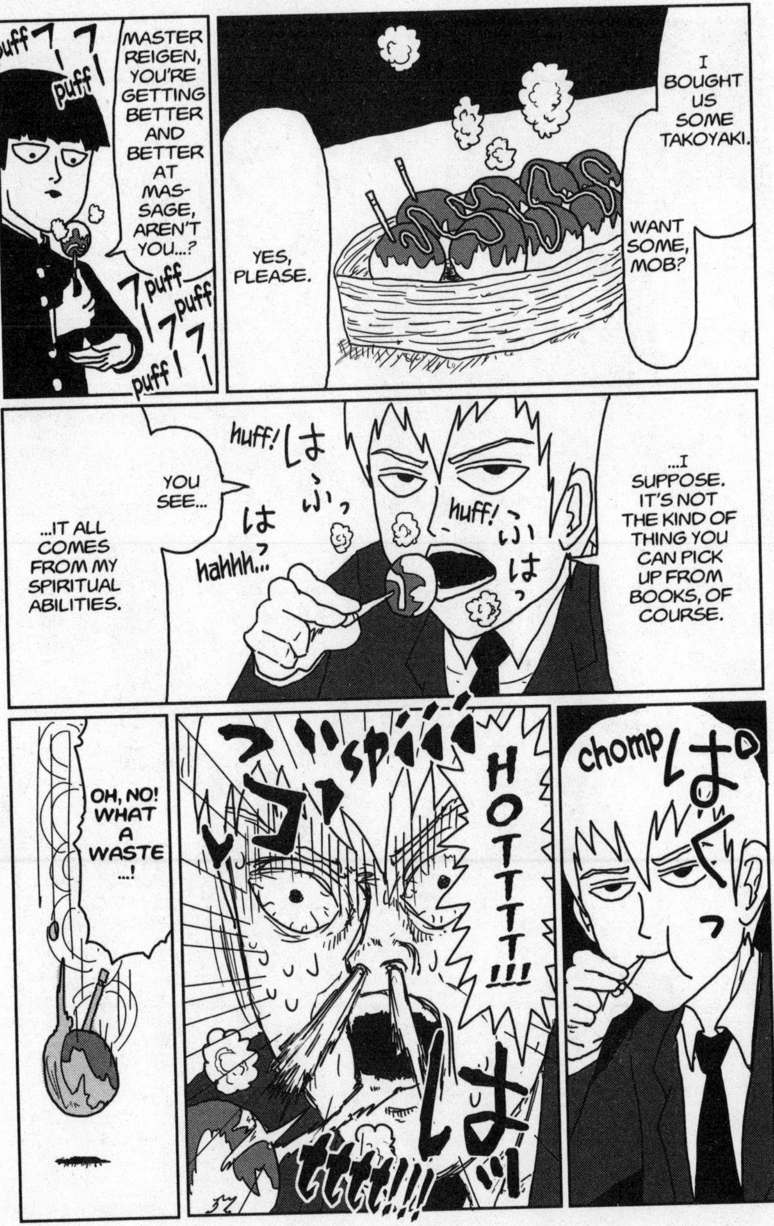
I BOUGHT US SOME TAKOYAKI.
WANT SOME, MOB?
YES, PLEASE.
puff puff
MASTER REIGEN, YOU'RE GETTING BETTER AND BETTER AT MAS-SAGE, AREN'T YOU...?
puff puff puff
...I SUPPOSE. IT'S NOT THE KIND OF THING YOU CAN PICK UP FROM BOOKS, OF COURSE.
huff! ふはっ
huff! はふっ
はっ hahhh...
YOU SEE...
...IT ALL COMES FROM MY SPIRITUAL ABILITIES.
chomp ぱくっ
spiiii
HOTTTTT!!!
ttttt!!!
OH, NO! WHAT A WASTE...!

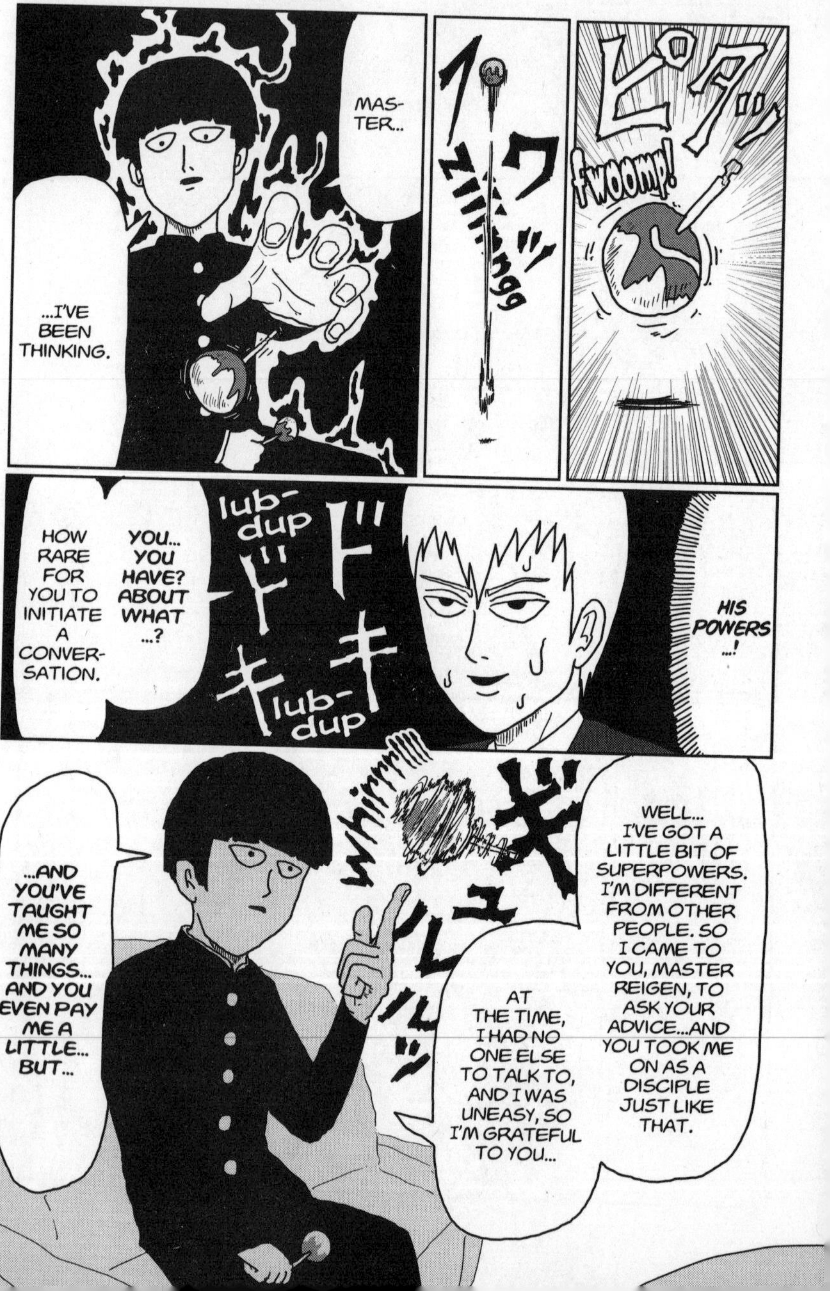
ピタッ
fwoomp!
MAS-TER...
...I'VE BEEN THINKING.
HIS POWERS ...!
ドキドキ
lub-dup
lub-dup
YOU... YOU HAVE? ABOUT WHAT ...?
HOW RARE FOR YOU TO INITIATE A CONVERSATION.
whirrrr
WELL... I'VE GOT A LITTLE BIT OF SUPERPOWERS. I'M DIFFERENT FROM OTHER PEOPLE. SO I CAME TO YOU, MASTER REIGEN, TO ASK YOUR ADVICE...AND YOU TOOK ME ON AS A DISCIPLE JUST LIKE THAT.
AT THE TIME, I HAD NO ONE ELSE TO TALK TO, AND I WAS UNEASY, SO I'M GRATEFUL TO YOU...
...AND YOU'VE TAUGHT ME SO MANY THINGS... AND YOU EVEN PAY ME A LITTLE... BUT...

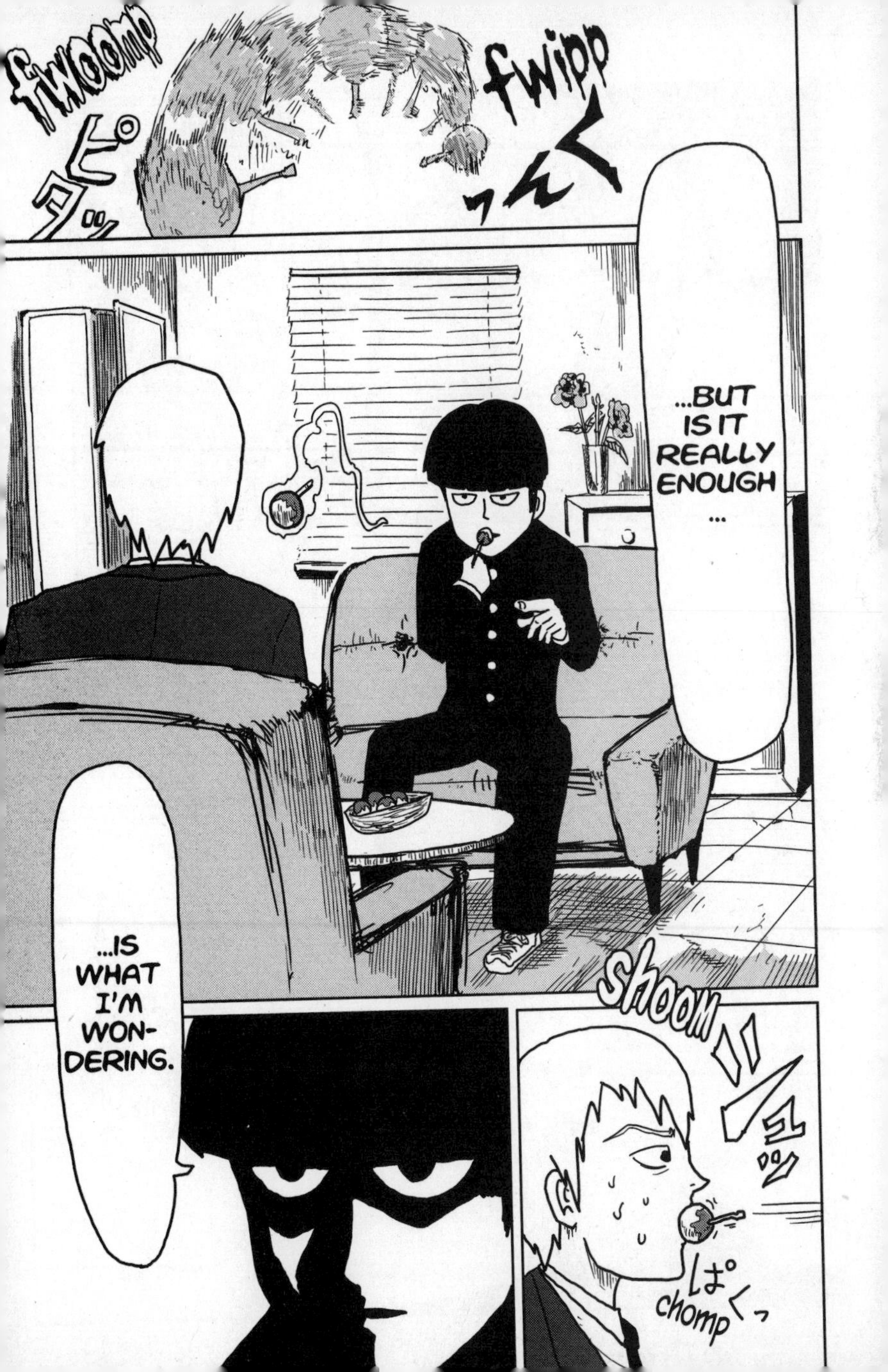
fwipp
fwoomp
...BUT IS IT REALLY ENOUGH ...
...IS WHAT I'M WON-DERING.
SHOOM
chomp
ぱくっ

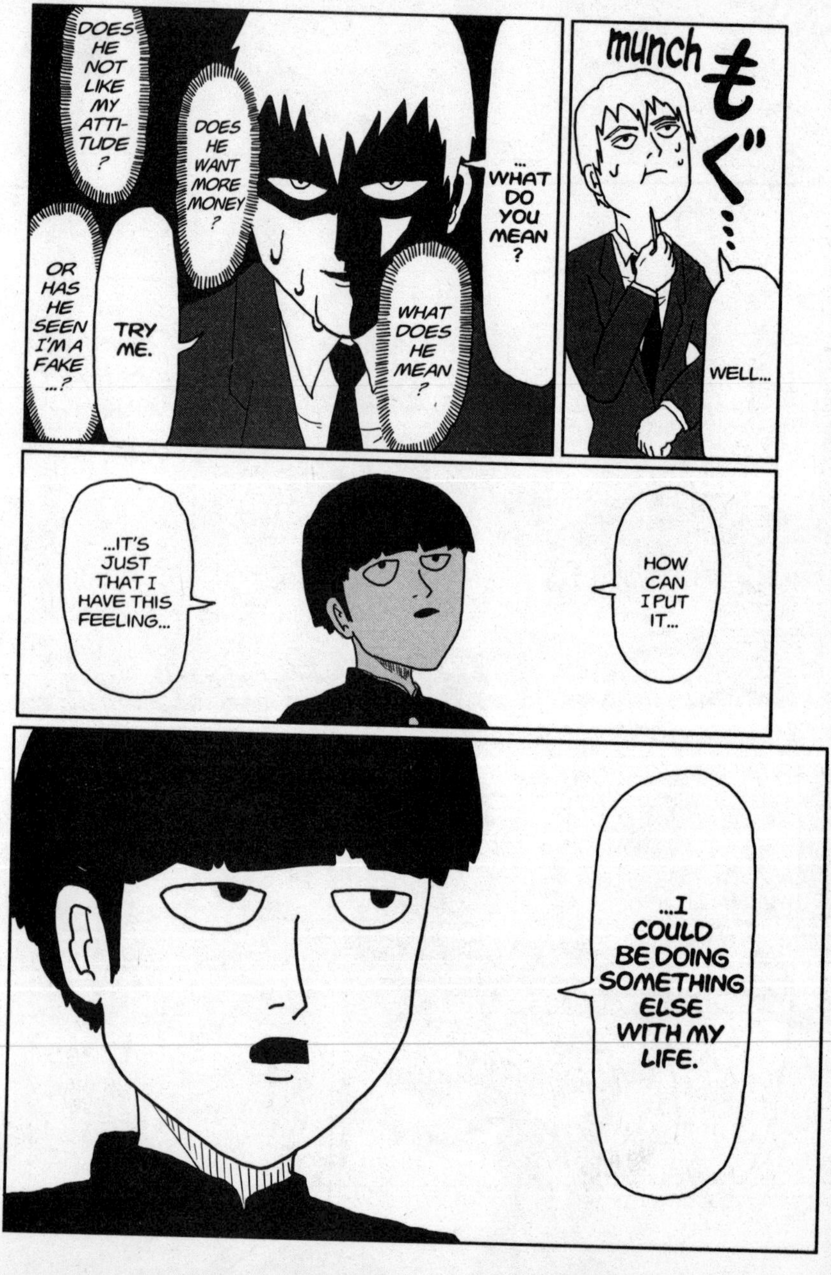
munch
もぐ…
WELL...
...WHAT DO YOU MEAN?
WHAT DOES HE MEAN?
DOES HE WANT MORE MONEY?
DOES HE NOT LIKE MY ATTITUDE?
TRY ME.
OR HAS HE SEEN I'M A FAKE ...?
HOW CAN I PUT IT...
...IT'S JUST THAT I HAVE THIS FEELING...
...I COULD BE DOING SOMETHING ELSE WITH MY LIFE.

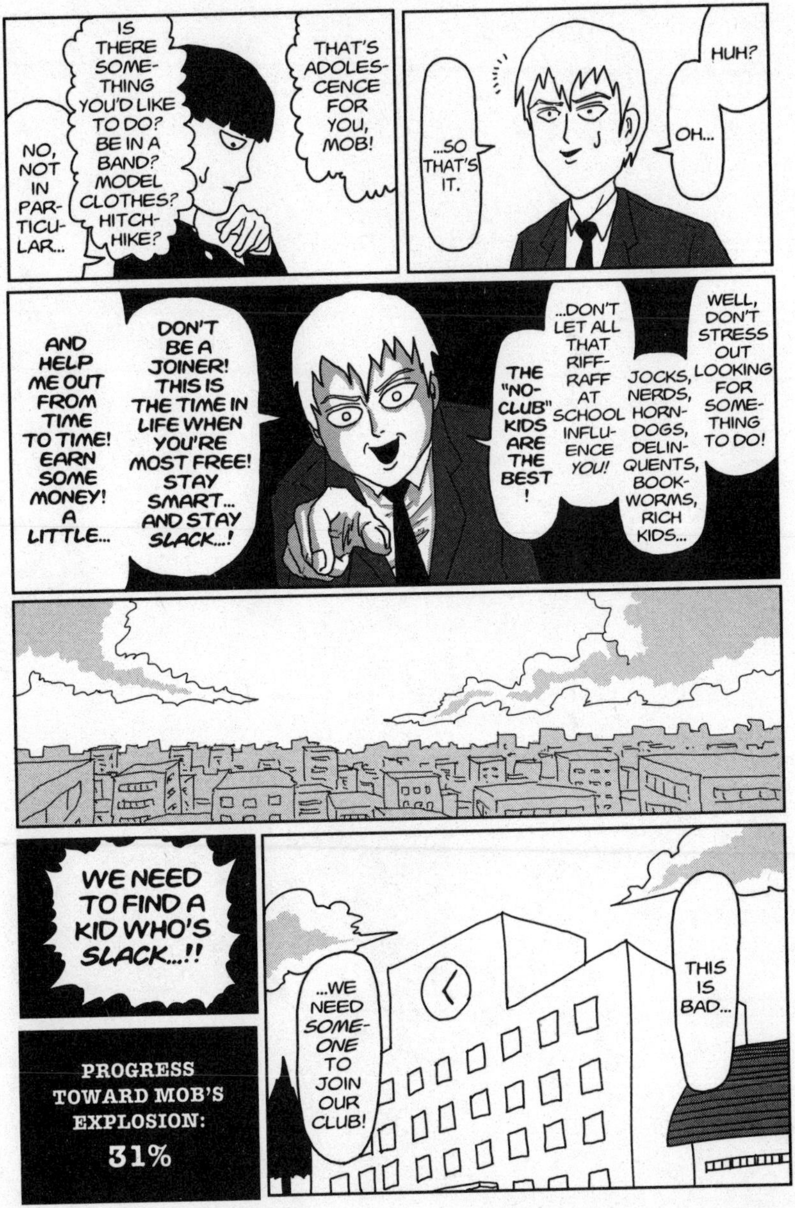
HUH?
OH...
...SO THAT'S IT.
THAT'S ADOLESCENCE FOR YOU, MOB!
IS THERE SOMETHING YOU'D LIKE TO DO? BE IN A BAND? MODEL CLOTHES? HITCHHIKE?
NO, NOT IN PARTICULAR...
WELL, DON'T STRESS OUT LOOKING FOR SOMETHING TO DO!
JOCKS, NERDS, HORNDOGS, DELINQUENTS, BOOKWORMS, RICH KIDS...
...DON'T LET ALL THAT RIFFRAFF AT SCHOOL INFLUENCE *YOU!*
THE "NO-CLUB" KIDS ARE THE BEST!
DON'T BE A JOINER! THIS IS THE TIME IN LIFE WHEN YOU'RE MOST FREE! STAY SMART... AND STAY *SLACK*...!
AND HELP ME OUT FROM TIME TO TIME! EARN SOME MONEY! A LITTLE...
THIS IS BAD...
...WE NEED SOMEONE TO JOIN OUR CLUB!
WE NEED TO FIND A KID WHO'S *SLACK*...!!
PROGRESS TOWARD MOB'S EXPLOSION: 31%

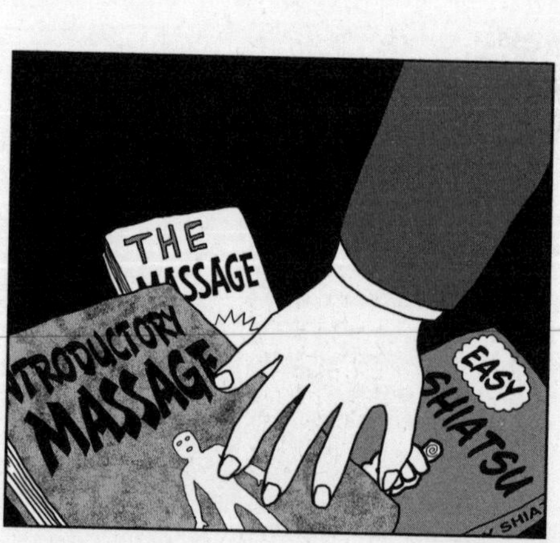
THE
ASSAGE
NTRODUCTORY
MASSAGE
EASY
SHIATSU
SHIAT

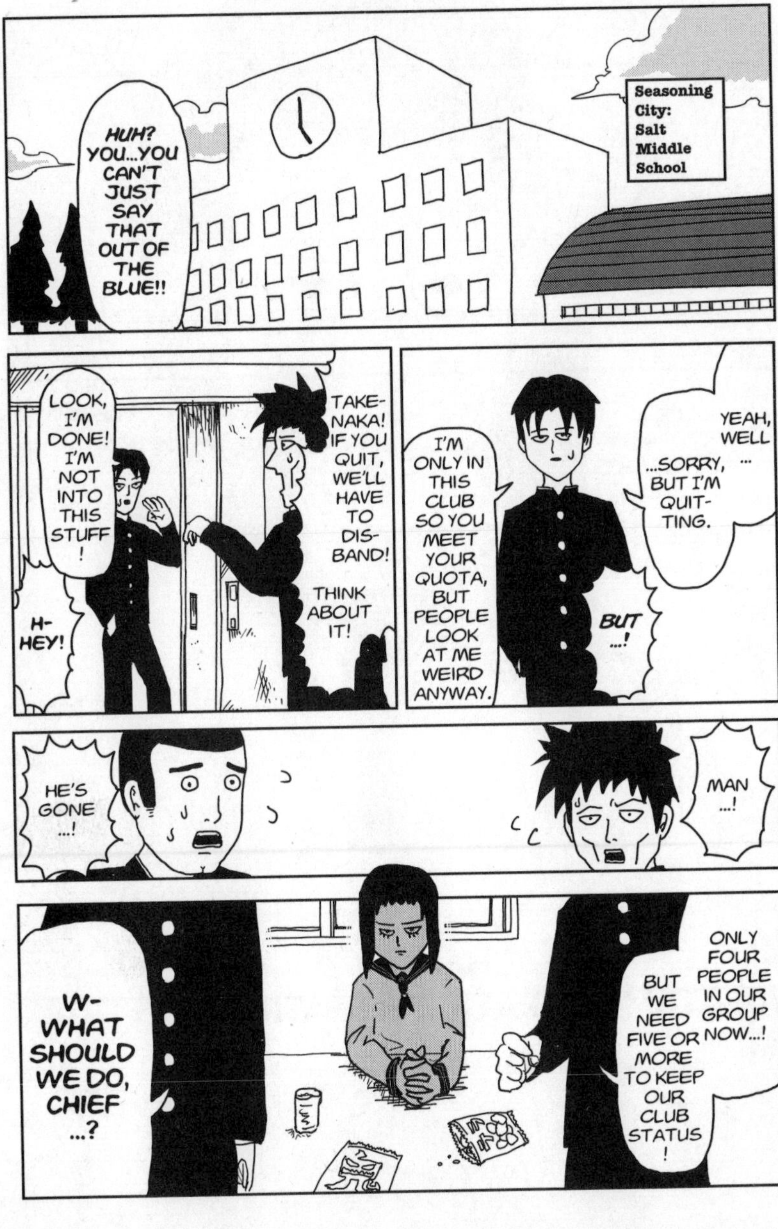
Seasoning City: Salt Middle School
HUH? YOU...YOU CAN'T JUST SAY THAT OUT OF THE BLUE!!
YEAH, WELL ...
...SORRY, BUT I'M QUITTING.
BUT ...!
I'M ONLY IN THIS CLUB SO YOU MEET YOUR QUOTA, BUT PEOPLE LOOK AT ME WEIRD ANYWAY.
TAKENAKA! IF YOU QUIT, WE'LL HAVE TO DISBAND!
THINK ABOUT IT!
LOOK, I'M DONE! I'M NOT INTO THIS STUFF!
H-HEY!
MAN ...!
HE'S GONE ...!
ONLY FOUR PEOPLE IN OUR GROUP NOW...!
BUT WE NEED FIVE OR MORE TO KEEP OUR CLUB STATUS!
W-WHAT SHOULD WE DO, CHIEF ...?

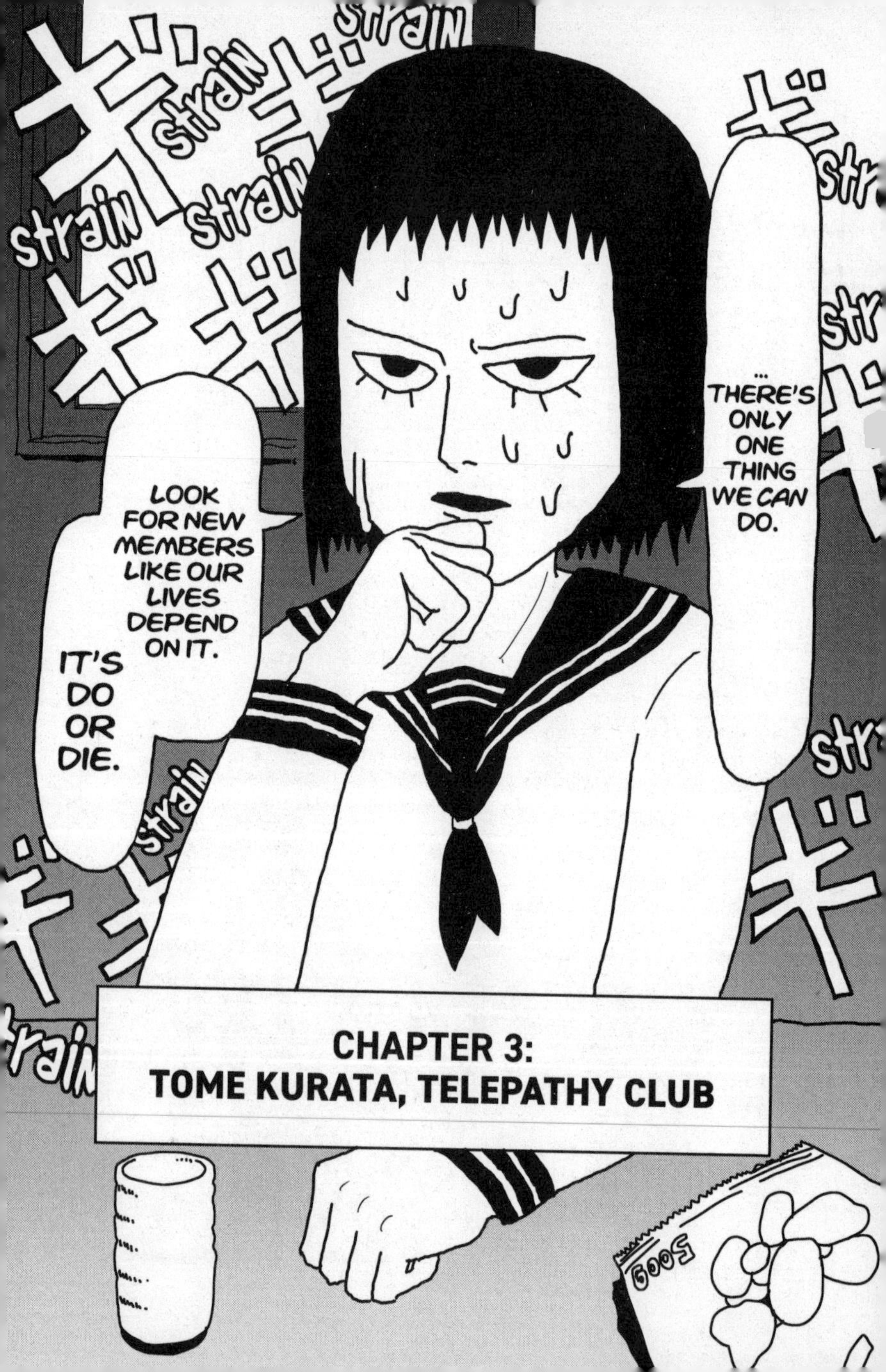
strain strain strain strain
... THERE'S ONLY ONE THING WE CAN DO.
LOOK FOR NEW MEMBERS LIKE OUR LIVES DEPEND ON IT.
IT'S DO OR DIE.
strain strain

CHAPTER 3: TOME KURATA, TELEPATHY CLUB

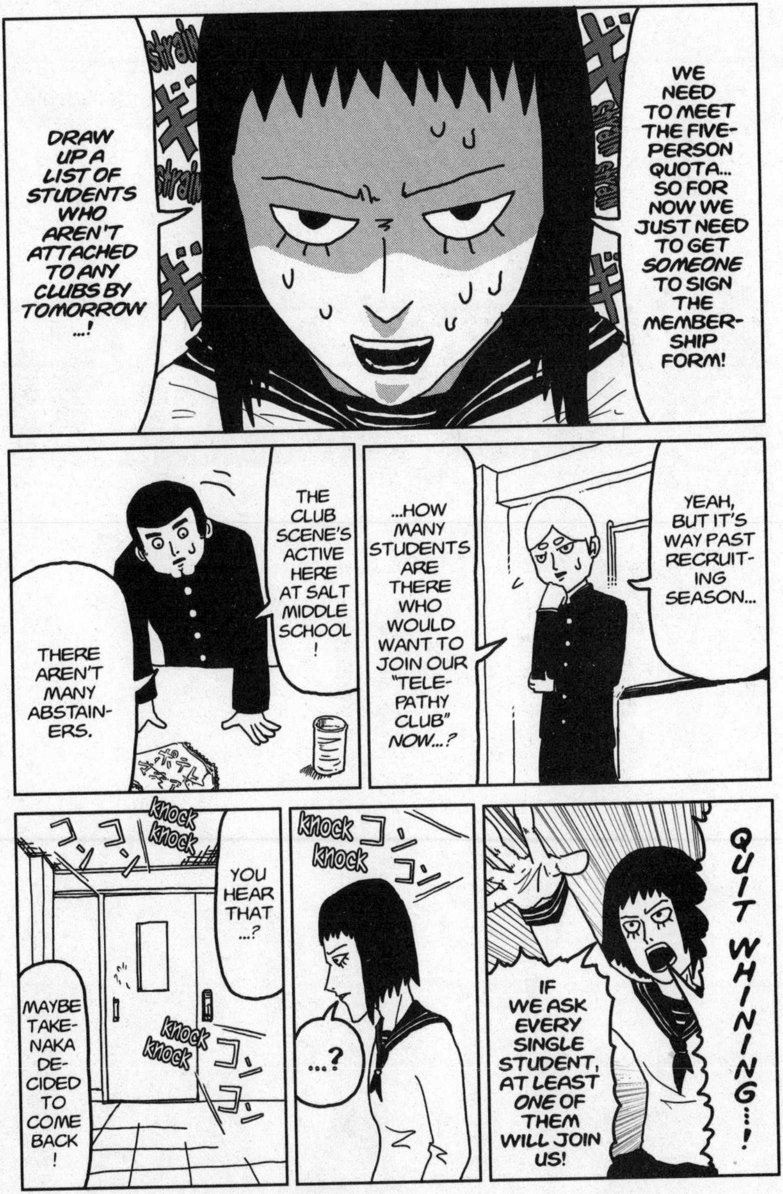
strain
WE NEED TO MEET THE FIVE-PERSON QUOTA... SO FOR NOW WE JUST NEED TO GET SOMEONE TO SIGN THE MEMBERSHIP FORM!
DRAW UP A LIST OF STUDENTS WHO AREN'T ATTACHED TO ANY CLUBS BY TOMORROW ...!
YEAH, BUT IT'S WAY PAST RECRUITING SEASON...
...HOW MANY STUDENTS ARE THERE WHO WOULD WANT TO JOIN OUR "TELEPATHY CLUB" NOW...?
THE CLUB SCENE'S ACTIVE HERE AT SALT MIDDLE SCHOOL!
THERE AREN'T MANY ABSTAINERS.
QUIT WHINING...!
IF WE ASK EVERY SINGLE STUDENT, AT LEAST ONE OF THEM WILL JOIN US!
knock knock
...?
knock knock
YOU HEAR THAT ...?
knock knock
MAYBE TAKENAKA DECIDED TO COME BACK!

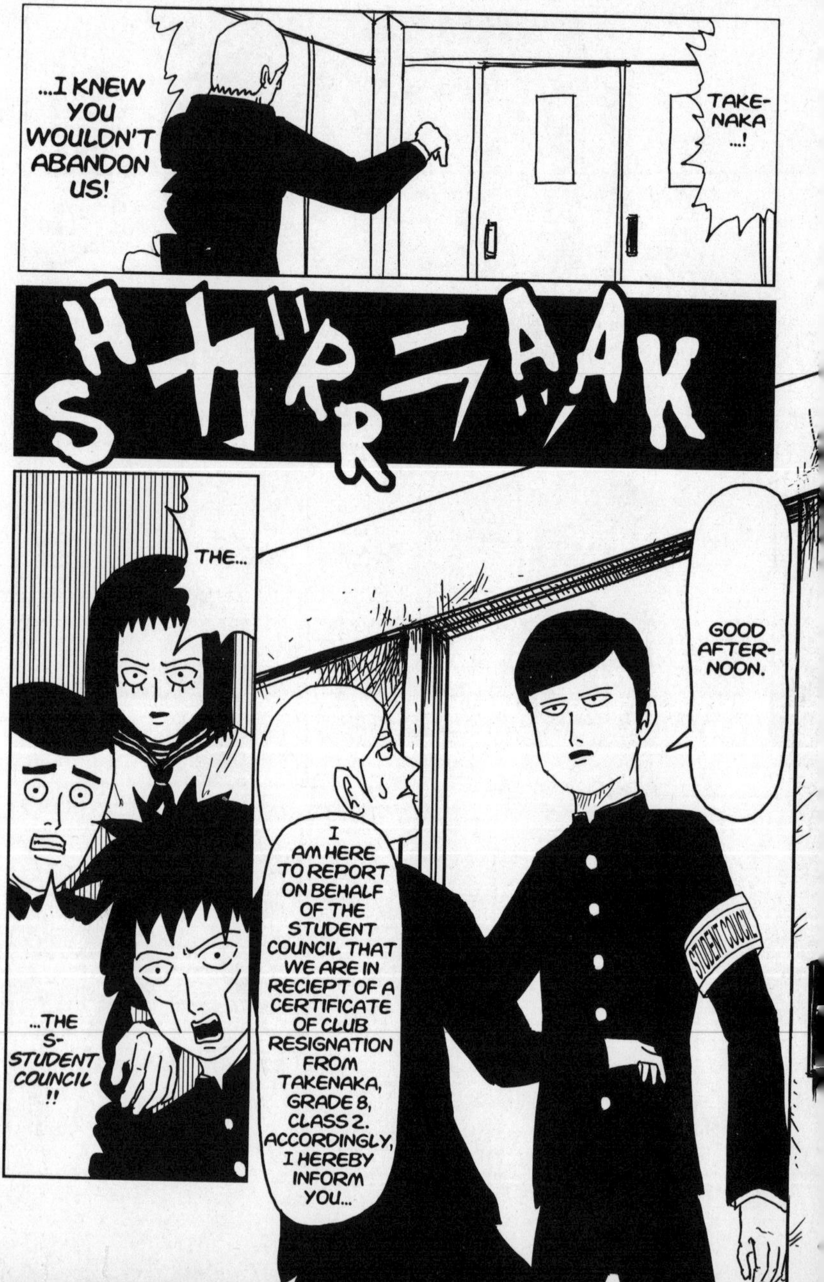
TAKENAKA...!
...I KNEW YOU WOULDN'T ABANDON US!
SHRRAAK
GOOD AFTERNOON.
I AM HERE TO REPORT ON BEHALF OF THE STUDENT COUNCIL THAT WE ARE IN RECIEPT OF A CERTIFICATE OF CLUB RESIGNATION FROM TAKENAKA, GRADE 8, CLASS 2. ACCORDINGLY, I HEREBY INFORM YOU...
STUDENT COUNCIL
THE...
...THE S-STUDENT COUNCIL!!

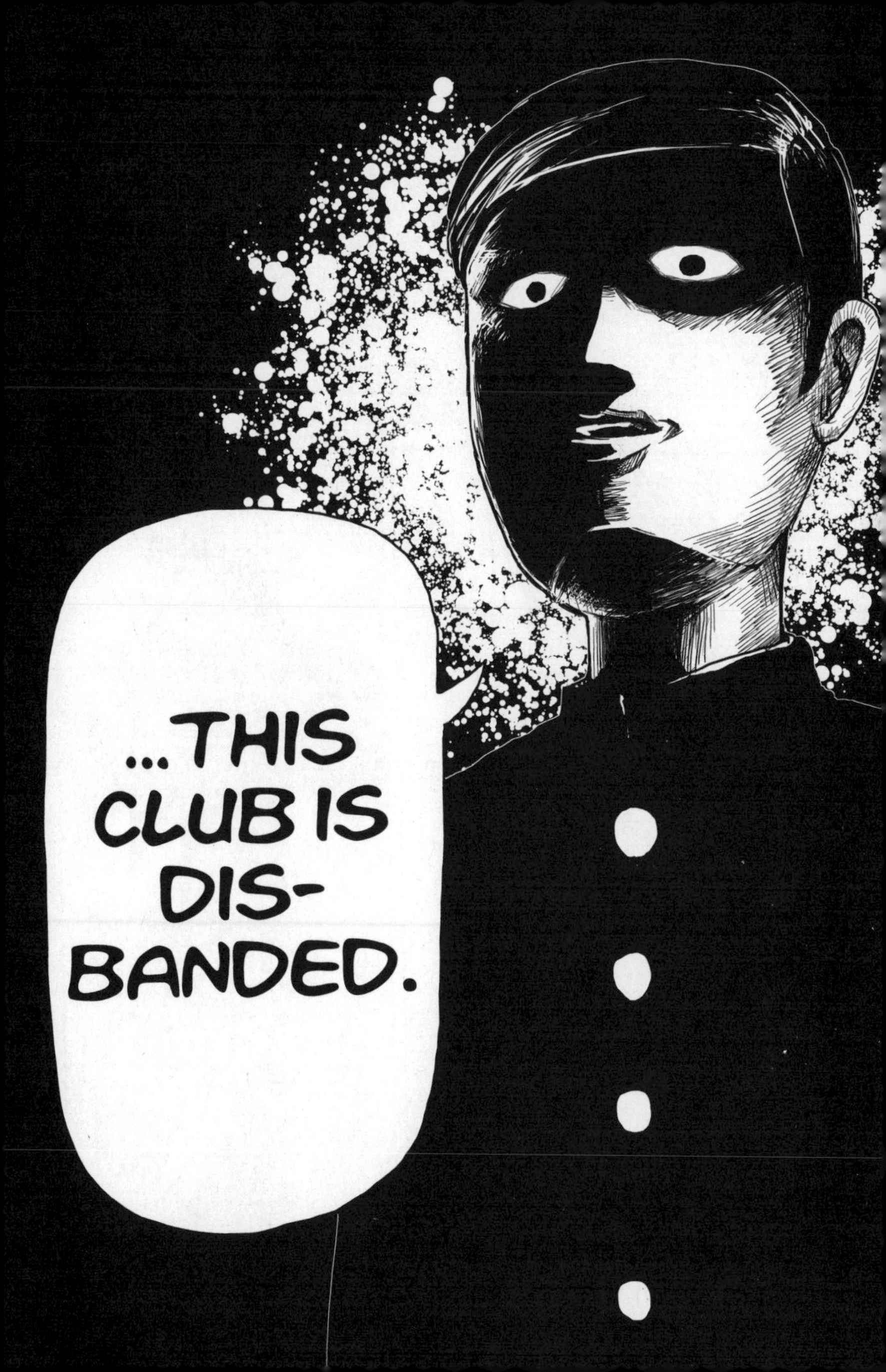
...THIS CLUB IS DIS- BANDED.

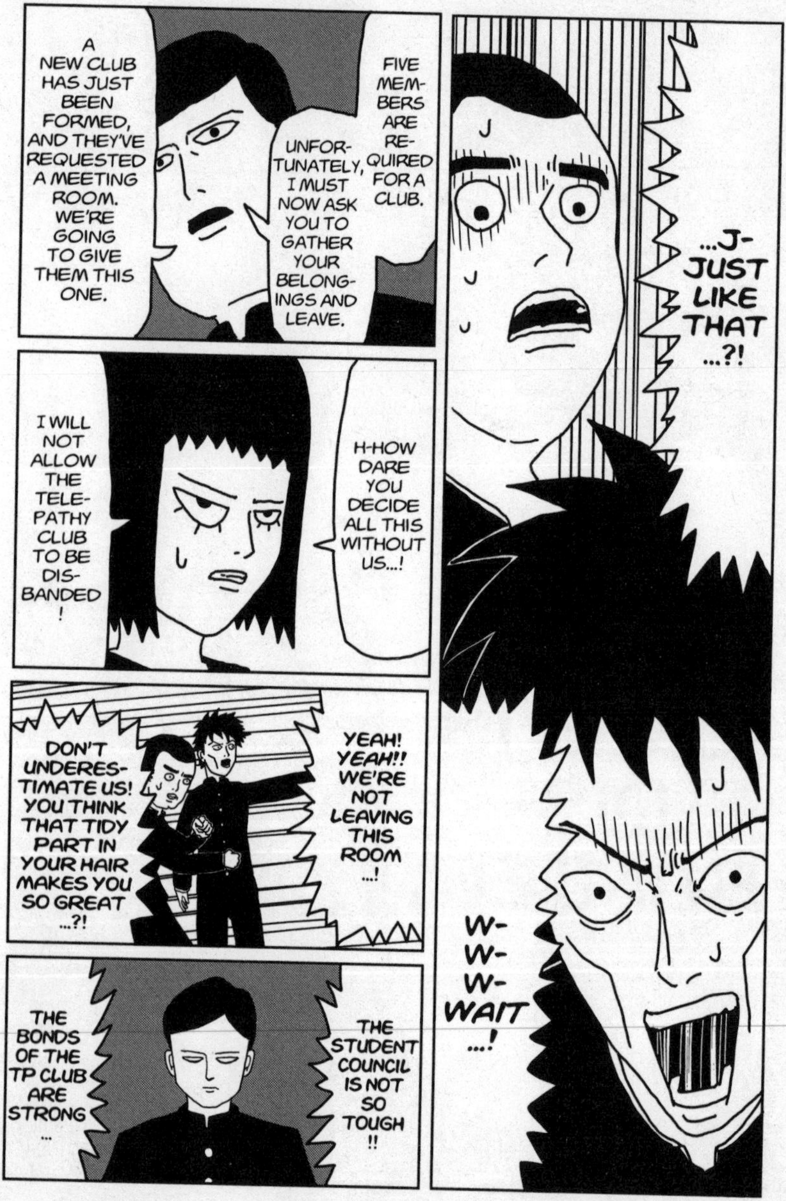
...J-JUST LIKE THAT...?!
W-W-W-WAIT...!
FIVE MEMBERS ARE REQUIRED FOR A CLUB.
UNFORTUNATELY, I MUST NOW ASK YOU TO GATHER YOUR BELONGINGS AND LEAVE.
A NEW CLUB HAS JUST BEEN FORMED, AND THEY'VE REQUESTED A MEETING ROOM. WE'RE GOING TO GIVE THEM THIS ONE.
H-HOW DARE YOU DECIDE ALL THIS WITHOUT US...!
I WILL NOT ALLOW THE TELEPATHY CLUB TO BE DISBANDED!
YEAH! YEAH!! WE'RE NOT LEAVING THIS ROOM...!
DON'T UNDERESTIMATE US! YOU THINK THAT TIDY PART IN YOUR HAIR MAKES YOU SO GREAT...?!
THE STUDENT COUNCIL IS NOT SO TOUGH!!
THE BONDS OF THE TP CLUB ARE STRONG...

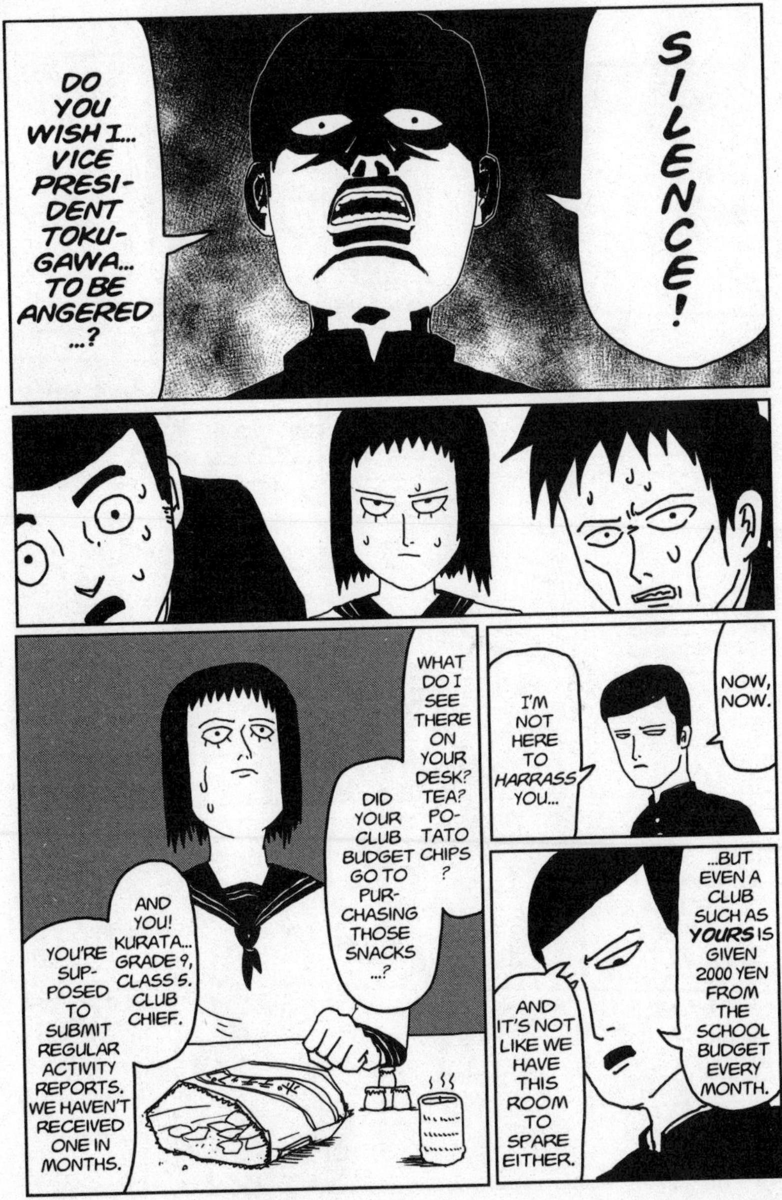
SILENCE!
DO YOU WISH I... VICE PRESIDENT TOKUGAWA... TO BE ANGERED ...?
NOW, NOW.
I'M NOT HERE TO *HARRASS* YOU...
...BUT EVEN A CLUB SUCH AS ***YOURS*** IS GIVEN 2000 YEN FROM THE SCHOOL BUDGET EVERY MONTH.
AND IT'S NOT LIKE WE HAVE THIS ROOM TO SPARE EITHER.
WHAT DO I SEE THERE ON YOUR DESK? TEA? POTATO CHIPS?
DID YOUR CLUB BUDGET GO TO PURCHASING THOSE SNACKS ...?
AND YOU! KURATA... GRADE 9, CLASS 5. CLUB CHIEF.
YOU'RE SUPPOSED TO SUBMIT REGULAR ACTIVITY REPORTS. WE HAVEN'T RECEIVED ONE IN MONTHS.

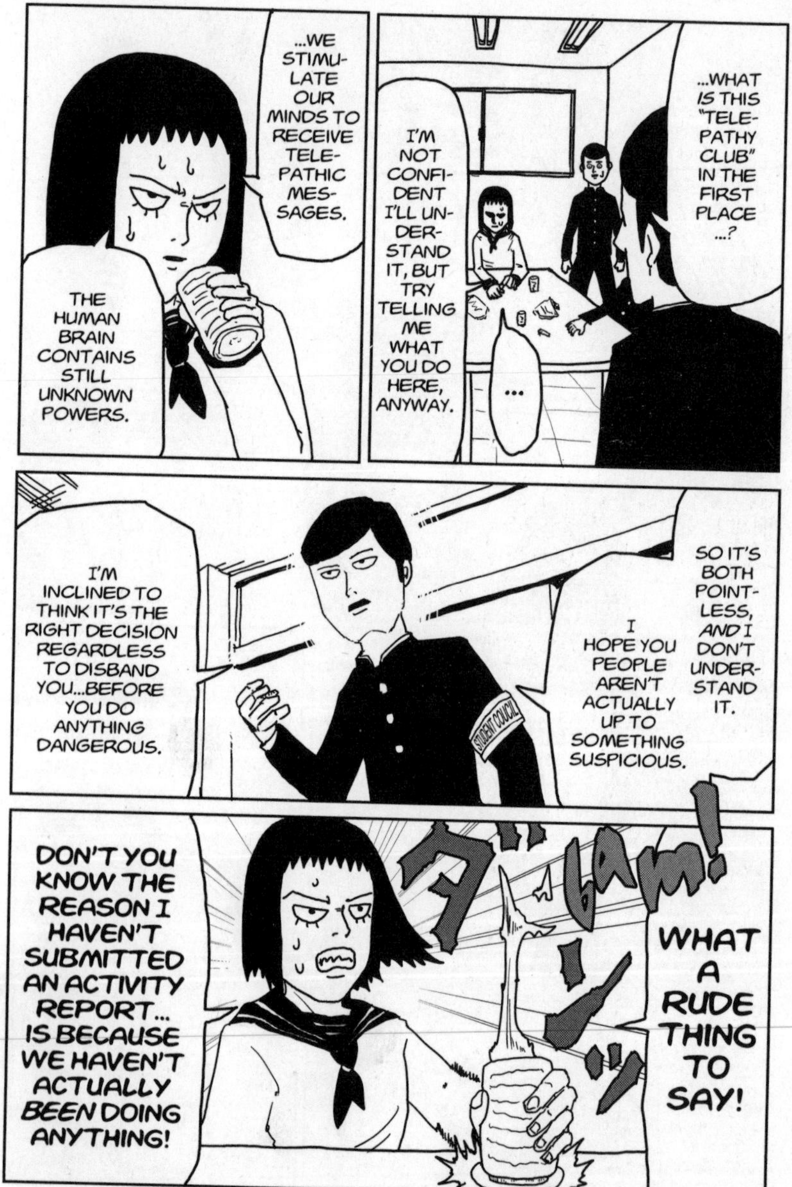
...WHAT IS THIS "TELEPATHY CLUB" IN THE FIRST PLACE ...?
I'M NOT CONFIDENT I'LL UNDERSTAND IT, BUT TRY TELLING ME WHAT YOU DO HERE, ANYWAY.
...
...WE STIMULATE OUR MINDS TO RECEIVE TELEPATHIC MESSAGES.
THE HUMAN BRAIN CONTAINS STILL UNKNOWN POWERS.
SO IT'S BOTH POINTLESS, AND I DON'T UNDERSTAND IT.
I HOPE YOU PEOPLE AREN'T ACTUALLY UP TO SOMETHING SUSPICIOUS.
I'M INCLINED TO THINK IT'S THE RIGHT DECISION REGARDLESS TO DISBAND YOU...BEFORE YOU DO ANYTHING DANGEROUS.
STUDENT COUNCIL
BAM!
WHAT A RUDE THING TO SAY!
DON'T YOU KNOW THE REASON I HAVEN'T SUBMITTED AN ACTIVITY REPORT... IS BECAUSE WE HAVEN'T ACTUALLY BEEN DOING ANYTHING!

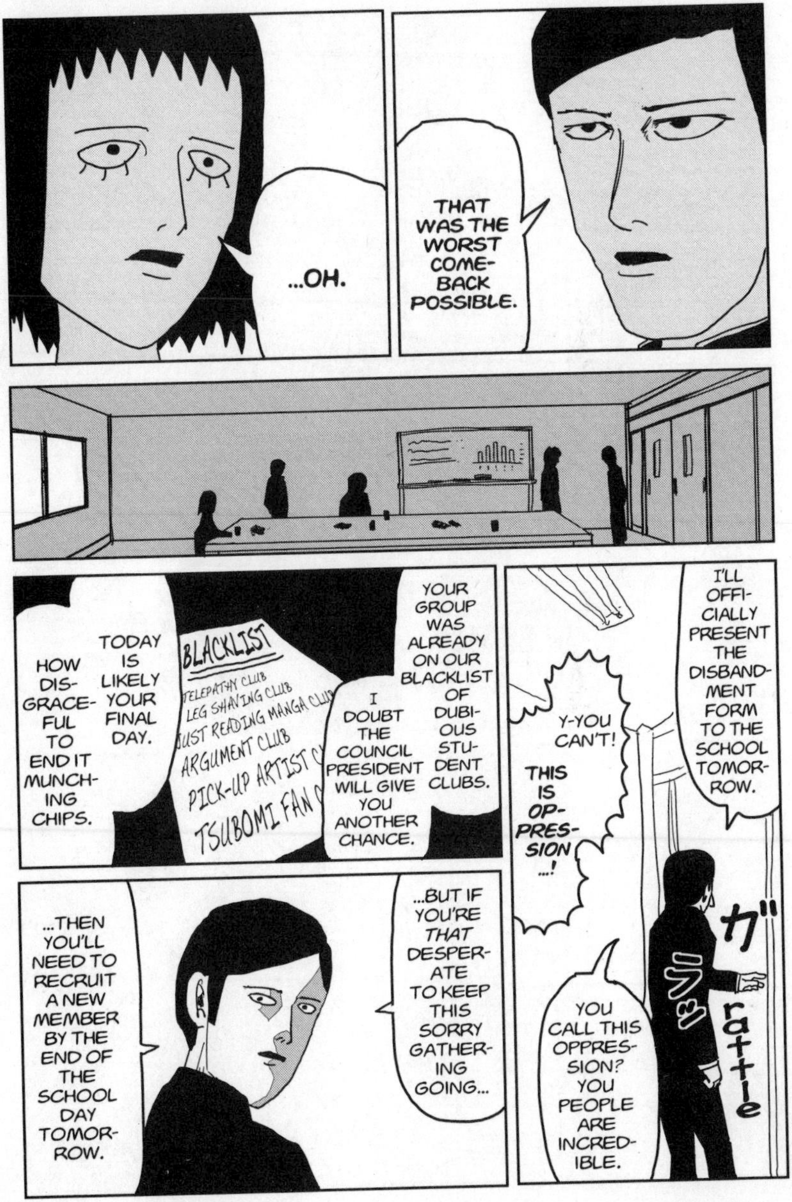
THAT WAS THE WORST COMEBACK POSSIBLE.
...OH.
I'LL OFFICIALLY PRESENT THE DISBANDMENT FORM TO THE SCHOOL TOMORROW.
Y-YOU CAN'T!
THIS IS OPPRESSION...!
YOU CALL THIS OPPRESSION? YOU PEOPLE ARE INCREDIBLE.
ガラッ
rattle
YOUR GROUP WAS ALREADY ON OUR BLACKLIST OF DUBIOUS STUDENT CLUBS.
I DOUBT THE COUNCIL PRESIDENT WILL GIVE YOU ANOTHER CHANCE.
BLACKLIST
TELEPATHY CLUB
LEG SHAVING CLUB
JUST READING MANGA CLUB
ARGUMENT CLUB
PICK-UP ARTIST C
TSUBOMI FAN C
TODAY IS LIKELY YOUR FINAL DAY.
HOW DISGRACEFUL TO END IT MUNCHING CHIPS.
...BUT IF YOU'RE THAT DESPERATE TO KEEP THIS SORRY GATHERING GOING...
...THEN YOU'LL NEED TO RECRUIT A NEW MEMBER BY THE END OF THE SCHOOL DAY TOMORROW.

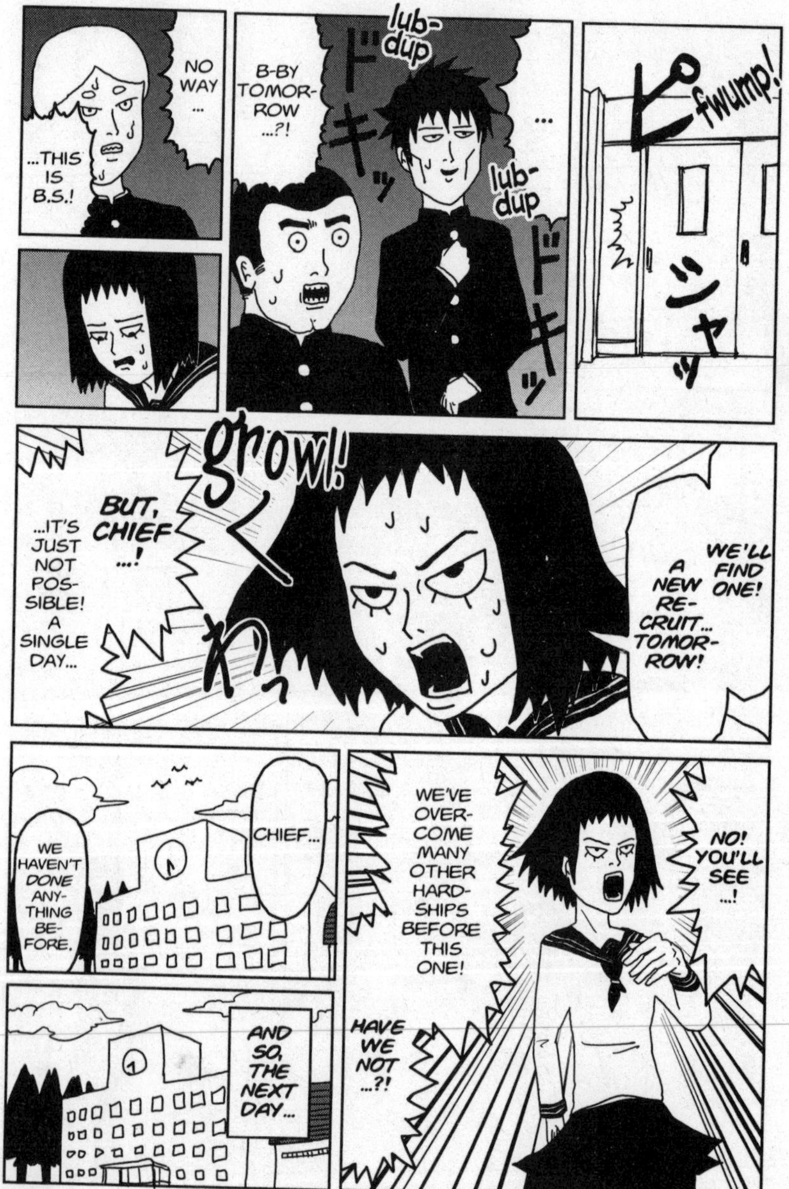
ピ
fwump!
シャッ
lub-dup
ドキッ
B-BY TOMORROW ...?!
...
lub-dup
ドキッ
NO WAY ...
...THIS IS B.S.!
WE'LL FIND ONE! A NEW RECRUIT... TOMORROW!
growl!
くわっ
BUT, CHIEF ...!
...IT'S JUST NOT POSSIBLE! A SINGLE DAY...
NO! YOU'LL SEE ...!
WE'VE OVERCOME MANY OTHER HARDSHIPS BEFORE THIS ONE!
HAVE WE NOT ...?!
CHIEF...
WE HAVEN'T *DONE* ANYTHING BEFORE.
AND SO, THE NEXT DAY...

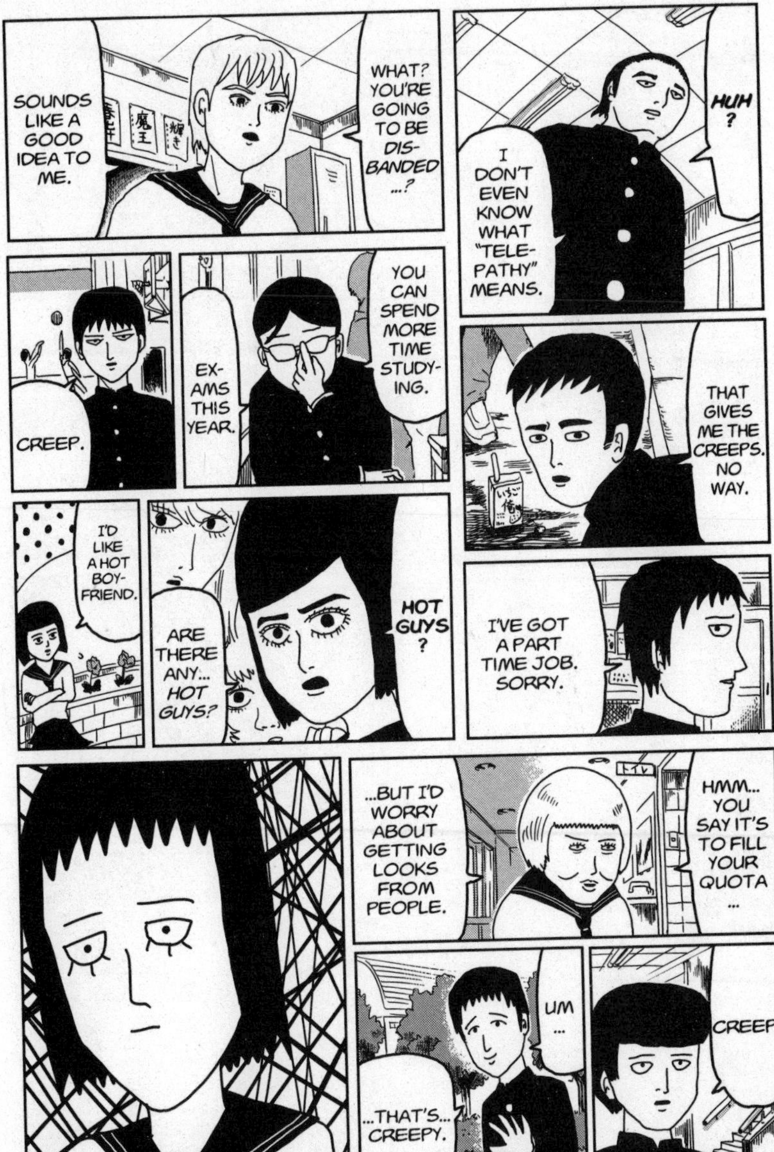
HUH?
I DON'T EVEN KNOW WHAT "TELEPATHY" MEANS.
WHAT? YOU'RE GOING TO BE DISBANDED ...?
SOUNDS LIKE A GOOD IDEA TO ME.
THAT GIVES ME THE CREEPS. NO WAY.
YOU CAN SPEND MORE TIME STUDYING.
EXAMS THIS YEAR.
CREEP.
I'VE GOT A PART TIME JOB. SORRY.
HOT GUYS?
ARE THERE ANY... HOT GUYS?
I'D LIKE A HOT BOYFRIEND.
HMM... YOU SAY IT'S TO FILL YOUR QUOTA ...
...BUT I'D WORRY ABOUT GETTING LOOKS FROM PEOPLE.
CREEP.
UM ...
...THAT'S... CREEPY.

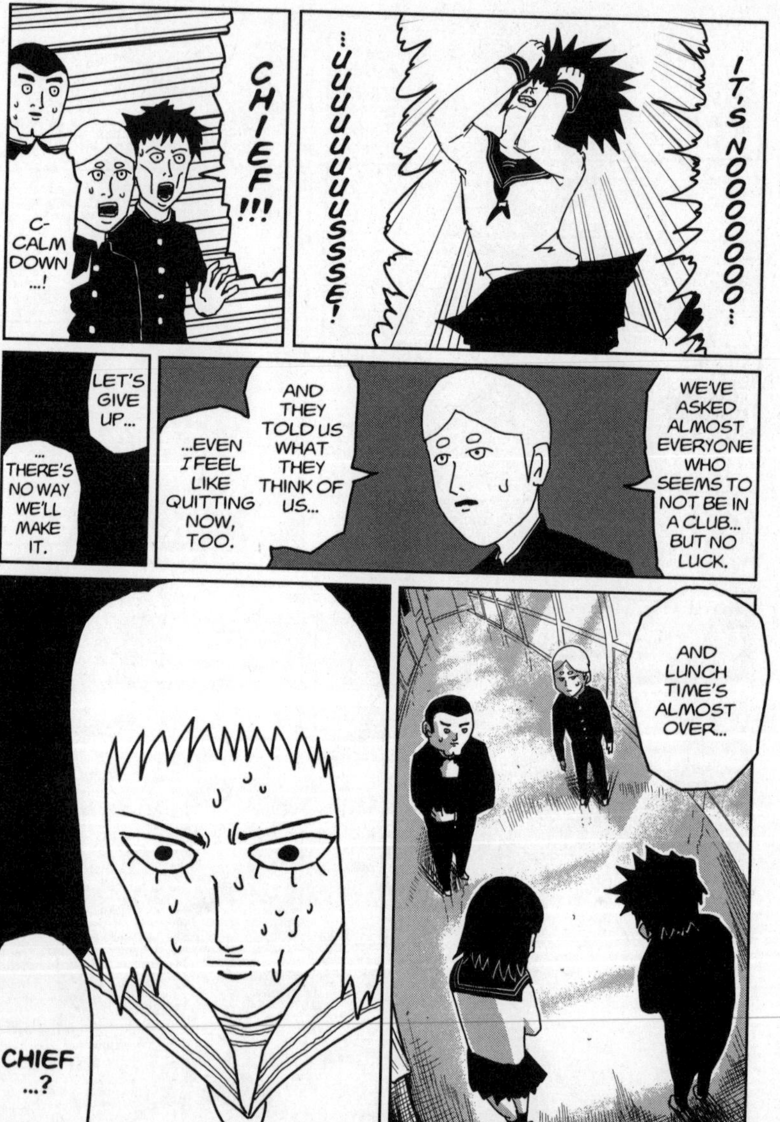
IT'S NOOOOOOOO...
...UUUUUUUSSSE!
CHIEF!!!
C-CALM DOWN...!
WE'VE ASKED ALMOST EVERYONE WHO SEEMS TO NOT BE IN A CLUB... BUT NO LUCK.
AND THEY TOLD US WHAT THEY THINK OF US...
...EVEN I FEEL LIKE QUITTING NOW, TOO.
LET'S GIVE UP...
...THERE'S NO WAY WE'LL MAKE IT.
AND LUNCH TIME'S ALMOST OVER...
CHIEF...?

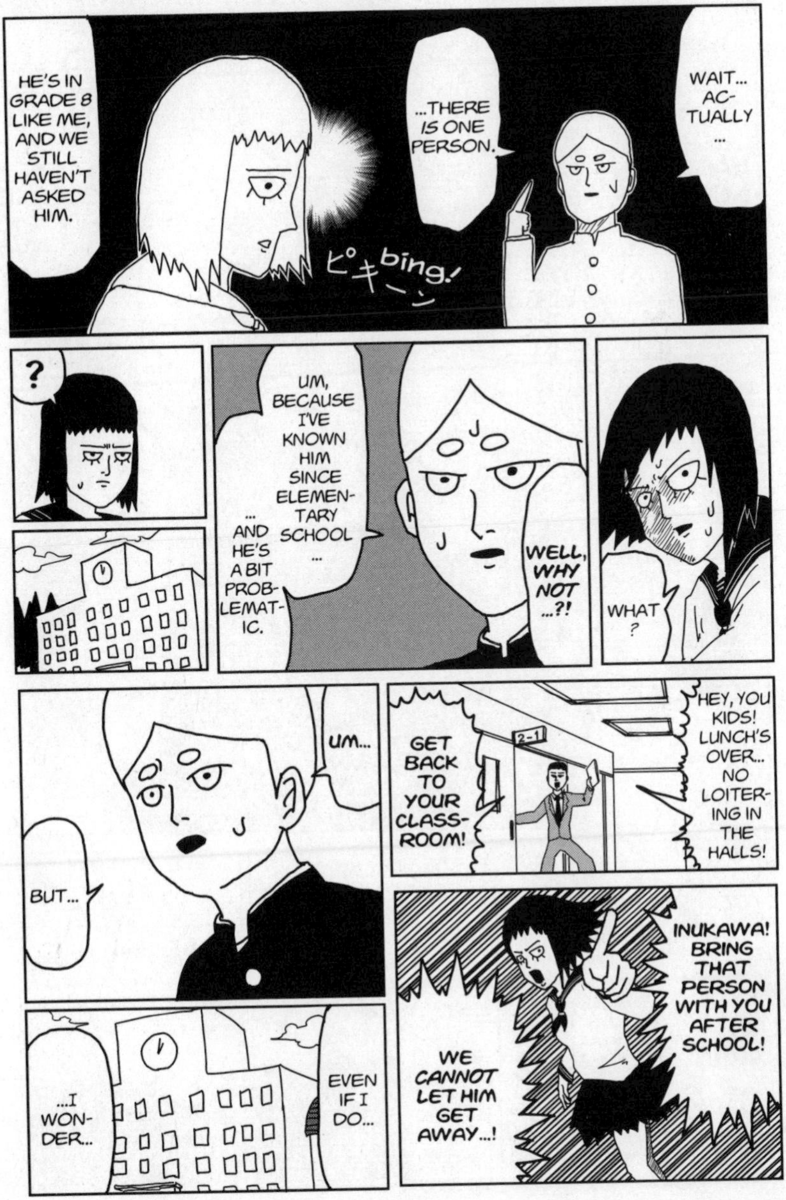
WAIT... ACTUALLY...
...THERE IS ONE PERSON.
ピキーン
bing!
HE'S IN GRADE 8 LIKE ME, AND WE STILL HAVEN'T ASKED HIM.
WHAT?
WELL, WHY NOT...?!
UM, BECAUSE I'VE KNOWN HIM SINCE ELEMENTARY SCHOOL...
...AND HE'S A BIT PROBLEMATIC.
?
HEY, YOU KIDS! LUNCH'S OVER... NO LOITERING IN THE HALLS!
2-1
GET BACK TO YOUR CLASSROOM!
INUKAWA! BRING THAT PERSON WITH YOU AFTER SCHOOL!
WE CANNOT LET HIM GET AWAY...!
UM...
BUT...
EVEN IF I DO...
...I WONDER...

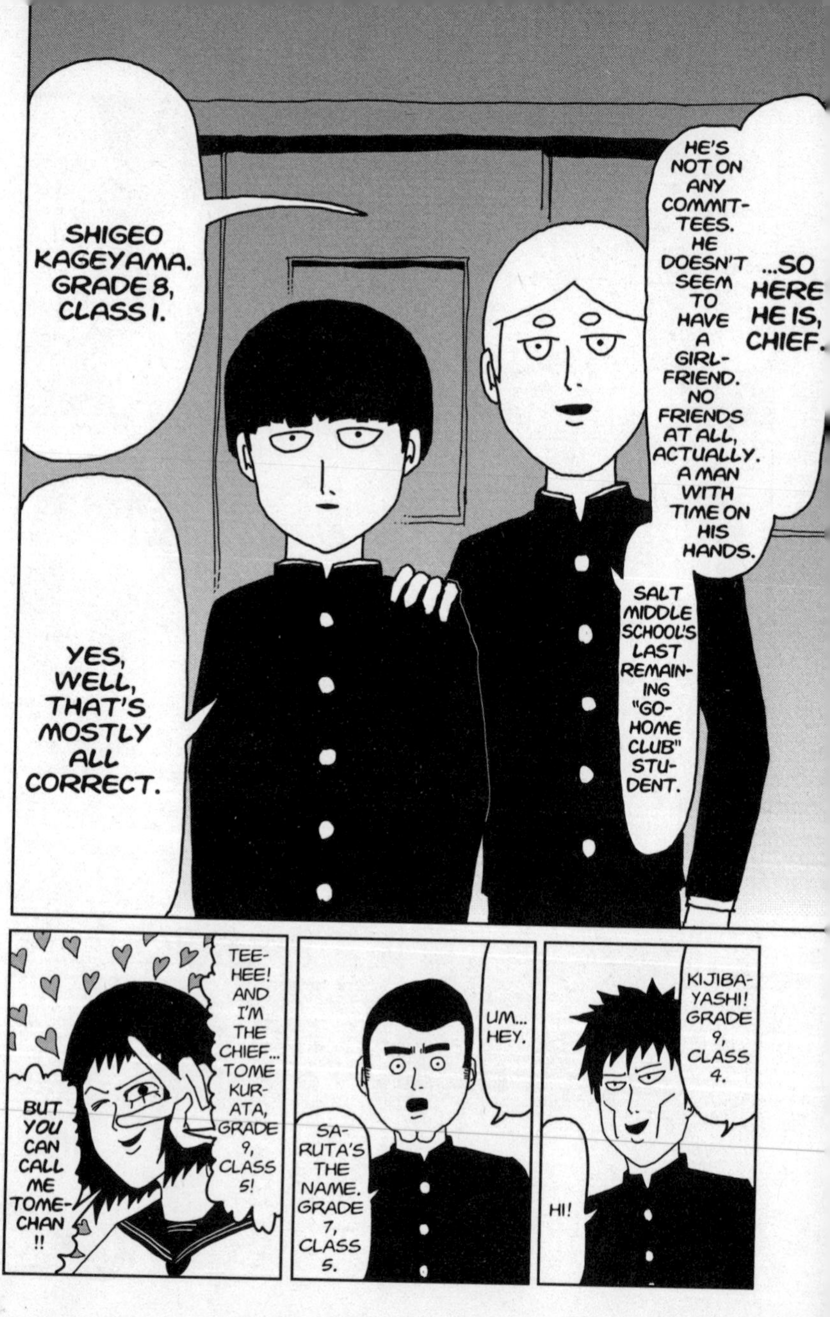
SHIGEO KAGEYAMA. GRADE 8, CLASS 1.
HE'S NOT ON ANY COMMIT-TEES. HE DOESN'T SEEM TO HAVE A GIRL-FRIEND. NO FRIENDS AT ALL, ACTUALLY. A MAN WITH TIME ON HIS HANDS.
SALT MIDDLE SCHOOL'S LAST REMAIN-ING "GO-HOME CLUB" STU-DENT.
...SO HERE HE IS, CHIEF.
YES, WELL, THAT'S MOSTLY ALL CORRECT.
KIJIBA-YASHI! GRADE 9, CLASS 4.
HI!
UM... HEY.
SA-RUTA'S THE NAME. GRADE 7, CLASS 5.
TEE-HEE! AND I'M THE CHIEF... TOME KUR-ATA, GRADE 9, CLASS 5!
BUT YOU CAN CALL ME TOME-CHAN !!

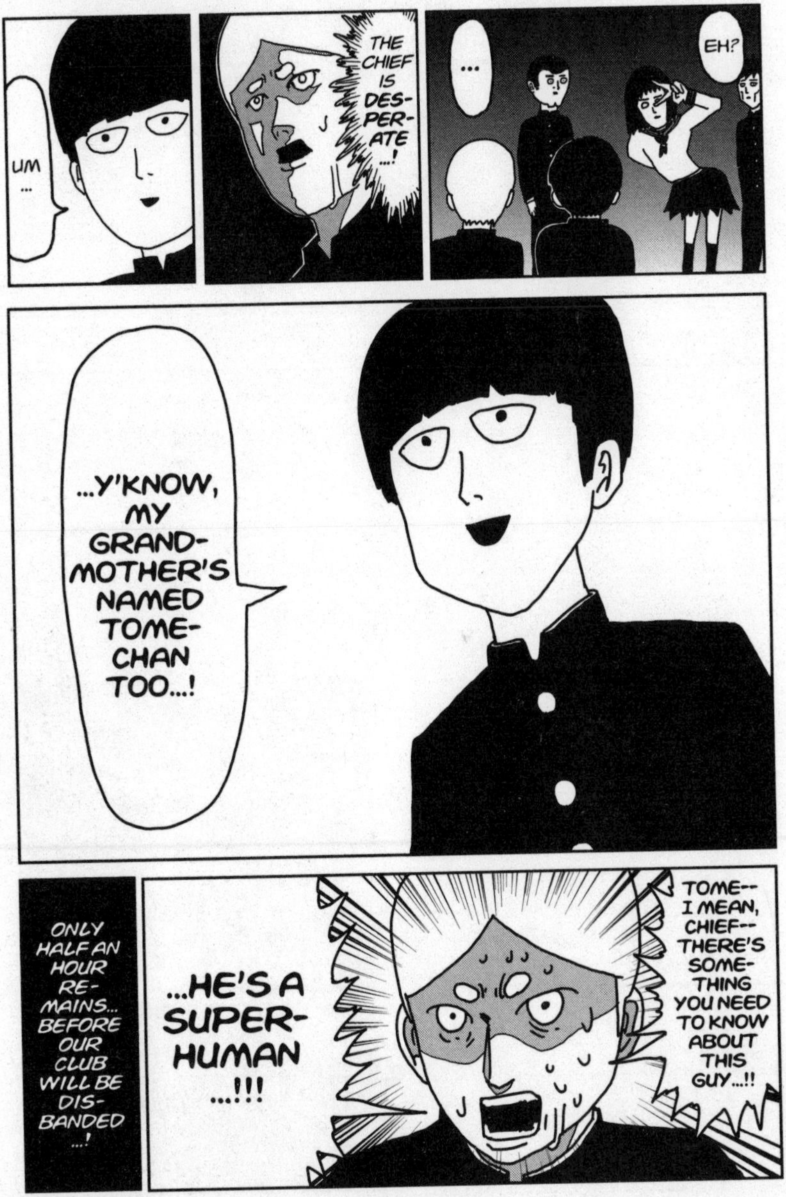
EH?
...
THE CHIEF IS DES-PER-ATE ...!
UM ...
...Y'KNOW, MY GRAND-MOTHER'S NAMED TOME-CHAN TOO...!
TOME-- I MEAN, CHIEF-- THERE'S SOME-THING YOU NEED TO KNOW ABOUT THIS GUY...!!
...HE'S A SUPER-HUMAN ...!!!
ONLY HALF AN HOUR RE-MAINS... BEFORE OUR CLUB WILL BE DIS-BANDED ...!

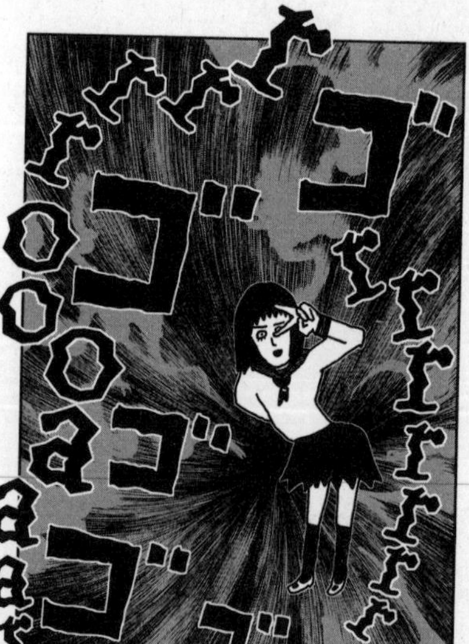

ゴ
ゴ
ゴ
ゴ
rrrrrr
oooa
aar

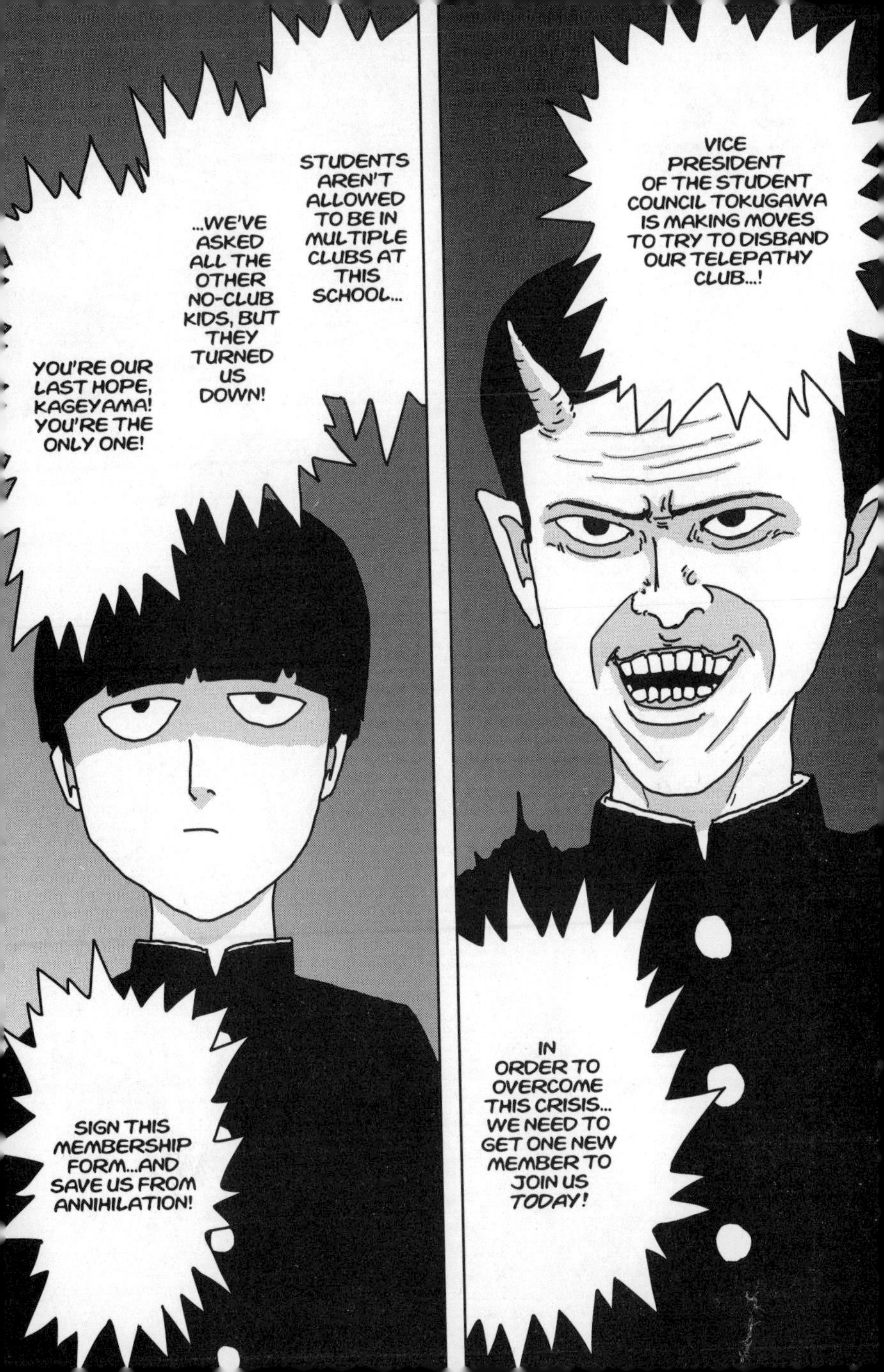
VICE PRESIDENT OF THE STUDENT COUNCIL TOKUGAWA IS MAKING MOVES TO TRY TO DISBAND OUR TELEPATHY CLUB...!
IN ORDER TO OVERCOME THIS CRISIS... WE NEED TO GET ONE NEW MEMBER TO JOIN US TODAY!
STUDENTS AREN'T ALLOWED TO BE IN MULTIPLE CLUBS AT THIS SCHOOL...
...WE'VE ASKED ALL THE OTHER NO-CLUB KIDS, BUT THEY TURNED US DOWN!
YOU'RE OUR LAST HOPE, KAGEYAMA! YOU'RE THE ONLY ONE!
SIGN THIS MEMBERSHIP FORM...AND SAVE US FROM ANNIHILATION!

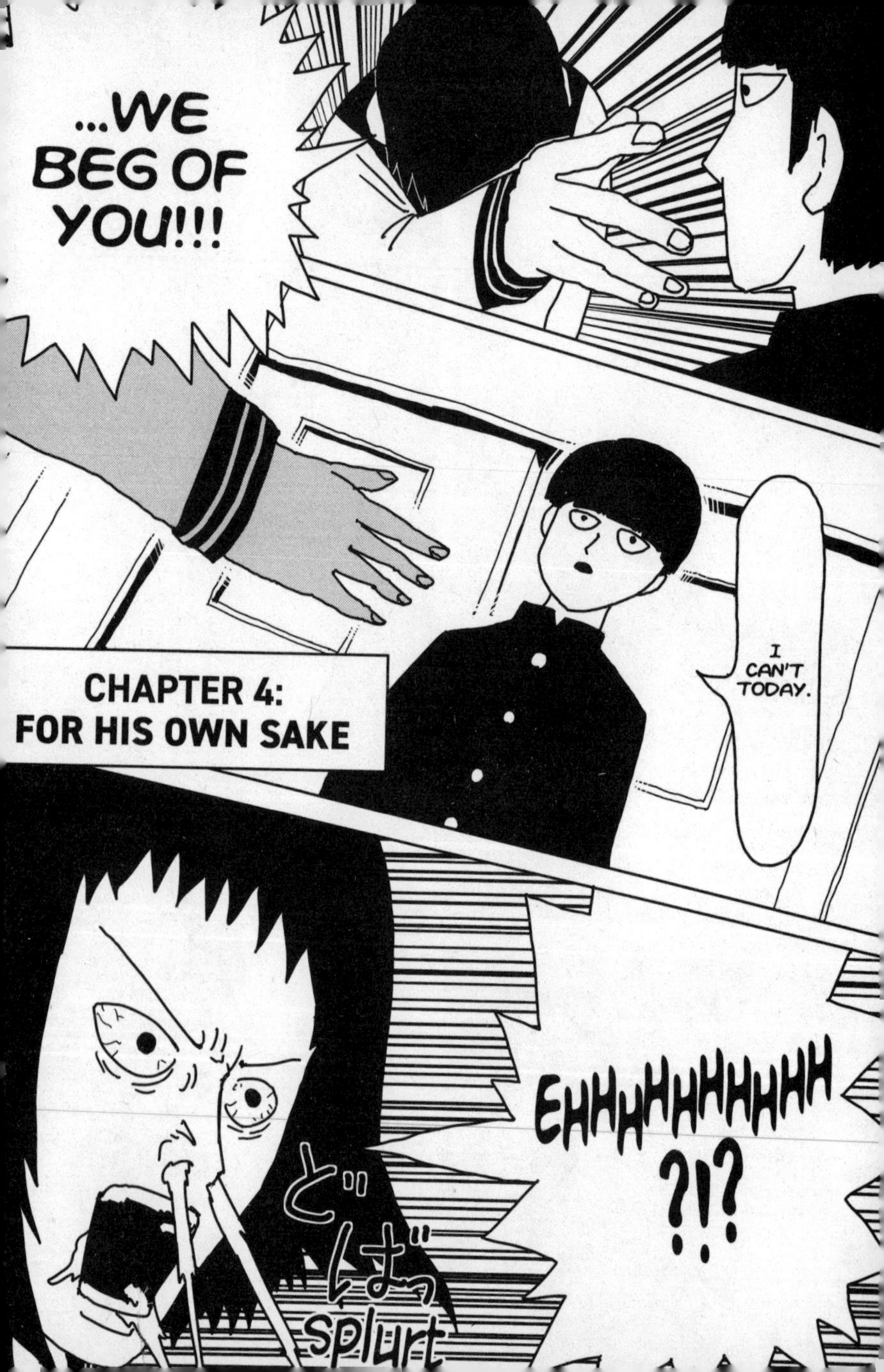
...WE BEG OF YOU!!!
I CAN'T TODAY.
CHAPTER 4: FOR HIS OWN SAKE
EHHHHHHHHHH ?!?
どばっ
splurt

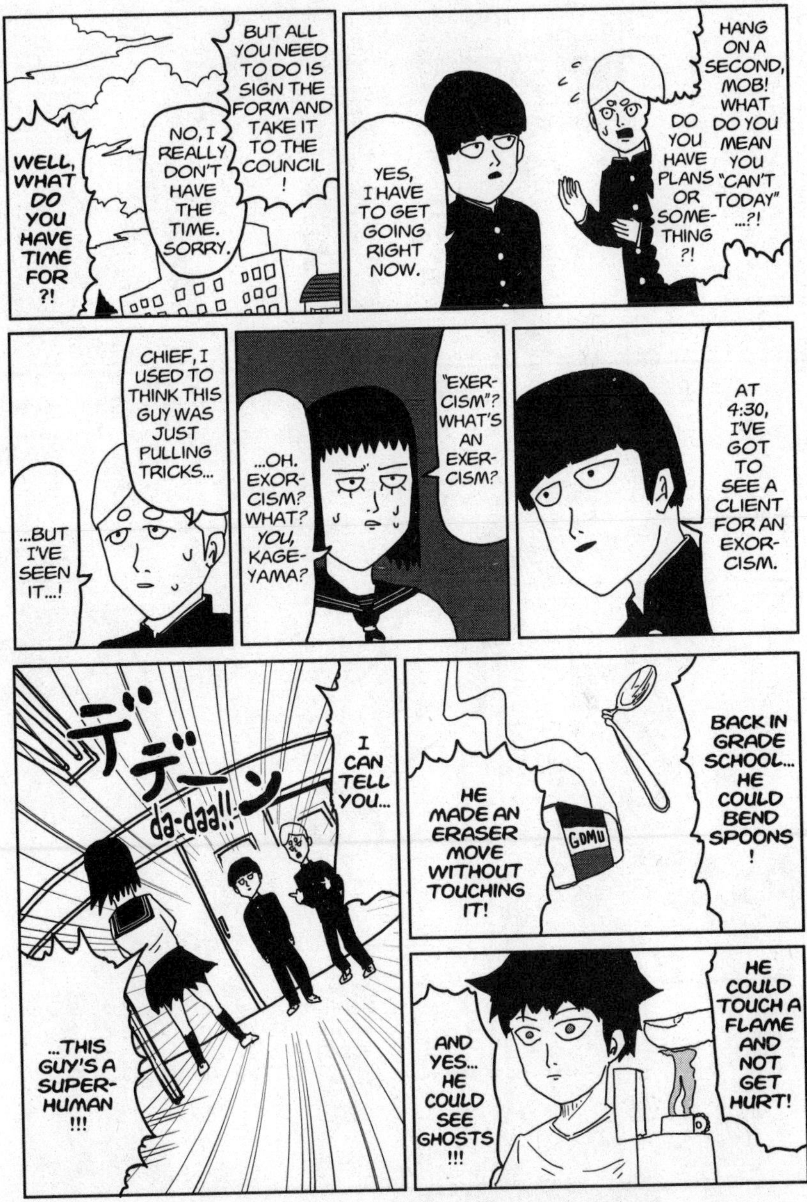
HANG ON A SECOND, MOB! WHAT DO YOU MEAN YOU "CAN'T TODAY" ...?!
DO YOU HAVE PLANS OR SOMETHING?!
YES, I HAVE TO GET GOING RIGHT NOW.
BUT ALL YOU NEED TO DO IS SIGN THE FORM AND TAKE IT TO THE COUNCIL!
NO, I REALLY DON'T HAVE THE TIME. SORRY.
WELL, WHAT DO YOU HAVE TIME FOR?!
AT 4:30, I'VE GOT TO SEE A CLIENT FOR AN EXORCISM.
"EXERCISM"? WHAT'S AN EXERCISM?
...OH. EXORCISM? WHAT? YOU, KAGEYAMA?
CHIEF, I USED TO THINK THIS GUY WAS JUST PULLING TRICKS...
...BUT I'VE SEEN IT...!
BACK IN GRADE SCHOOL... HE COULD BEND SPOONS!
HE MADE AN ERASER MOVE WITHOUT TOUCHING IT!
GOMU
HE COULD TOUCH A FLAME AND NOT GET HURT!
AND YES... HE COULD SEE GHOSTS!!!
I CAN TELL YOU...
デデーン
da-daa!!
...THIS GUY'S A SUPER-HUMAN!!!

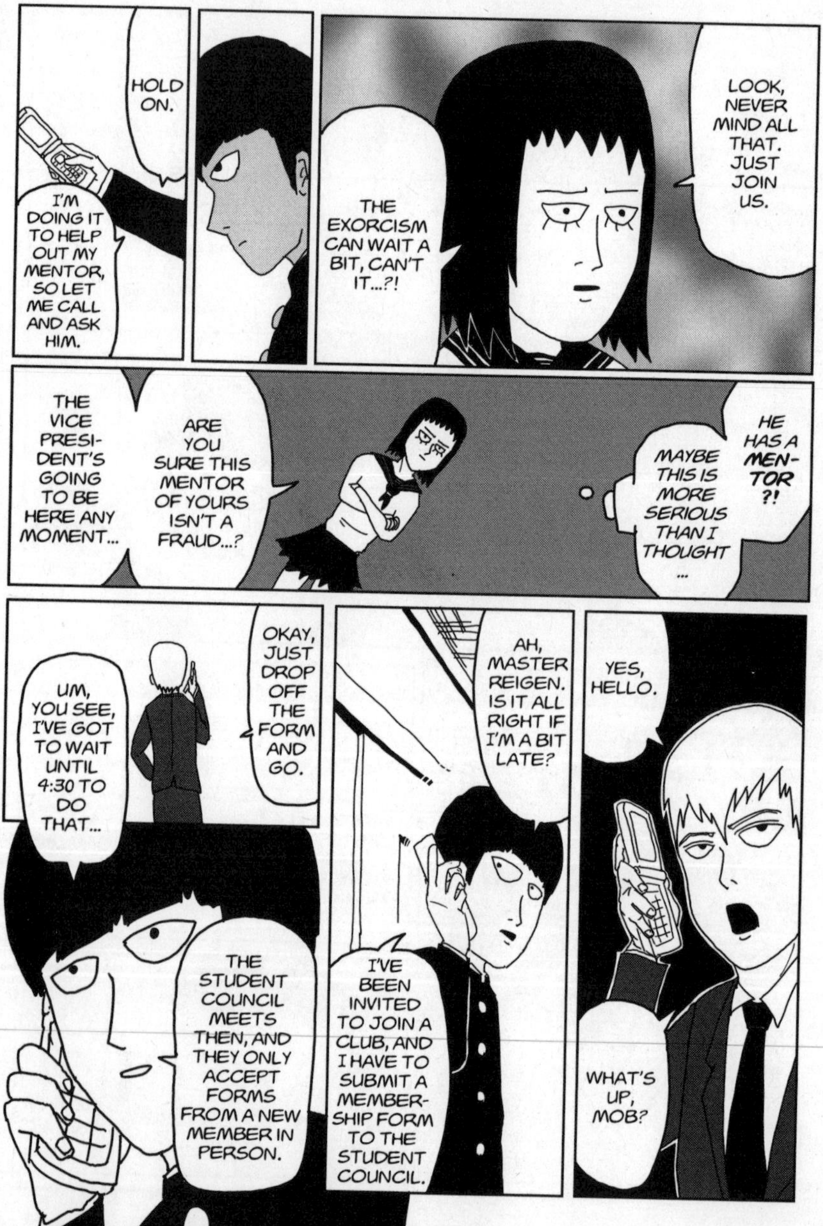
LOOK, NEVER MIND ALL THAT. JUST JOIN US.
THE EXORCISM CAN WAIT A BIT, CAN'T IT...?!
HOLD ON.
I'M DOING IT TO HELP OUT MY MENTOR, SO LET ME CALL AND ASK HIM.
HE HAS A *MENTOR*?!
MAYBE THIS IS MORE SERIOUS THAN I THOUGHT...
ARE YOU SURE THIS MENTOR OF YOURS ISN'T A FRAUD...?
THE VICE PRESIDENT'S GOING TO BE HERE ANY MOMENT...
YES, HELLO.
WHAT'S UP, MOB?
AH, MASTER REIGEN. IS IT ALL RIGHT IF I'M A BIT LATE?
I'VE BEEN INVITED TO JOIN A CLUB, AND I HAVE TO SUBMIT A MEMBERSHIP FORM TO THE STUDENT COUNCIL.
OKAY, JUST DROP OFF THE FORM AND GO.
UM, YOU SEE, I'VE GOT TO WAIT UNTIL 4:30 TO DO THAT...
THE STUDENT COUNCIL MEETS THEN, AND THEY ONLY ACCEPT FORMS FROM A NEW MEMBER IN PERSON.

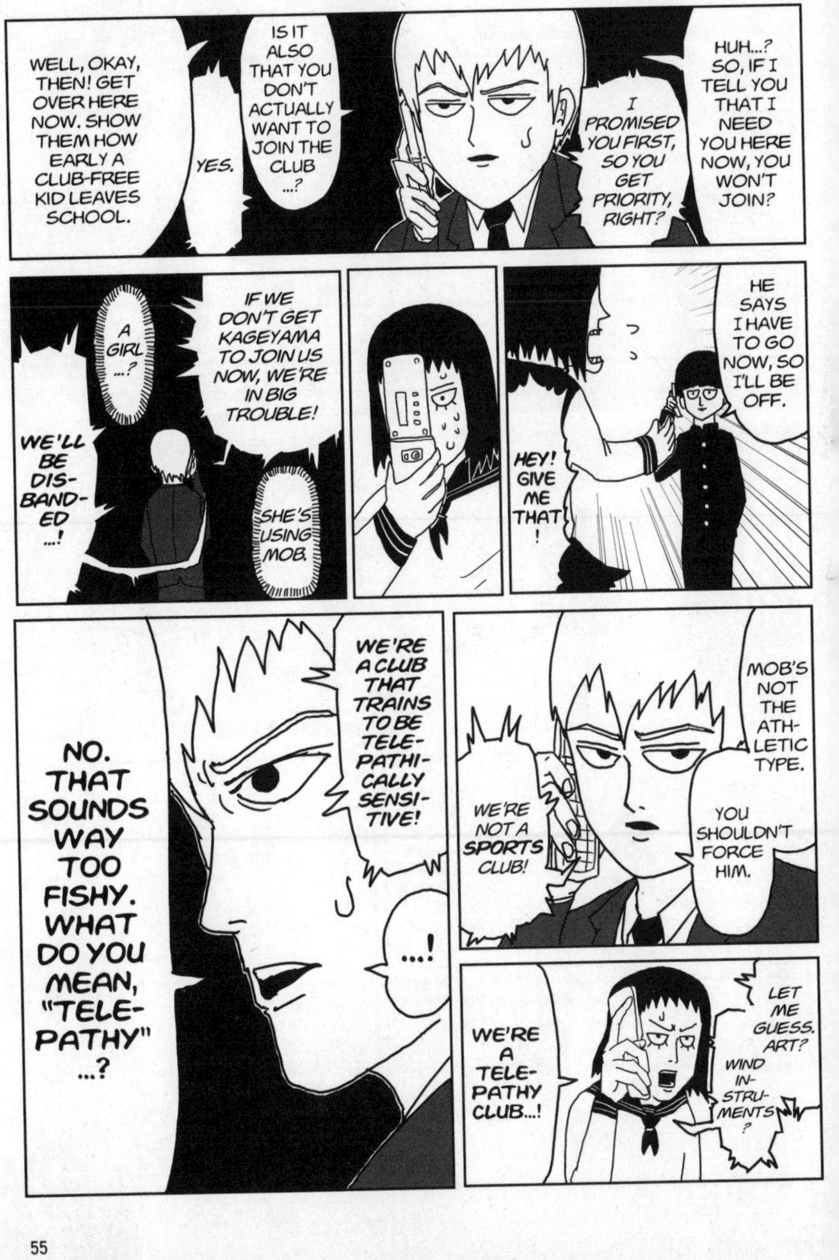
HUH...? SO, IF I TELL YOU THAT I NEED YOU HERE NOW, YOU WON'T JOIN?
I PROMISED YOU FIRST, SO YOU GET PRIORITY, RIGHT?
IS IT ALSO THAT YOU DON'T ACTUALLY WANT TO JOIN THE CLUB ...?
YES.
WELL, OKAY, THEN! GET OVER HERE NOW. SHOW THEM HOW EARLY A CLUB-FREE KID LEAVES SCHOOL.
HE SAYS I HAVE TO GO NOW, SO I'LL BE OFF.
HEY! GIVE ME THAT!
IF WE DON'T GET KAGEYAMA TO JOIN US NOW, WE'RE IN BIG TROUBLE!
A GIRL ...?
SHE'S USING MOB.
WE'LL BE DISBANDED ...!
MOB'S NOT THE ATHLETIC TYPE.
YOU SHOULDN'T FORCE HIM.
WE'RE NOT A SPORTS CLUB!
LET ME GUESS. ART?
WIND INSTRUMENTS?
WE'RE A TELEPATHY CLUB...!
WE'RE A CLUB THAT TRAINS TO BE TELEPATHICALLY SENSITIVE!
...!
NO. THAT SOUNDS WAY TOO FISHY. WHAT DO YOU MEAN, "TELEPATHY" ...?

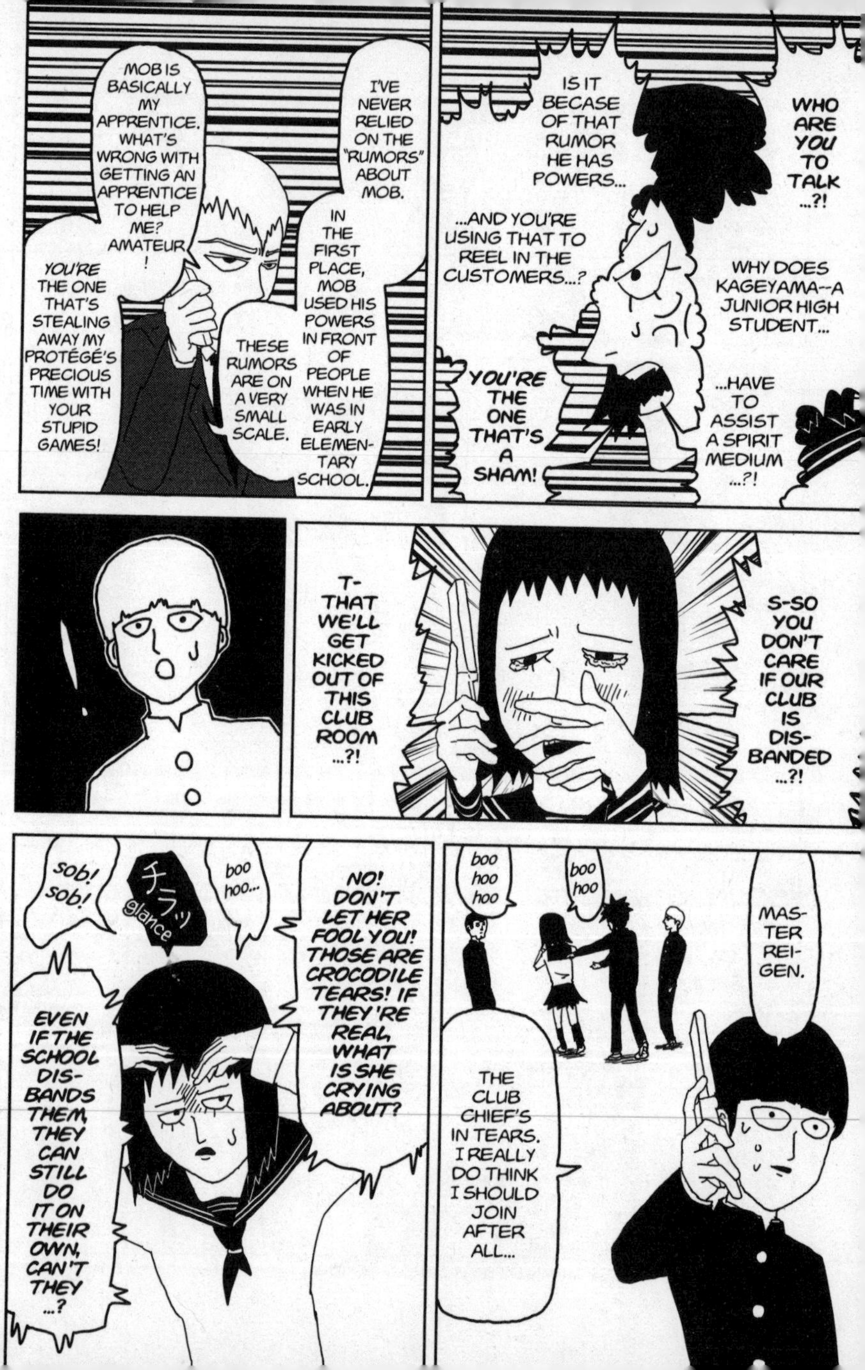
WHO ARE YOU TO TALK ...?!
IS IT BECASE OF THAT RUMOR HE HAS POWERS...
...AND YOU'RE USING THAT TO REEL IN THE CUSTOMERS...?
WHY DOES KAGEYAMA--A JUNIOR HIGH STUDENT...
...HAVE TO ASSIST A SPIRIT MEDIUM ...?!
YOU'RE THE ONE THAT'S A SHAM!
I'VE NEVER RELIED ON THE "RUMORS" ABOUT MOB.
IN THE FIRST PLACE, MOB USED HIS POWERS IN FRONT OF PEOPLE WHEN HE WAS IN EARLY ELEMEN-TARY SCHOOL.
THESE RUMORS ARE ON A VERY SMALL SCALE.
MOB IS BASICALLY MY APPRENTICE. WHAT'S WRONG WITH GETTING AN APPRENTICE TO HELP ME? AMATEUR!
YOU'RE THE ONE THAT'S STEALING AWAY MY PROTÉGÉ'S PRECIOUS TIME WITH YOUR STUPID GAMES!
S-SO YOU DON'T CARE IF OUR CLUB IS DIS-BANDED ...?!
T-THAT WE'LL GET KICKED OUT OF THIS CLUB ROOM ...?!
MAS-TER REI-GEN.
boo hoo
boo hoo hoo
THE CLUB CHIEF'S IN TEARS. I REALLY DO THINK I SHOULD JOIN AFTER ALL...
NO! DON'T LET HER FOOL YOU! THOSE ARE CROCODILE TEARS! IF THEY'RE REAL, WHAT IS SHE CRYING ABOUT?
boo hoo...
チラッ
glance
sob! sob!
EVEN IF THE SCHOOL DIS-BANDS THEM, THEY CAN STILL DO IT ON THEIR OWN, CAN'T THEY ...?

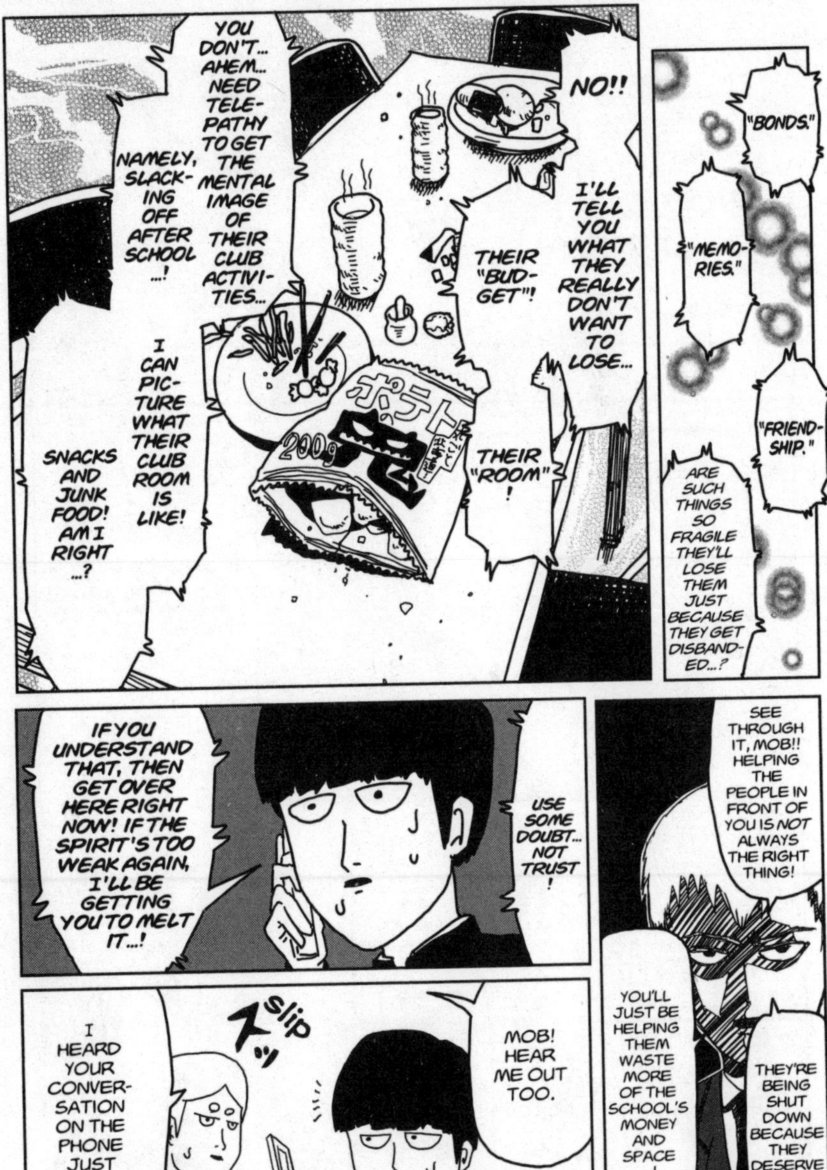
"BONDS."
"MEMORIES."
"FRIENDSHIP."
ARE SUCH THINGS SO FRAGILE THEY'LL LOSE THEM JUST BECAUSE THEY GET DISBANDED...?
NO!!
I'LL TELL YOU WHAT THEY REALLY DON'T WANT TO LOSE...
THEIR "BUDGET"!
THEIR "ROOM"!
YOU DON'T... AHEM... NEED TELEPATHY TO GET THE MENTAL IMAGE OF THEIR CLUB ACTIVITIES...
NAMELY, SLACKING OFF AFTER SCHOOL...!
I CAN PICTURE WHAT THEIR CLUB ROOM IS LIKE!
SNACKS AND JUNK FOOD! AM I RIGHT...?
SEE THROUGH IT, MOB!! HELPING THE PEOPLE IN FRONT OF YOU IS NOT ALWAYS THE RIGHT THING!
THEY'RE BEING SHUT DOWN BECAUSE THEY DESERVE IT.
YOU'LL JUST BE HELPING THEM WASTE MORE OF THE SCHOOL'S MONEY AND SPACE...!
USE SOME DOUBT... NOT TRUST!
IF YOU UNDERSTAND THAT, THEN GET OVER HERE RIGHT NOW! IF THE SPIRIT'S TOO WEAK AGAIN, I'LL BE GETTING YOU TO MELT IT...!
MOB! HEAR ME OUT TOO.
スッ
slip
I HEARD YOUR CONVERSATION ON THE PHONE JUST NOW...

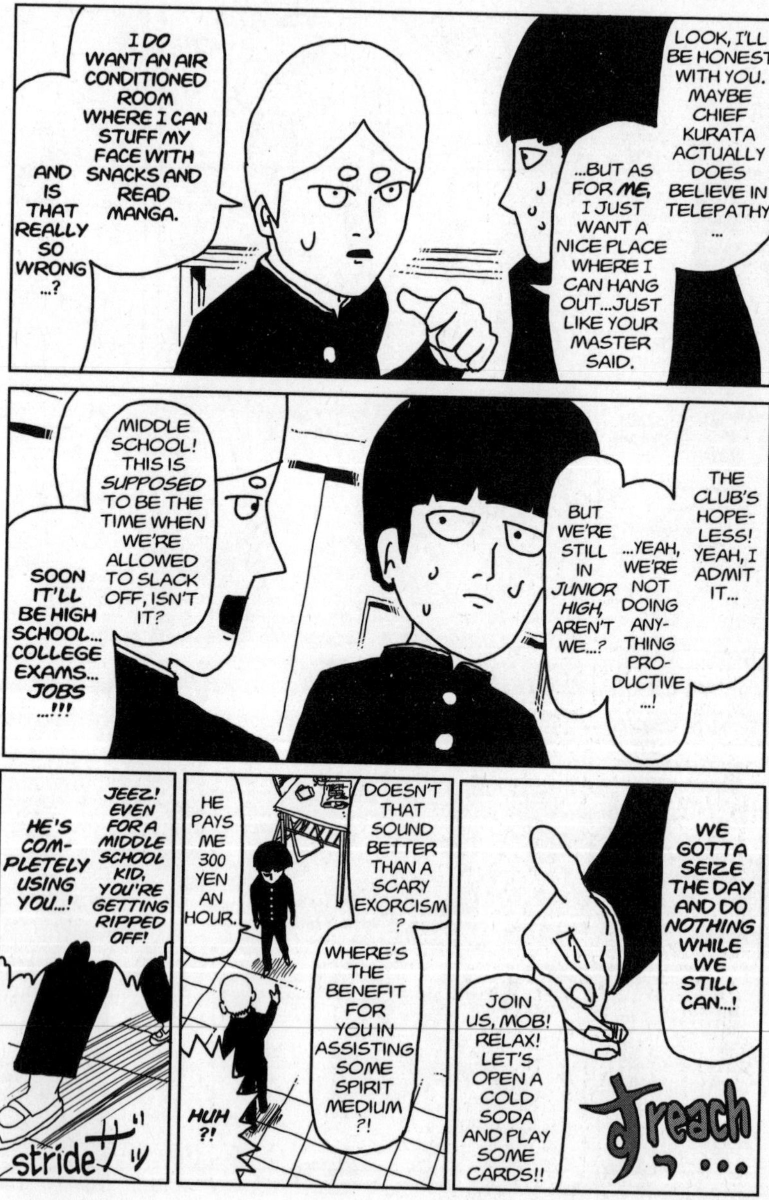
LOOK, I'LL BE HONEST WITH YOU. MAYBE CHIEF KURATA ACTUALLY DOES BELIEVE IN TELEPATHY...
...BUT AS FOR *ME*, I JUST WANT A NICE PLACE WHERE I CAN HANG OUT...JUST LIKE YOUR MASTER SAID.
I DO WANT AN AIR CONDITIONED ROOM WHERE I CAN STUFF MY FACE WITH SNACKS AND READ MANGA.
AND IS THAT REALLY SO WRONG...?
THE CLUB'S HOPELESS! YEAH, I ADMIT IT...
...YEAH, WE'RE NOT DOING ANYTHING PRODUCTIVE...!
BUT WE'RE STILL IN *JUNIOR HIGH*, AREN'T WE...?
MIDDLE SCHOOL! THIS IS *SUPPOSED* TO BE THE TIME WHEN WE'RE ALLOWED TO SLACK OFF, ISN'T IT?
SOON IT'LL BE HIGH SCHOOL... COLLEGE EXAMS... JOBS...!!!
WE GOTTA SEIZE THE DAY AND DO *NOTHING* WHILE WE STILL CAN...!
JOIN US, MOB! RELAX! LET'S OPEN A COLD SODA AND PLAY SOME CARDS!!
reach...
DOESN'T THAT SOUND BETTER THAN A SCARY EXORCISM?
WHERE'S THE BENEFIT FOR YOU IN ASSISTING SOME SPIRIT MEDIUM?!
HE PAYS ME 300 YEN AN HOUR.
HUH?!
JEEZ! EVEN FOR A MIDDLE SCHOOL KID, YOU'RE GETTING RIPPED OFF!
HE'S COMPLETELY USING YOU...!
stride

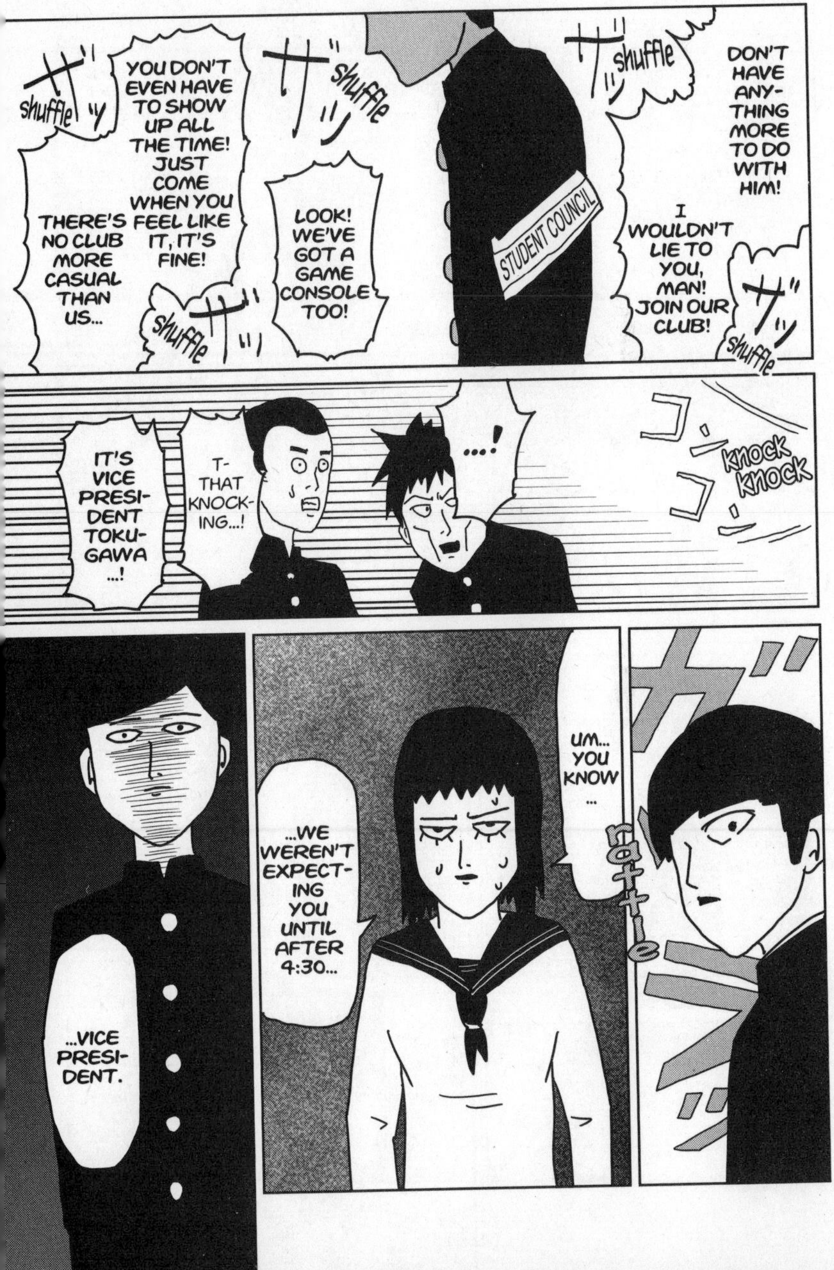
DON'T HAVE ANYTHING MORE TO DO WITH HIM!
I WOULDN'T LIE TO YOU, MAN! JOIN OUR CLUB!
shuffle
shuffle
STUDENT COUNCIL
shuffle
LOOK! WE'VE GOT A GAME CONSOLE TOO!
shuffle
YOU DON'T EVEN HAVE TO SHOW UP ALL THE TIME! JUST COME WHEN YOU FEEL LIKE IT, IT'S FINE!
shuffle
THERE'S NO CLUB MORE CASUAL THAN US...
knock knock
...!
T-THAT KNOCKING...!
IT'S VICE PRESIDENT TOKUGAWA...!
rattle
UM... YOU KNOW...
...WE WEREN'T EXPECTING YOU UNTIL AFTER 4:30...
...VICE PRESIDENT.

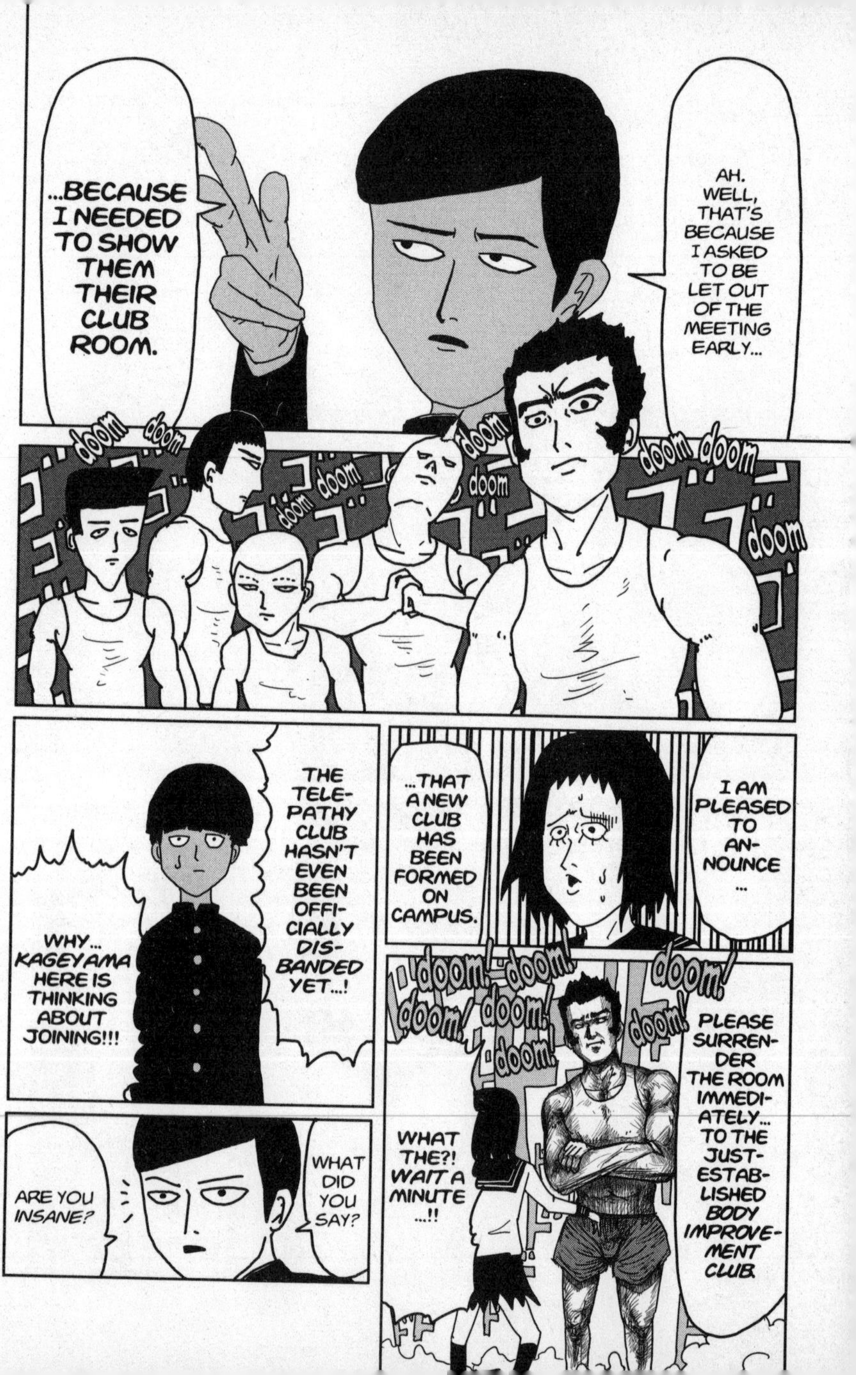
AH. WELL, THAT'S BECAUSE I ASKED TO BE LET OUT OF THE MEETING EARLY...
...BECAUSE I NEEDED TO SHOW THEM THEIR CLUB ROOM.
doom doom
doom
doom
doom doom
doom
doom doom
I AM PLEASED TO ANNOUNCE ...
...THAT A NEW CLUB HAS BEEN FORMED ON CAMPUS.
THE TELE-PATHY CLUB HASN'T EVEN BEEN OFFI-CIALLY DIS-BANDED YET...!
WHY... KAGEYAMA HERE IS THINKING ABOUT JOINING!!!
doom! doom! doom!
doom! doom! doom! doom!
PLEASE SURREN-DER THE ROOM IMMEDI-ATELY... TO THE JUST-ESTAB-LISHED BODY IMPROVE-MENT CLUB.
WHAT THE?! WAIT A MINUTE ...!!
WHAT DID YOU SAY?
ARE YOU INSANE?

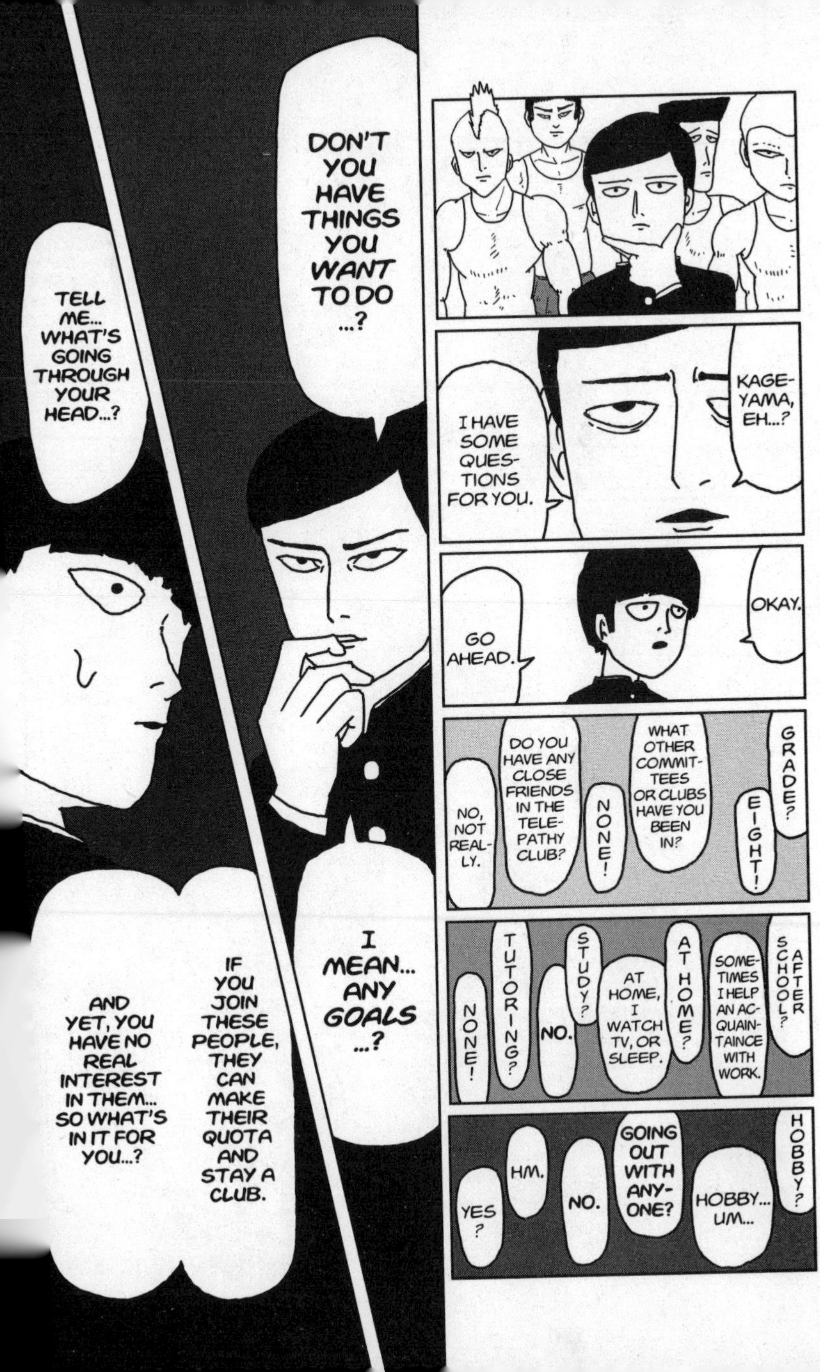
KAGEYAMA, EH...?
I HAVE SOME QUESTIONS FOR YOU.
OKAY.
GO AHEAD.
GRADE?
EIGHT!
WHAT OTHER COMMITTEES OR CLUBS HAVE YOU BEEN IN?
NONE!
DO YOU HAVE ANY CLOSE FRIENDS IN THE TELEPATHY CLUB?
NO, NOT REALLY.
AFTER SCHOOL?
SOMETIMES I HELP AN ACQUAINTANCE WITH WORK.
AT HOME?
AT HOME, I WATCH TV, OR SLEEP.
STUDY?
NO.
TUTORING?
NONE!
HOBBY?
HOBBY... UM...
GOING OUT WITH ANYONE?
NO.
HM.
YES?
DON'T YOU HAVE THINGS YOU WANT TO DO ...?
I MEAN... ANY GOALS ...?
TELL ME... WHAT'S GOING THROUGH YOUR HEAD...?
IF YOU JOIN THESE PEOPLE, THEY CAN MAKE THEIR QUOTA AND STAY A CLUB.
AND YET, YOU HAVE NO REAL INTEREST IN THEM... SO WHAT'S IN IT FOR YOU...?

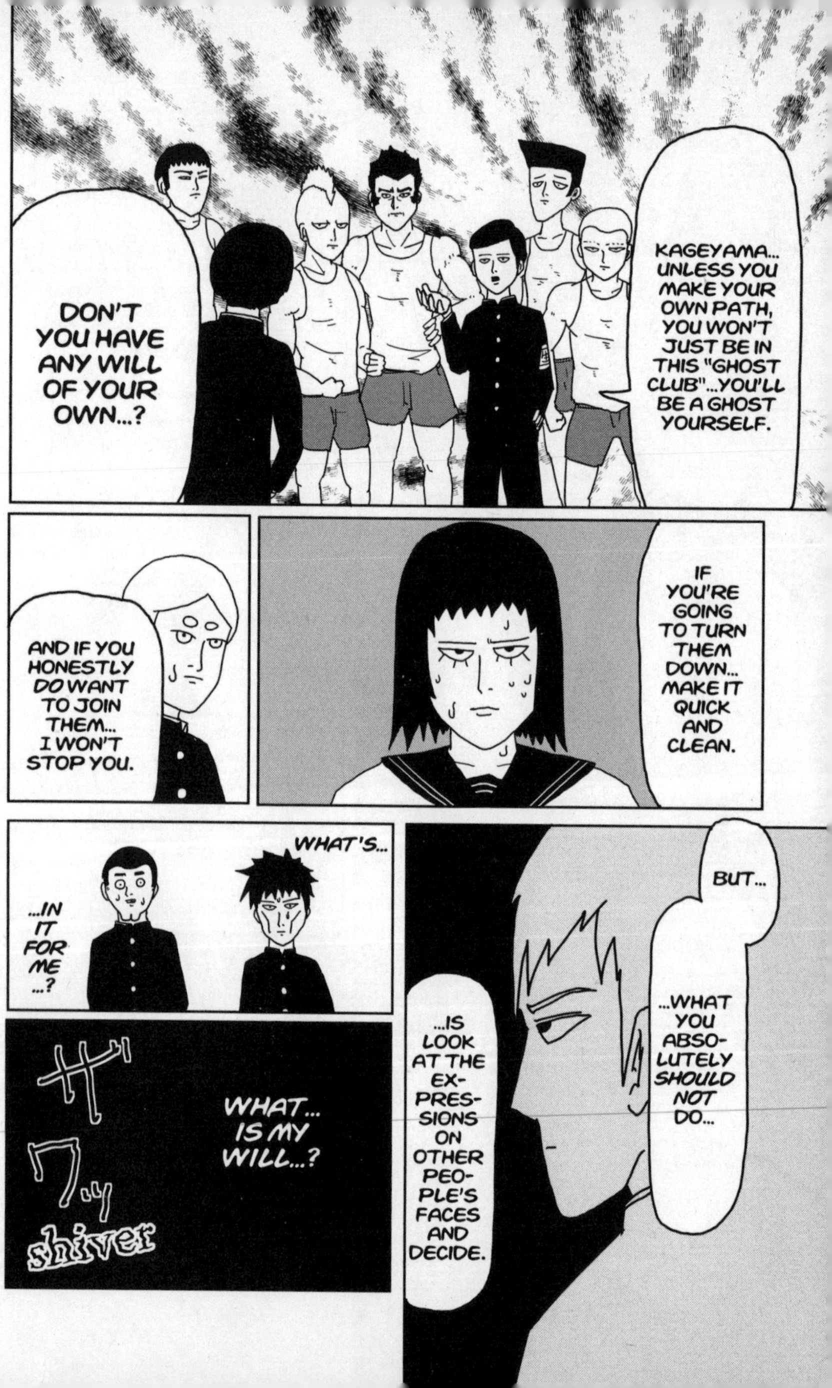
KAGEYAMA... UNLESS YOU MAKE YOUR OWN PATH, YOU WON'T JUST BE IN THIS "GHOST CLUB"...YOU'LL BE A GHOST YOURSELF.
DON'T YOU HAVE ANY WILL OF YOUR OWN...?
IF YOU'RE GOING TO TURN THEM DOWN... MAKE IT QUICK AND CLEAN.
AND IF YOU HONESTLY DO WANT TO JOIN THEM... I WON'T STOP YOU.
BUT...
...WHAT YOU ABSO-LUTELY SHOULD NOT DO...
...IS LOOK AT THE EX-PRES-SIONS ON OTHER PEO-PLE'S FACES AND DECIDE.
WHAT'S...
...IN IT FOR ME ...?
ザワッ
shiver
WHAT... IS MY WILL...?

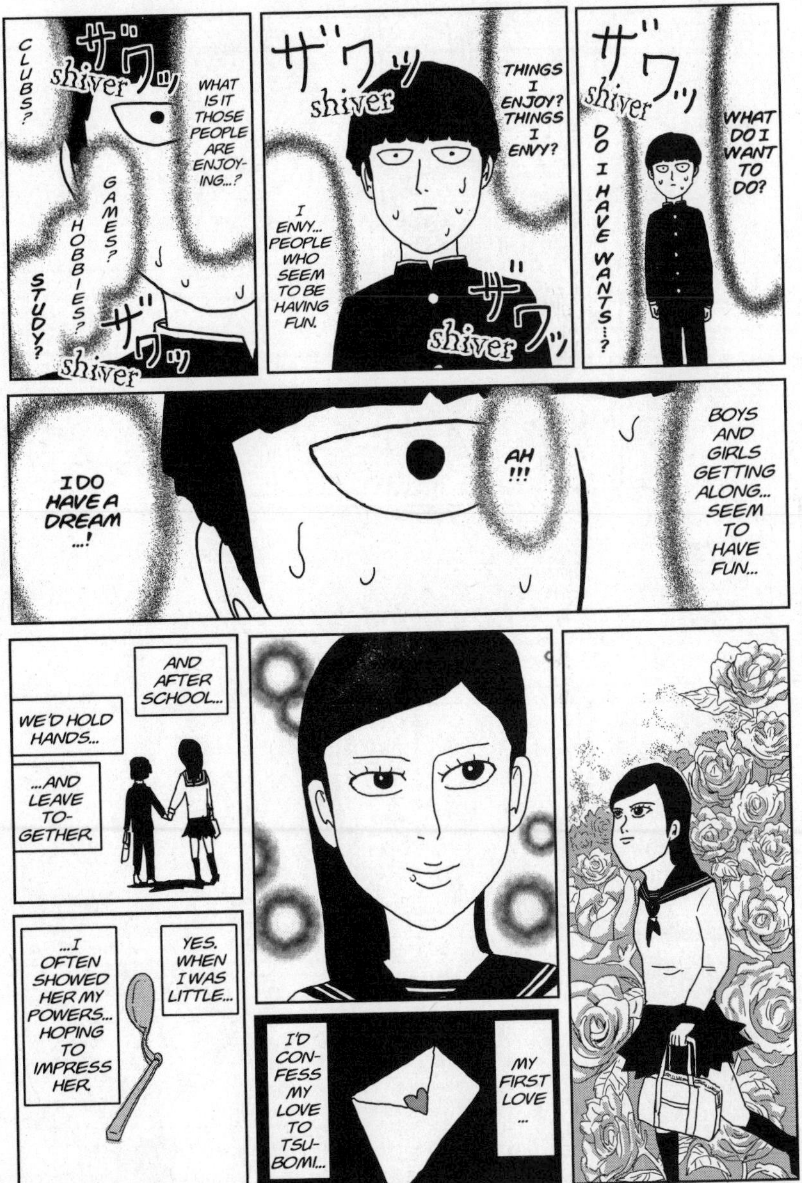
ザワッ
shiver
WHAT DO I WANT TO DO?
DO I HAVE WANTS...?
ザワッ
shiver
THINGS I ENJOY? THINGS I ENVY?
I ENVY... PEOPLE WHO SEEM TO BE HAVING FUN.
ザワッ
shiver
ザワッ
shiver
WHAT IS IT THOSE PEOPLE ARE ENJOYING...?
CLUBS?
GAMES?
HOBBIES?
STUDY?
ザワッ
shiver
BOYS AND GIRLS GETTING ALONG... SEEM TO HAVE FUN...
AH!!!
I DO HAVE A DREAM...!
MY FIRST LOVE...
I'D CONFESS MY LOVE TO TSUBOMI...
AND AFTER SCHOOL...
WE'D HOLD HANDS...
...AND LEAVE TOGETHER.
YES. WHEN I WAS LITTLE...
...I OFTEN SHOWED HER MY POWERS... HOPING TO IMPRESS HER.

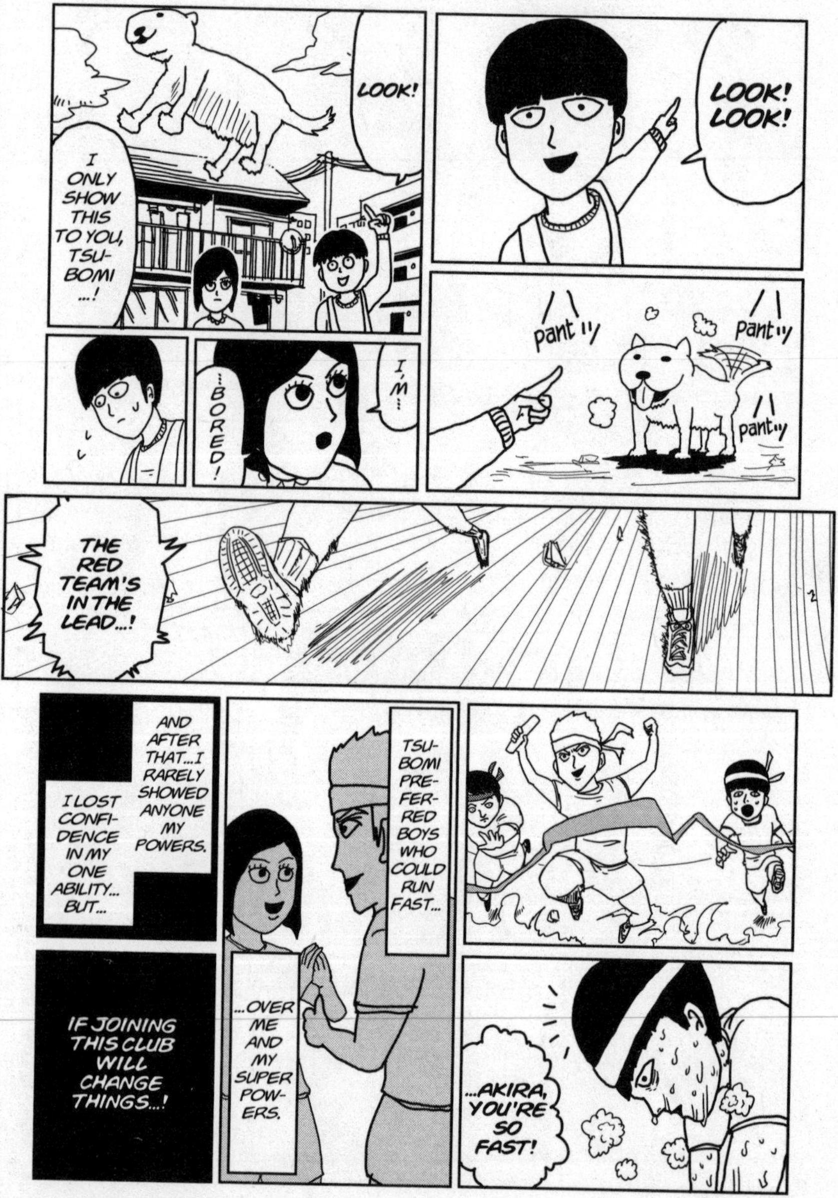
LOOK! LOOK!
LOOK!
I ONLY SHOW THIS TO YOU, TSUBOMI...!
pant
pant
pant
I, M...
...BORED!
THE RED TEAM'S IN THE LEAD...!
TSUBOMI PREFERRED BOYS WHO COULD RUN FAST...
...OVER ME AND MY SUPER POWERS.
AND AFTER THAT...I RARELY SHOWED ANYONE MY POWERS.
I LOST CONFIDENCE IN MY ONE ABILITY... BUT...
...AKIRA, YOU'RE SO FAST!
IF JOINING THIS CLUB WILL CHANGE THINGS...!

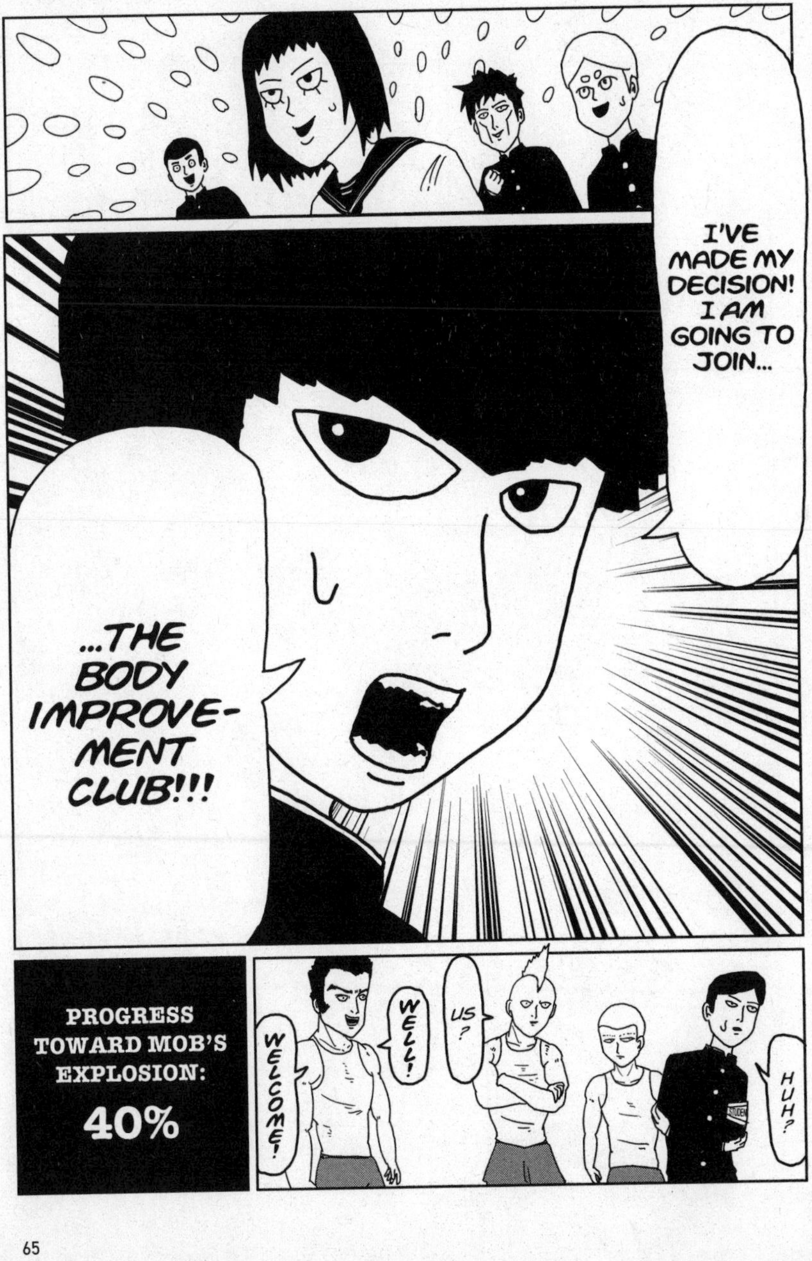
I'VE MADE MY DECISION! I AM GOING TO JOIN...
...THE BODY IMPROVE-MENT CLUB!!!
HUH?
US?
WELL!
WELCOME!
PROGRESS TOWARD MOB'S EXPLOSION:
40%

Meanwhile

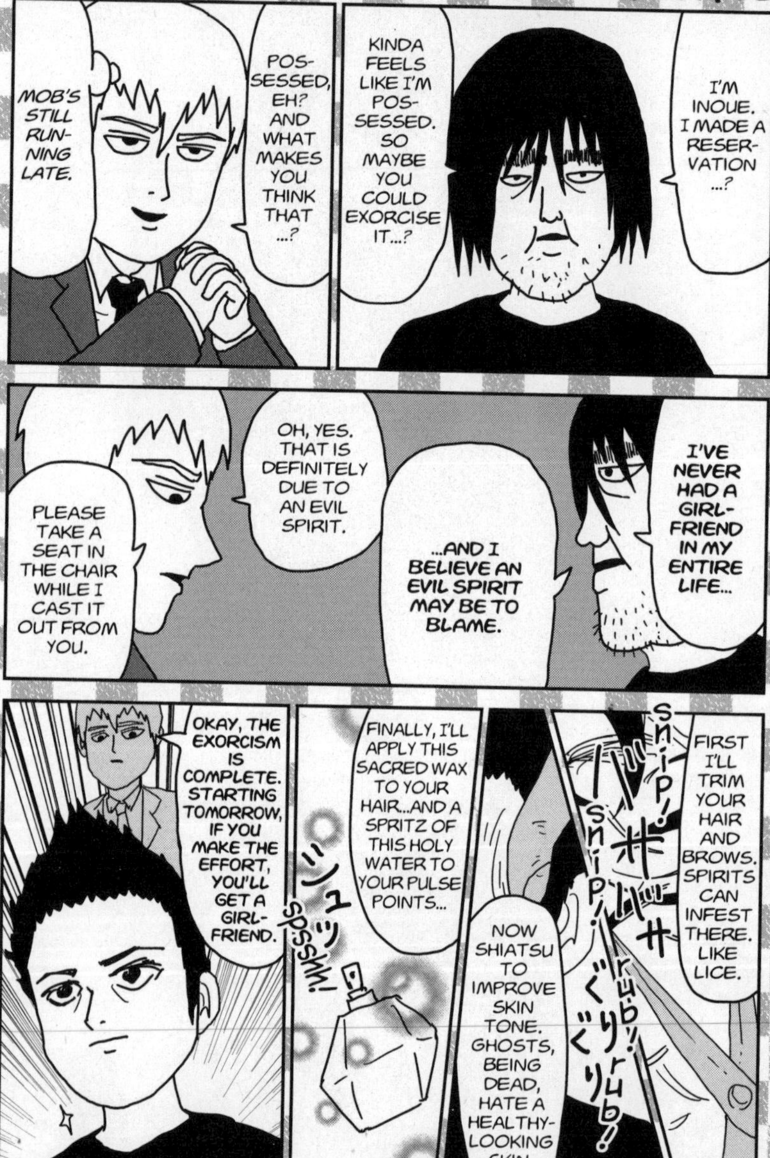

I'M INOUE. I MADE A RESERVATION...?
KINDA FEELS LIKE I'M POSSESSED. SO MAYBE YOU COULD EXORCISE IT...?
POSSESSED, EH? AND WHAT MAKES YOU THINK THAT...?
MOB'S STILL RUNNING LATE.
I'VE NEVER HAD A GIRLFRIEND IN MY ENTIRE LIFE...
...AND I BELIEVE AN EVIL SPIRIT MAY BE TO BLAME.
OH, YES. THAT IS DEFINITELY DUE TO AN EVIL SPIRIT.
PLEASE TAKE A SEAT IN THE CHAIR WHILE I CAST IT OUT FROM YOU.
FIRST I'LL TRIM YOUR HAIR AND BROWS. SPIRITS CAN INFEST THERE. LIKE LICE.
snip! snip!
rub! rub!
ぐりぐり
NOW SHIATSU TO IMPROVE SKIN TONE. GHOSTS, BEING DEAD, HATE A HEALTHY-LOOKING SKIN.
FINALLY, I'LL APPLY THIS SACRED WAX TO YOUR HAIR...AND A SPRITZ OF THIS HOLY WATER TO YOUR PULSE POINTS...
シュッ
spssshh!
OKAY, THE EXORCISM IS COMPLETE. STARTING TOMORROW, IF YOU MAKE THE EFFORT, YOU'LL GET A GIRLFRIEND.

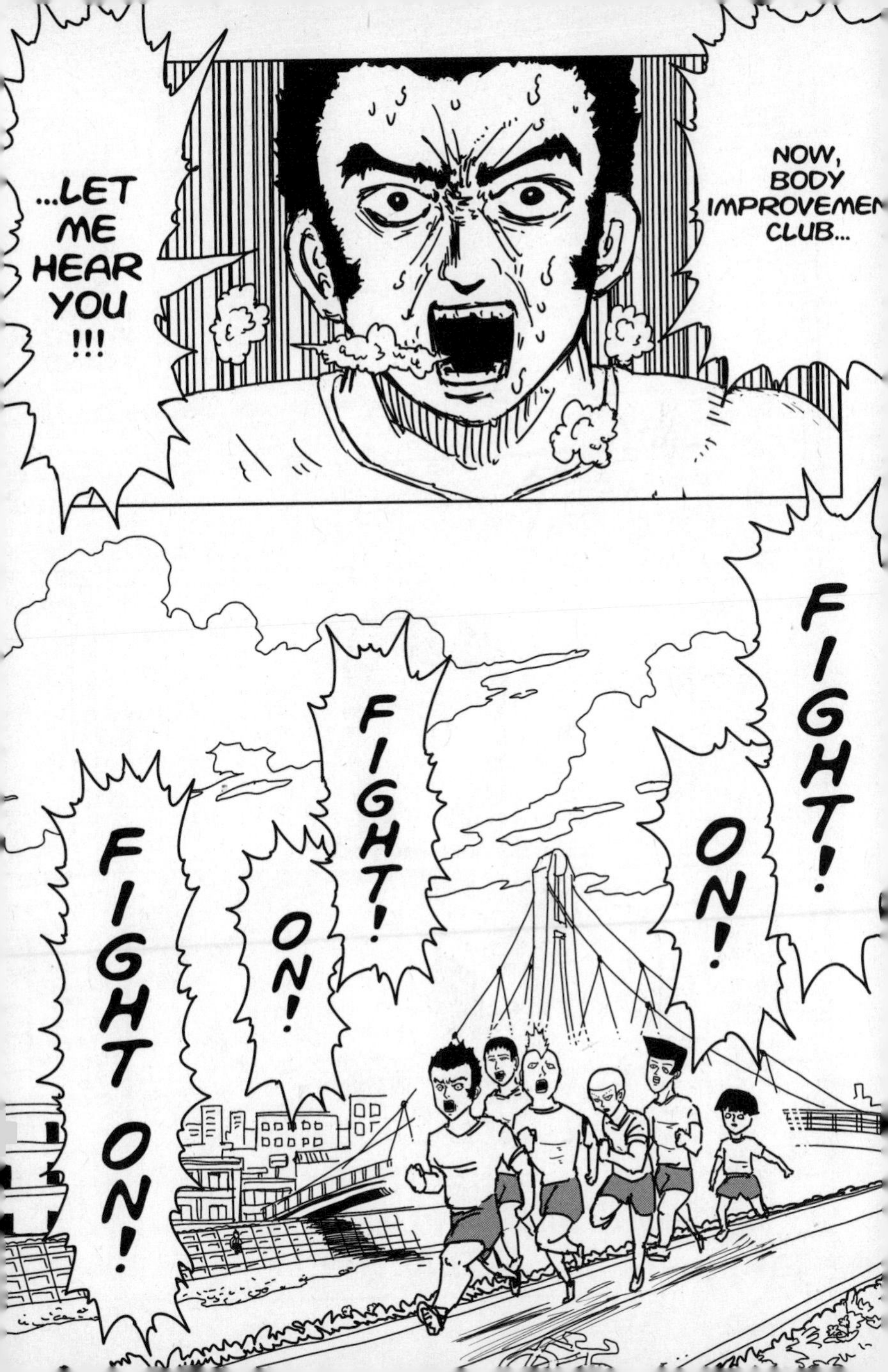
NOW, BODY IMPROVEMEN CLUB...
...LET ME HEAR YOU!!!
FIGHT!
ON!
FIGHT!
ON!
FIGHT ON!

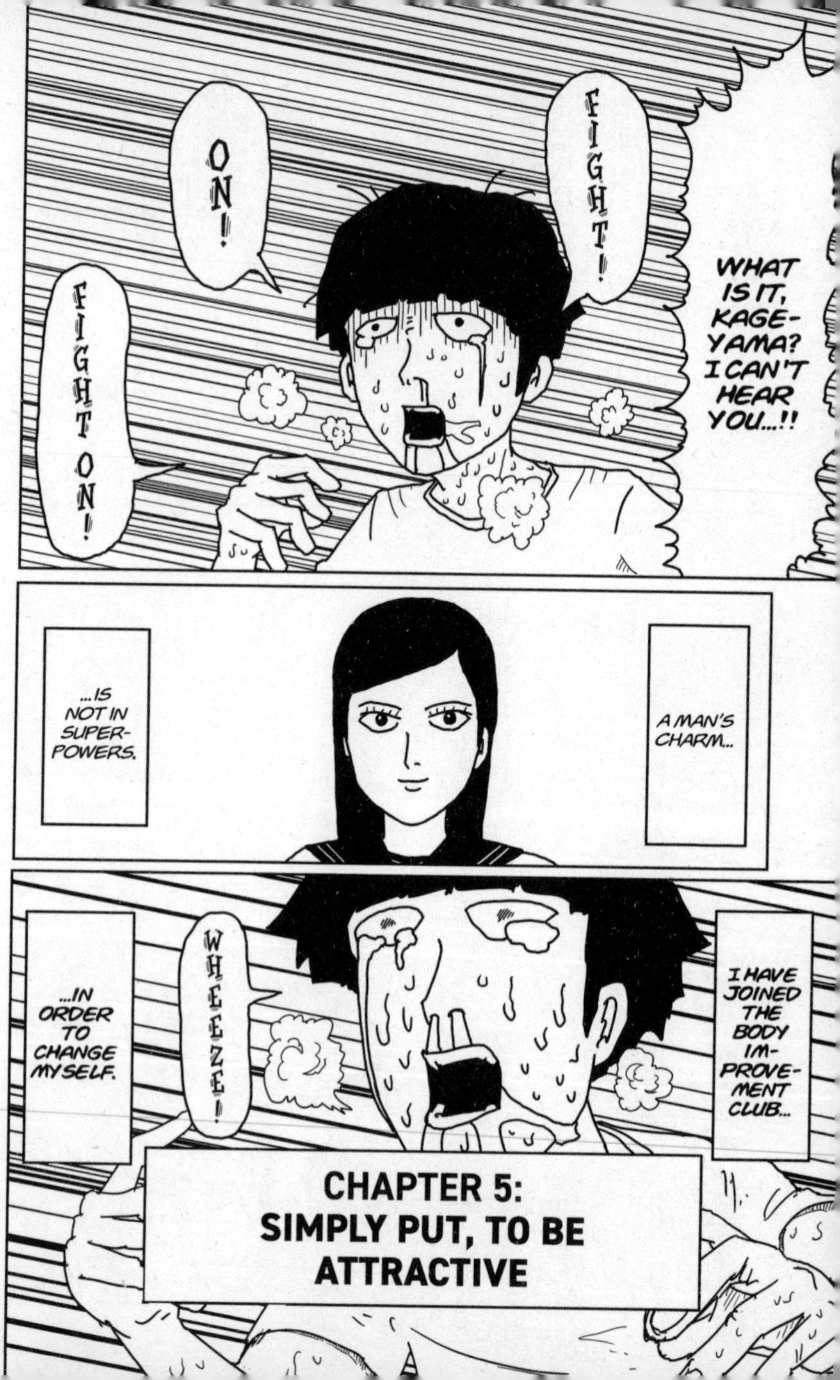
WHAT IS IT, KAGE-YAMA? I CAN'T HEAR YOU...!!
FIGHT!
ON!
FIGHT ON!
A MAN'S CHARM...
...IS NOT IN SUPER-POWERS.
I HAVE JOINED THE BODY IM-PROVE-MENT CLUB...
WHEEZE!
...IN ORDER TO CHANGE MYSELF.
CHAPTER 5:
SIMPLY PUT, TO BE ATTRACTIVE

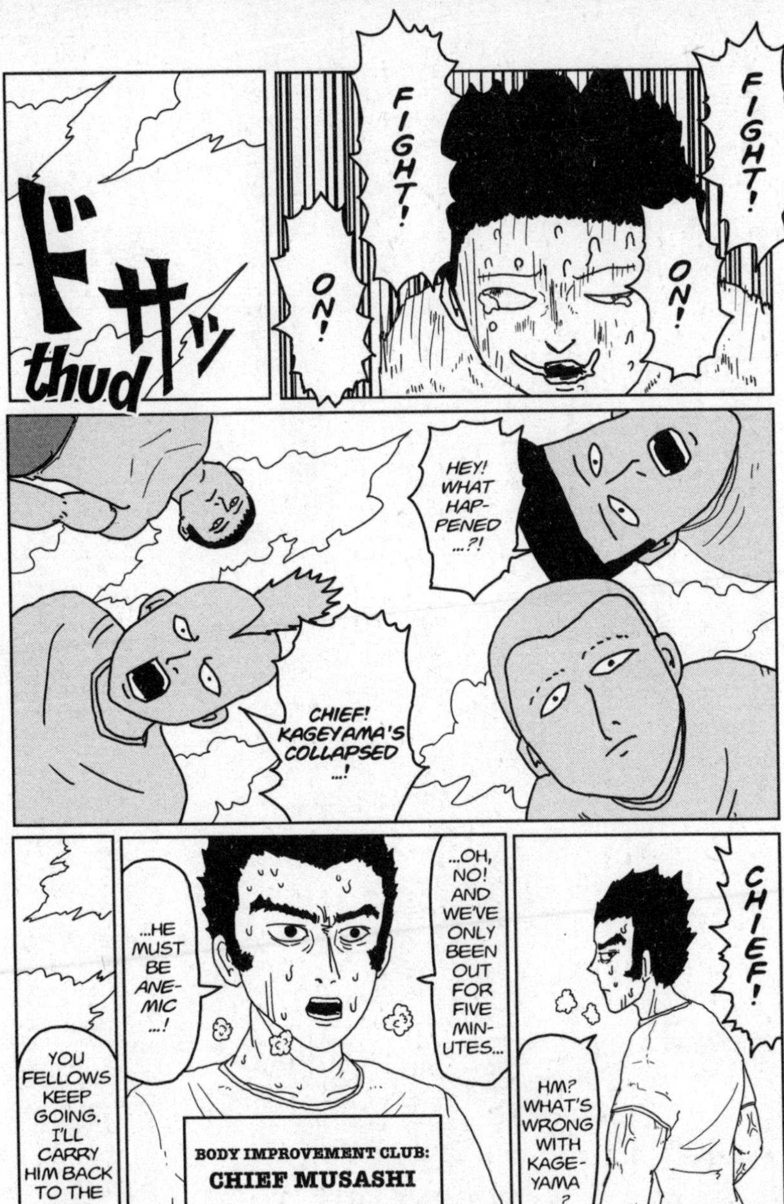
FIGHT! ON!
FIGHT! ON!
ドサッ
thud
HEY! WHAT HAP-PENED ...?!
CHIEF! KAGEYAMA'S COLLAPSED ...!
CHIEF!
HM? WHAT'S WRONG WITH KAGE-YAMA ...?
...OH, NO! AND WE'VE ONLY BEEN OUT FOR FIVE MIN-UTES...
...HE MUST BE ANE-MIC ...!
BODY IMPROVEMENT CLUB:
CHIEF MUSASHI
YOU FELLOWS KEEP GOING. I'LL CARRY HIM BACK TO THE CLUB ROOM.

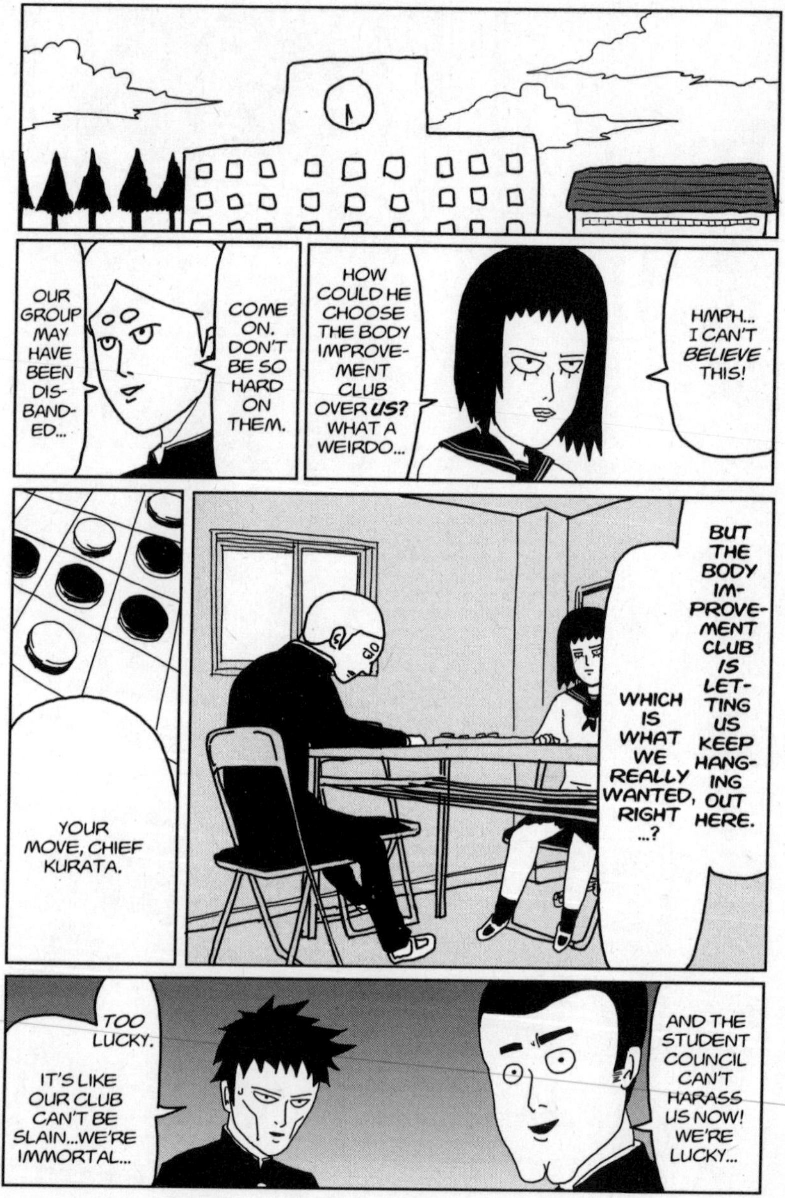
HMPH... I CAN'T BELIEVE THIS!
HOW COULD HE CHOOSE THE BODY IMPROVEMENT CLUB OVER US? WHAT A WEIRDO...
COME ON. DON'T BE SO HARD ON THEM.
OUR GROUP MAY HAVE BEEN DISBANDED...
BUT THE BODY IMPROVEMENT CLUB IS LETTING US KEEP HANGING OUT HERE.
WHICH IS WHAT WE REALLY WANTED, RIGHT...?
YOUR MOVE, CHIEF KURATA.
AND THE STUDENT COUNCIL CAN'T HARASS US NOW! WE'RE LUCKY...
TOO LUCKY.
IT'S LIKE OUR CLUB CAN'T BE SLAIN...WE'RE IMMORTAL...

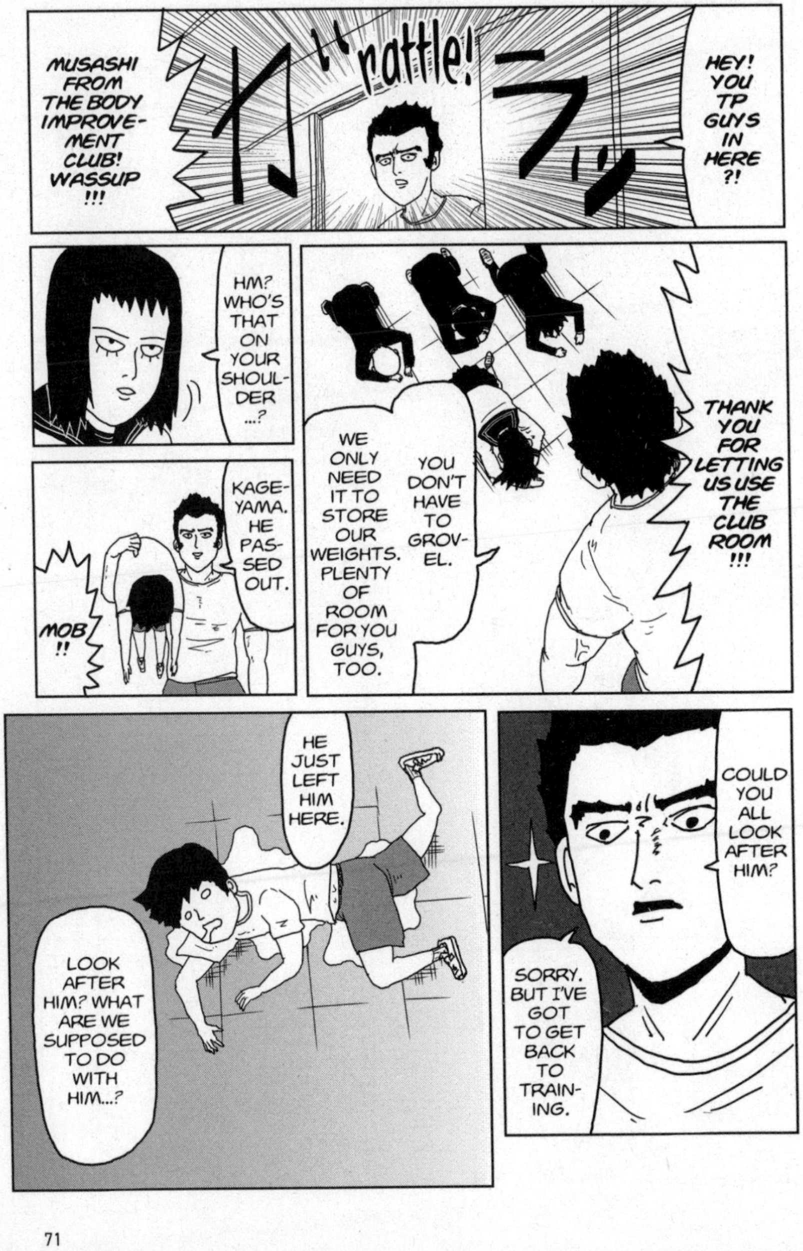
HEY! YOU TP GUYS IN HERE?!
rattle!
MUSASHI FROM THE BODY IMPROVEMENT CLUB! WASSUP!!!
THANK YOU FOR LETTING US USE THE CLUB ROOM!!!
YOU DON'T HAVE TO GROVEL.
WE ONLY NEED IT TO STORE OUR WEIGHTS. PLENTY OF ROOM FOR YOU GUYS, TOO.
HM? WHO'S THAT ON YOUR SHOULDER...?
KAGEYAMA. HE PASSED OUT.
MOB!!
COULD YOU ALL LOOK AFTER HIM?
SORRY. BUT I'VE GOT TO GET BACK TO TRAINING.
HE JUST LEFT HIM HERE.
LOOK AFTER HIM? WHAT ARE WE SUPPOSED TO DO WITH HIM...?

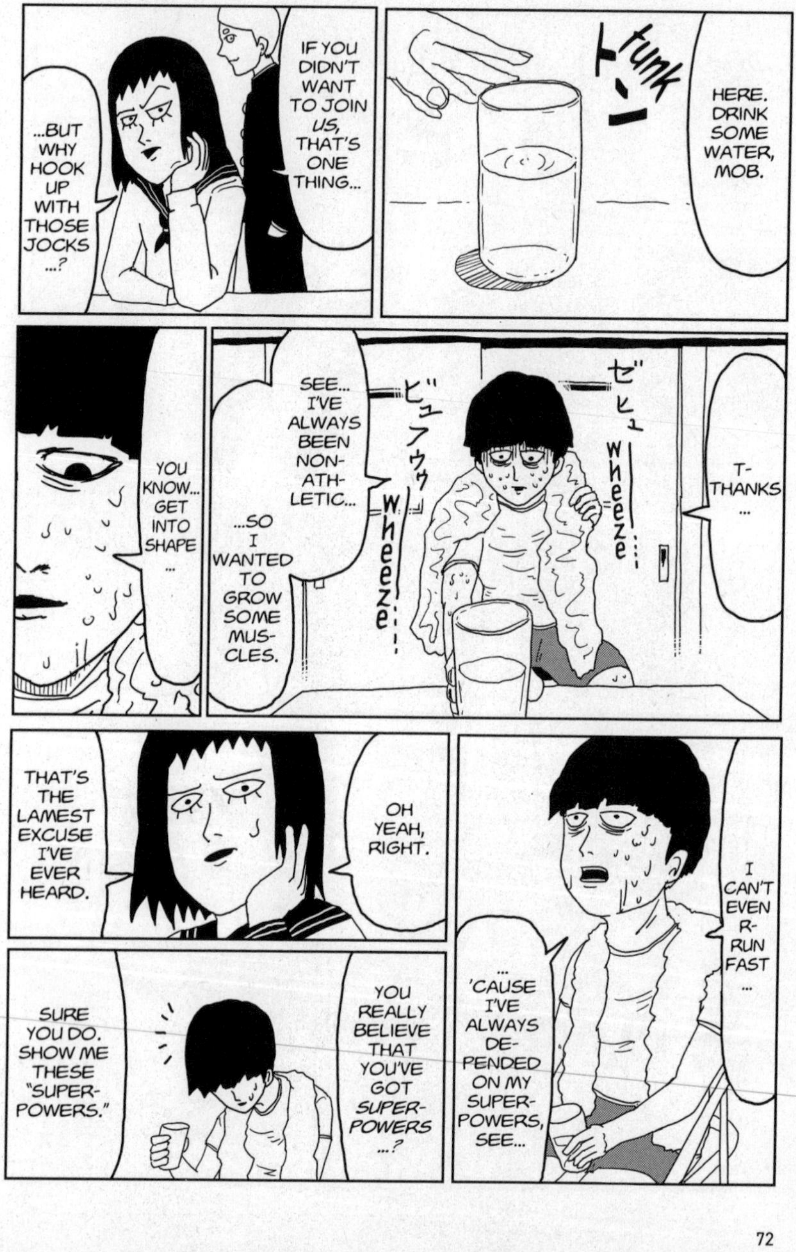
トン
tunk
HERE. DRINK SOME WATER, MOB.
IF YOU DIDN'T WANT TO JOIN *US*, THAT'S ONE THING...
...BUT WHY HOOK UP WITH THOSE JOCKS...?
T-THANKS...
ゼヒュ
wheeze...
SEE... I'VE ALWAYS BEEN NON-ATHLETIC...
ビュアウゥ
wheeze...
...SO I WANTED TO GROW SOME MUSCLES.
YOU KNOW... GET INTO SHAPE...
I CAN'T EVEN R-RUN FAST...
...'CAUSE I'VE ALWAYS DEPENDED ON MY SUPERPOWERS, SEE...
OH YEAH, RIGHT.
THAT'S THE LAMEST EXCUSE I'VE EVER HEARD.
YOU REALLY BELIEVE THAT YOU'VE GOT SUPERPOWERS...?
SURE YOU DO. SHOW ME THESE "SUPERPOWERS."

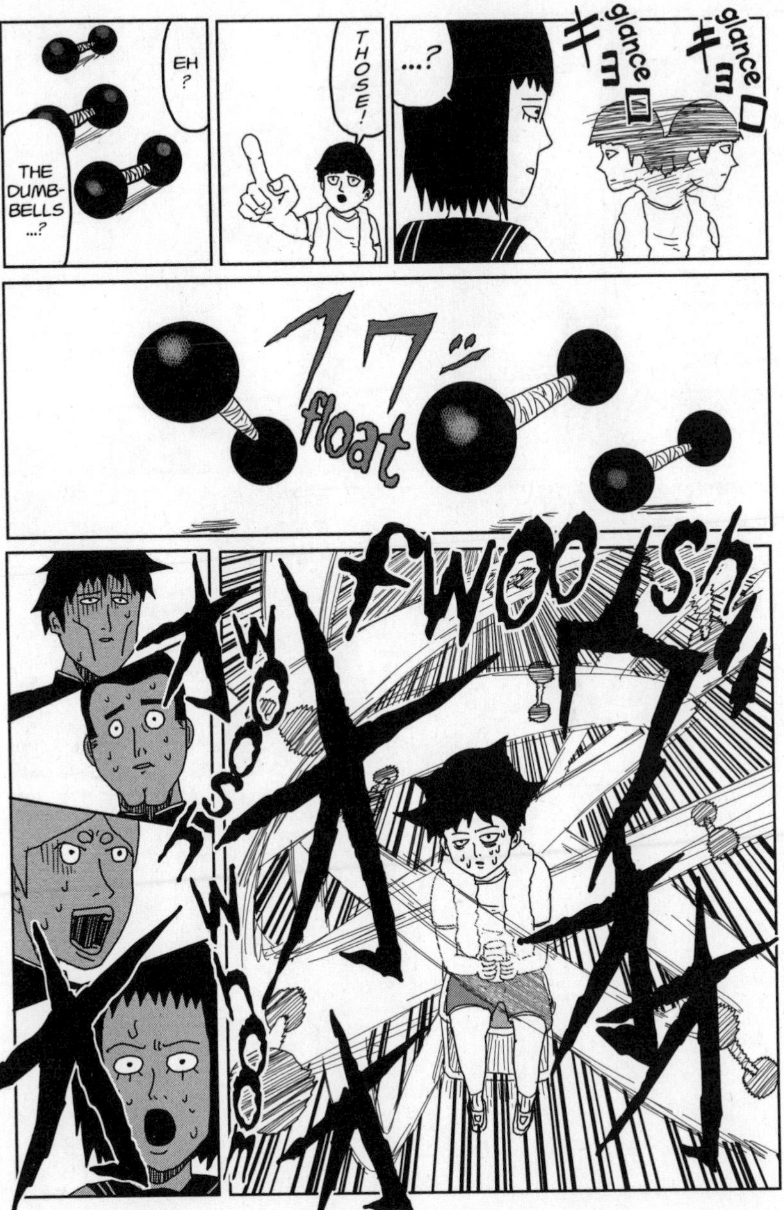
キョロ glance
キョロ glance
...?
THOSE!
EH?
THE DUMB-BELLS ...?
フワ float
FWOOSH
WHOOSH

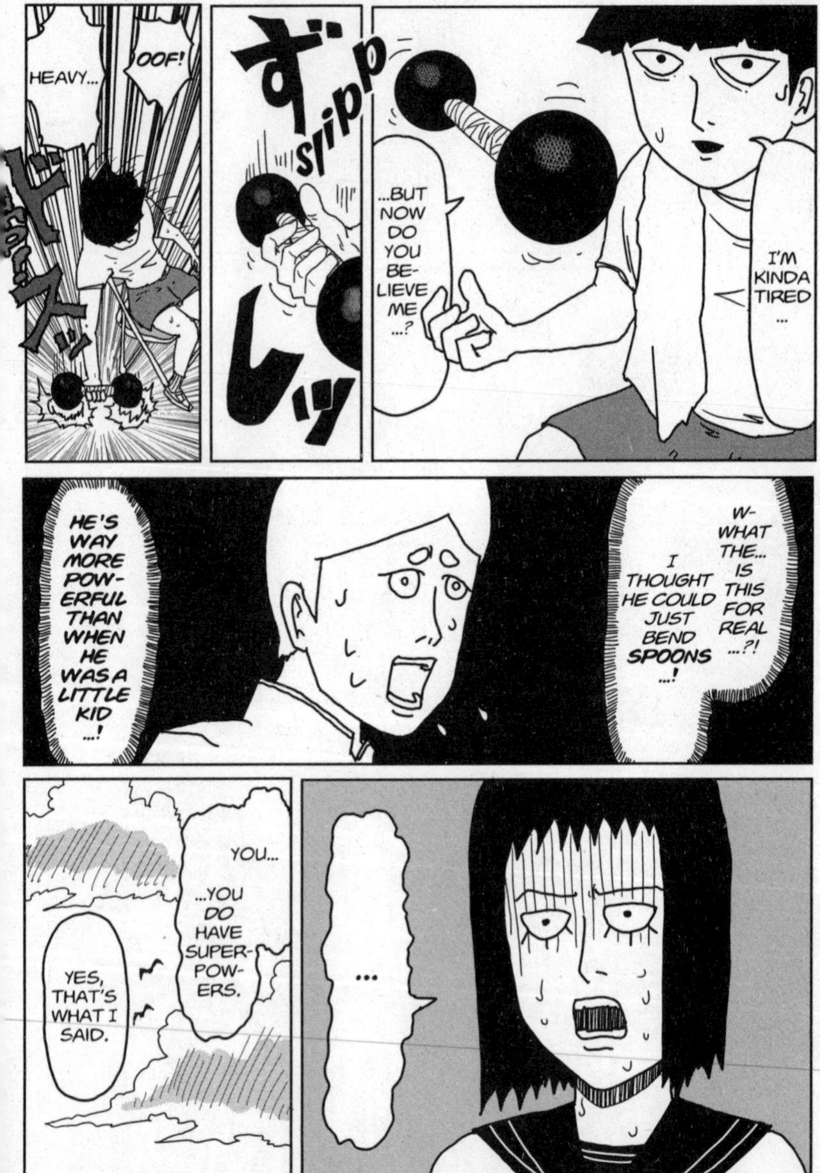
I'M KINDA TIRED ...
...BUT NOW DO YOU BE-LIEVE ME ...?
ず
slipp
しッ
OOF!
HEAVY...
W-WHAT THE... IS THIS FOR REAL ...?!
I THOUGHT HE COULD JUST BEND SPOONS ...!
HE'S WAY MORE POW-ERFUL THAN WHEN HE WAS A LITTLE KID ...!
...
YOU...
...YOU DO HAVE SUPER-POW-ERS.
YES, THAT'S WHAT I SAID.

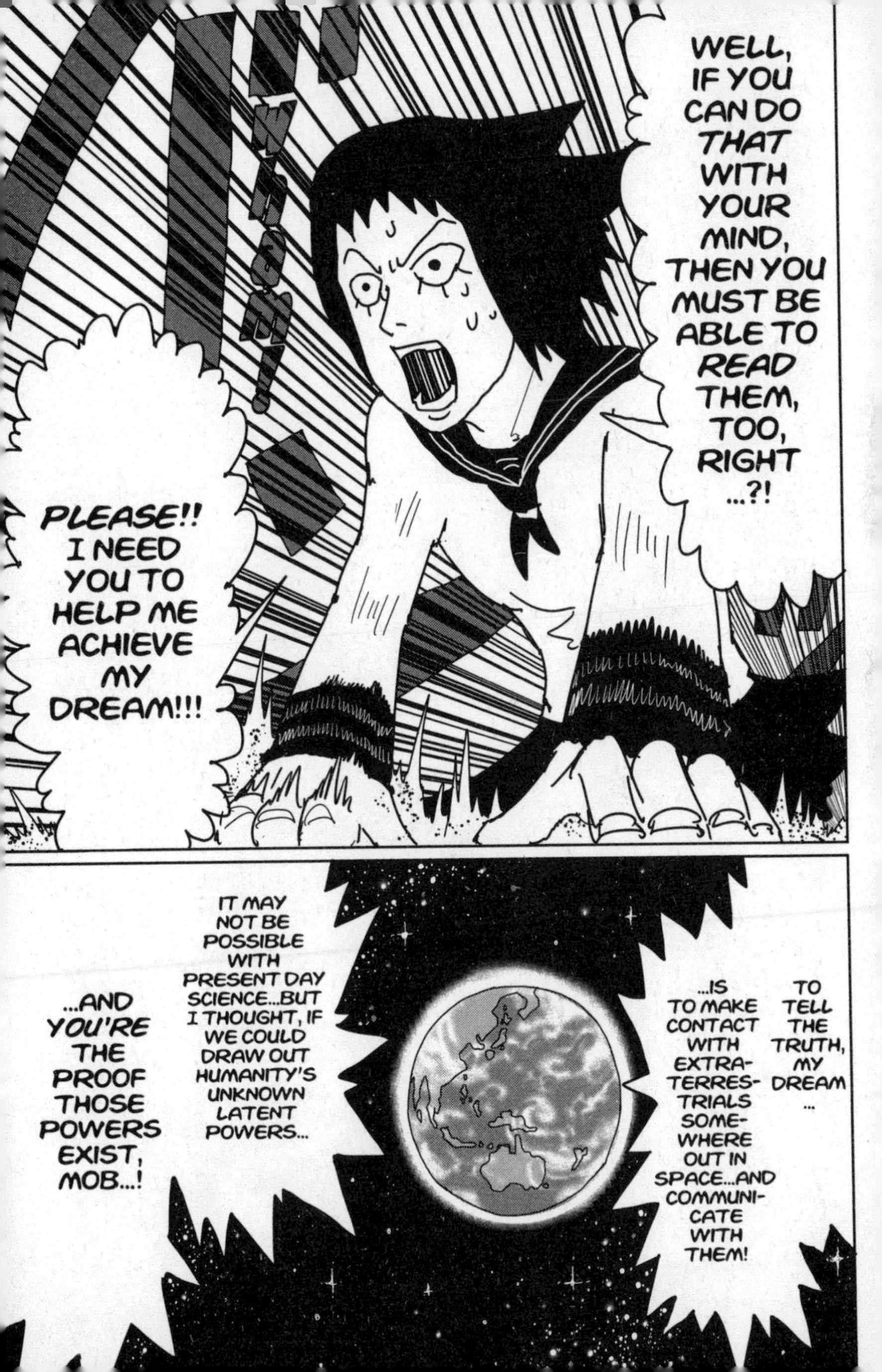
WELL, IF YOU CAN DO *THAT* WITH YOUR MIND, THEN YOU MUST BE ABLE TO *READ* THEM, TOO, RIGHT ...?!
PLEASE!! I NEED YOU TO HELP ME ACHIEVE MY DREAM!!!
TO TELL THE TRUTH, MY DREAM ...
...IS TO MAKE CONTACT WITH EXTRA-TERRES-TRIALS SOME-WHERE OUT IN SPACE...AND COMMUNI-CATE WITH THEM!
IT MAY NOT BE POSSIBLE WITH PRESENT DAY SCIENCE...BUT I THOUGHT, IF WE COULD DRAW OUT HUMANITY'S UNKNOWN LATENT POWERS...
...AND *YOU'RE* THE PROOF THOSE POWERS EXIST, MOB...!

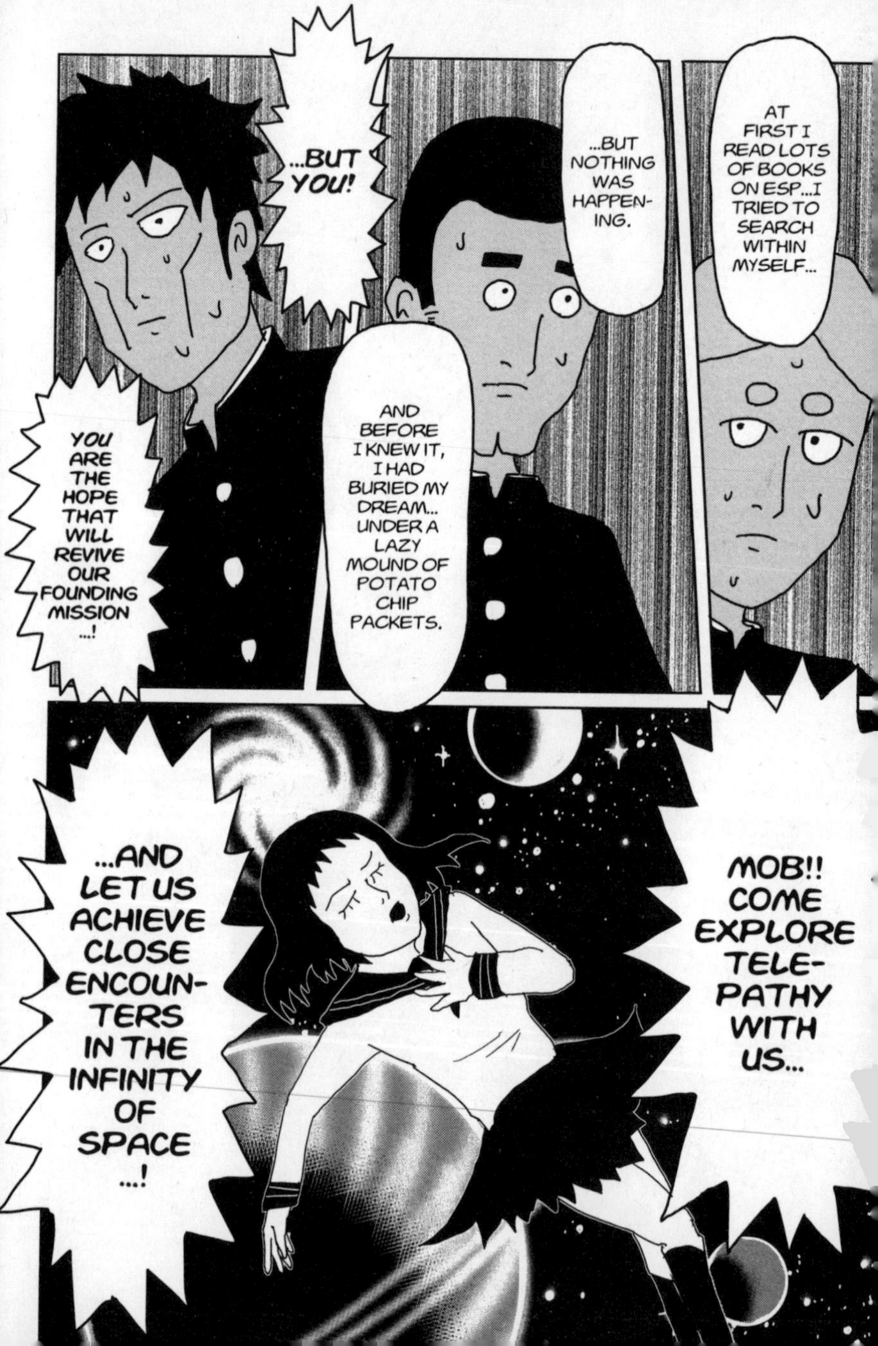
AT FIRST I READ LOTS OF BOOKS ON ESP...I TRIED TO SEARCH WITHIN MYSELF...
...BUT NOTHING WAS HAPPEN-ING.
AND BEFORE I KNEW IT, I HAD BURIED MY DREAM... UNDER A LAZY MOUND OF POTATO CHIP PACKETS.
...BUT YOU!
YOU ARE THE HOPE THAT WILL REVIVE OUR FOUNDING MISSION ...!
MOB!! COME EXPLORE TELE-PATHY WITH US...
...AND LET US ACHIEVE CLOSE ENCOUN-TERS IN THE INFINITY OF SPACE ...!

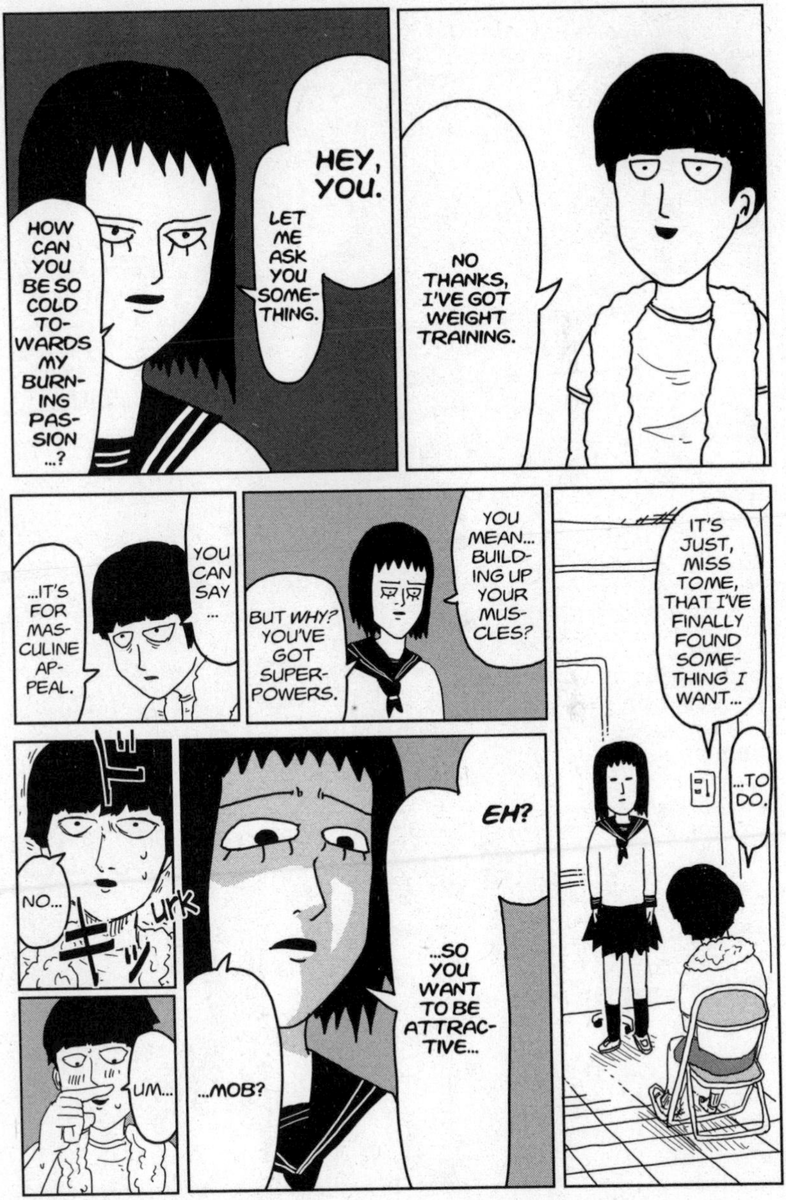

NO THANKS, I'VE GOT WEIGHT TRAINING.
HEY, YOU.
LET ME ASK YOU SOME-THING.
HOW CAN YOU BE SO COLD TO-WARDS MY BURN-ING PAS-SION ...?
IT'S JUST, MISS TOME, THAT I'VE FINALLY FOUND SOME-THING I WANT...
...TO DO.
YOU MEAN... BUILD-ING UP YOUR MUS-CLES?
BUT WHY? YOU'VE GOT SUPER-POWERS.
YOU CAN SAY ...
...IT'S FOR MAS-CULINE AP-PEAL.
EH?
...SO YOU WANT TO BE ATTRAC-TIVE...
...MOB?
NO...
urk
UM...

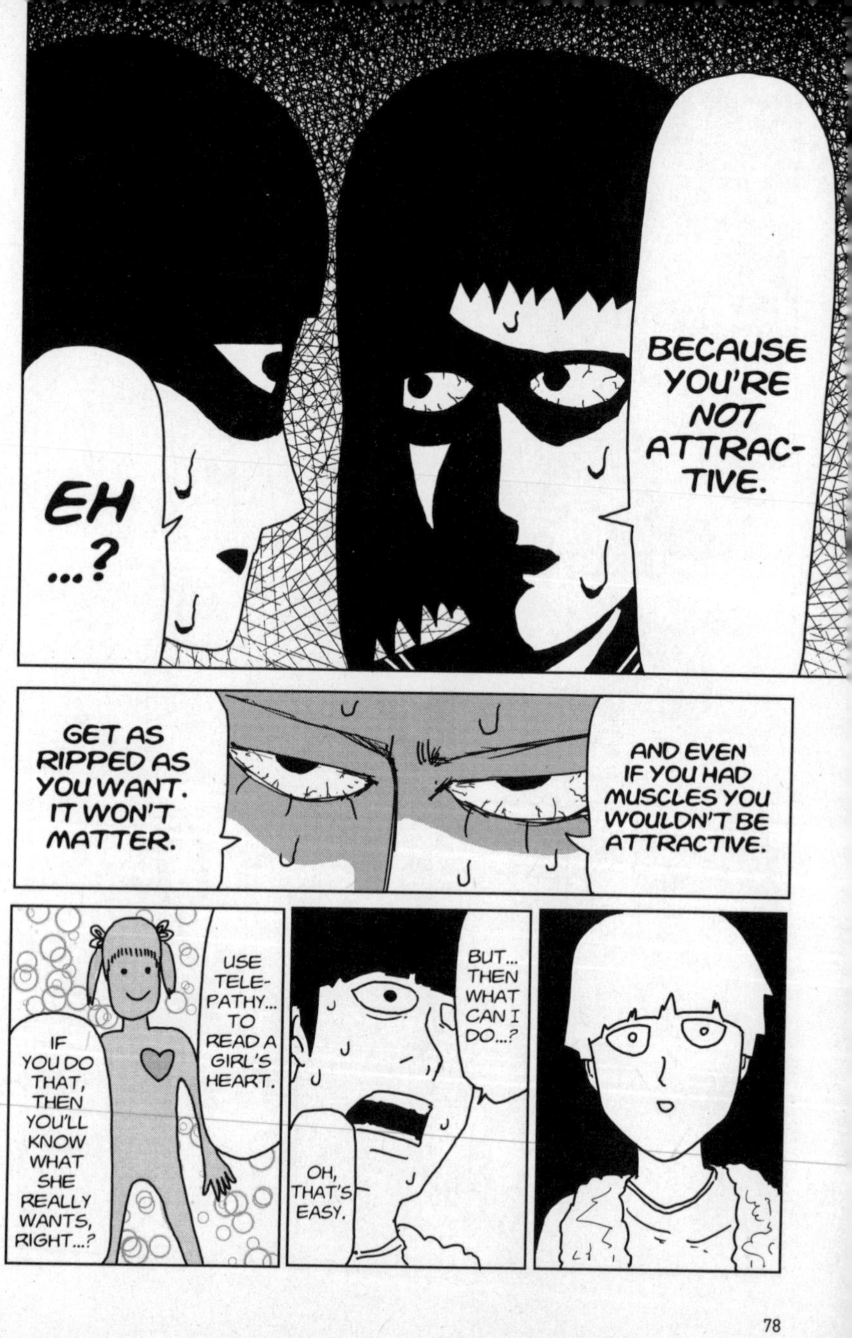
BECAUSE YOU'RE NOT ATTRAC-TIVE.
EH ...?
AND EVEN IF YOU HAD MUSCLES YOU WOULDN'T BE ATTRACTIVE.
GET AS RIPPED AS YOU WANT. IT WON'T MATTER.
BUT... THEN WHAT CAN I DO...?
OH, THAT'S EASY.
USE TELE-PATHY... TO READ A GIRL'S HEART.
IF YOU DO THAT, THEN YOU'LL KNOW WHAT SHE REALLY WANTS, RIGHT...?

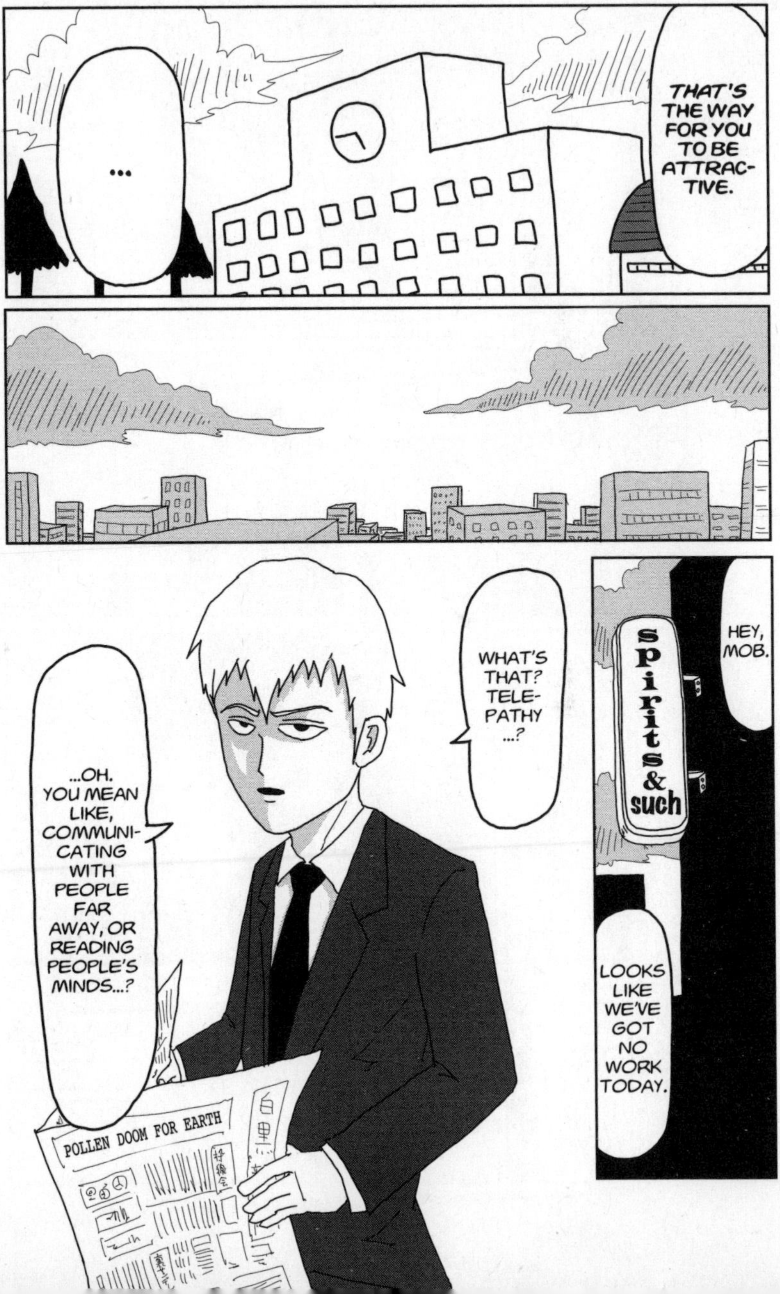
THAT'S THE WAY FOR YOU TO BE ATTRACTIVE.
...
spirits & such
HEY, MOB.
LOOKS LIKE WE'VE GOT NO WORK TODAY.
WHAT'S THAT? TELEPATHY ...?
...OH. YOU MEAN LIKE, COMMUNICATING WITH PEOPLE FAR AWAY, OR READING PEOPLE'S MINDS...?
POLLEN DOOM FOR EARTH

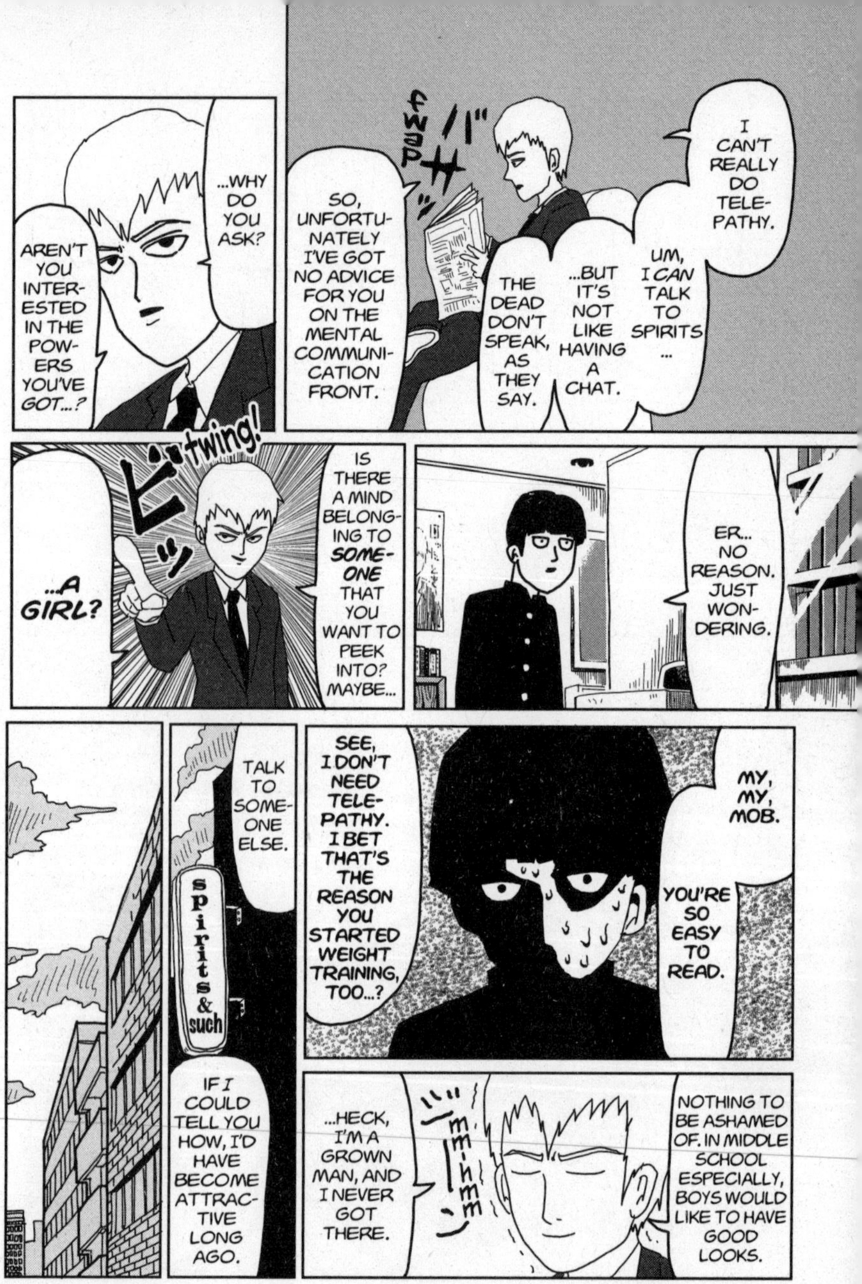
I CAN'T REALLY DO TELEPATHY.
UM, I *CAN* TALK TO SPIRITS...
...BUT IT'S NOT LIKE HAVING A CHAT.
THE DEAD DON'T SPEAK, AS THEY SAY.
fwap
SO, UNFORTUNATELY I'VE GOT NO ADVICE FOR YOU ON THE MENTAL COMMUNICATION FRONT.
...WHY DO YOU ASK?
AREN'T YOU INTERESTED IN THE POWERS YOU'VE GOT...?
ER... NO REASON. JUST WONDERING.
twing!
IS THERE A MIND BELONGING TO ***SOMEONE*** THAT YOU WANT TO PEEK INTO? MAYBE...
...A ***GIRL?***
MY, MY, MOB.
YOU'RE SO EASY TO READ.
SEE, I DON'T NEED TELEPATHY. I BET THAT'S THE REASON YOU STARTED WEIGHT TRAINING, TOO...?
NOTHING TO BE ASHAMED OF. IN MIDDLE SCHOOL ESPECIALLY, BOYS WOULD LIKE TO HAVE GOOD LOOKS.
m-hmm
...HECK, I'M A GROWN MAN, AND I NEVER GOT THERE.
TALK TO SOMEONE ELSE.
spirits & such
IF *I* COULD TELL YOU HOW, I'D HAVE BECOME ATTRACTIVE LONG AGO.

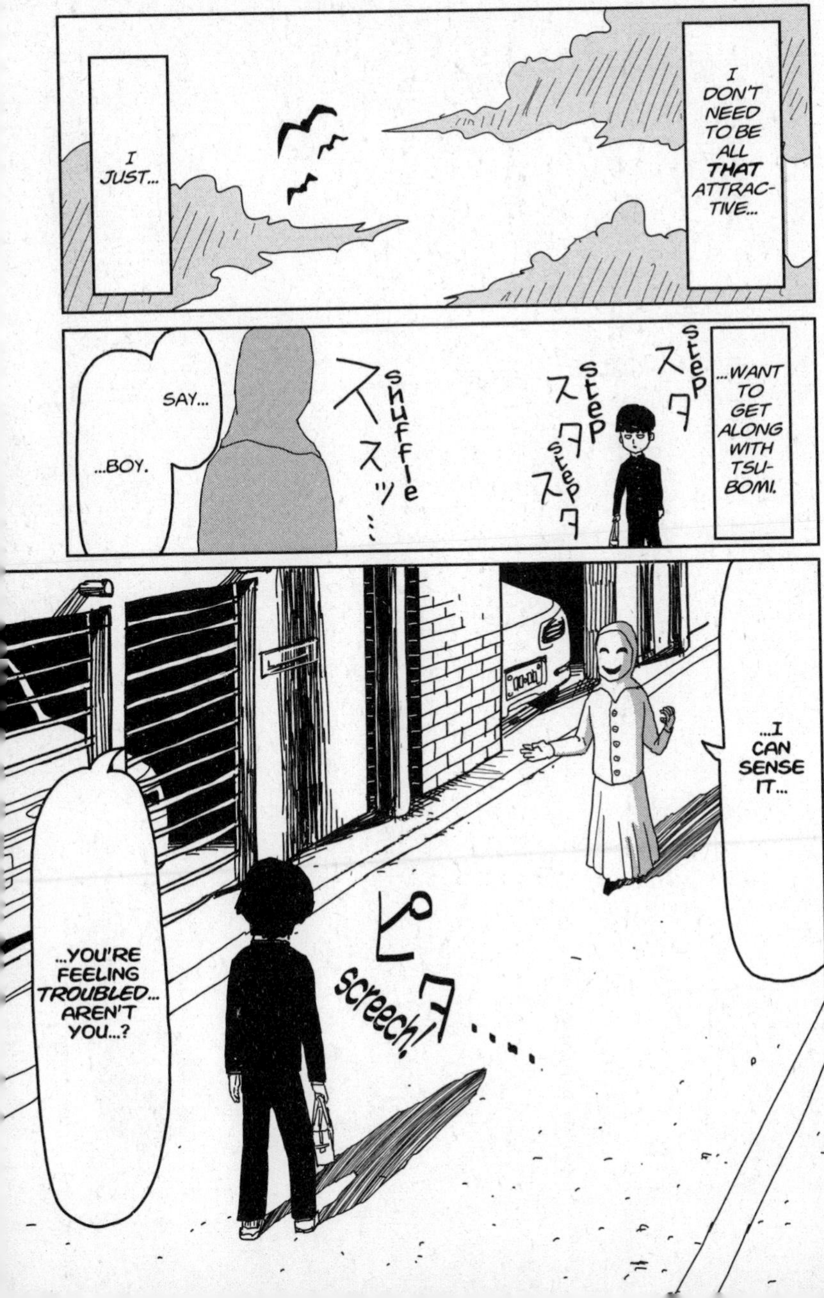
I DON'T NEED TO BE ALL THAT ATTRACTIVE...
I JUST...
...WANT TO GET ALONG WITH TSU-BOMI.
step
step
step
shuffle
SAY...
...BOY.
...I CAN SENSE IT...
screech!
...YOU'RE FEELING TROUBLED... AREN'T YOU...?

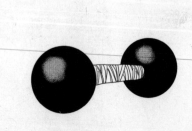

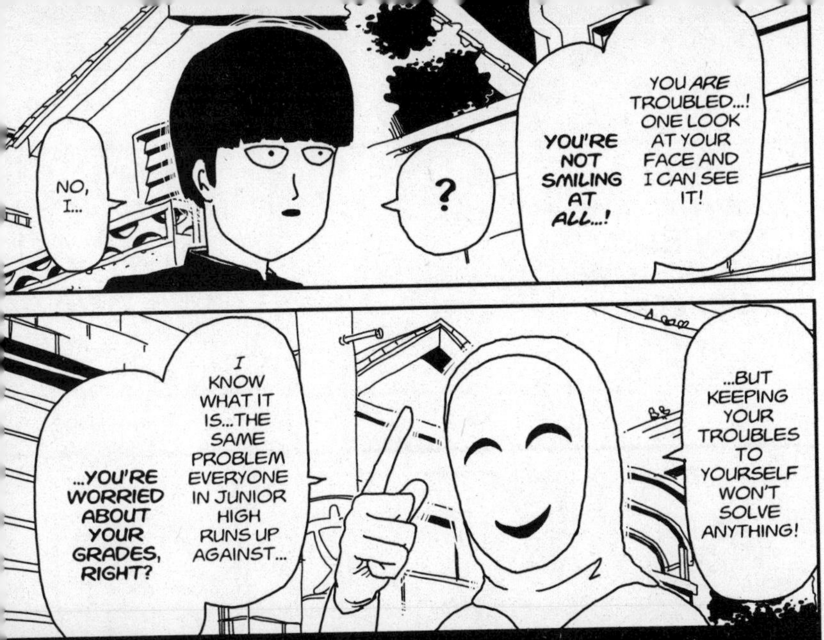
YOU ARE TROUBLED...! ONE LOOK AT YOUR FACE AND I CAN SEE IT!
YOU'RE NOT SMILING AT ALL...!
?
NO, I...
...BUT KEEPING YOUR TROUBLES TO YOURSELF WON'T SOLVE ANYTHING!
I KNOW WHAT IT IS...THE SAME PROBLEM EVERYONE IN JUNIOR HIGH RUNS UP AGAINST...
...YOU'RE WORRIED ABOUT YOUR GRADES, RIGHT?

CHAPTER 6: INVITATION TO A GATHERING

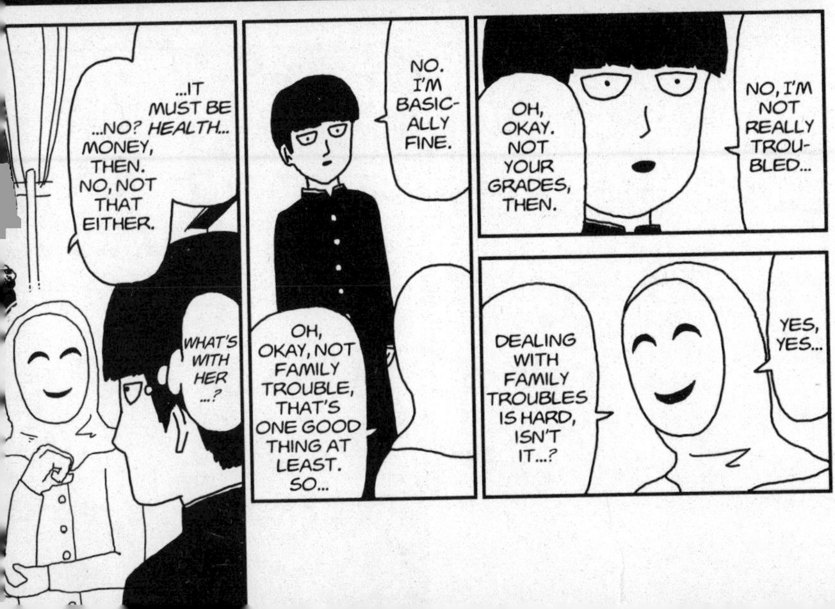
NO, I'M NOT REALLY TROU-BLED...
OH, OKAY. NOT YOUR GRADES, THEN.
YES, YES...
DEALING WITH FAMILY TROUBLES IS HARD, ISN'T IT...?
NO. I'M BASIC-ALLY FINE.
OH, OKAY, NOT FAMILY TROUBLE, THAT'S ONE GOOD THING AT LEAST. SO...
...IT MUST BE HEALTH... ...NO? MONEY, THEN. NO, NOT THAT EITHER.
WHAT'S WITH HER ...?

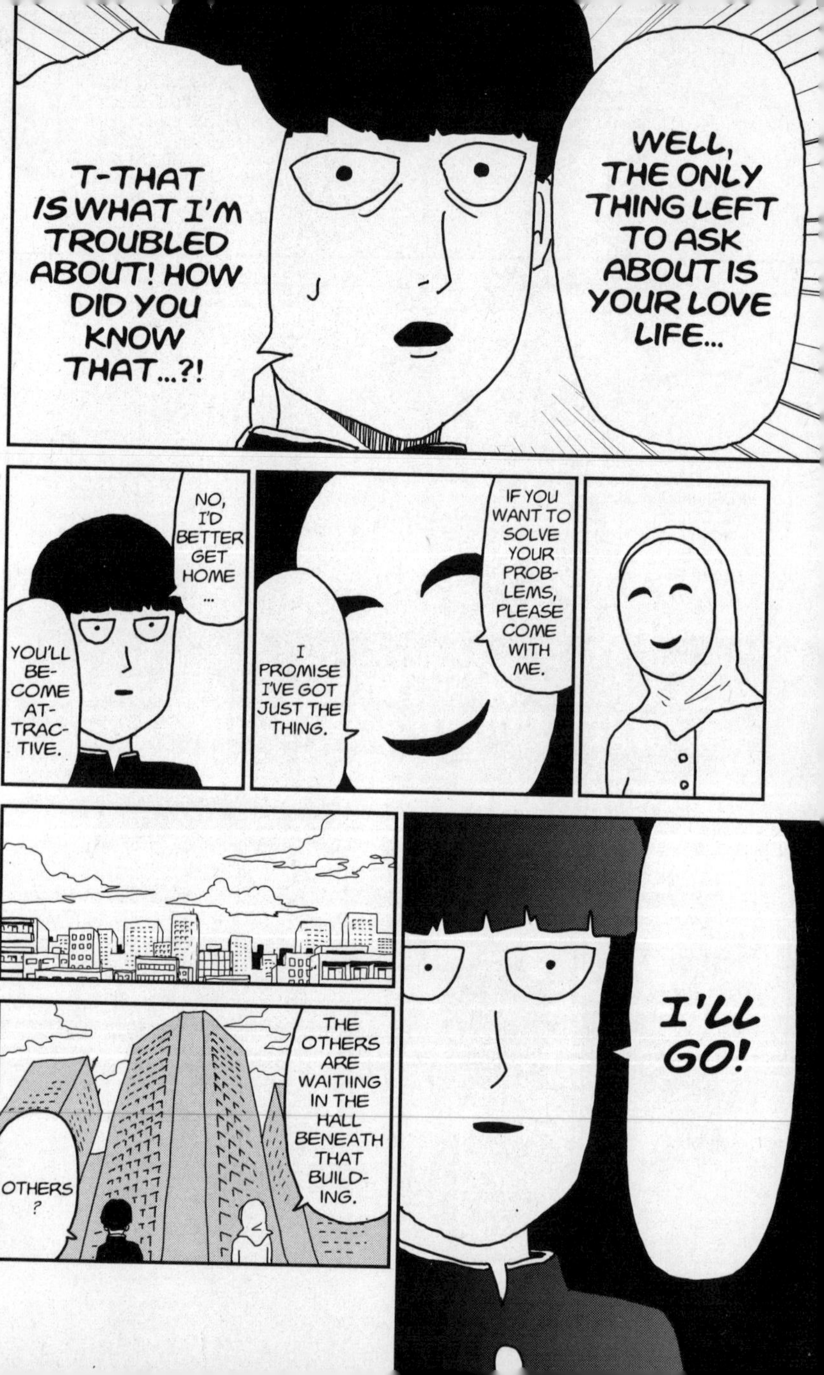
WELL, THE ONLY THING LEFT TO ASK ABOUT IS YOUR LOVE LIFE...
T-THAT IS WHAT I'M TROUBLED ABOUT! HOW DID YOU KNOW THAT...?!
IF YOU WANT TO SOLVE YOUR PROBLEMS, PLEASE COME WITH ME.
I PROMISE I'VE GOT JUST THE THING.
NO, I'D BETTER GET HOME ...
YOU'LL BECOME ATTRACTIVE.
I'LL GO!
THE OTHERS ARE WAITIING IN THE HALL BENEATH THAT BUILDING.
OTHERS?

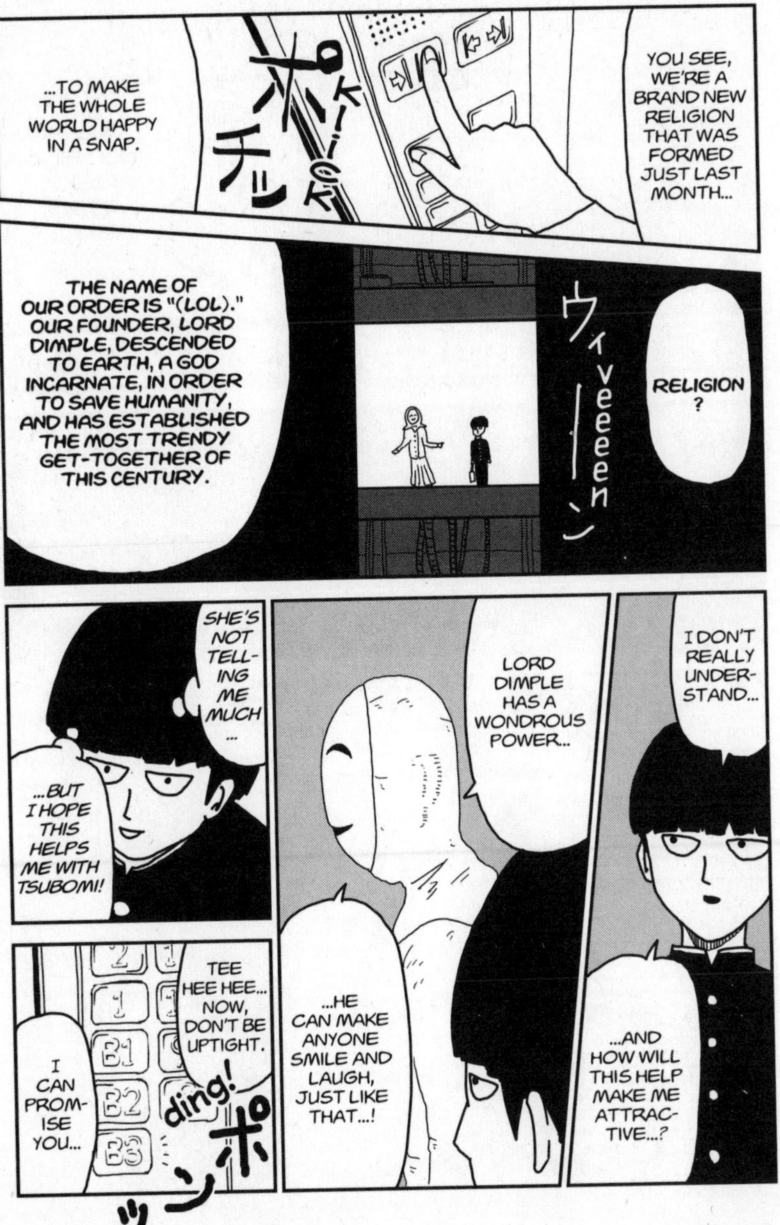
YOU SEE, WE'RE A BRAND NEW RELIGION THAT WAS FORMED JUST LAST MONTH...
ポチッ
KLICK
...TO MAKE THE WHOLE WORLD HAPPY IN A SNAP.
RELIGION?
ウィーン
Viveeeen
THE NAME OF OUR ORDER IS "(LOL)." OUR FOUNDER, LORD DIMPLE, DESCENDED TO EARTH, A GOD INCARNATE, IN ORDER TO SAVE HUMANITY, AND HAS ESTABLISHED THE MOST TRENDY GET-TOGETHER OF THIS CENTURY.
I DON'T REALLY UNDER-STAND...
...AND HOW WILL THIS HELP MAKE ME ATTRAC-TIVE...?
LORD DIMPLE HAS A WONDROUS POWER...
...HE CAN MAKE ANYONE SMILE AND LAUGH, JUST LIKE THAT...!
SHE'S NOT TELL-ING ME MUCH...
...BUT I HOPE THIS HELPS ME WITH TSUBOMI!
TEE HEE HEE... NOW, DON'T BE UPTIGHT.
I CAN PROM-ISE YOU...
ding!

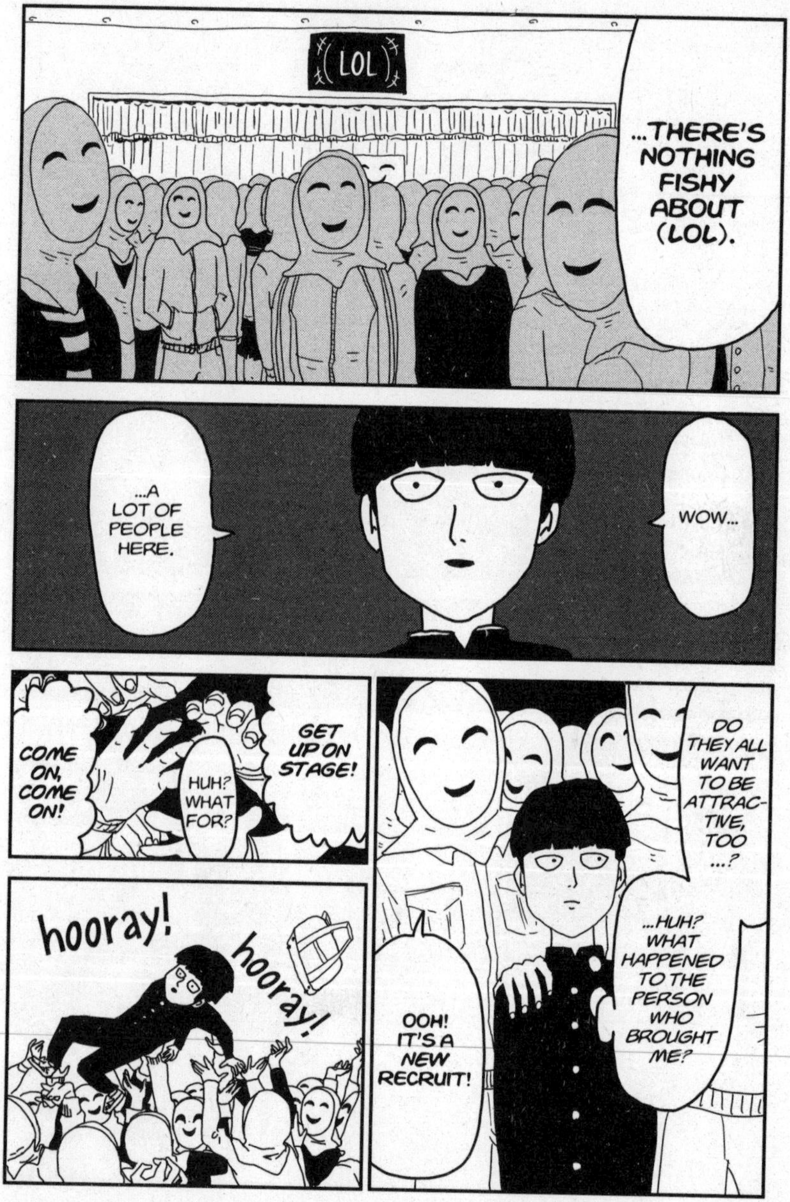
(LOL)
...THERE'S NOTHING FISHY ABOUT (LOL).
WOW...
...A LOT OF PEOPLE HERE.
DO THEY ALL WANT TO BE ATTRACTIVE, TOO ...?
...HUH? WHAT HAPPENED TO THE PERSON WHO BROUGHT ME?
OOH! IT'S A NEW RECRUIT!
GET UP ON STAGE!
HUH? WHAT FOR?
COME ON, COME ON!
hooray!
hooray!

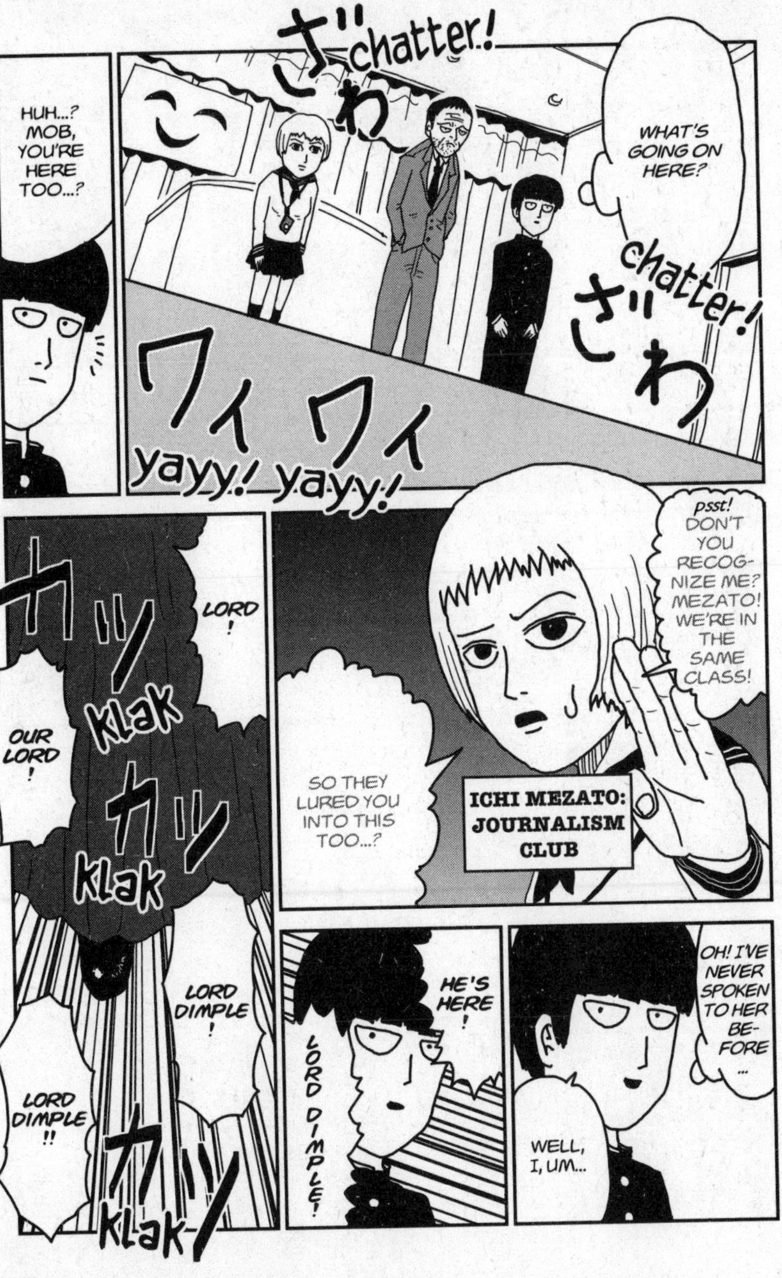
ざわ chatter!
WHAT'S GOING ON HERE?
ざわ chatter!
ワイワイ yayy! yayy!
HUH...? MOB, YOU'RE HERE TOO...?
psst! DON'T YOU RECOG-NIZE ME? MEZATO! WE'RE IN THE SAME CLASS!
ICHI MEZATO: JOURNALISM CLUB
SO THEY LURED YOU INTO THIS TOO...?
OH! I'VE NEVER SPOKEN TO HER BE-FORE ...
WELL, I, UM...
HE'S HERE!
LORD DIMPLE!
LORD!
カッ KLAK
OUR LORD!
カッ KLAK
LORD DIMPLE!
LORD DIMPLE!!
カッ KLAK

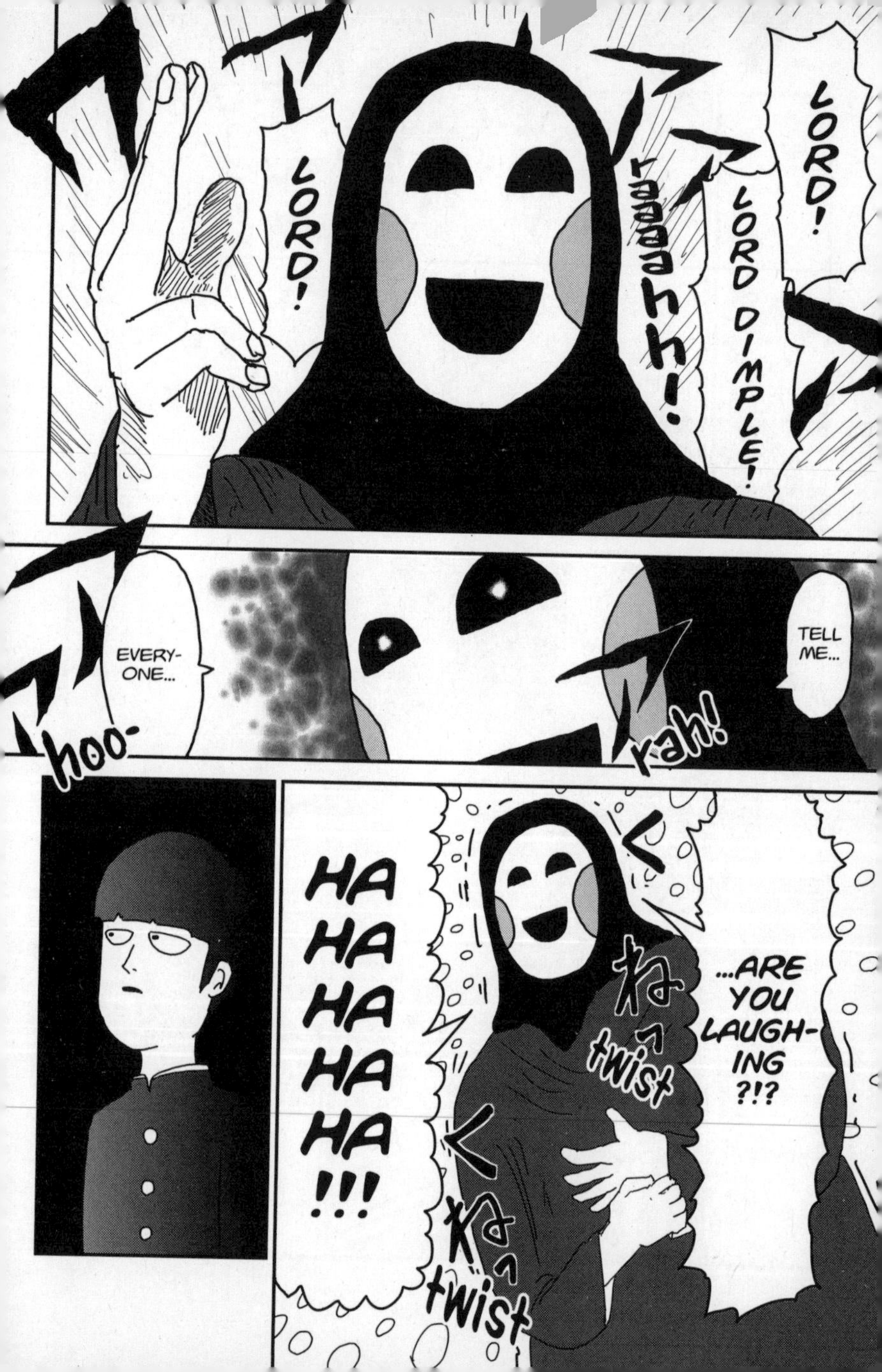
LORD!
LORD DIMPLE!
kyaaaahh!
LORD!
TELL ME...
rah!
EVERY-ONE...
hoo-
...ARE YOU LAUGH-ING?!?
HA HA HA HA HA HA!!!
twist
twist

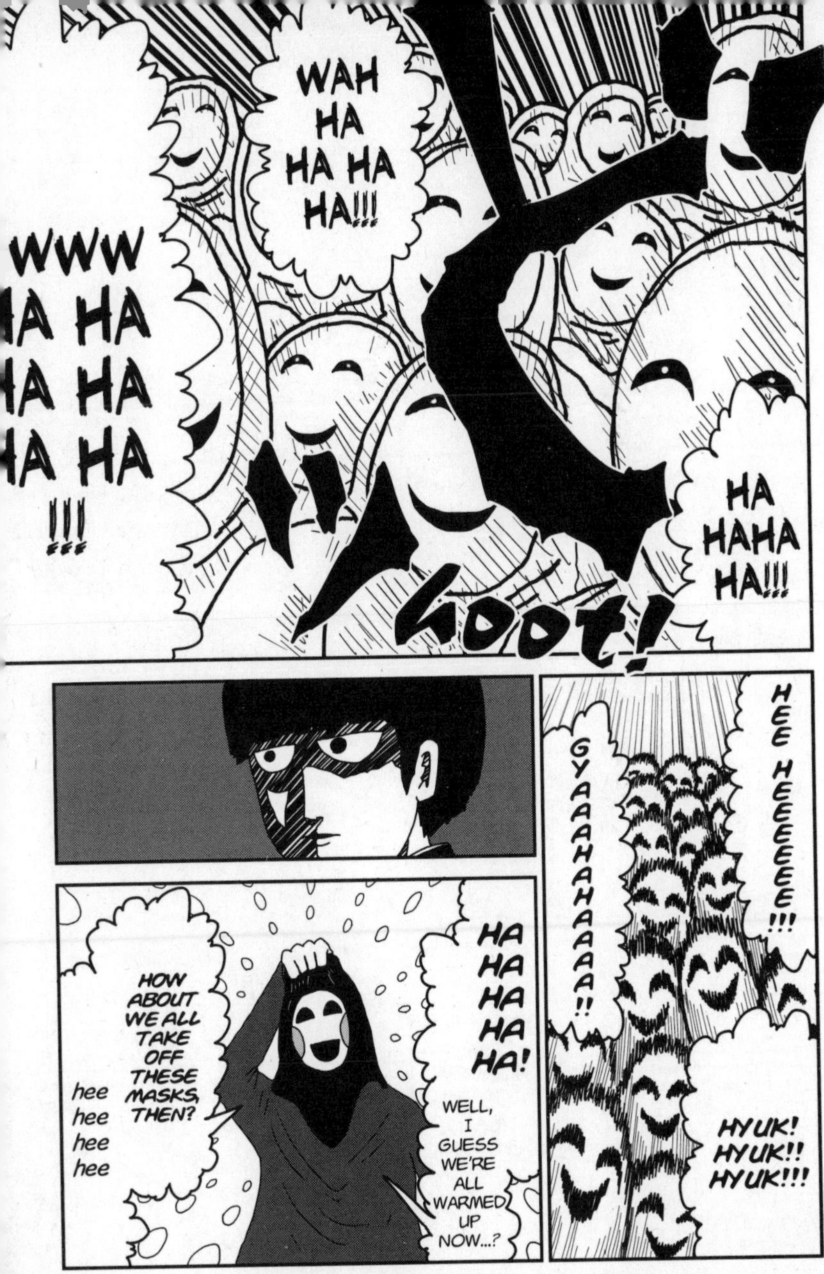
WAH HA HA HA HA!!!
HA HAHA HA!!!
WWW HA HA HA HA HA HA !!!
GOOT!
HEE HEEEEEE!!!
GYAAAAHAHAAAAA!!
HYUK! HYUK!! HYUK!!!
HA HA HA HA HA!
WELL, I GUESS WE'RE ALL WARMED UP NOW...?
HOW ABOUT WE ALL TAKE OFF THESE MASKS, THEN?
hee hee hee hee

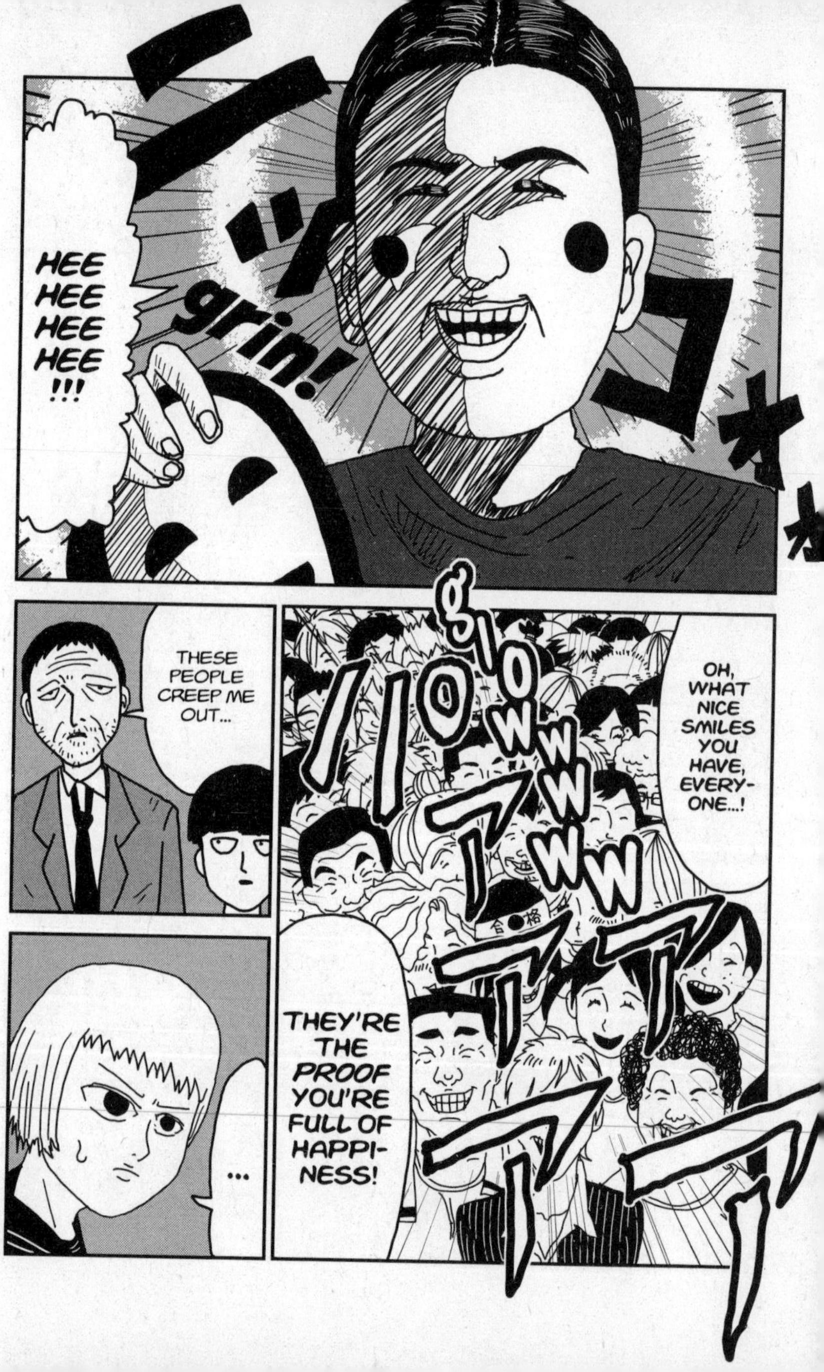
grin!
HEE HEE HEE HEE!!!
OH, WHAT NICE SMILES YOU HAVE, EVERYONE...!
glowwwwww
THEY'RE THE PROOF YOU'RE FULL OF HAPPINESS!
THESE PEOPLE CREEP ME OUT...
...

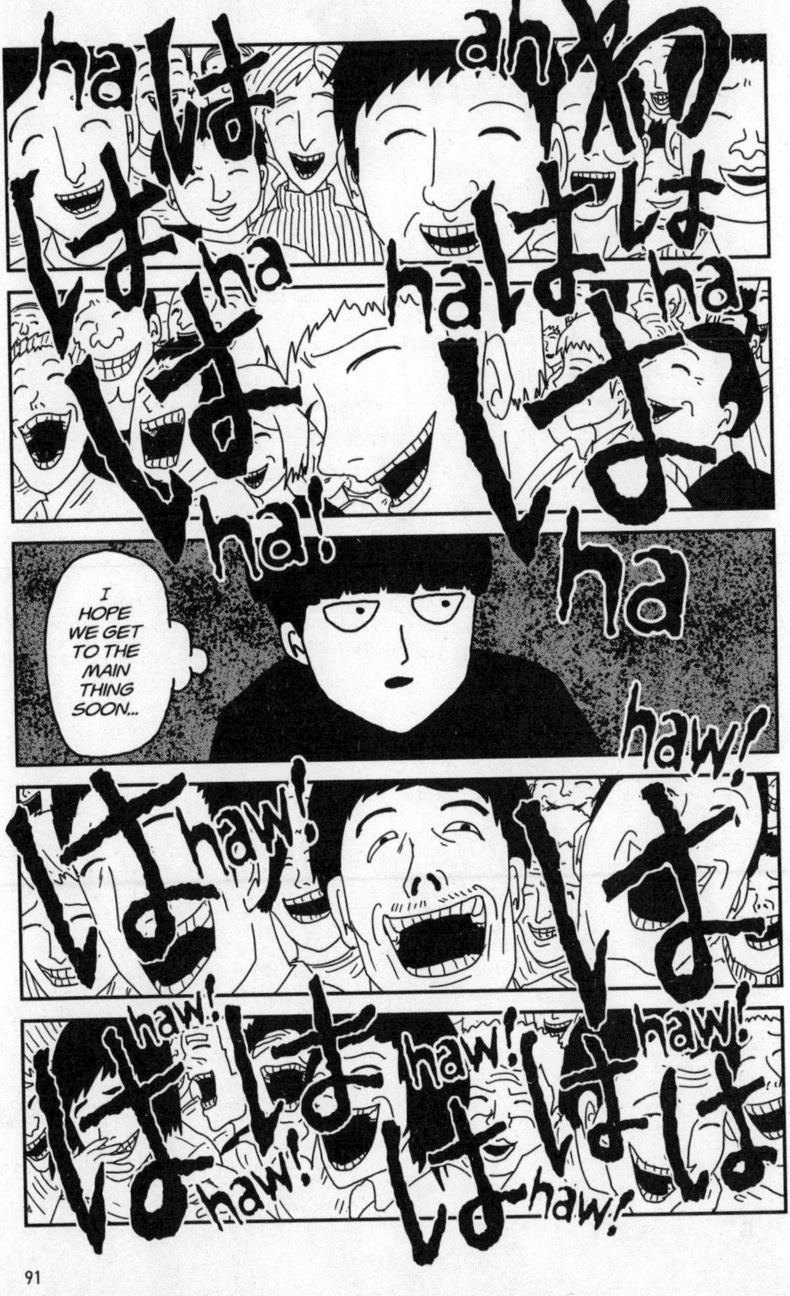
ah
ha!
ha
ha!
ha!
ha
I HOPE WE GET TO THE MAIN THING SOON...
haw!
haw!
haw!
haw!
haw!
haw!
haw!

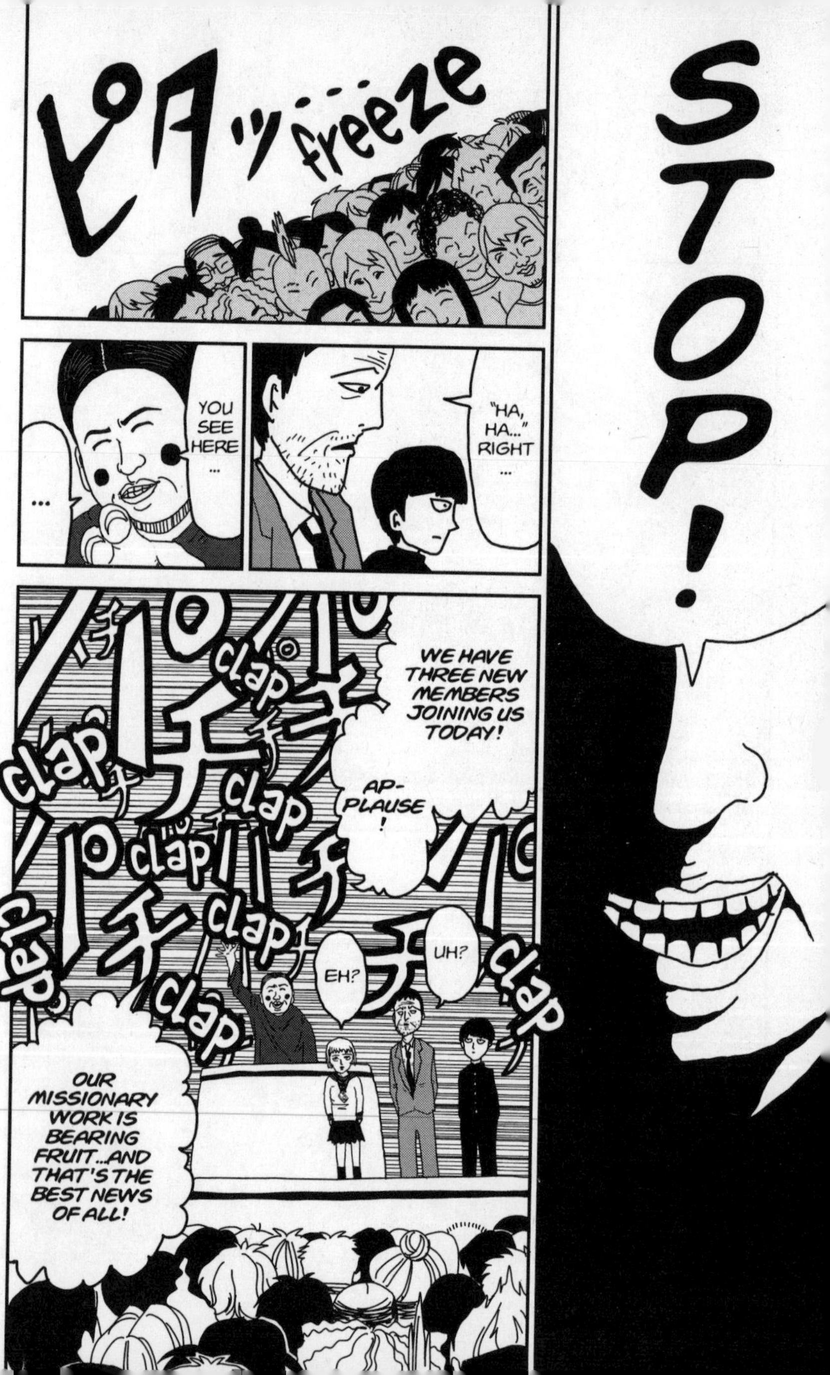
STOP!
ピタッ
freeze
"HA, HA..." RIGHT...
YOU SEE HERE...
...
WE HAVE THREE NEW MEMBERS JOINING US TODAY!
AP-PLAUSE!
clap clap clap clap clap clap clap clap
UH?
EH?
OUR MISSIONARY WORK IS BEARING FRUIT...AND THAT'S THE BEST NEWS OF ALL!

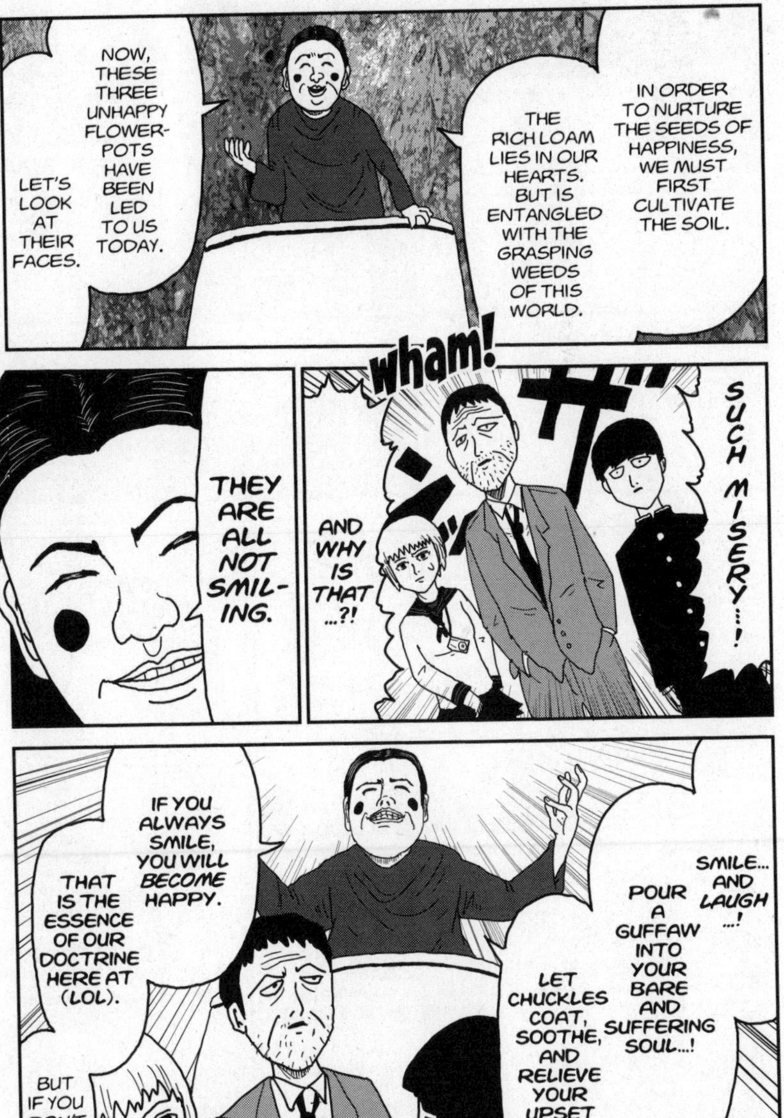
IN ORDER TO NURTURE THE SEEDS OF HAPPINESS, WE MUST FIRST CULTIVATE THE SOIL.
THE RICH LOAM LIES IN OUR HEARTS. BUT IS ENTANGLED WITH THE GRASPING WEEDS OF THIS WORLD.
NOW, THESE THREE UNHAPPY FLOWER-POTS HAVE BEEN LED TO US TODAY.
LET'S LOOK AT THEIR FACES.
wham!
SUCH MISERY...!
AND WHY IS THAT...?!
THEY ARE ALL NOT SMILING.
SMILE... AND LAUGH...!
POUR A GUFFAW INTO YOUR BARE AND SUFFERING SOUL...!
LET CHUCKLES COAT, SOOTHE, AND RELIEVE YOUR UPSET HEAD...!!
IF YOU ALWAYS SMILE, YOU WILL BECOME HAPPY.
THAT IS THE ESSENCE OF OUR DOCTRINE HERE AT (LOL).
BUT IF YOU DON'T LAUGH...

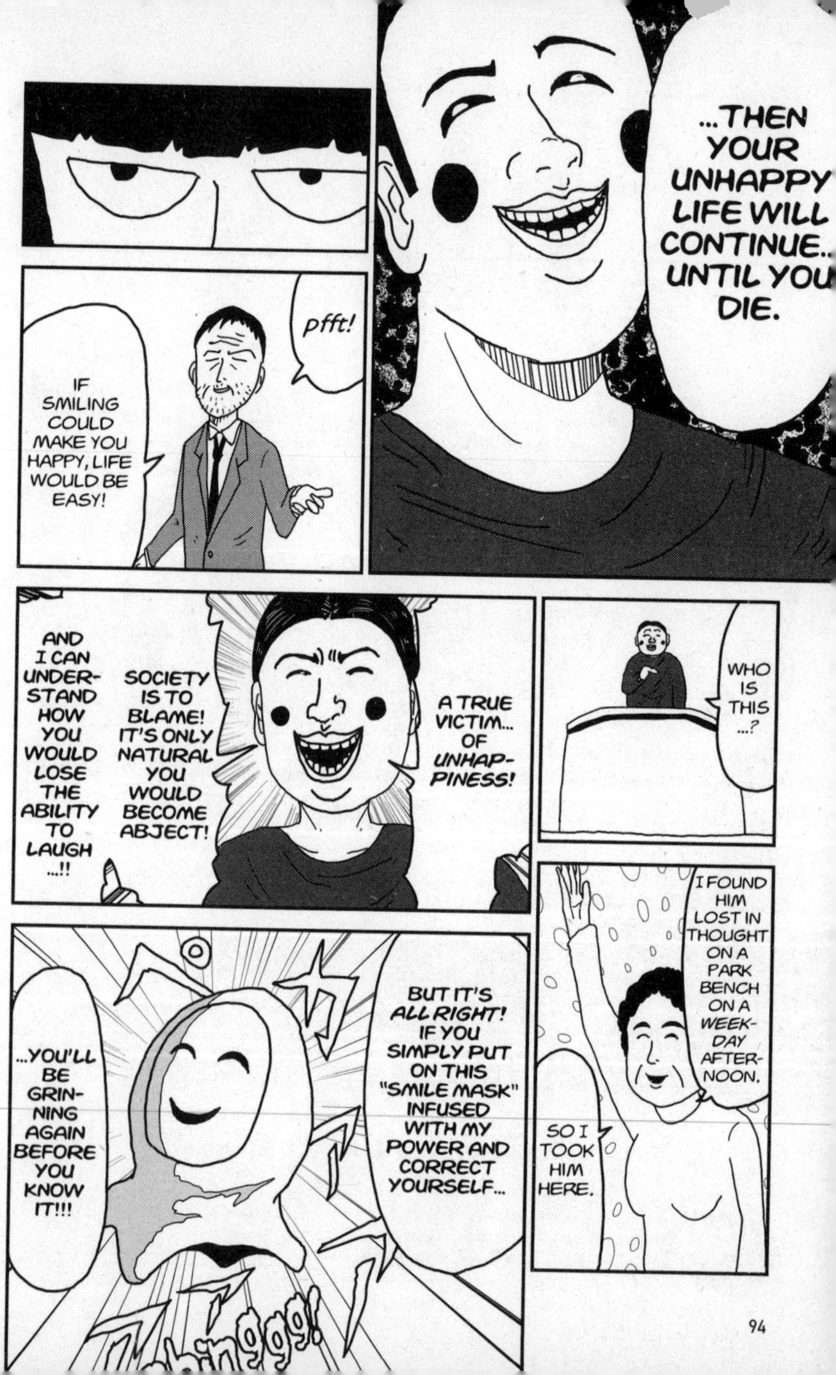
...THEN YOUR UNHAPPY LIFE WILL CONTINUE... UNTIL YOU DIE.
pfft!
IF SMILING COULD MAKE YOU HAPPY, LIFE WOULD BE EASY!
WHO IS THIS ...?
A TRUE VICTIM... OF UNHAPPINESS!
SOCIETY IS TO BLAME! IT'S ONLY NATURAL YOU WOULD BECOME ABJECT!
AND I CAN UNDERSTAND HOW YOU WOULD LOSE THE ABILITY TO LAUGH ...!!
I FOUND HIM LOST IN THOUGHT ON A PARK BENCH ON A WEEKDAY AFTERNOON.
SO I TOOK HIM HERE.
BUT IT'S ALL RIGHT! IF YOU SIMPLY PUT ON THIS "SMILE MASK" INFUSED WITH MY POWER AND CORRECT YOURSELF...
...YOU'LL BE GRINNING AGAIN BEFORE YOU KNOW IT!!!

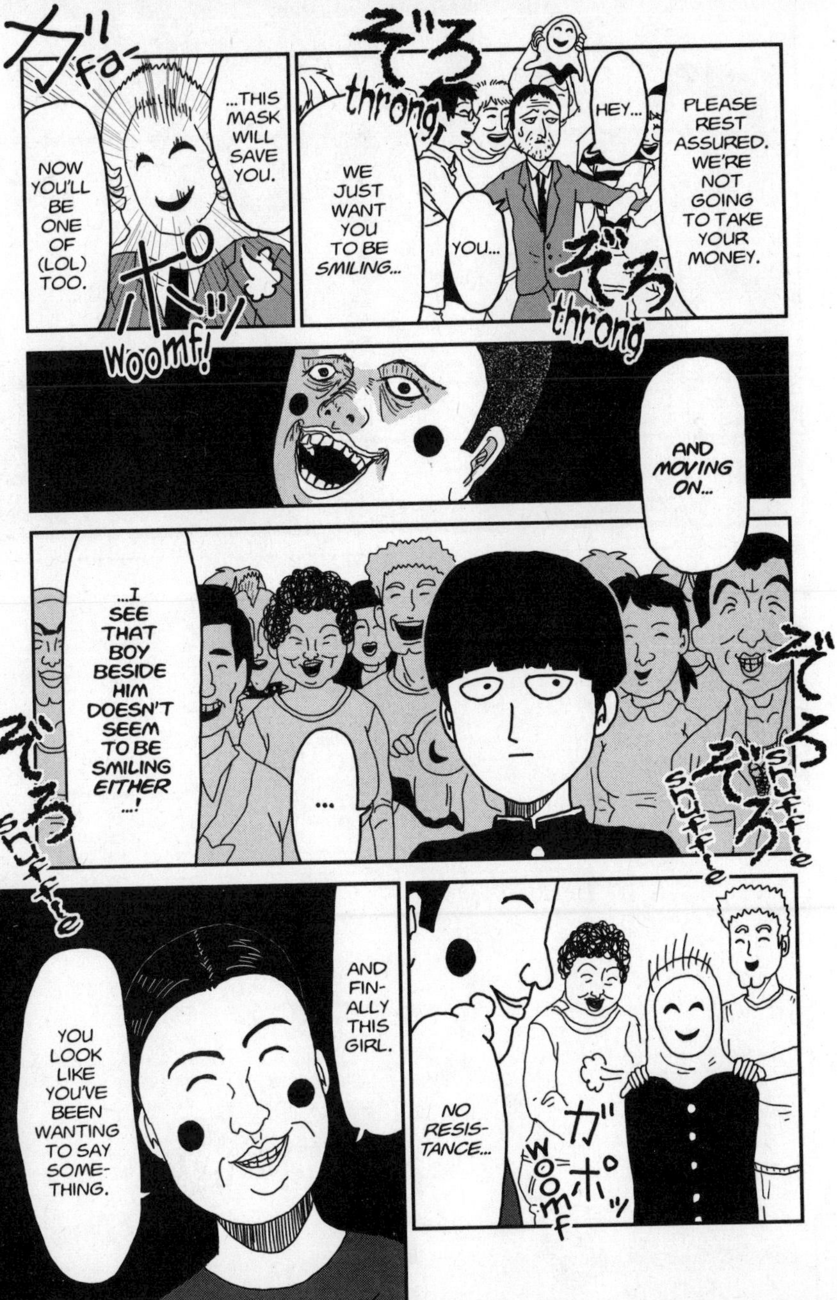
ぞろ
throng
PLEASE REST ASSURED. WE'RE NOT GOING TO TAKE YOUR MONEY.
HEY...
YOU...
WE JUST WANT YOU TO BE SMILING...
ぞろ
throng
ガ
fa
...THIS MASK WILL SAVE YOU.
NOW YOU'LL BE ONE OF (LOL) TOO.
ポッ
woomf!
AND MOVING ON...
ぞろ
shuffle
ぞろ
shuffle
...I SEE THAT BOY BESIDE HIM DOESN'T SEEM TO BE SMILING EITHER...!
...
ぞろ
shuffle
AND FIN-ALLY THIS GIRL.
NO RESIS-TANCE...
ガポッ
woomf
YOU LOOK LIKE YOU'VE BEEN WANTING TO SAY SOME-THING.

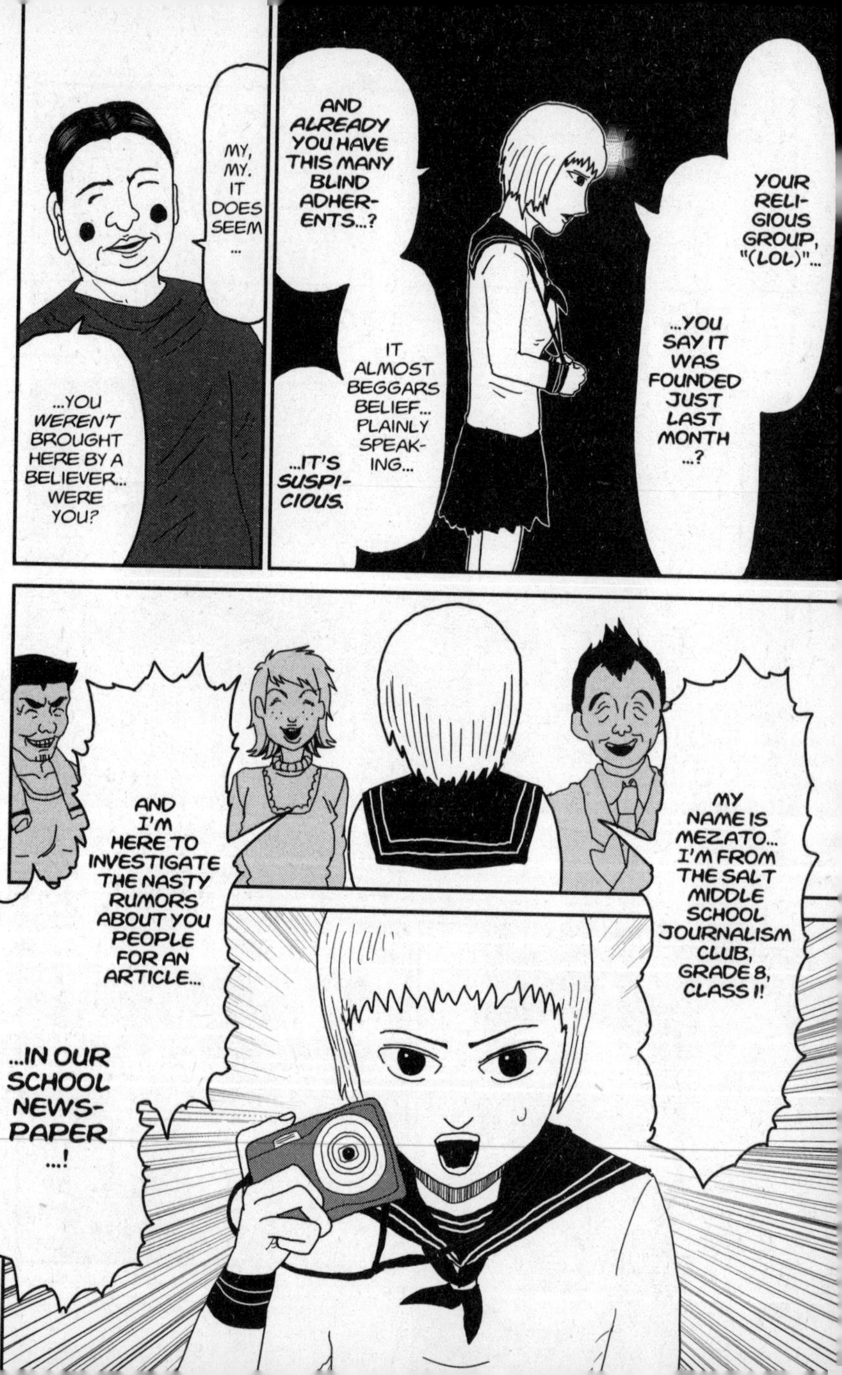
YOUR RELIGIOUS GROUP, "(LOL)"...
...YOU SAY IT WAS FOUNDED JUST LAST MONTH...?
AND ALREADY YOU HAVE THIS MANY BLIND ADHERENTS...?
IT ALMOST BEGGARS BELIEF... PLAINLY SPEAKING...
...IT'S SUSPICIOUS.
MY, MY. IT DOES SEEM...
...YOU WEREN'T BROUGHT HERE BY A BELIEVER... WERE YOU?
MY NAME IS MEZATO... I'M FROM THE SALT MIDDLE SCHOOL JOURNALISM CLUB, GRADE 8, CLASS 1!
AND I'M HERE TO INVESTIGATE THE NASTY RUMORS ABOUT YOU PEOPLE FOR AN ARTICLE...
...IN OUR SCHOOL NEWSPAPER...!

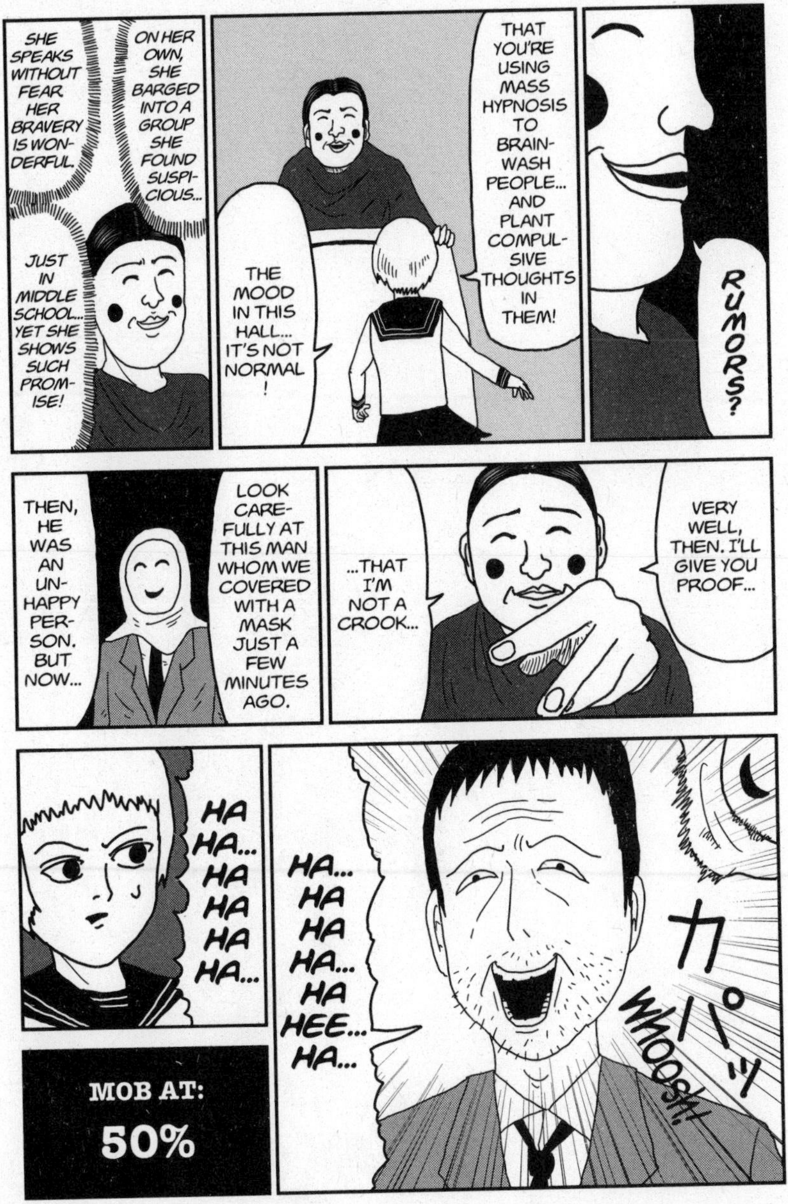
RUMORS?
THAT YOU'RE USING MASS HYPNOSIS TO BRAIN-WASH PEOPLE... AND PLANT COMPUL-SIVE THOUGHTS IN THEM!
THE MOOD IN THIS HALL... IT'S NOT NORMAL!
ON HER OWN, SHE BARGED INTO A GROUP SHE FOUND SUSPI-CIOUS...
SHE SPEAKS WITHOUT FEAR HER BRAVERY IS WON-DERFUL.
JUST IN MIDDLE SCHOOL... YET SHE SHOWS SUCH PROM-ISE!
VERY WELL, THEN. I'LL GIVE YOU PROOF...
...THAT I'M NOT A CROOK...
LOOK CARE-FULLY AT THIS MAN WHOM WE COVERED WITH A MASK JUST A FEW MINUTES AGO.
THEN, HE WAS AN UN-HAPPY PER-SON. BUT NOW...
カパッ
WHOOSH!
HA... HA HA HA... HA HEE... HA...
HA HA... HA HA HA HA...
MOB AT: 50%

Example of a nice smile

CHAPTER 7: MOOD OF THE GROUP

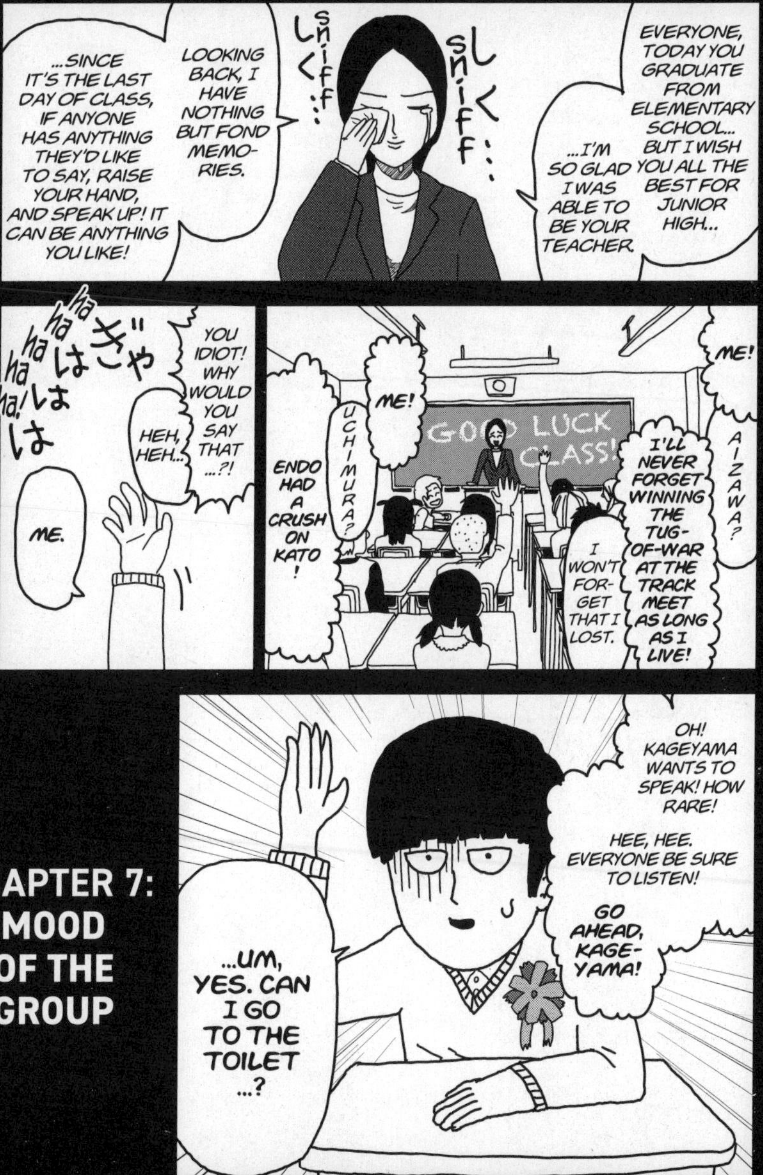
EVERYONE, TODAY YOU GRADUATE FROM ELEMENTARY SCHOOL... BUT I WISH YOU ALL THE BEST FOR JUNIOR HIGH...
...I'M SO GLAD I WAS ABLE TO BE YOUR TEACHER.
しくsniff...
しくsniff...
LOOKING BACK, I HAVE NOTHING BUT FOND MEMORIES.
...SINCE IT'S THE LAST DAY OF CLASS, IF ANYONE HAS ANYTHING THEY'D LIKE TO SAY, RAISE YOUR HAND, AND SPEAK UP! IT CAN BE ANYTHING YOU LIKE!
ME!
AIZAWA?
I'LL NEVER FORGET WINNING THE TUG-OF-WAR AT THE TRACK MEET AS LONG AS I LIVE!
I WON'T FORGET THAT I LOST.
GOOD LUCK CLASS!
ME!
UCHIMURA?
ENDO HAD A CRUSH ON KATO!
ぎゃははは ha ha ha ha ha!
YOU IDIOT! WHY WOULD YOU SAY THAT...?!
HEH, HEH...
ME.
OH! KAGEYAMA WANTS TO SPEAK! HOW RARE!
HEE, HEE. EVERYONE BE SURE TO LISTEN!
GO AHEAD, KAGE-YAMA!
...UM, YES. CAN I GO TO THE TOILET...?

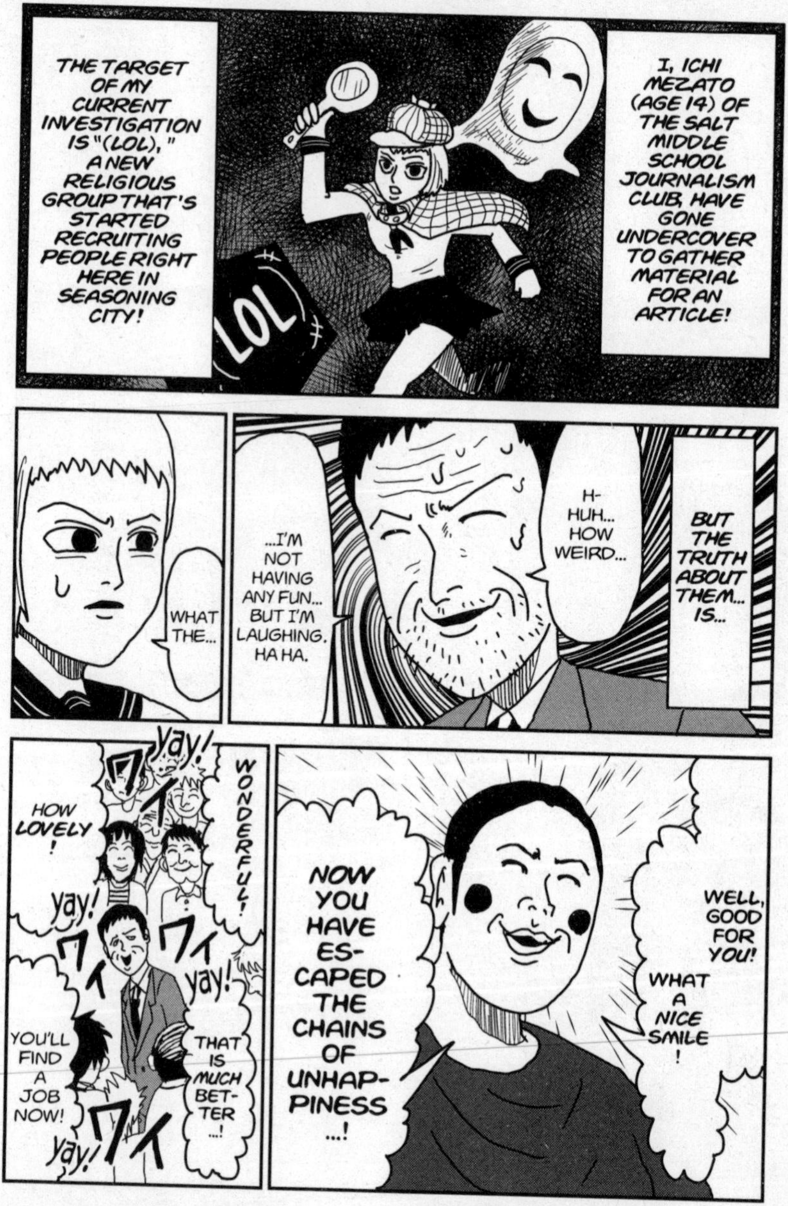
I, ICHI MEZATO (AGE 14) OF THE SALT MIDDLE SCHOOL JOURNALISM CLUB, HAVE GONE UNDERCOVER TO GATHER MATERIAL FOR AN ARTICLE!
THE TARGET OF MY CURRENT INVESTIGATION IS "(LOL)," A NEW RELIGIOUS GROUP THAT'S STARTED RECRUITING PEOPLE RIGHT HERE IN SEASONING CITY!
(LOL)
BUT THE TRUTH ABOUT THEM... IS...
H-HUH... HOW WEIRD...
...I'M NOT HAVING ANY FUN... BUT I'M LAUGHING. HA HA.
WHAT THE...
WELL, GOOD FOR YOU!
WHAT A NICE SMILE!
NOW YOU HAVE ES-CAPED THE CHAINS OF UNHAP-PINESS...!
WONDERFUL!
yay!
ワイ
HOW LOVELY!
yay!
ワイ
ワイ
yay!
THAT IS MUCH BET-TER...!
YOU'LL FIND A JOB NOW!
ワイ
yay!

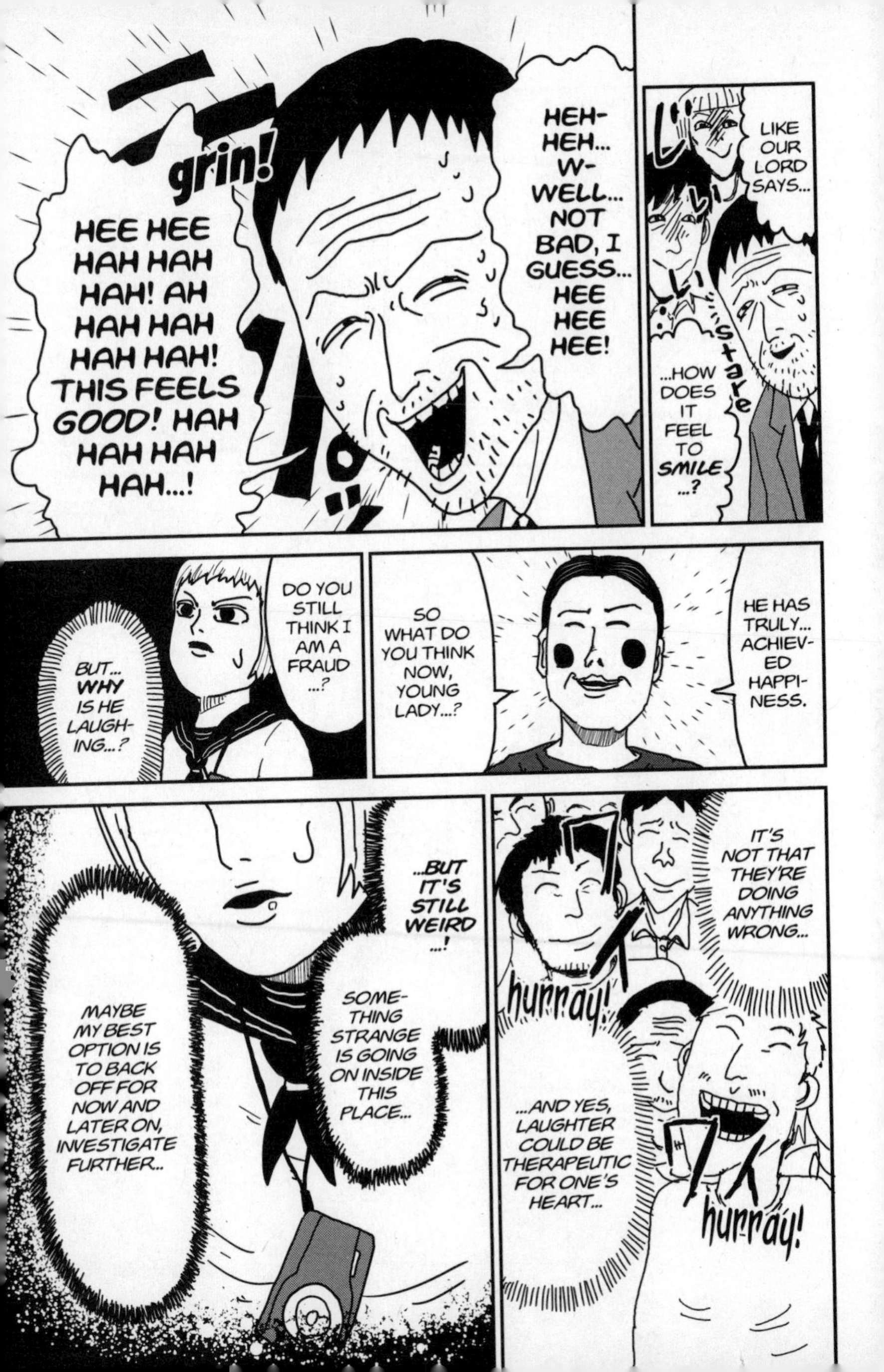
LIKE OUR LORD SAYS...
...HOW DOES IT FEEL TO SMILE...?
stare
HEH-HEH... W-WELL... NOT BAD, I GUESS... HEE HEE HEE!
grin!
HEE HEE HAH HAH HAH! AH HAH HAH HAH HAH! THIS FEELS GOOD! HAH HAH HAH HAH...!
HE HAS TRULY... ACHIEVED HAPPINESS.
SO WHAT DO YOU THINK NOW, YOUNG LADY...?
DO YOU STILL THINK I AM A FRAUD...?
BUT... WHY IS HE LAUGHING...?
IT'S NOT THAT THEY'RE DOING ANYTHING WRONG...
hurray!
...AND YES, LAUGHTER COULD BE THERAPEUTIC FOR ONE'S HEART...
hurray!
...BUT IT'S STILL WEIRD...!
SOMETHING STRANGE IS GOING ON INSIDE THIS PLACE...
MAYBE MY BEST OPTION IS TO BACK OFF FOR NOW AND LATER ON, INVESTIGATE FURTHER...

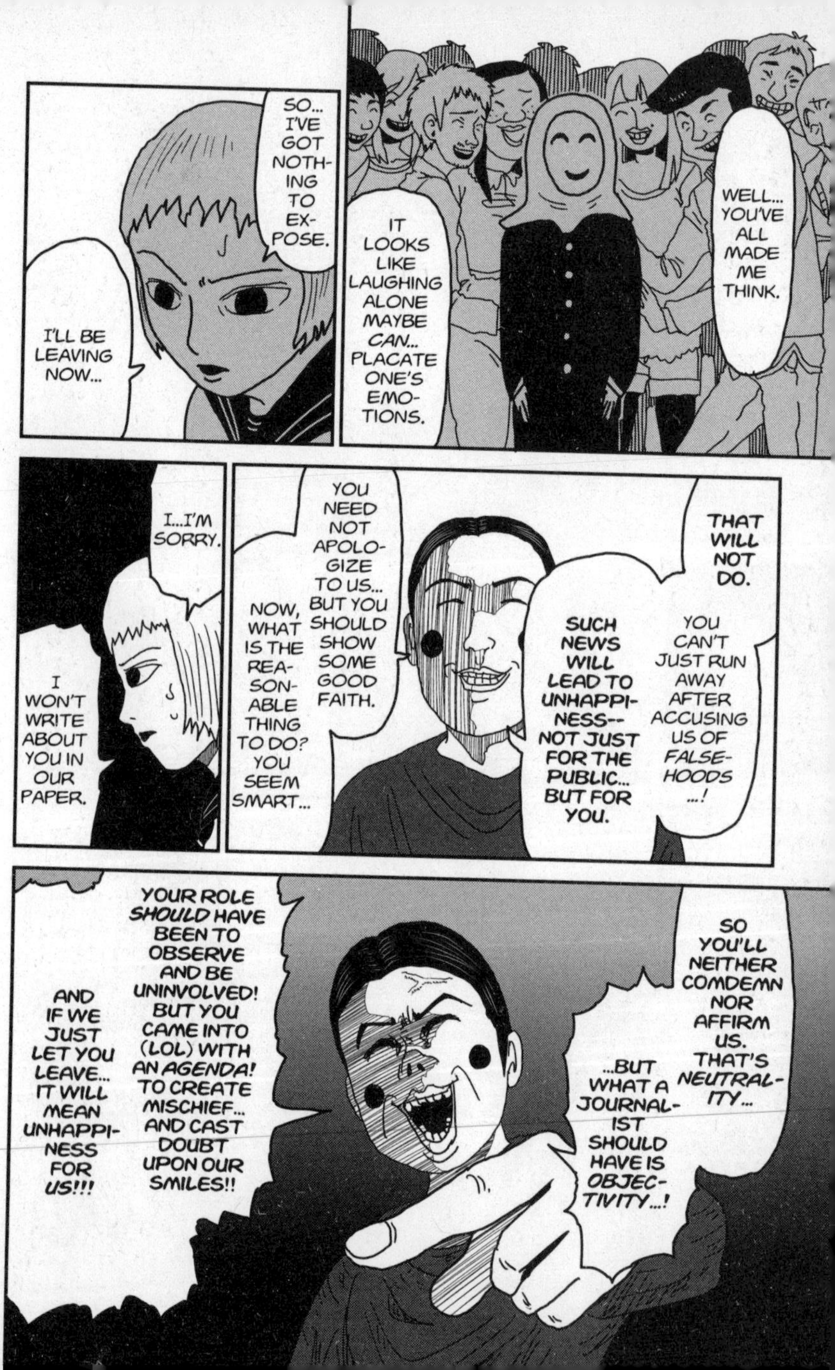
WELL... YOU'VE ALL MADE ME THINK.
IT LOOKS LIKE LAUGHING ALONE MAYBE CAN... PLACATE ONE'S EMOTIONS.
SO... I'VE GOT NOTHING TO EXPOSE.
I'LL BE LEAVING NOW...
THAT WILL NOT DO.
YOU CAN'T JUST RUN AWAY AFTER ACCUSING US OF FALSEHOODS ...!
SUCH NEWS WILL LEAD TO UNHAPPINESS-- NOT JUST FOR THE PUBLIC... BUT FOR YOU.
YOU NEED NOT APOLOGIZE TO US... BUT YOU SHOULD SHOW SOME GOOD FAITH.
NOW, WHAT IS THE REASONABLE THING TO DO? YOU SEEM SMART...
I...I'M SORRY.
I WON'T WRITE ABOUT YOU IN OUR PAPER.
SO YOU'LL NEITHER COMDEMN NOR AFFIRM US. THAT'S NEUTRALITY...
...BUT WHAT A JOURNALIST SHOULD HAVE IS OBJECTIVITY...!
YOUR ROLE SHOULD HAVE BEEN TO OBSERVE AND BE UNINVOLVED! BUT YOU CAME INTO (LOL) WITH AN AGENDA! TO CREATE MISCHIEF... AND CAST DOUBT UPON OUR SMILES!!
AND IF WE JUST LET YOU LEAVE... IT WILL MEAN UNHAPPINESS FOR US!!!

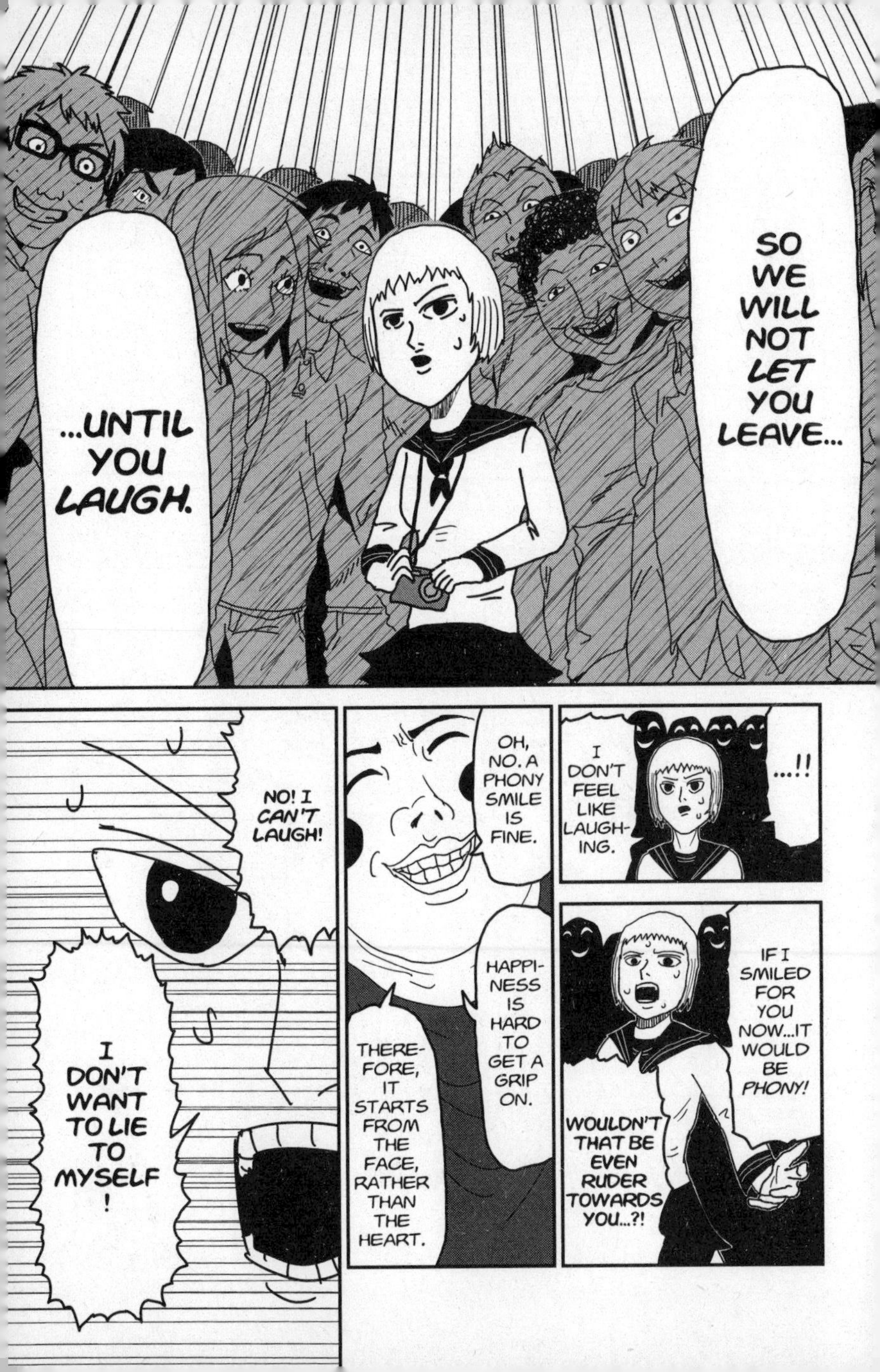
SO WE WILL NOT LET YOU LEAVE...
...UNTIL YOU LAUGH.
...!!
I DON'T FEEL LIKE LAUGHING.
IF I SMILED FOR YOU NOW...IT WOULD BE PHONY!
WOULDN'T THAT BE EVEN RUDER TOWARDS YOU...?!
OH, NO. A PHONY SMILE IS FINE.
HAPPINESS IS HARD TO GET A GRIP ON.
THEREFORE, IT STARTS FROM THE FACE, RATHER THAN THE HEART.
NO! I CAN'T LAUGH!
I DON'T WANT TO LIE TO MYSELF!

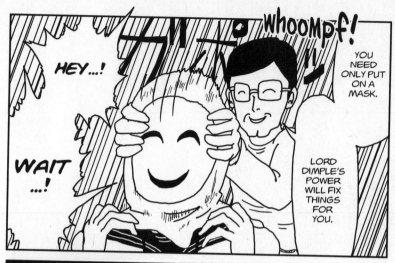

whoompf!

HEY...!

WAIT ...!

YOU NEED ONLY PUT ON A MASK.

LORD DIMPLE'S POWER WILL FIX THINGS FOR YOU.

MY MOUTH IS MOVING OF ITS OWN WILL...

WHAT THE... I'M... SMILING...

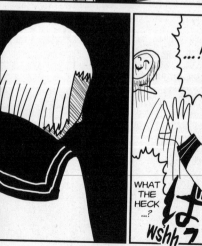

....!

WHAT THE HECK ...?

wshh

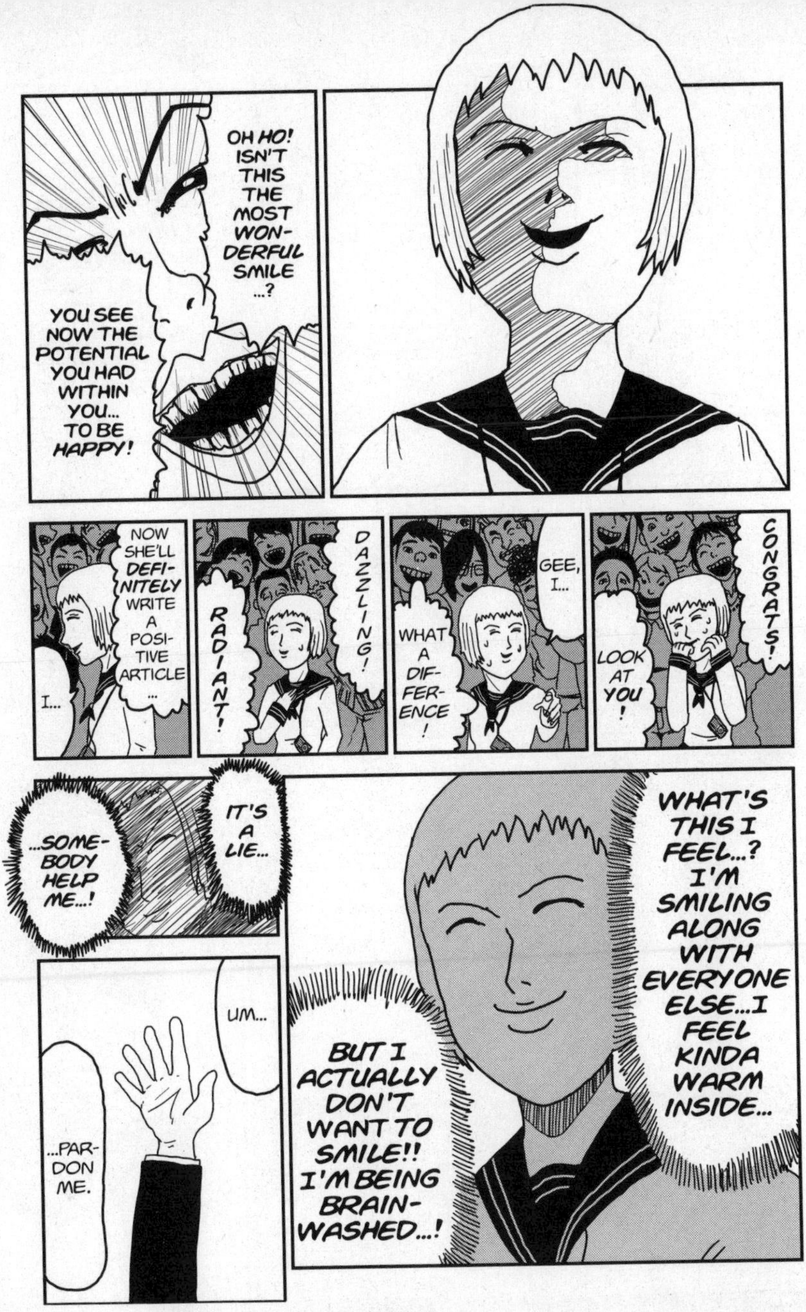
OH HO! ISN'T THIS THE MOST WONDERFUL SMILE ...?
YOU SEE NOW THE POTENTIAL YOU HAD WITHIN YOU... TO BE HAPPY!
CONGRATS!
LOOK AT YOU!
GEE, I...
WHAT A DIFFERENCE!
DAZZLING!
RADIANT!
NOW SHE'LL DEFINITELY WRITE A POSITIVE ARTICLE ...
I...
WHAT'S THIS I FEEL...? I'M SMILING ALONG WITH EVERYONE ELSE...I FEEL KINDA WARM INSIDE...
BUT I ACTUALLY DON'T WANT TO SMILE!! I'M BEING BRAINWASHED...!
IT'S A LIE...
...SOMEBODY HELP ME...!
UM...
...PARDON ME.

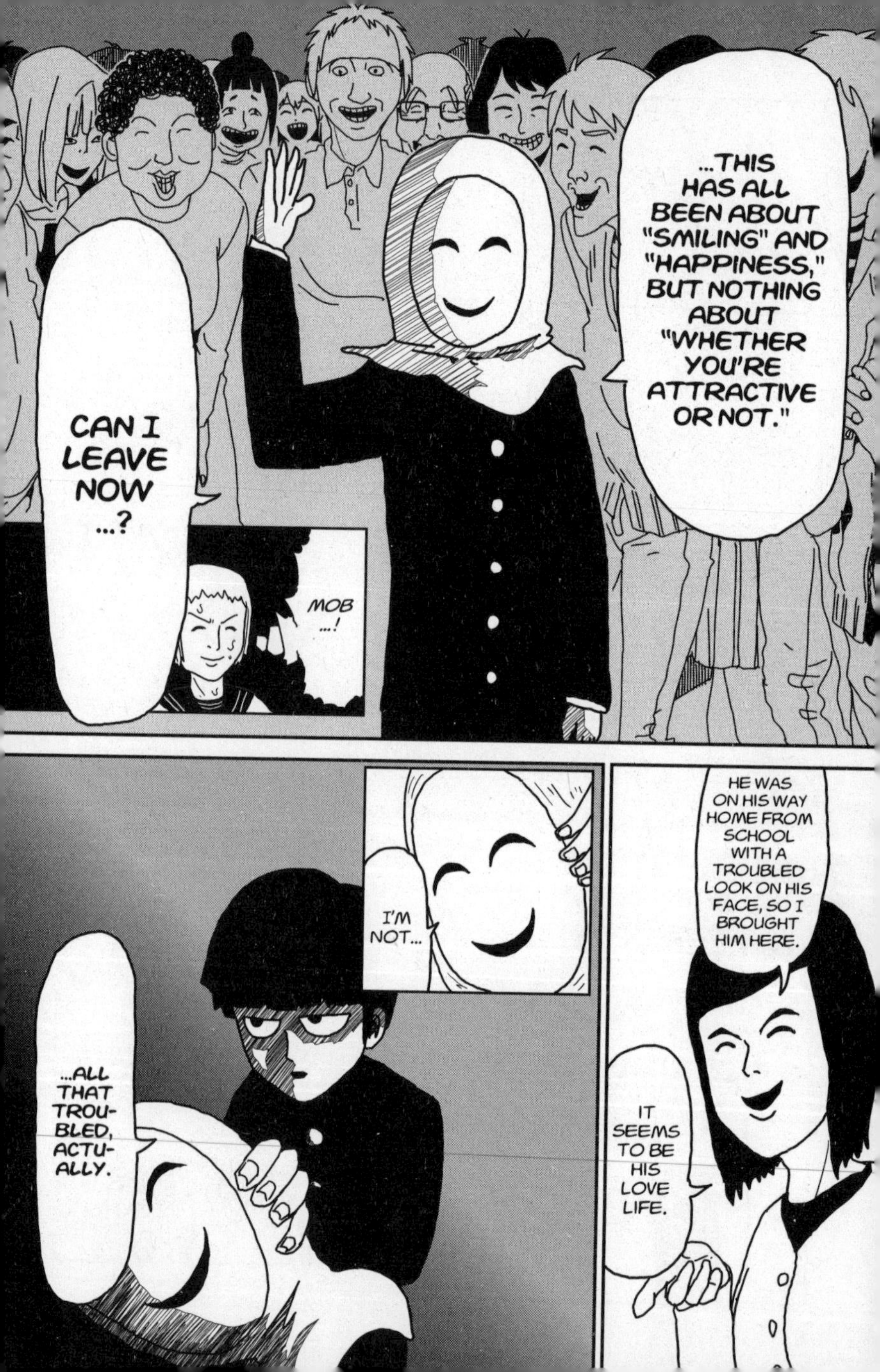
...THIS HAS ALL BEEN ABOUT "SMILING" AND "HAPPINESS," BUT NOTHING ABOUT "WHETHER YOU'RE ATTRACTIVE OR NOT."
CAN I LEAVE NOW ...?
MOB ...!
HE WAS ON HIS WAY HOME FROM SCHOOL WITH A TROUBLED LOOK ON HIS FACE, SO I BROUGHT HIM HERE.
IT SEEMS TO BE HIS LOVE LIFE.
I'M NOT...
...ALL THAT TROU-BLED, ACTU-ALLY.

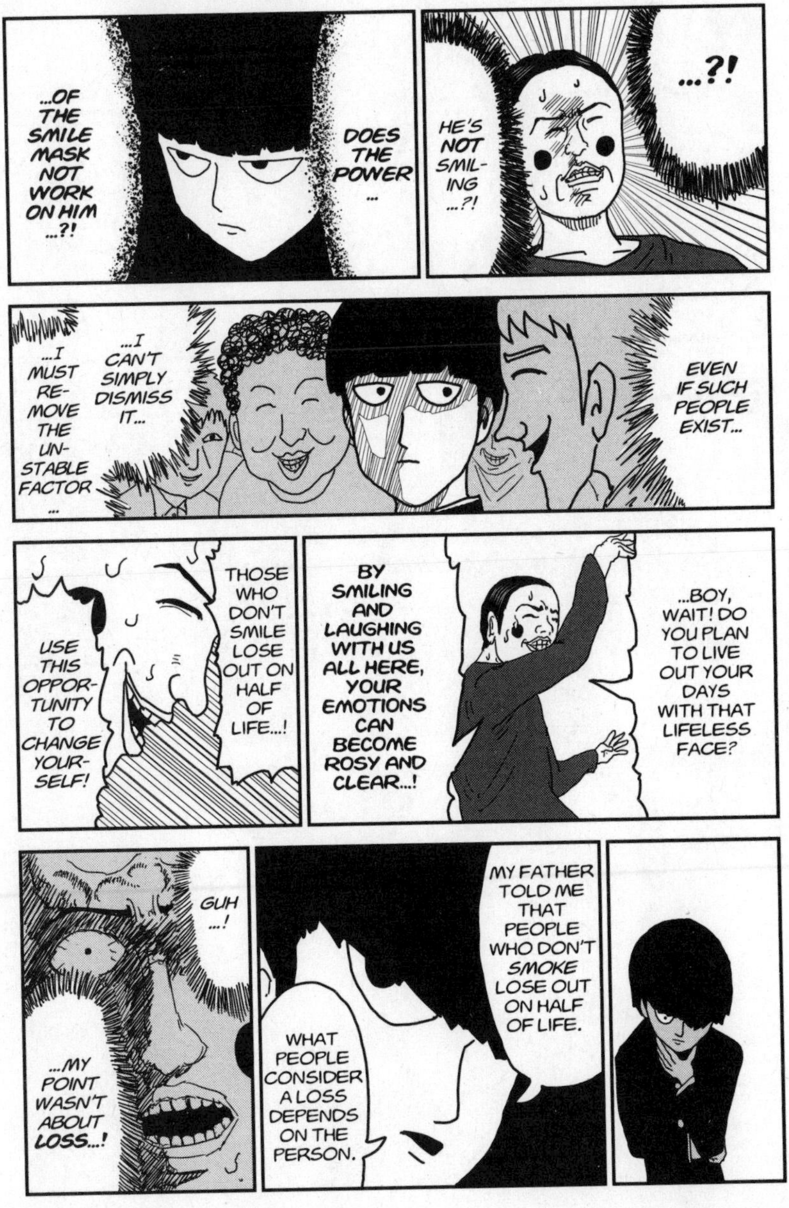
...?!
HE'S NOT SMILING ...?!
DOES THE POWER ...
...OF THE SMILE MASK NOT WORK ON HIM ...?!
EVEN IF SUCH PEOPLE EXIST...
...I CAN'T SIMPLY DISMISS IT...
...I MUST REMOVE THE UNSTABLE FACTOR ...
...BOY, WAIT! DO YOU PLAN TO LIVE OUT YOUR DAYS WITH THAT LIFELESS FACE?
BY SMILING AND LAUGHING WITH US ALL HERE, YOUR EMOTIONS CAN BECOME ROSY AND CLEAR...!
THOSE WHO DON'T SMILE LOSE OUT ON HALF OF LIFE...!
USE THIS OPPORTUNITY TO CHANGE YOURSELF!
MY FATHER TOLD ME THAT PEOPLE WHO DON'T *SMOKE* LOSE OUT ON HALF OF LIFE.
WHAT PEOPLE CONSIDER A LOSS DEPENDS ON THE PERSON.
GUH ...!
...MY POINT WASN'T ABOUT *LOSS*...!

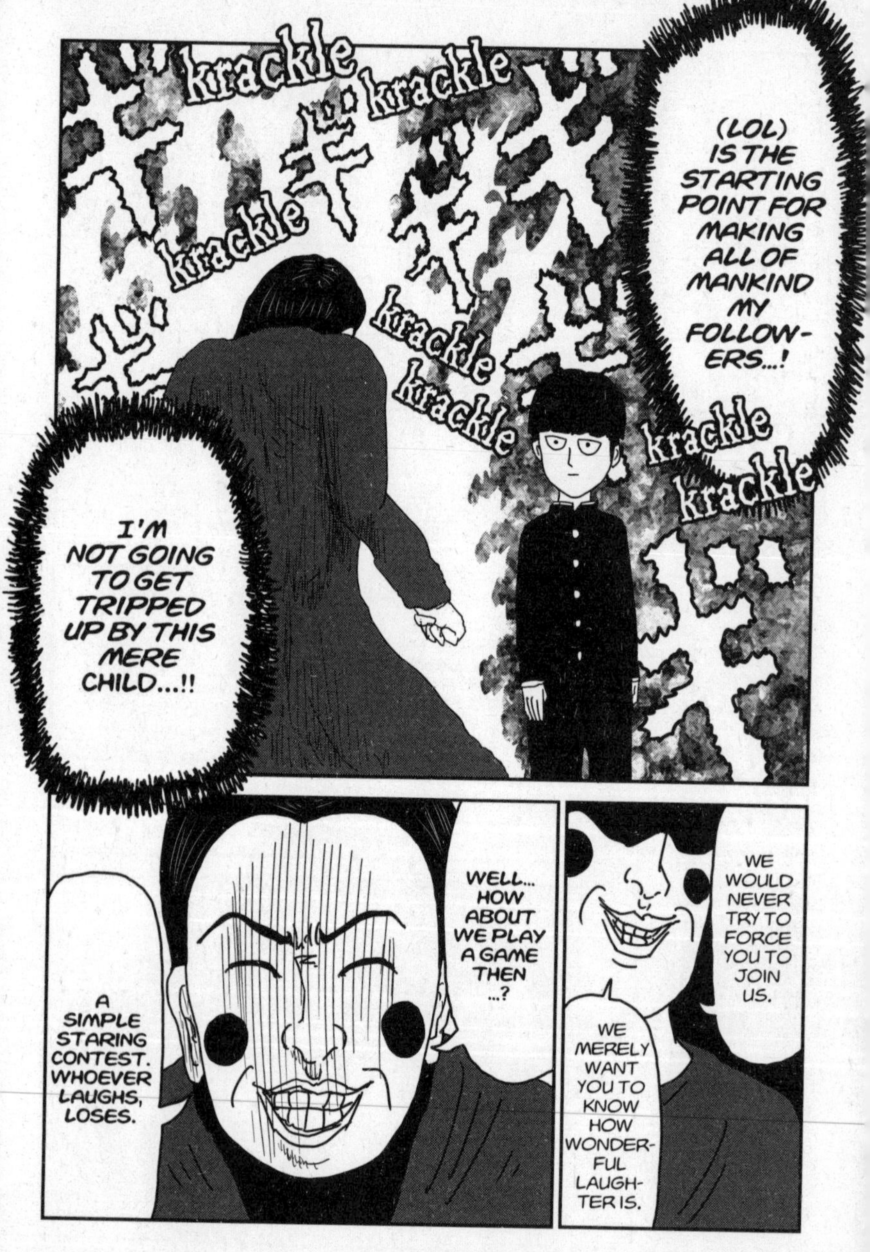
krackle
krackle
(LOL) IS THE STARTING POINT FOR MAKING ALL OF MANKIND MY FOLLOWERS...!
krackle
krackle
krackle
krackle
krackle
I'M NOT GOING TO GET TRIPPED UP BY THIS MERE CHILD...!!
WE WOULD NEVER TRY TO FORCE YOU TO JOIN US.
WE MERELY WANT YOU TO KNOW HOW WONDERFUL LAUGHTER IS.
WELL... HOW ABOUT WE PLAY A GAME THEN ...?
A SIMPLE STARING CONTEST. WHOEVER LAUGHS, LOSES.

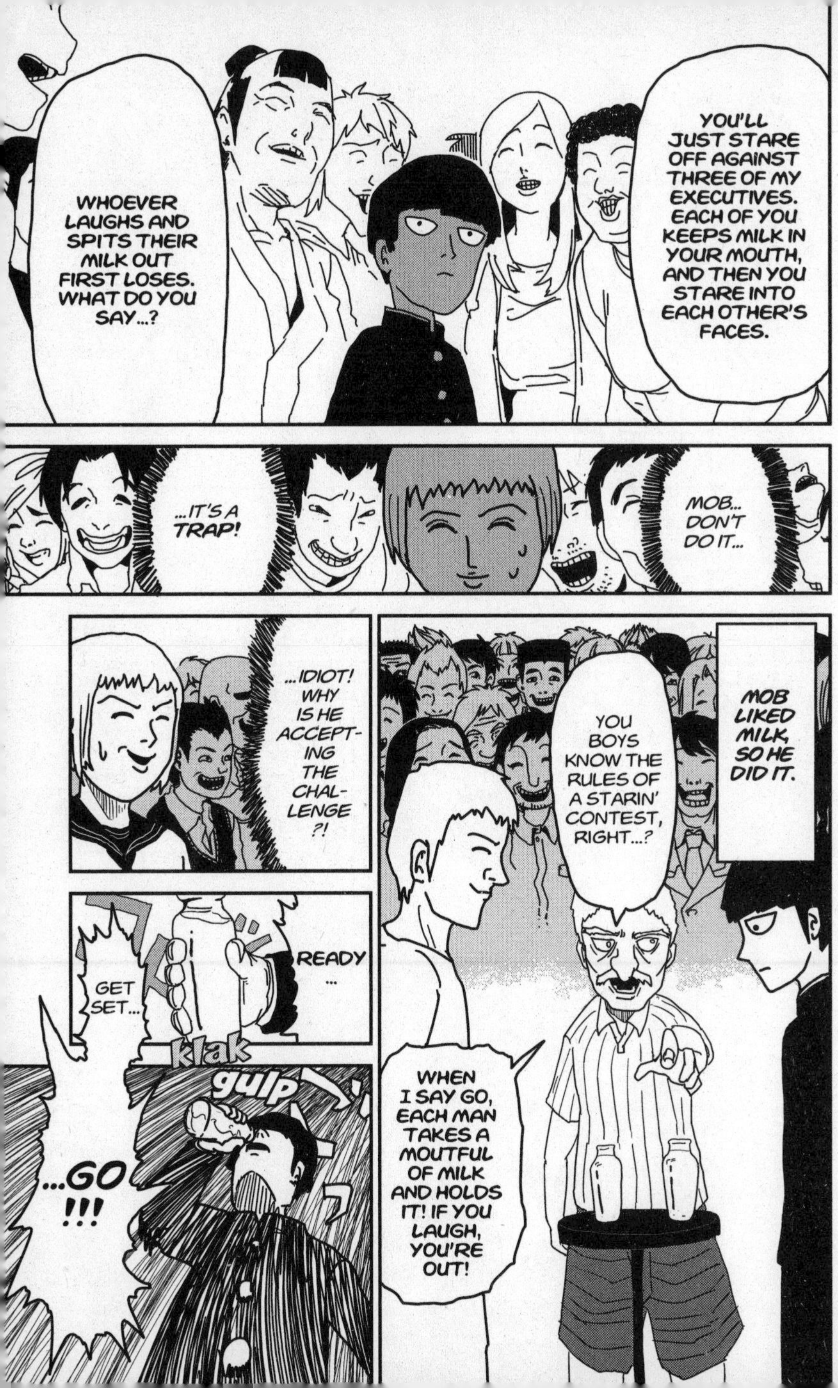
YOU'LL JUST STARE OFF AGAINST THREE OF MY EXECUTIVES. EACH OF YOU KEEPS MILK IN YOUR MOUTH, AND THEN YOU STARE INTO EACH OTHER'S FACES.
WHOEVER LAUGHS AND SPITS THEIR MILK OUT FIRST LOSES. WHAT DO YOU SAY...?
MOB... DON'T DO IT...
...IT'S A TRAP!
MOB LIKED MILK, SO HE DID IT.
YOU BOYS KNOW THE RULES OF A STARIN' CONTEST, RIGHT...?
WHEN I SAY GO, EACH MAN TAKES A MOUTFUL OF MILK AND HOLDS IT! IF YOU LAUGH, YOU'RE OUT!
...IDIOT! WHY IS HE ACCEPT-ING THE CHAL-LENGE ?!
READY ...
GET SET...
klak
gulp
...GO !!!

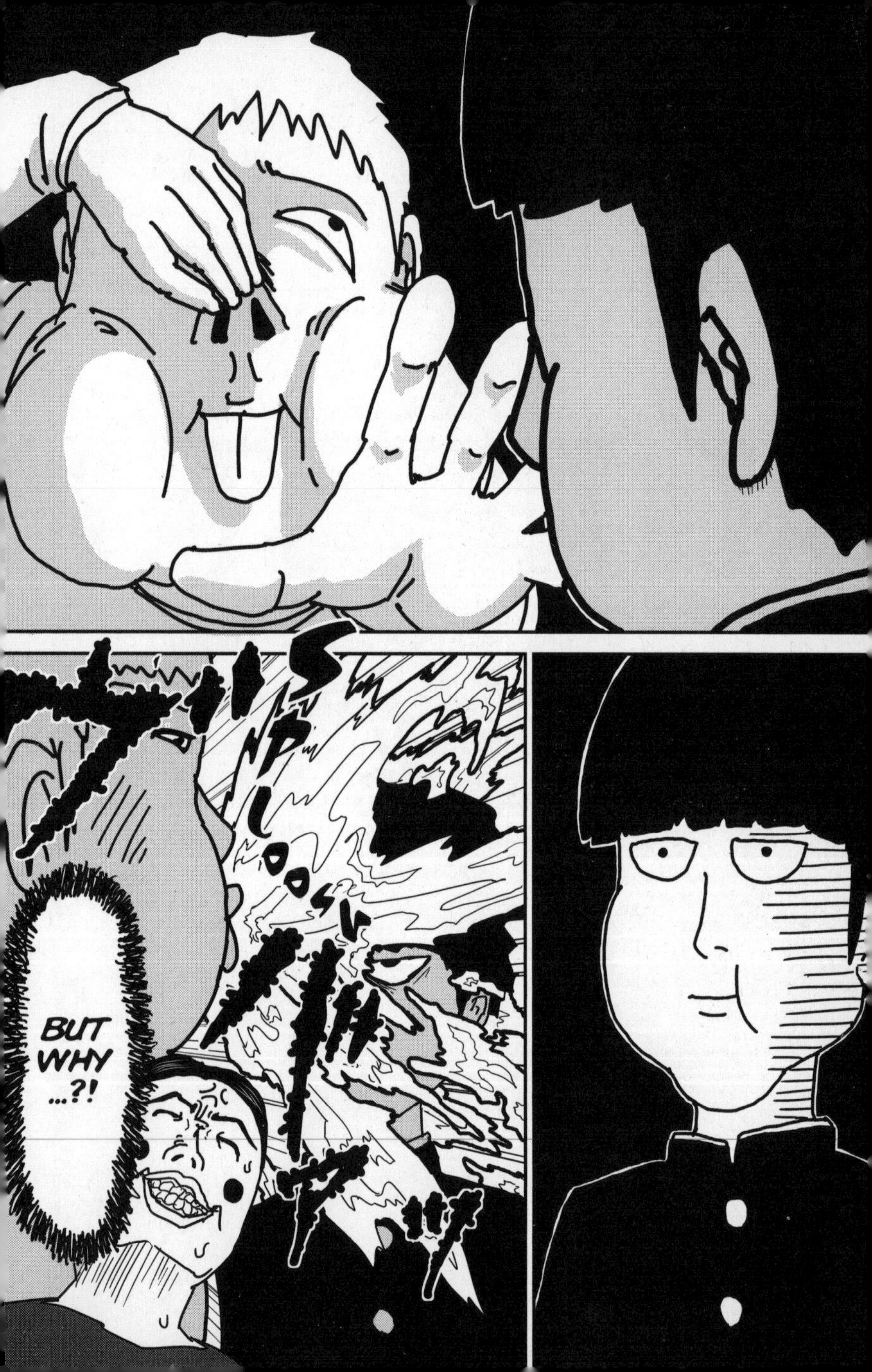
BUT WHY ...?!

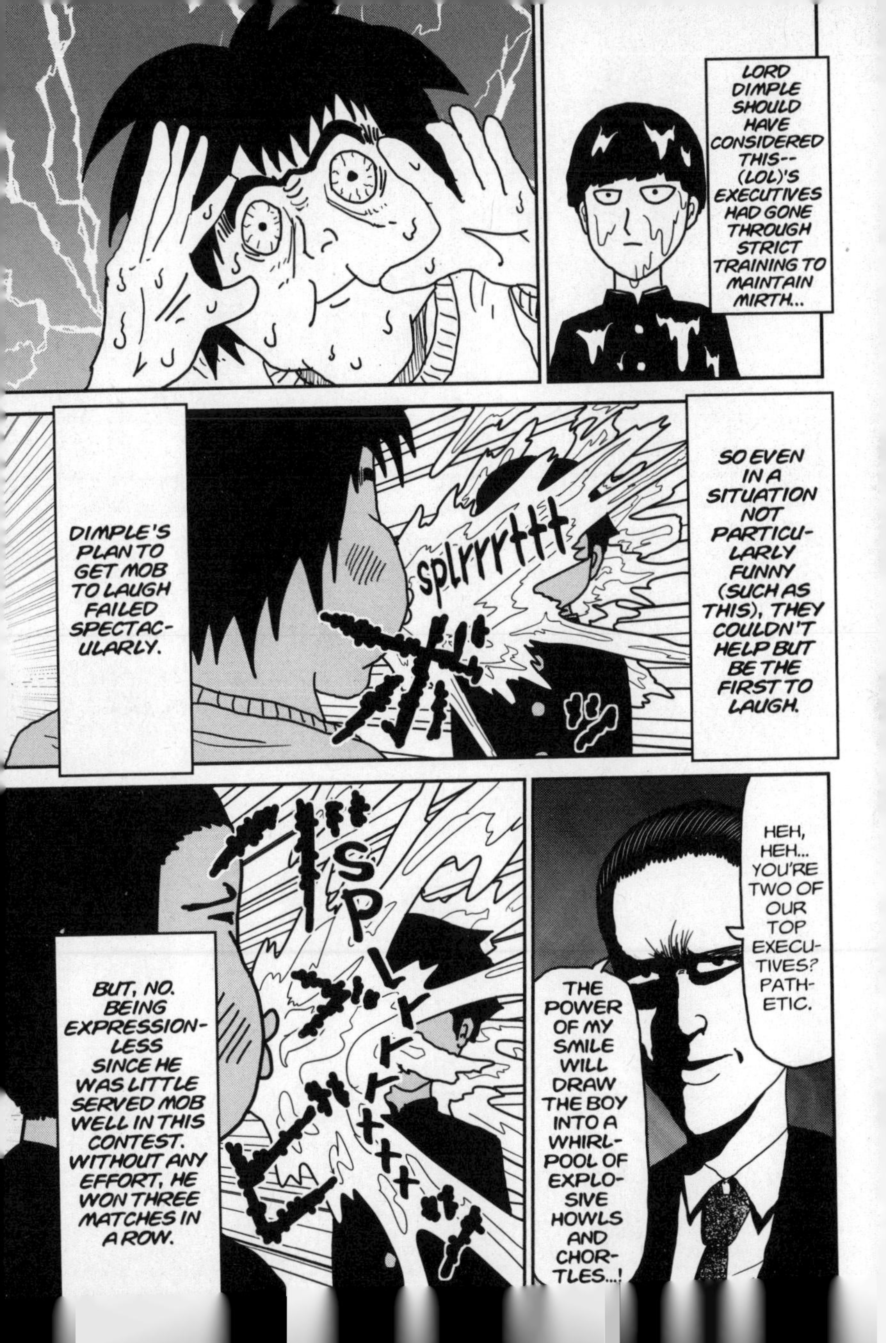
LORD DIMPLE SHOULD HAVE CONSIDERED THIS--(LOL)'S EXECUTIVES HAD GONE THROUGH STRICT TRAINING TO MAINTAIN MIRTH...
SO EVEN IN A SITUATION NOT PARTICULARLY FUNNY (SUCH AS THIS), THEY COULDN'T HELP BUT BE THE FIRST TO LAUGH.
splrrrttt
DIMPLE'S PLAN TO GET MOB TO LAUGH FAILED SPECTACULARLY.
HEH, HEH... YOU'RE TWO OF OUR TOP EXECUTIVES? PATHETIC.
THE POWER OF MY SMILE WILL DRAW THE BOY INTO A WHIRLPOOL OF EXPLOSIVE HOWLS AND CHORTLES...!
SPLYYYttt
BUT, NO. BEING EXPRESSIONLESS SINCE HE WAS LITTLE SERVED MOB WELL IN THIS CONTEST. WITHOUT ANY EFFORT, HE WON THREE MATCHES IN A ROW.

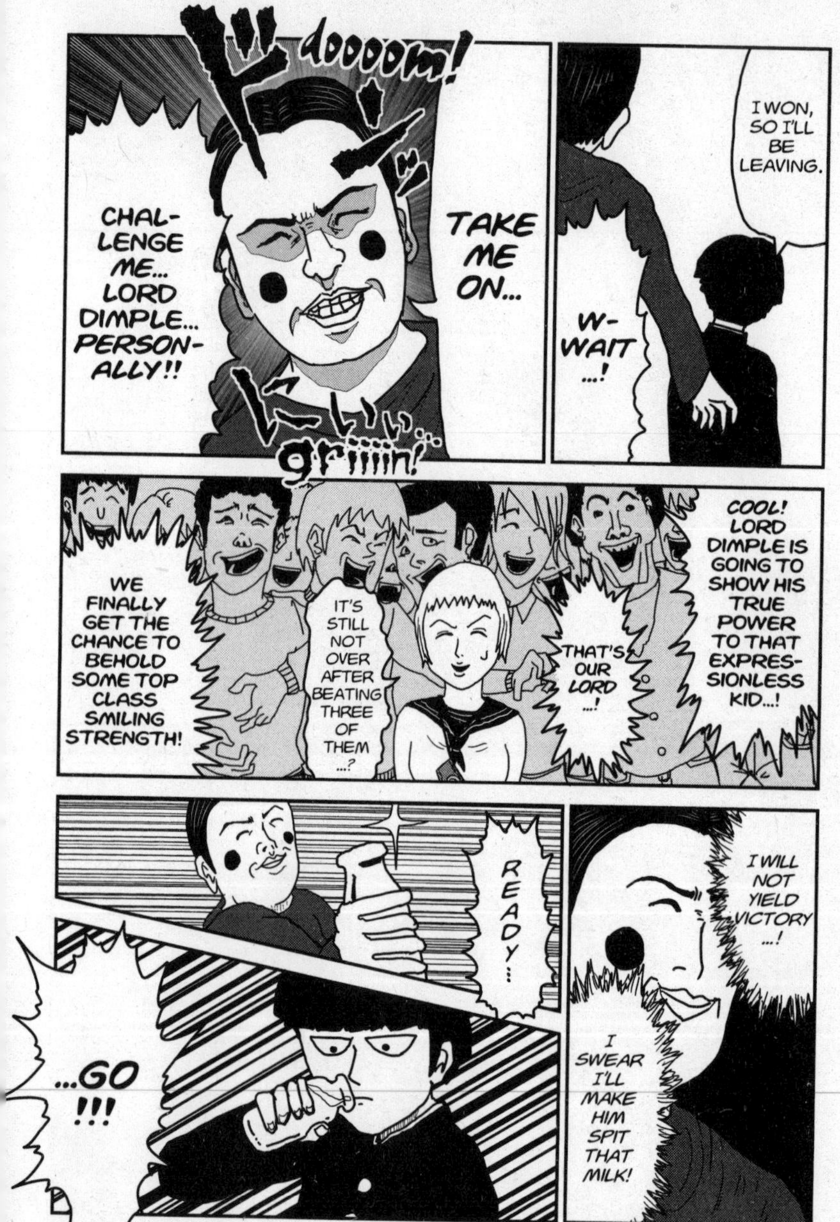
I WON, SO I'LL BE LEAVING.
W-WAIT ...!
doooom!
TAKE ME ON...
CHAL-LENGE ME... LORD DIMPLE... PERSON-ALLY!!
griiiin!
COOL! LORD DIMPLE IS GOING TO SHOW HIS TRUE POWER TO THAT EXPRES-SIONLESS KID...!
THAT'S OUR LORD ...!
IT'S STILL NOT OVER AFTER BEATING THREE OF THEM ...?
WE FINALLY GET THE CHANCE TO BEHOLD SOME TOP CLASS SMILING STRENGTH!
I WILL NOT YIELD VICTORY ...!
I SWEAR I'LL MAKE HIM SPIT THAT MILK!
READY...
...GO !!!

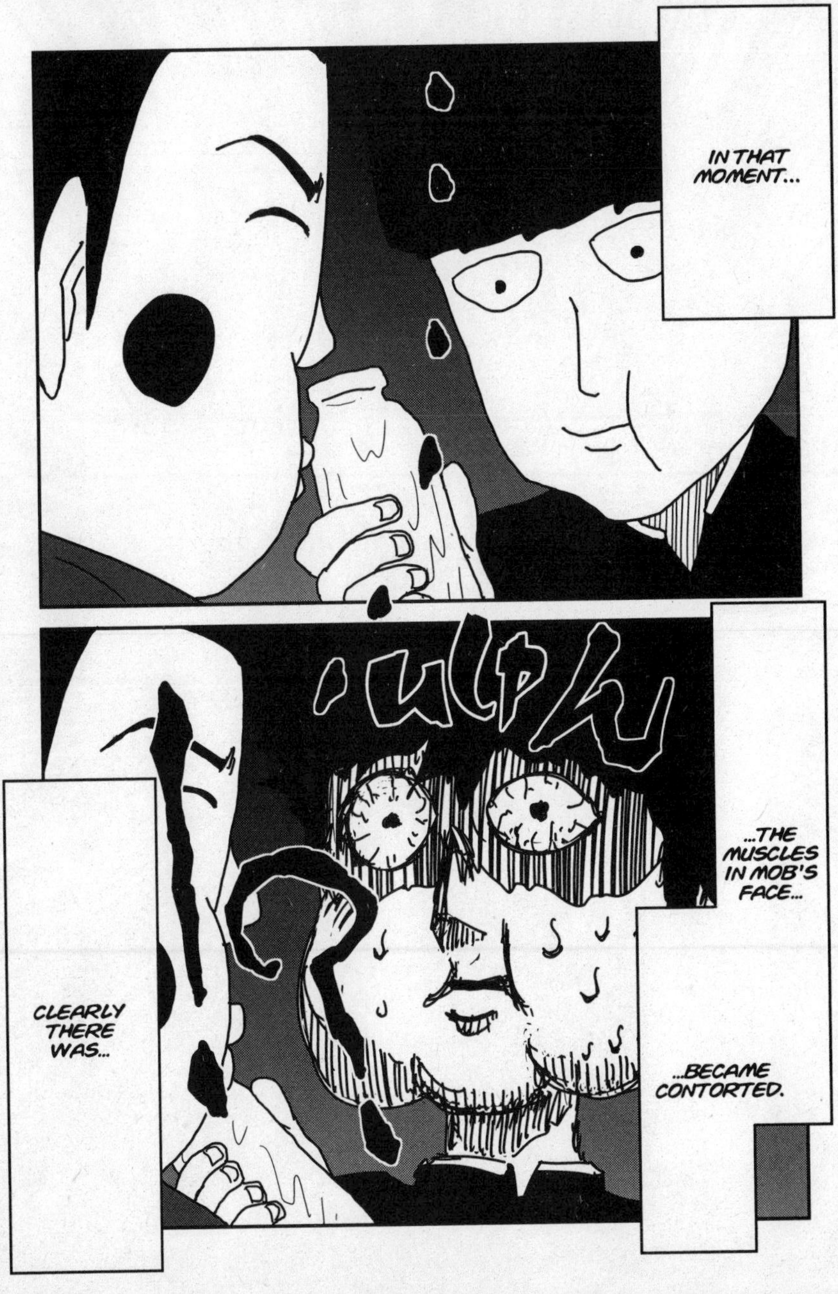
IN THAT MOMENT...
...THE MUSCLES IN MOB'S FACE...
...BECAME CONTORTED.
CLEARLY THERE WAS...

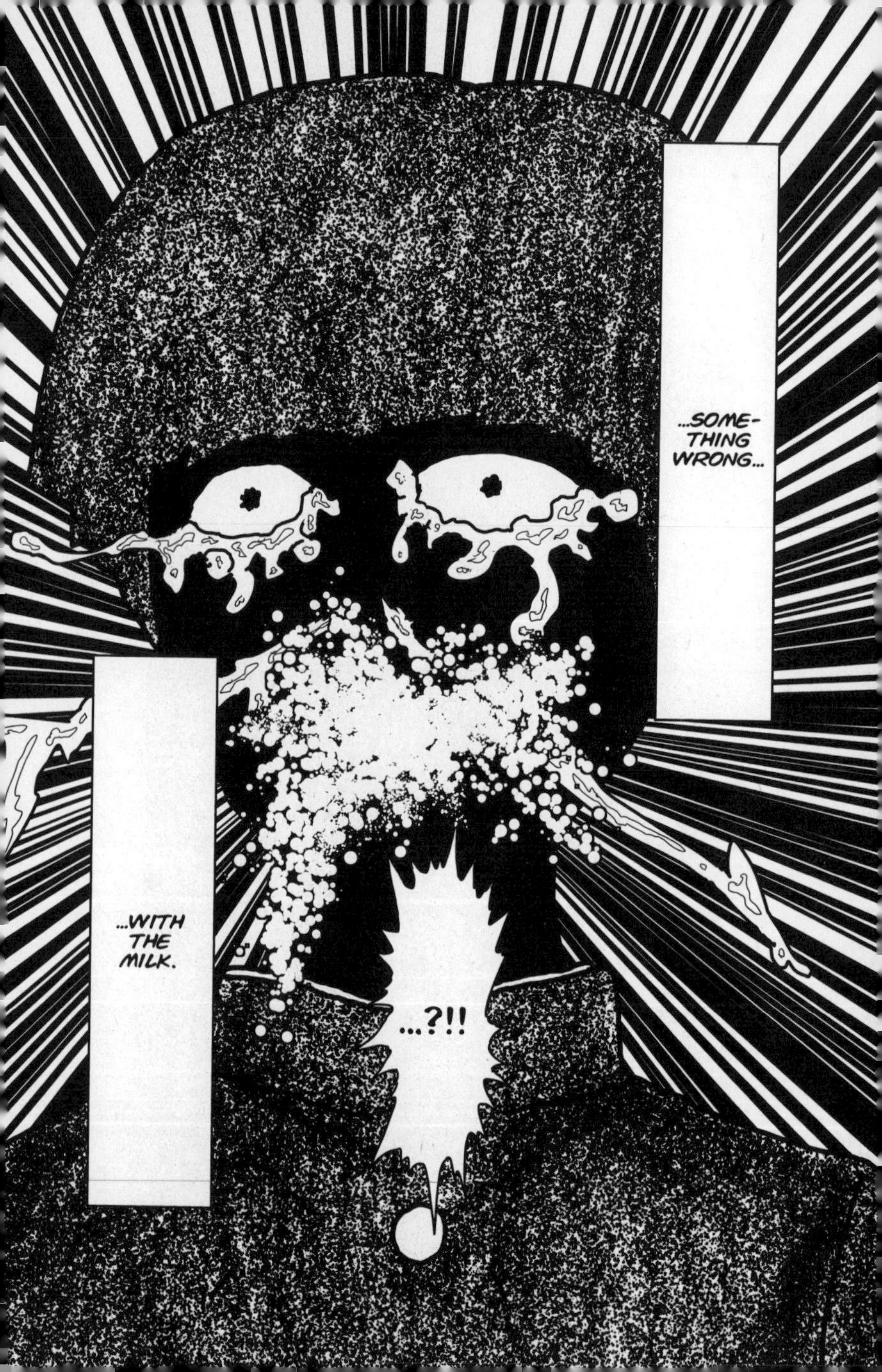
...SOME-THING WRONG...
...WITH THE MILK.
...?!!

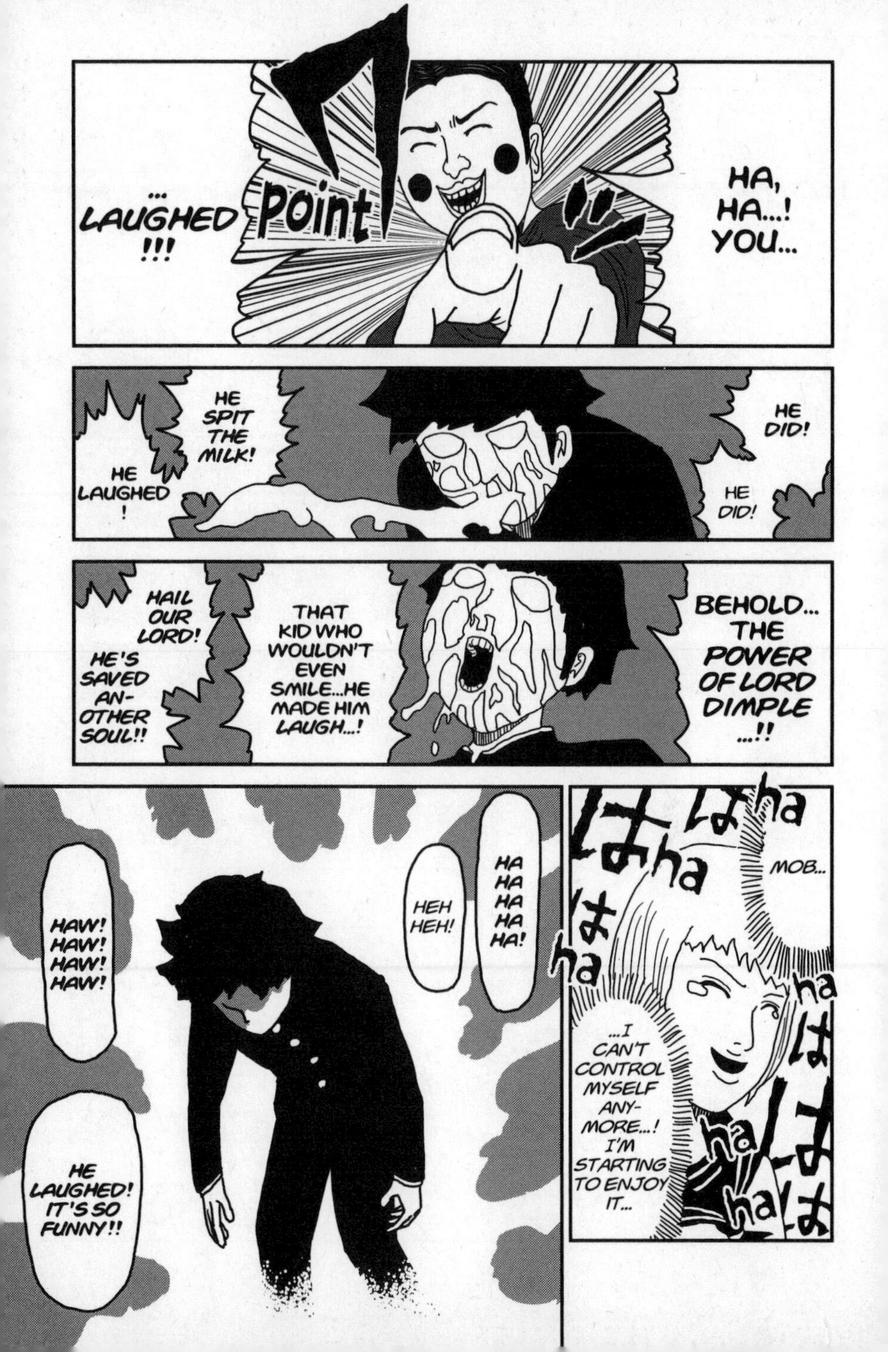
HA, HA...! YOU...
Point
...LAUGHED!!!
HE DID!
HE DID!
HE SPIT THE MILK!
HE LAUGHED!
BEHOLD... THE POWER OF LORD DIMPLE ...!!
THAT KID WHO WOULDN'T EVEN SMILE...HE MADE HIM LAUGH...!
HAIL OUR LORD!
HE'S SAVED AN-OTHER SOUL!!
はha はha はha
MOB...
はha はha はha
...I CAN'T CONTROL MYSELF ANY-MORE...! I'M STARTING TO ENJOY IT...
HA HA HA HA HA!
HEH HEH!
HAW! HAW! HAW! HAW!
HE LAUGHED! IT'S SO FUNNY!!

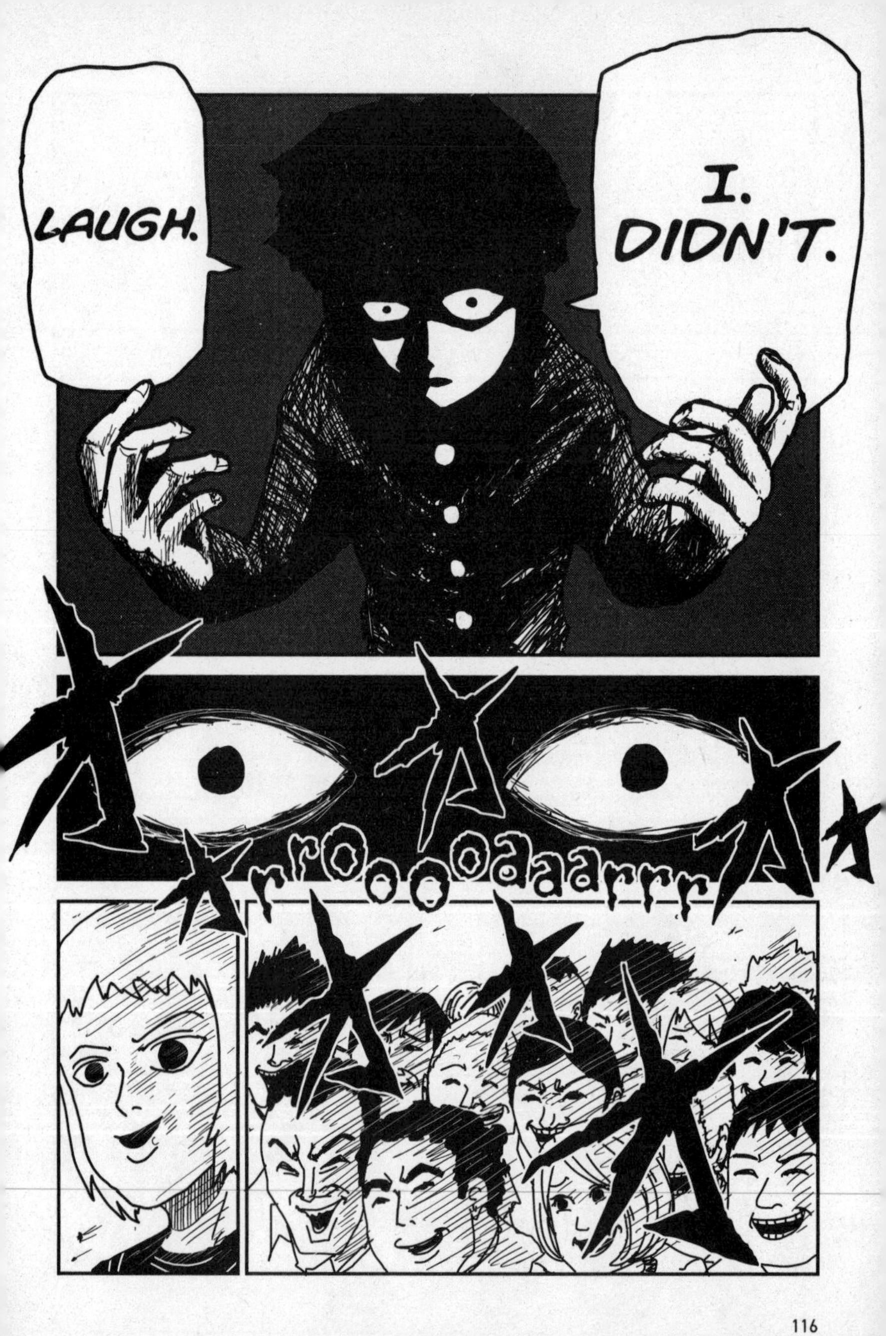
I. DIDN'T.
LAUGH.
rrOooooaaarrr

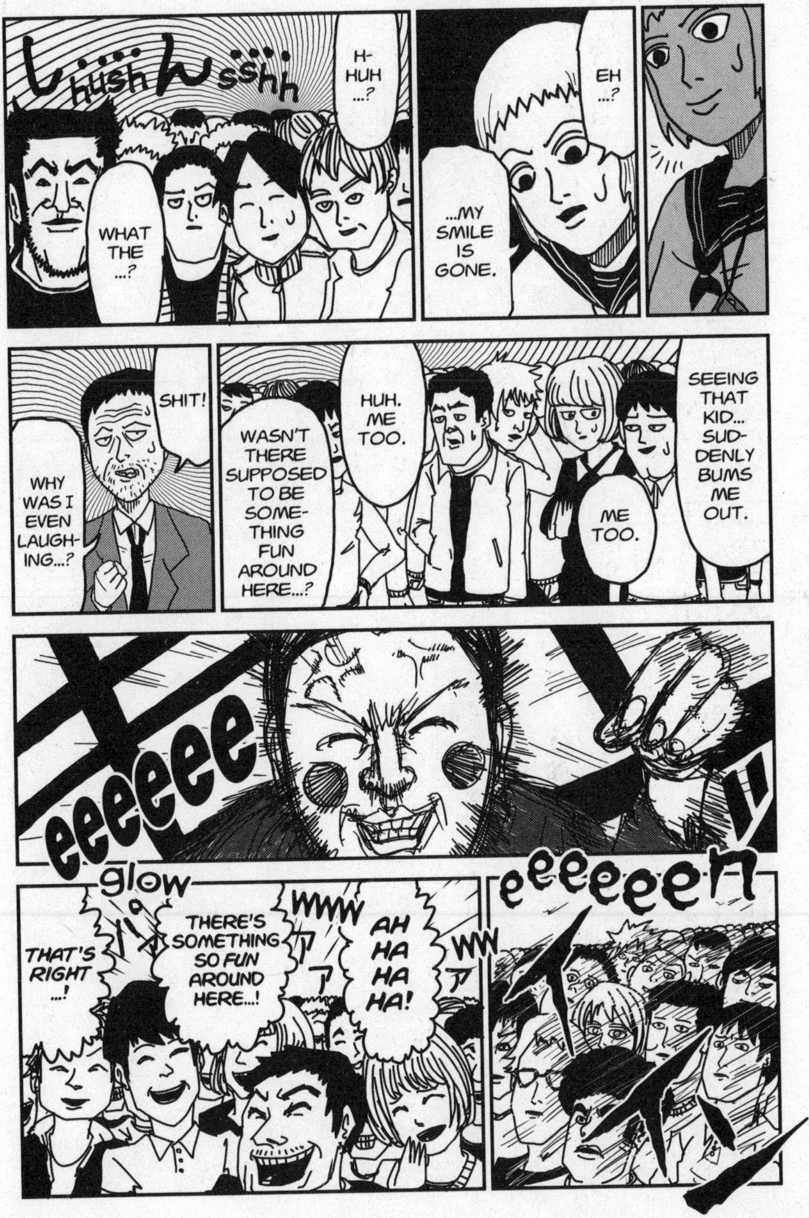
EH ...?
...MY SMILE IS GONE.
hush hush...
H-HUH ...?
WHAT THE ...?
SEEING THAT KID... SUDDENLY BUMS ME OUT.
ME TOO.
HUH. ME TOO.
WASN'T THERE SUPPOSED TO BE SOMETHING FUN AROUND HERE...?
SHIT!
WHY WAS I EVEN LAUGHING...?
eeeeee
eeeeeen
www
AH HA HA HA!
www
THERE'S SOMETHING SO FUN AROUND HERE...!
glow
THAT'S RIGHT ...!

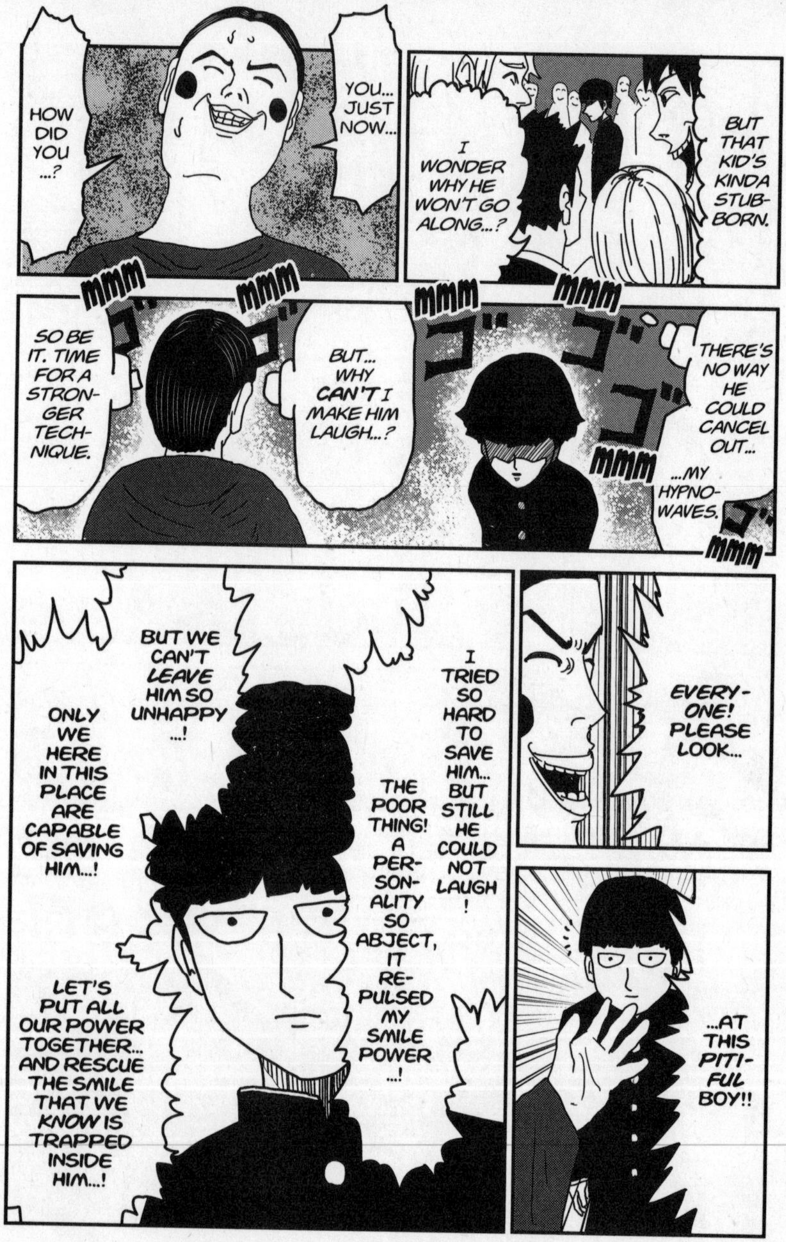

BUT THAT KID'S KINDA STUBBORN.
I WONDER WHY HE WON'T GO ALONG...?
YOU... JUST NOW...
HOW DID YOU ...?
MMM
ゴ
THERE'S NO WAY HE COULD CANCEL OUT...
...MY HYPNO-WAVES.
MMM
ゴ
MMM
ゴ
MMM
ゴ
BUT... WHY CAN'T I MAKE HIM LAUGH...?
MMM
ゴ
MMM
SO BE IT. TIME FOR A STRONGER TECHNIQUE.
EVERY-ONE! PLEASE LOOK...
...AT THIS PITIFUL BOY!!
I TRIED SO HARD TO SAVE HIM... BUT STILL HE COULD NOT LAUGH!
THE POOR THING! A PERSONALITY SO ABJECT, IT REPULSED MY SMILE POWER...!
BUT WE CAN'T LEAVE HIM SO UNHAPPY...!
ONLY WE HERE IN THIS PLACE ARE CAPABLE OF SAVING HIM...!
LET'S PUT ALL OUR POWER TOGETHER... AND RESCUE THE SMILE THAT WE KNOW IS TRAPPED INSIDE HIM...!

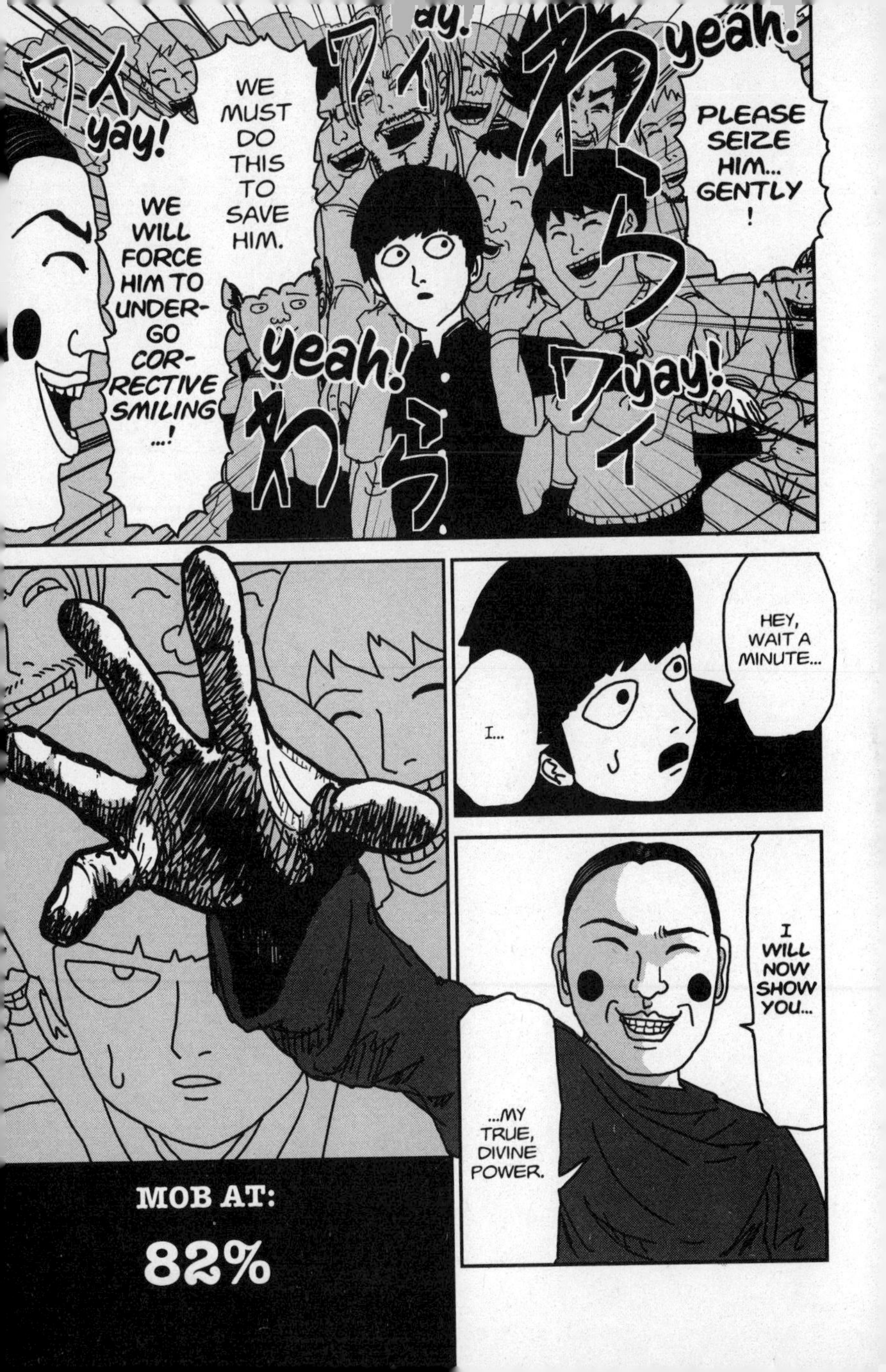
yeah!
わら
PLEASE SEIZE HIM... GENTLY!
ay!
ワイ
WE MUST DO THIS TO SAVE HIM.
yay!
ワイ
WE WILL FORCE HIM TO UNDER-GO COR-RECTIVE SMILING...!
yay!
ワイ
yeah!
わら
HEY, WAIT A MINUTE...
I...
I WILL NOW SHOW YOU...
...MY TRUE, DIVINE POWER.
MOB AT:
82%

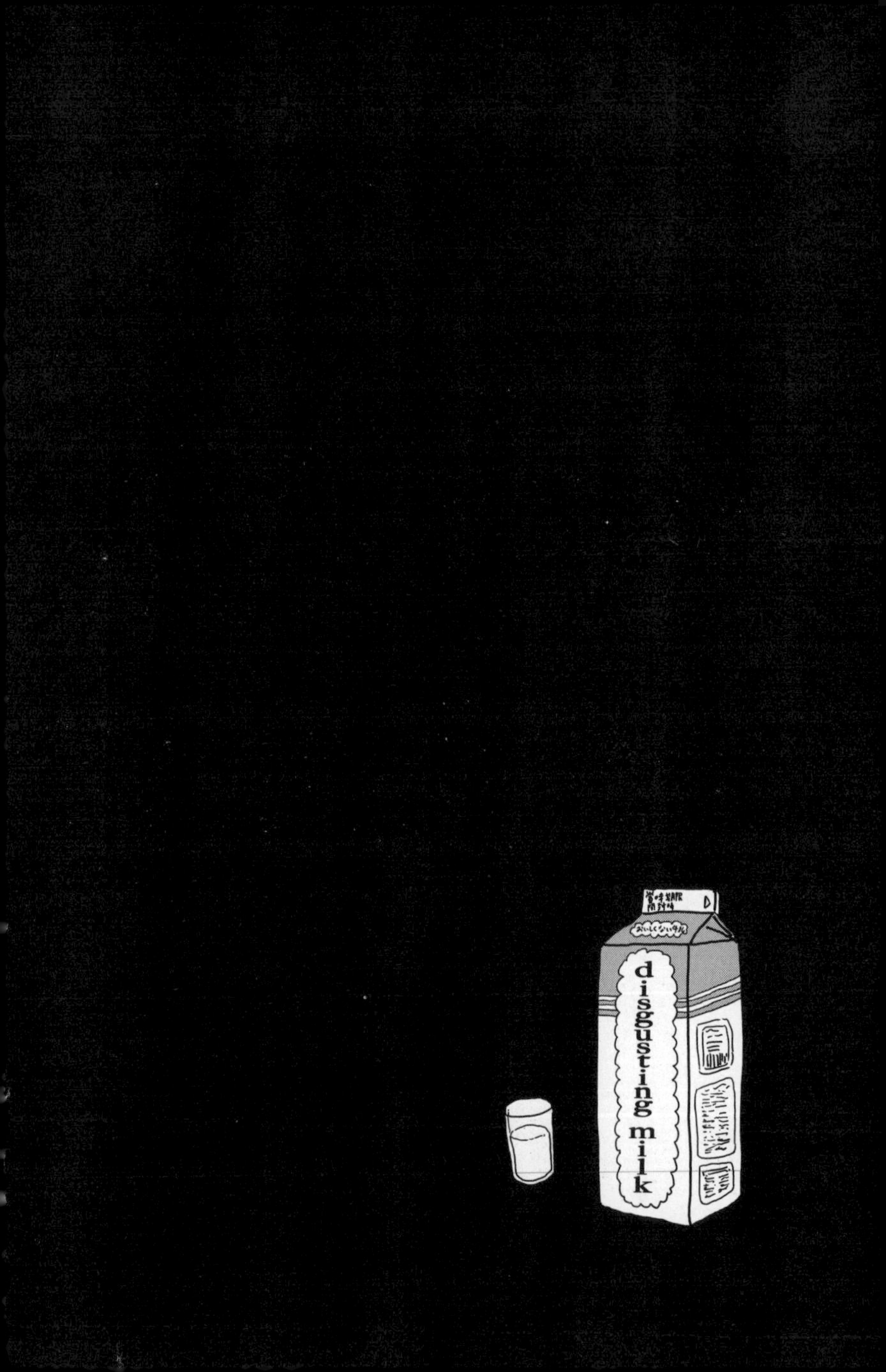
おいしくない牛乳
disgusting milk

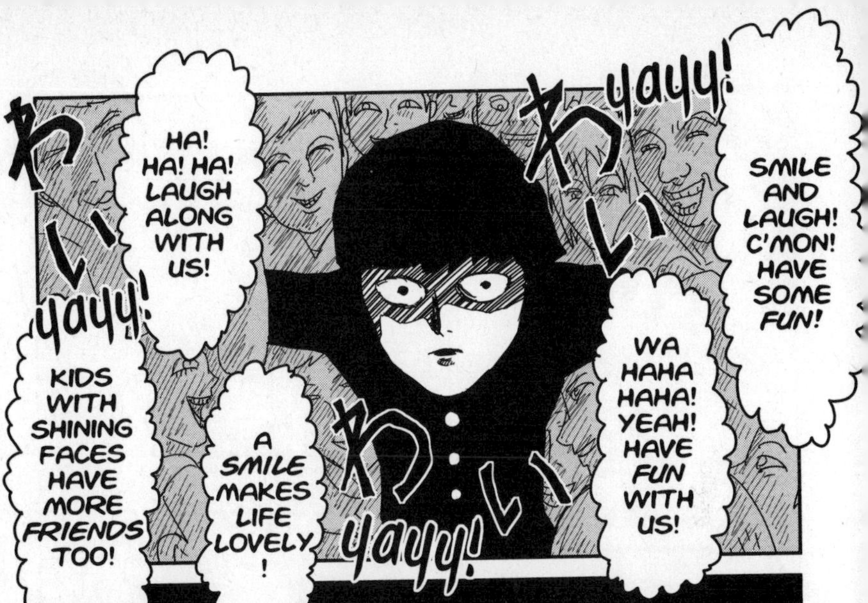
わい yayy!
SMILE AND LAUGH! C'MON! HAVE SOME FUN!
HA! HA! HA! LAUGH ALONG WITH US!
わい yayy!
WA HAHA HAHA! YEAH! HAVE FUN WITH US!
わい yayy!
A SMILE MAKES LIFE LOVELY!
KIDS WITH SHINING FACES HAVE MORE FRIENDS TOO!

CHAPTER 8: BREAKDOWN

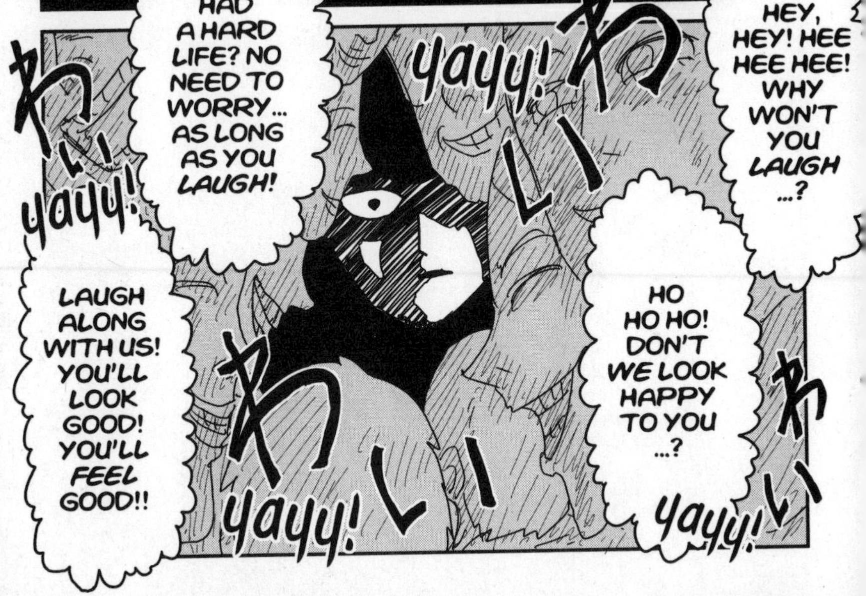
HEY, HEY! HEE HEE HEE! WHY WON'T YOU LAUGH ...?
わい yayy!
HAD A HARD LIFE? NO NEED TO WORRY... AS LONG AS YOU LAUGH!
わい yayy!
わい yayy!
HO HO HO! DON'T WE LOOK HAPPY TO YOU ...?
わい yayy!
LAUGH ALONG WITH US! YOU'LL LOOK GOOD! YOU'LL FEEL GOOD!!

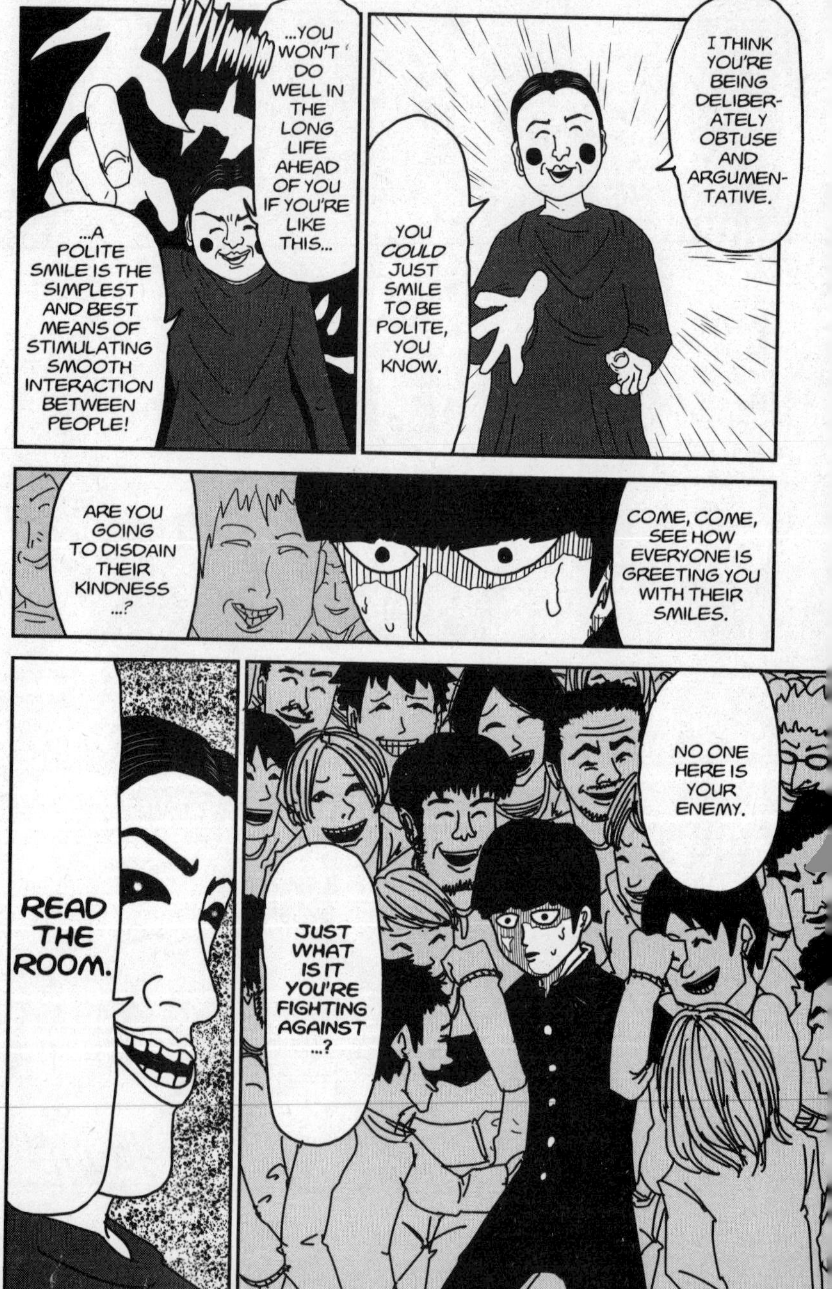
I THINK YOU'RE BEING DELIBER-ATELY OBTUSE AND ARGUMEN-TATIVE.
YOU COULD JUST SMILE TO BE POLITE, YOU KNOW.
...YOU WON'T DO WELL IN THE LONG LIFE AHEAD OF YOU IF YOU'RE LIKE THIS...
...A POLITE SMILE IS THE SIMPLEST AND BEST MEANS OF STIMULATING SMOOTH INTERACTION BETWEEN PEOPLE!
COME, COME, SEE HOW EVERYONE IS GREETING YOU WITH THEIR SMILES.
ARE YOU GOING TO DISDAIN THEIR KINDNESS ...?
NO ONE HERE IS YOUR ENEMY.
JUST WHAT IS IT YOU'RE FIGHTING AGAINST ...?
READ THE ROOM.

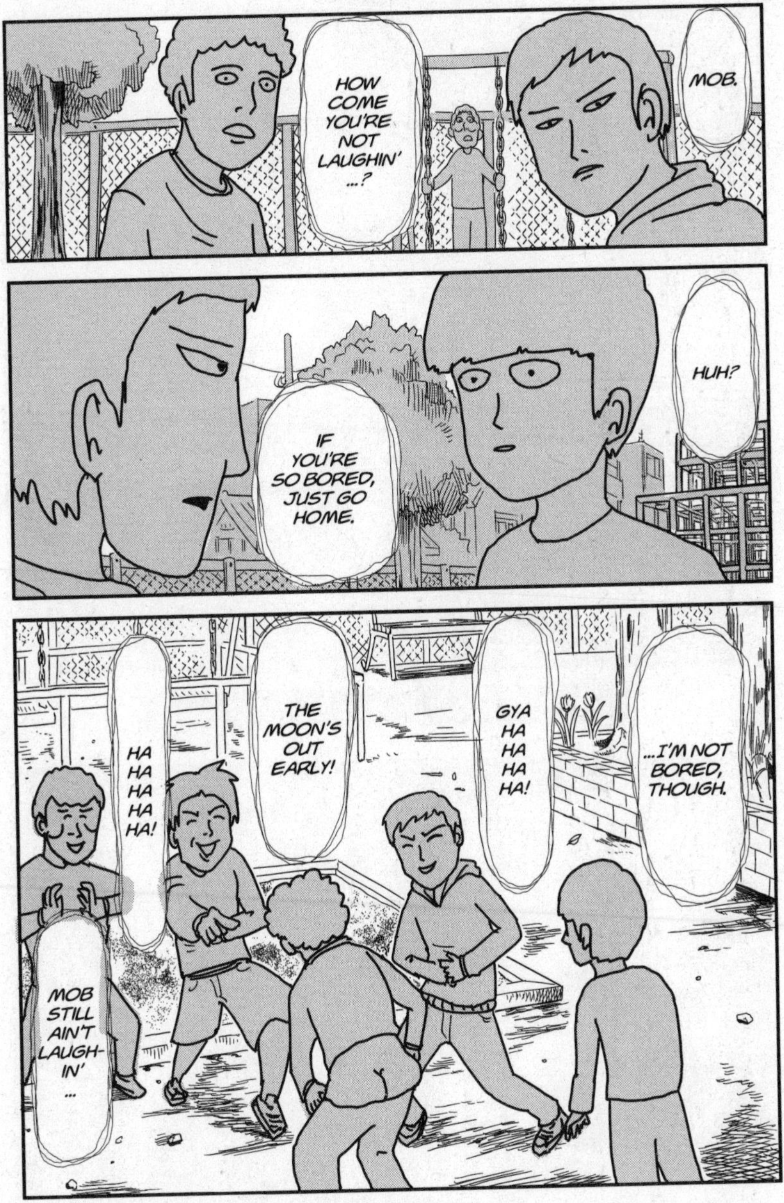
MOB.
HOW COME YOU'RE NOT LAUGHIN' ...?
HUH?
IF YOU'RE SO BORED, JUST GO HOME.
...I'M NOT BORED, THOUGH.
GYA HA HA HA HA!
THE MOON'S OUT EARLY!
HA HA HA HA HA!
MOB STILL AIN'T LAUGHIN' ...

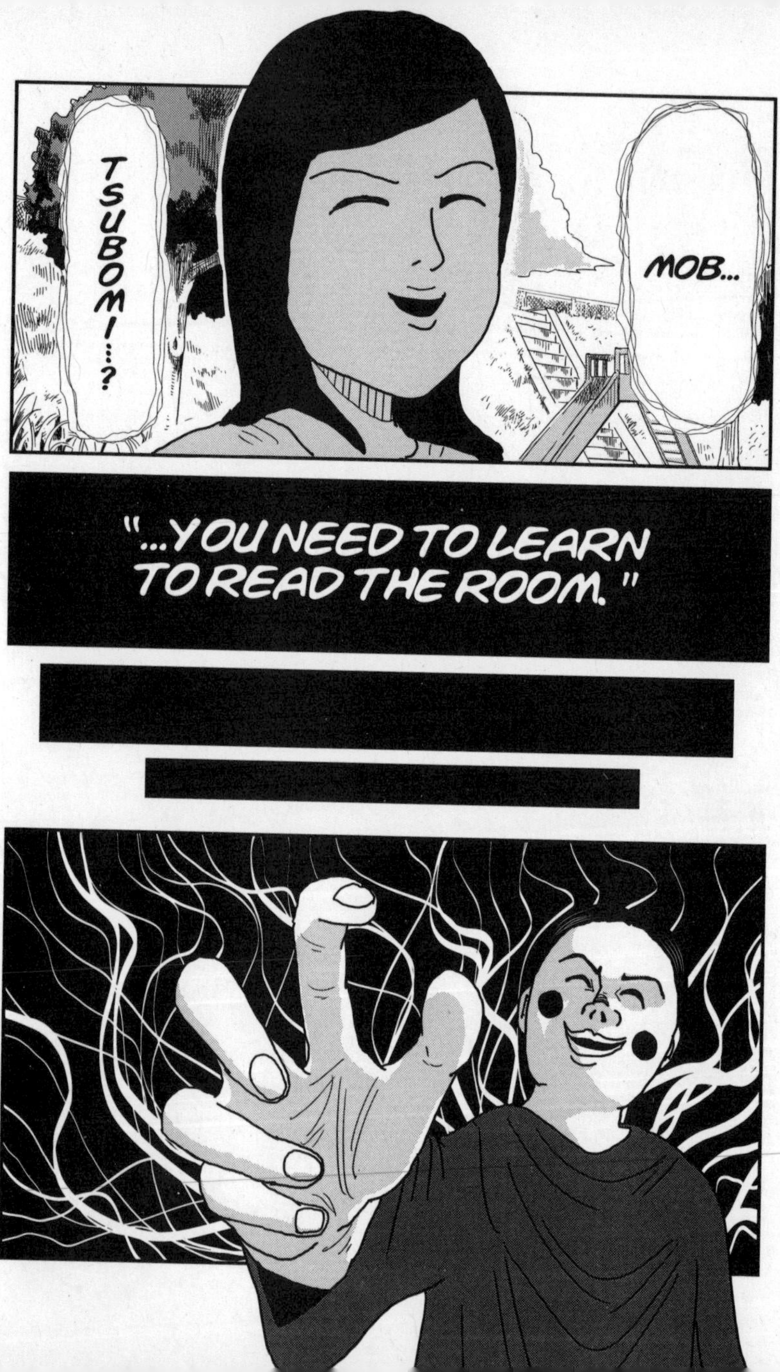
MOB...
TSUBOMI...?
"...YOU NEED TO LEARN TO READ THE ROOM."

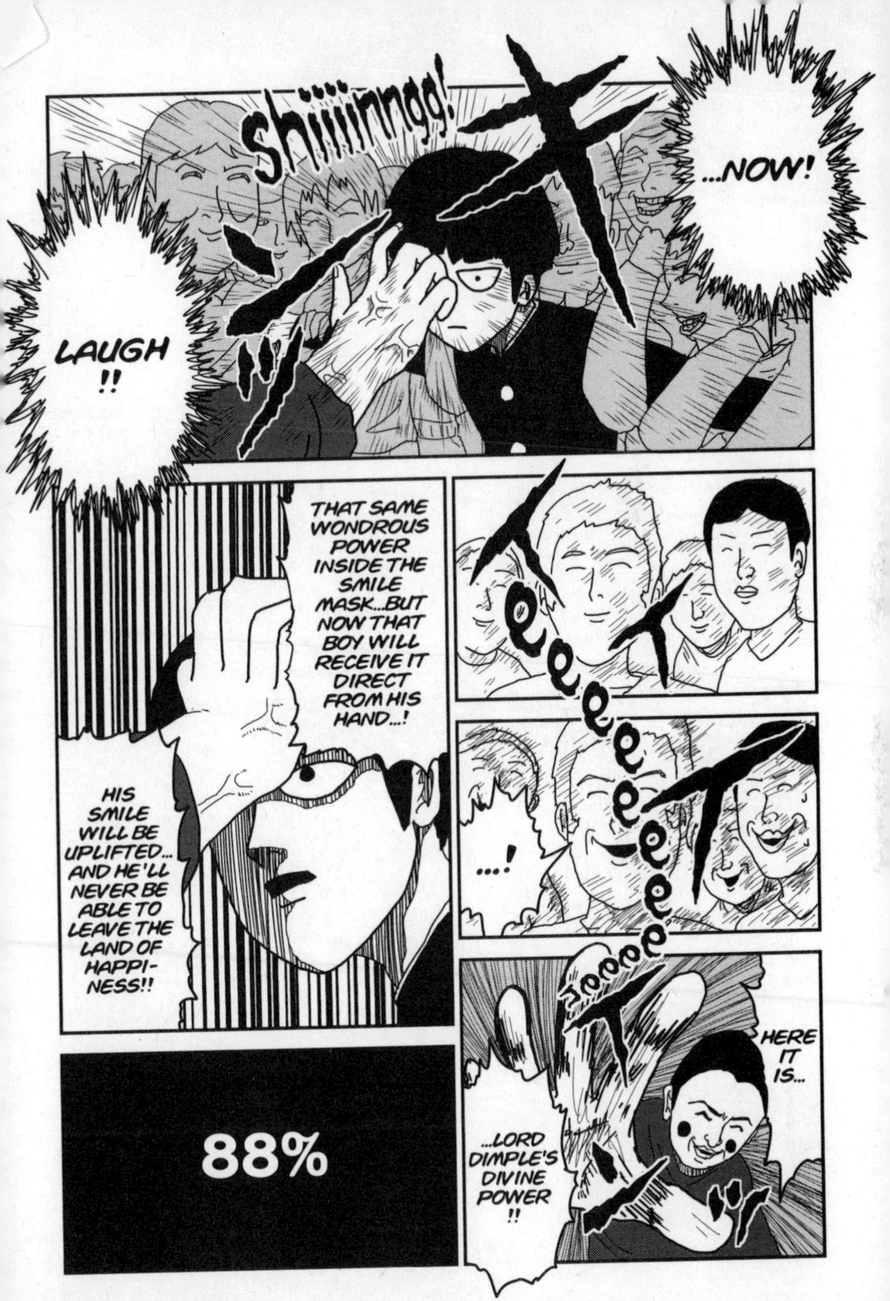
Shiiiinngg!
...NOW!
LAUGH!!
Eeeeeeeeeeeeeeeeeee
...!
HERE IT IS...
...LORD DIMPLE'S DIVINE POWER!!
THAT SAME WONDROUS POWER INSIDE THE SMILE MASK...BUT NOW THAT BOY WILL RECEIVE IT DIRECT FROM HIS HAND...!
HIS SMILE WILL BE UPLIFTED... AND HE'LL NEVER BE ABLE TO LEAVE THE LAND OF HAPPINESS!!
88%

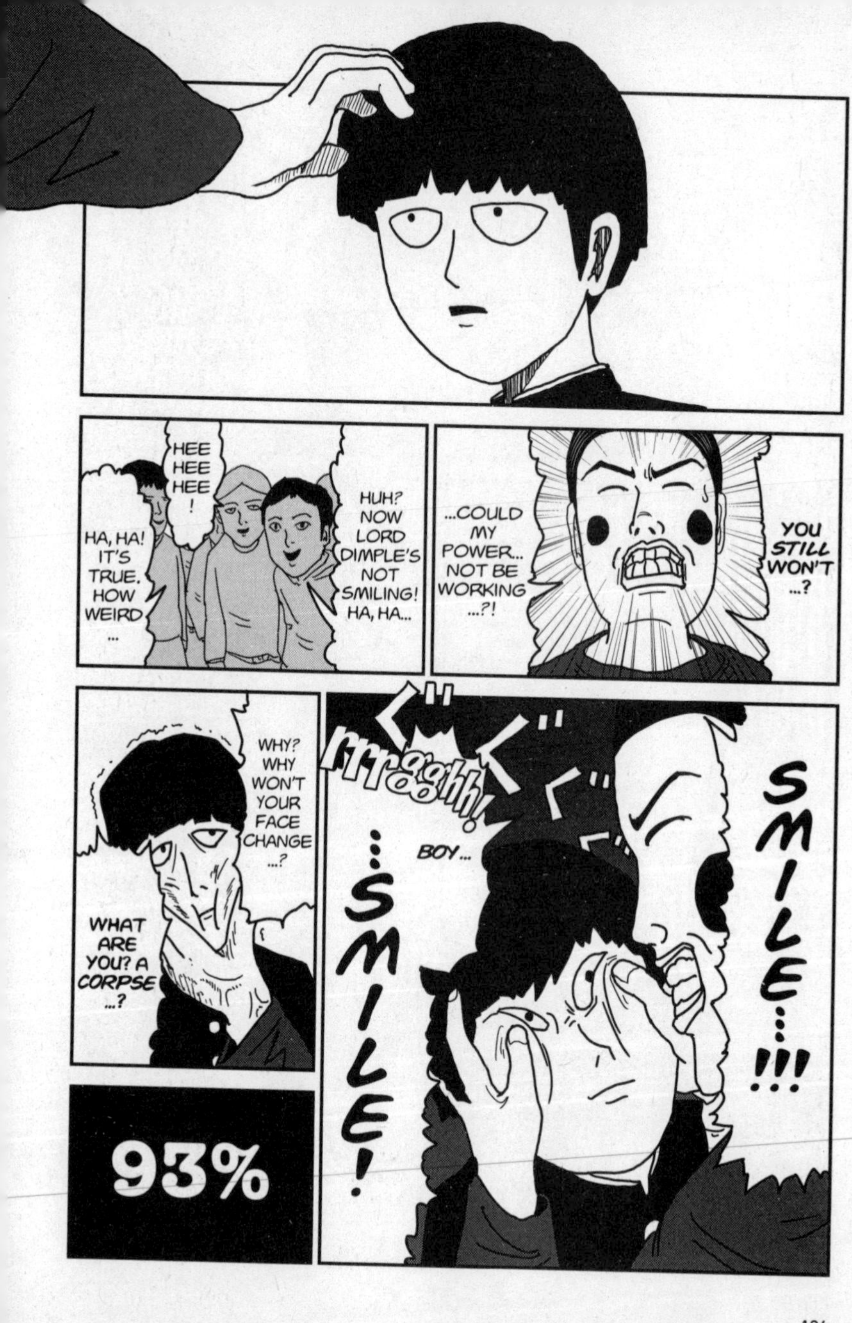

YOU STILL WON'T ...?
...COULD MY POWER... NOT BE WORKING ...?!
HUH? NOW LORD DIMPLE'S NOT SMILING! HA, HA...
HEE HEE HEE !
HA, HA! IT'S TRUE. HOW WEIRD ...
rrragghh!
SMILE...!!!
BOY...
...SMILE!
WHY? WHY WON'T YOUR FACE CHANGE ...?
WHAT ARE YOU? A CORPSE ...?
93%

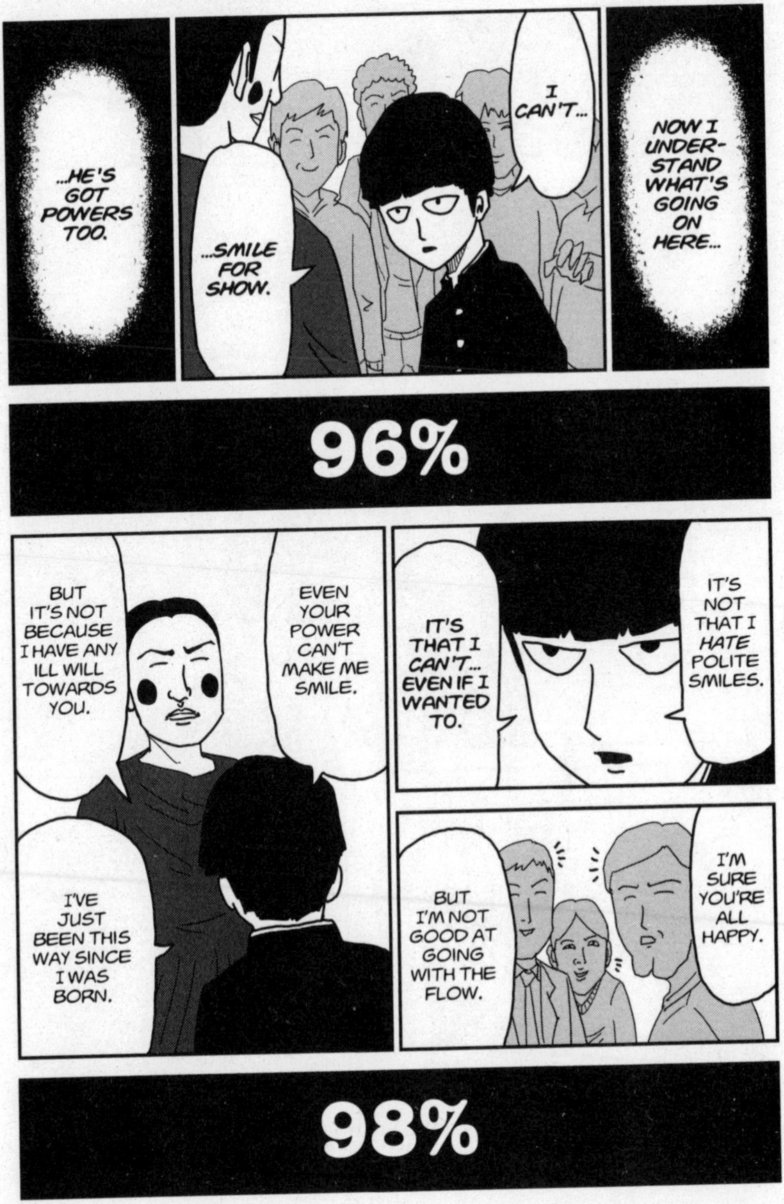
NOW I UNDERSTAND WHAT'S GOING ON HERE...
I CAN'T...
...SMILE FOR SHOW.
...HE'S GOT POWERS TOO.
96%
IT'S NOT THAT I *HATE* POLITE SMILES.
IT'S THAT I *CAN'T*... EVEN IF I WANTED TO.
I'M SURE YOU'RE ALL HAPPY.
BUT I'M NOT GOOD AT GOING WITH THE FLOW.
EVEN YOUR POWER CAN'T MAKE ME SMILE.
BUT IT'S NOT BECAUSE I HAVE ANY ILL WILL TOWARDS YOU.
I'VE JUST BEEN THIS WAY SINCE I WAS BORN.
98%

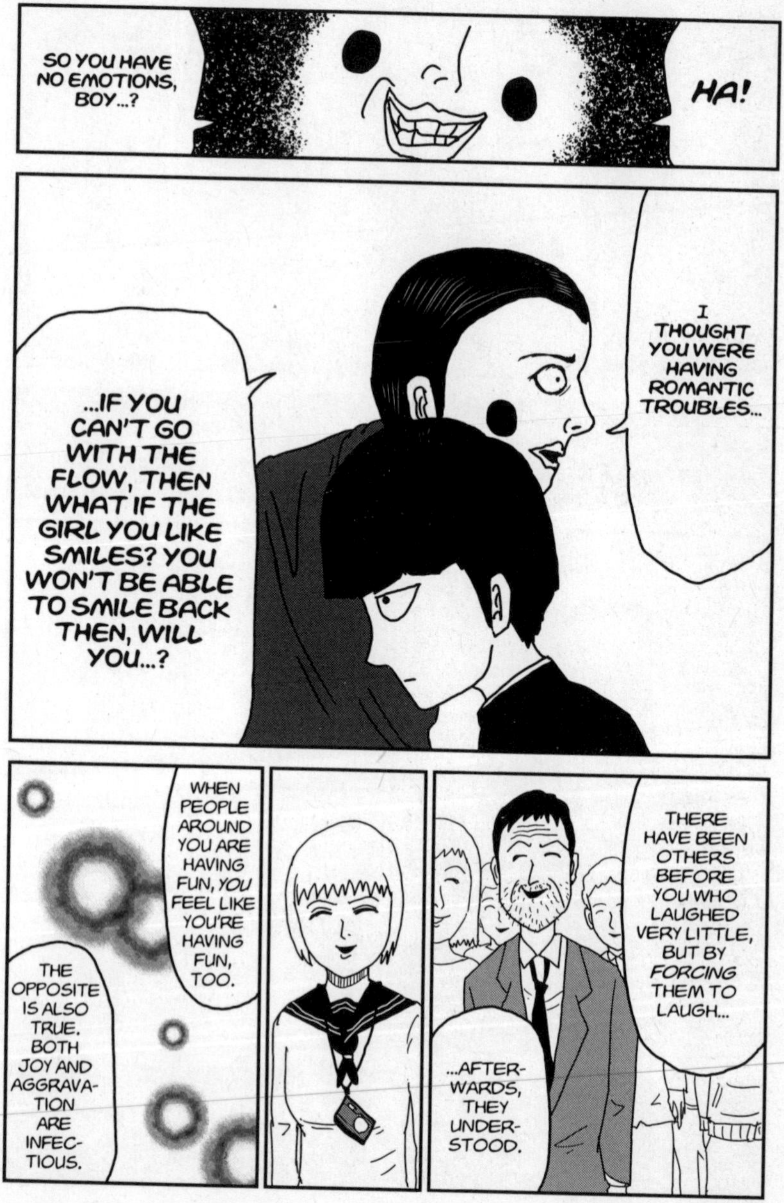
HA!
SO YOU HAVE NO EMOTIONS, BOY...?
I THOUGHT YOU WERE HAVING ROMANTIC TROUBLES...
...IF YOU CAN'T GO WITH THE FLOW, THEN WHAT IF THE GIRL YOU LIKE SMILES? YOU WON'T BE ABLE TO SMILE BACK THEN, WILL YOU...?
THERE HAVE BEEN OTHERS BEFORE YOU WHO LAUGHED VERY LITTLE, BUT BY *FORCING* THEM TO LAUGH...
...AFTER-WARDS, THEY UNDER-STOOD.
WHEN PEOPLE AROUND YOU ARE HAVING FUN, *YOU* FEEL LIKE YOU'RE HAVING FUN, TOO.
THE OPPOSITE IS ALSO TRUE. BOTH JOY AND AGGRAVA-TION ARE INFEC-TIOUS.

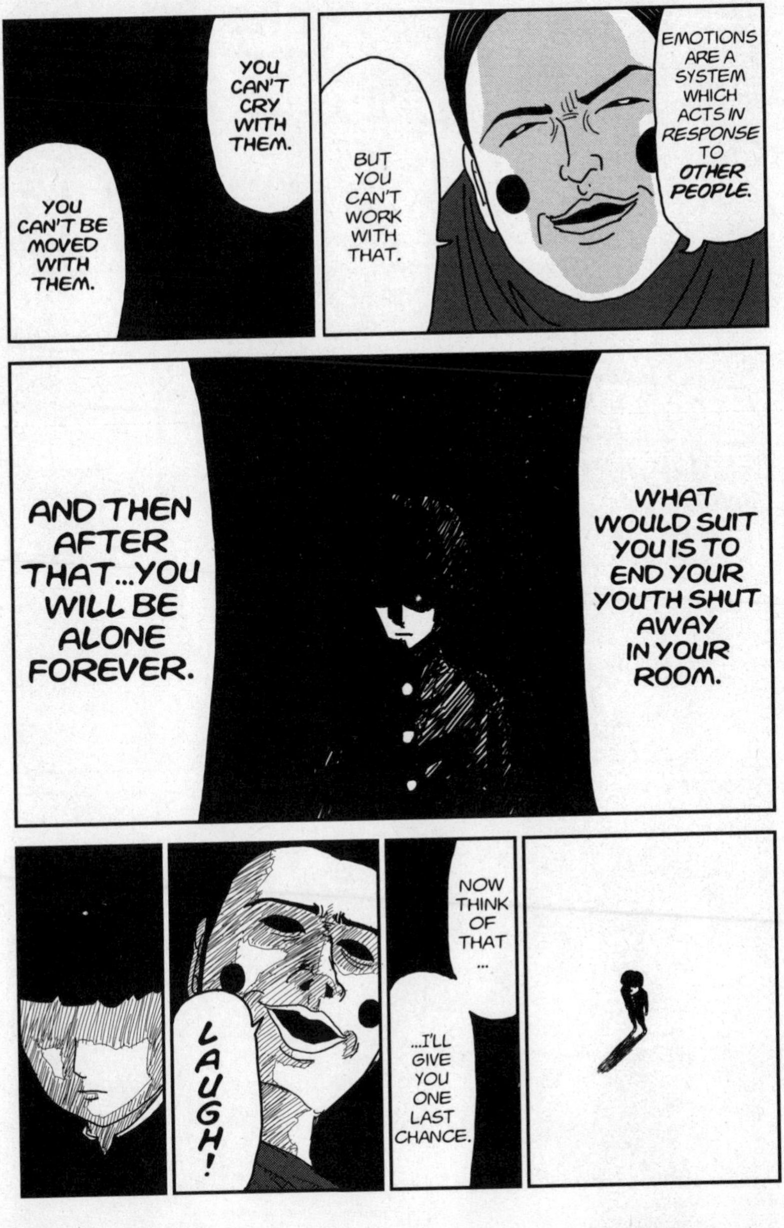
EMOTIONS ARE A SYSTEM WHICH ACTS IN RESPONSE TO OTHER PEOPLE.
BUT YOU CAN'T WORK WITH THAT.
YOU CAN'T CRY WITH THEM.
YOU CAN'T BE MOVED WITH THEM.
WHAT WOULD SUIT YOU IS TO END YOUR YOUTH SHUT AWAY IN YOUR ROOM.
AND THEN AFTER THAT...YOU WILL BE ALONE FOREVER.
NOW THINK OF THAT ...
...I'LL GIVE YOU ONE LAST CHANCE.
LAUGH!

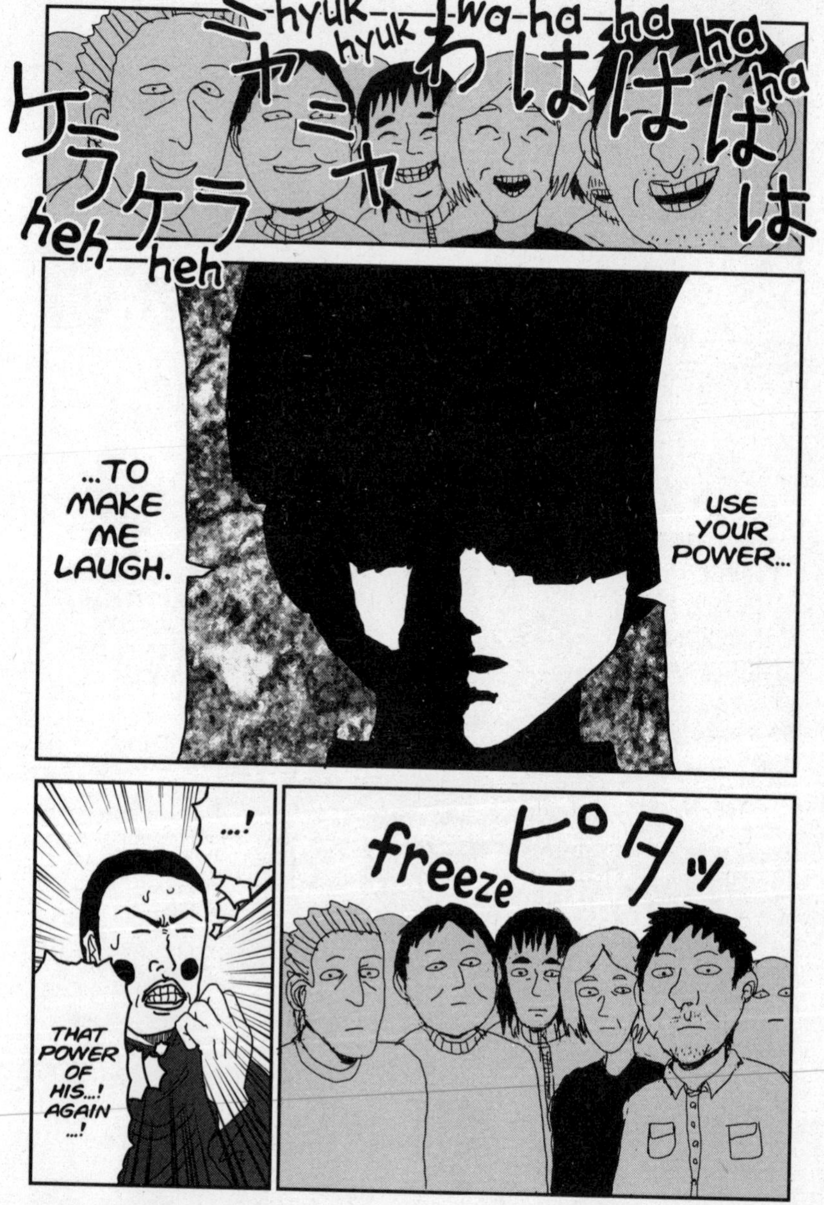
わははははは
wa-ha-ha-ha-ha-ha
ニャニャ
hyuk hyuk
ケラケラ
heh heh
USE YOUR POWER...
...TO MAKE ME LAUGH.
freeze
ピタッ
...!
THAT POWER OF HIS...! AGAIN ...!

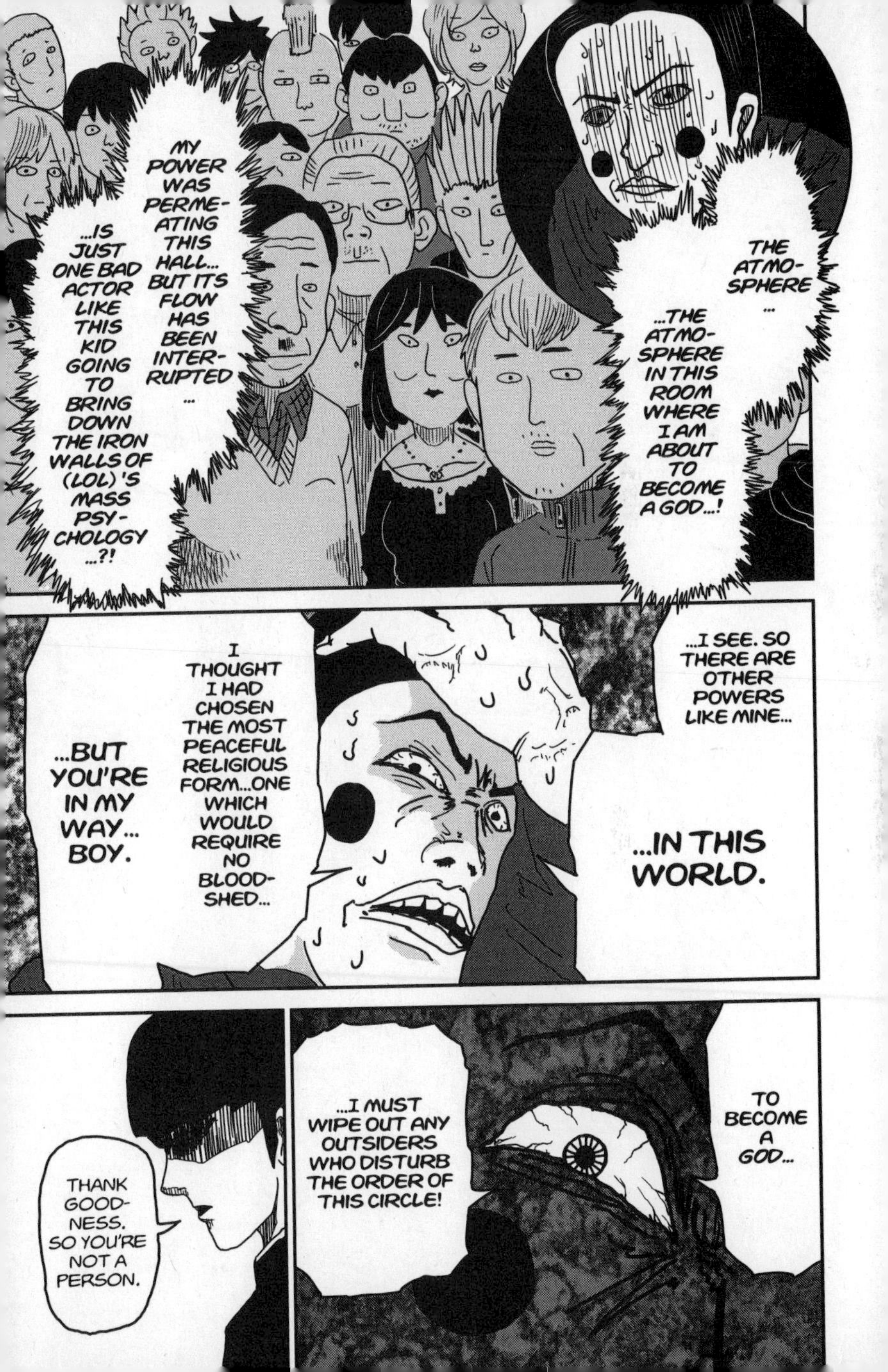
THE ATMOSPHERE...
...THE ATMOSPHERE IN THIS ROOM WHERE I AM ABOUT TO BECOME A GOD...!
MY POWER WAS PERMEATING THIS HALL... BUT ITS FLOW HAS BEEN INTERRUPTED...
...IS JUST ONE BAD ACTOR LIKE THIS KID GOING TO BRING DOWN THE IRON WALLS OF (LOL)'S MASS PSYCHOLOGY...?!
...I SEE. SO THERE ARE OTHER POWERS LIKE MINE...
...IN THIS WORLD.
I THOUGHT I HAD CHOSEN THE MOST PEACEFUL RELIGIOUS FORM...ONE WHICH WOULD REQUIRE NO BLOODSHED...
...BUT YOU'RE IN MY WAY... BOY.
TO BECOME A GOD...
...I MUST WIPE OUT ANY OUTSIDERS WHO DISTURB THE ORDER OF THIS CIRCLE!
THANK GOODNESS. SO YOU'RE NOT A PERSON.

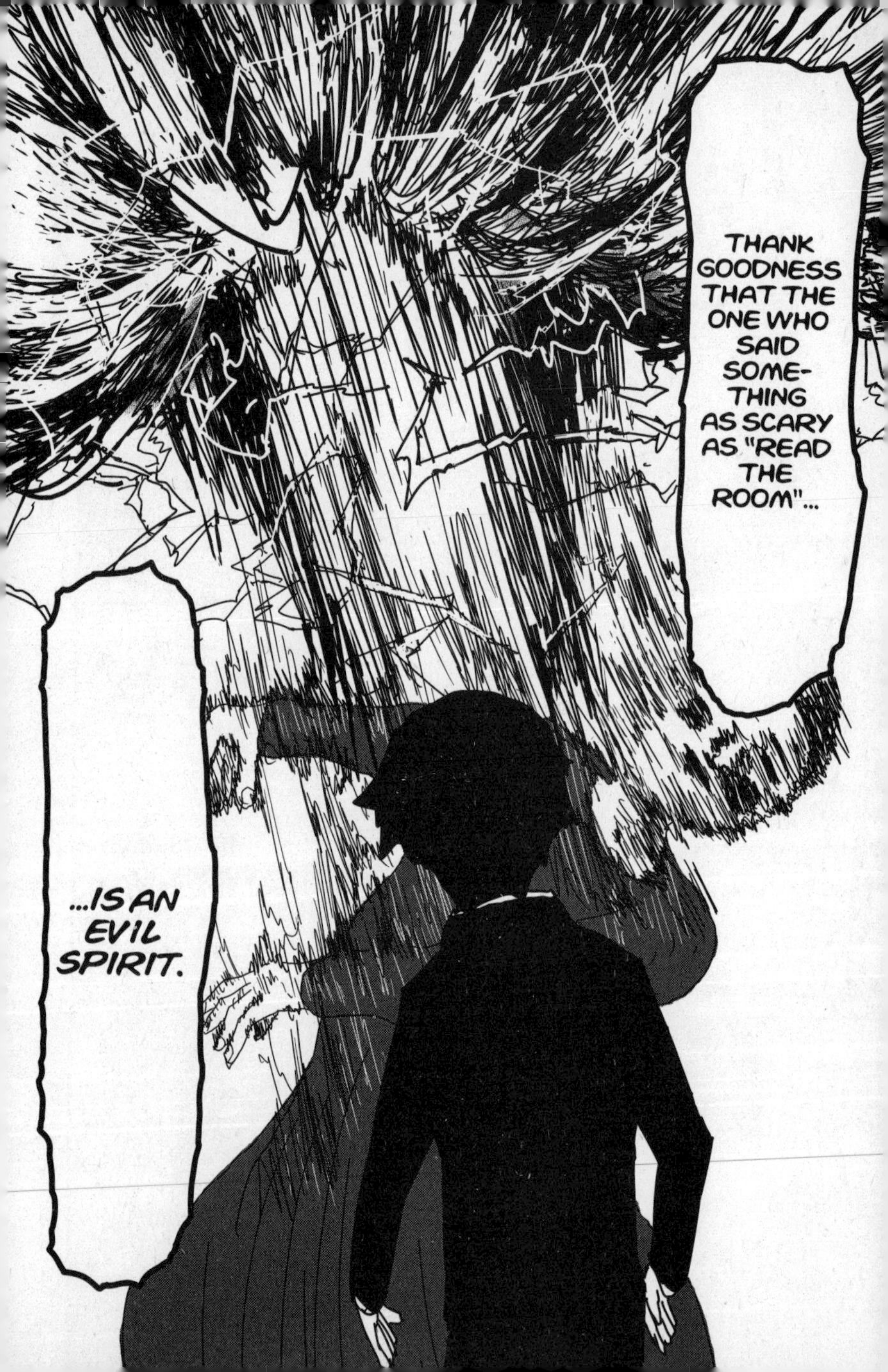
THANK GOODNESS THAT THE ONE WHO SAID SOME-THING AS SCARY AS "READ THE ROOM"...
...IS AN EVIL SPIRIT.

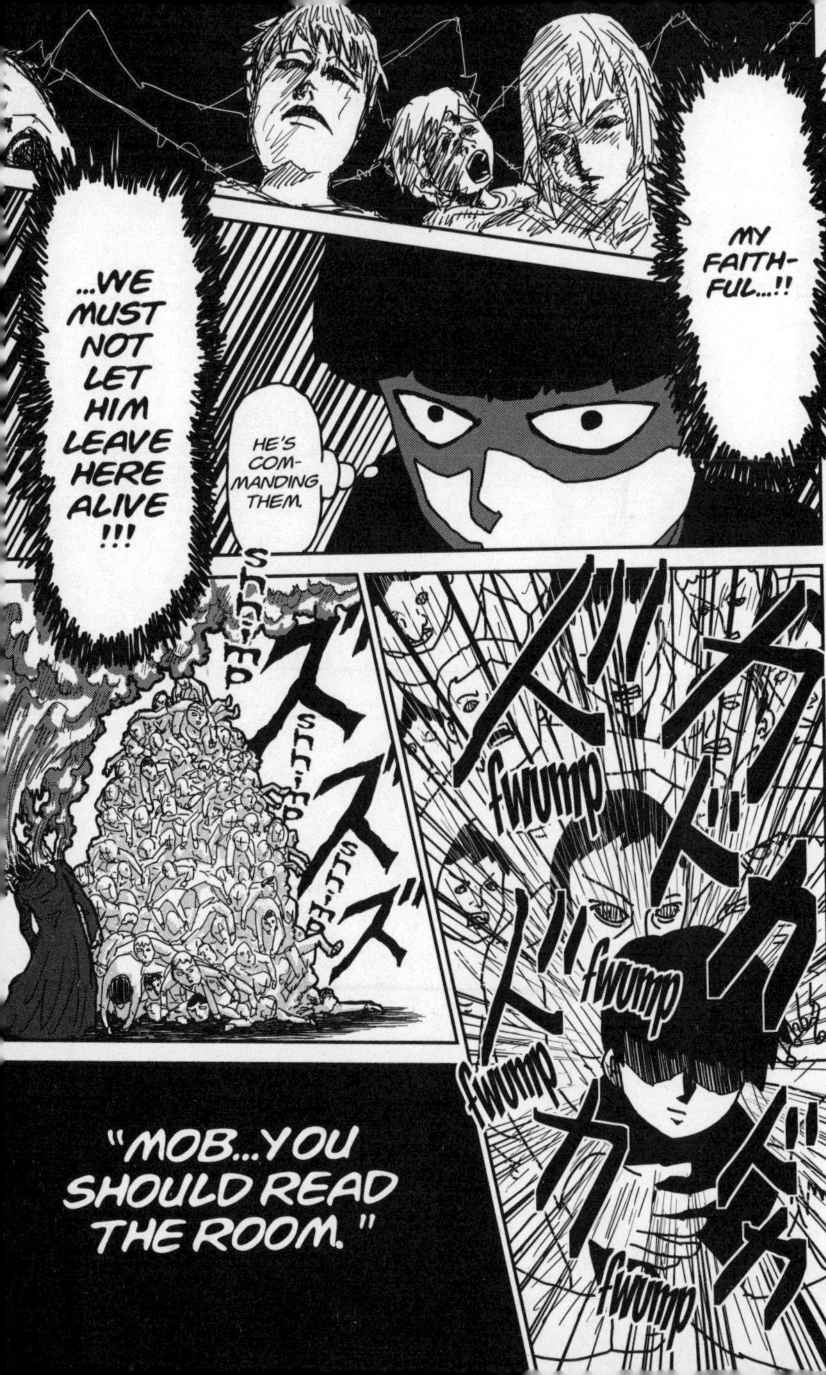
MY FAITH-FUL...!!
...WE MUST NOT LET HIM LEAVE HERE ALIVE!!!
HE'S COM-MANDING THEM.
fwump
fwump
fwump
fwump
shhimp
shhimp
shhimp
"MOB...YOU SHOULD READ THE ROOM."

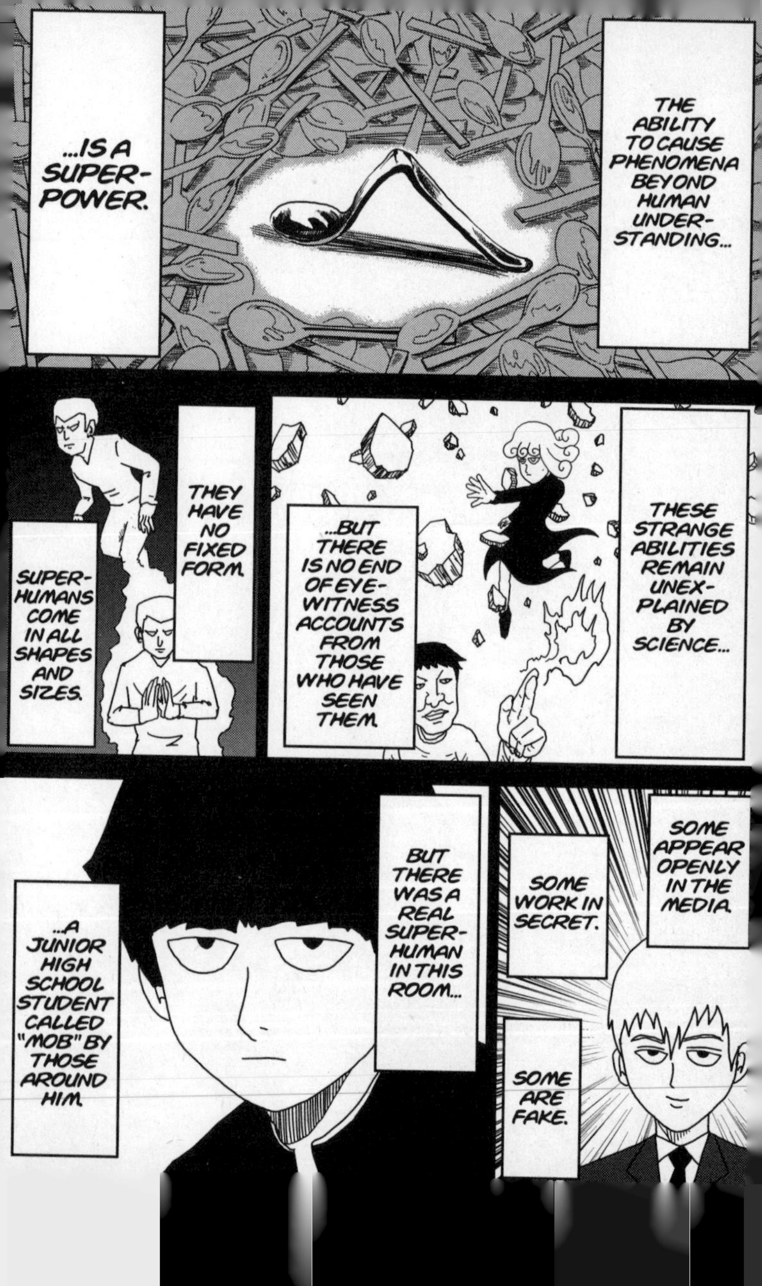
THE ABILITY TO CAUSE PHENOMENA BEYOND HUMAN UNDER-STANDING...
...IS A SUPER-POWER.
THESE STRANGE ABILITIES REMAIN UNEX-PLAINED BY SCIENCE...
...BUT THERE IS NO END OF EYE-WITNESS ACCOUNTS FROM THOSE WHO HAVE SEEN THEM.
THEY HAVE NO FIXED FORM.
SUPER-HUMANS COME IN ALL SHAPES AND SIZES.
SOME APPEAR OPENLY IN THE MEDIA.
SOME WORK IN SECRET.
SOME ARE FAKE.
BUT THERE WAS A REAL SUPER-HUMAN IN THIS ROOM...
...A JUNIOR HIGH SCHOOL STUDENT CALLED "MOB" BY THOSE AROUND HIM.

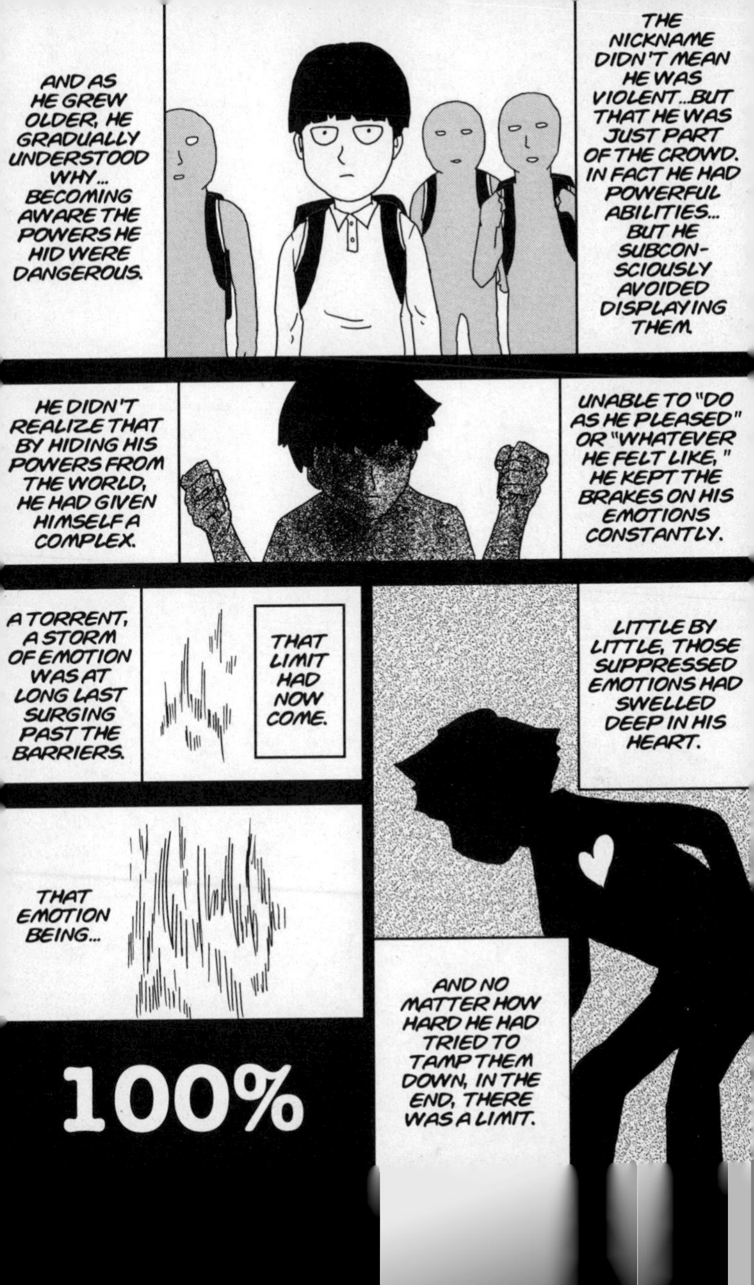
THE NICKNAME DIDN'T MEAN HE WAS VIOLENT...BUT THAT HE WAS JUST PART OF THE CROWD. IN FACT HE HAD POWERFUL ABILITIES... BUT HE SUBCON-SCIOUSLY AVOIDED DISPLAYING THEM.
AND AS HE GREW OLDER, HE GRADUALLY UNDERSTOOD WHY... BECOMING AWARE THE POWERS HE HID WERE DANGEROUS.
UNABLE TO "DO AS HE PLEASED" OR "WHATEVER HE FELT LIKE," HE KEPT THE BRAKES ON HIS EMOTIONS CONSTANTLY.
HE DIDN'T REALIZE THAT BY HIDING HIS POWERS FROM THE WORLD, HE HAD GIVEN HIMSELF A COMPLEX.
LITTLE BY LITTLE, THOSE SUPPRESSED EMOTIONS HAD SWELLED DEEP IN HIS HEART.
AND NO MATTER HOW HARD HE HAD TRIED TO TAMP THEM DOWN, IN THE END, THERE WAS A LIMIT.
THAT LIMIT HAD NOW COME.
A TORRENT, A STORM OF EMOTION WAS AT LONG LAST SURGING PAST THE BARRIERS.
THAT EMOTION BEING...
100%

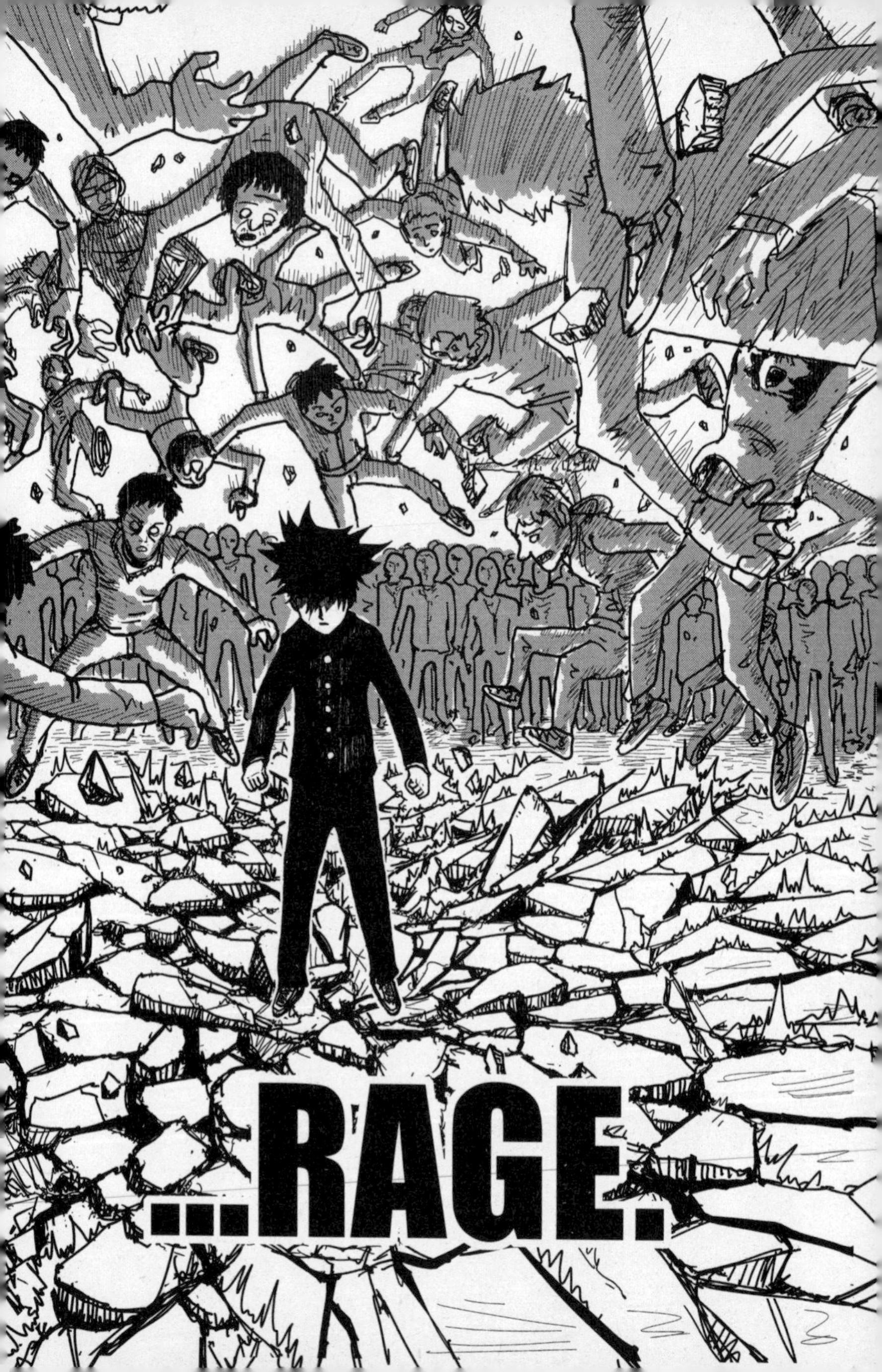
...RAGE.

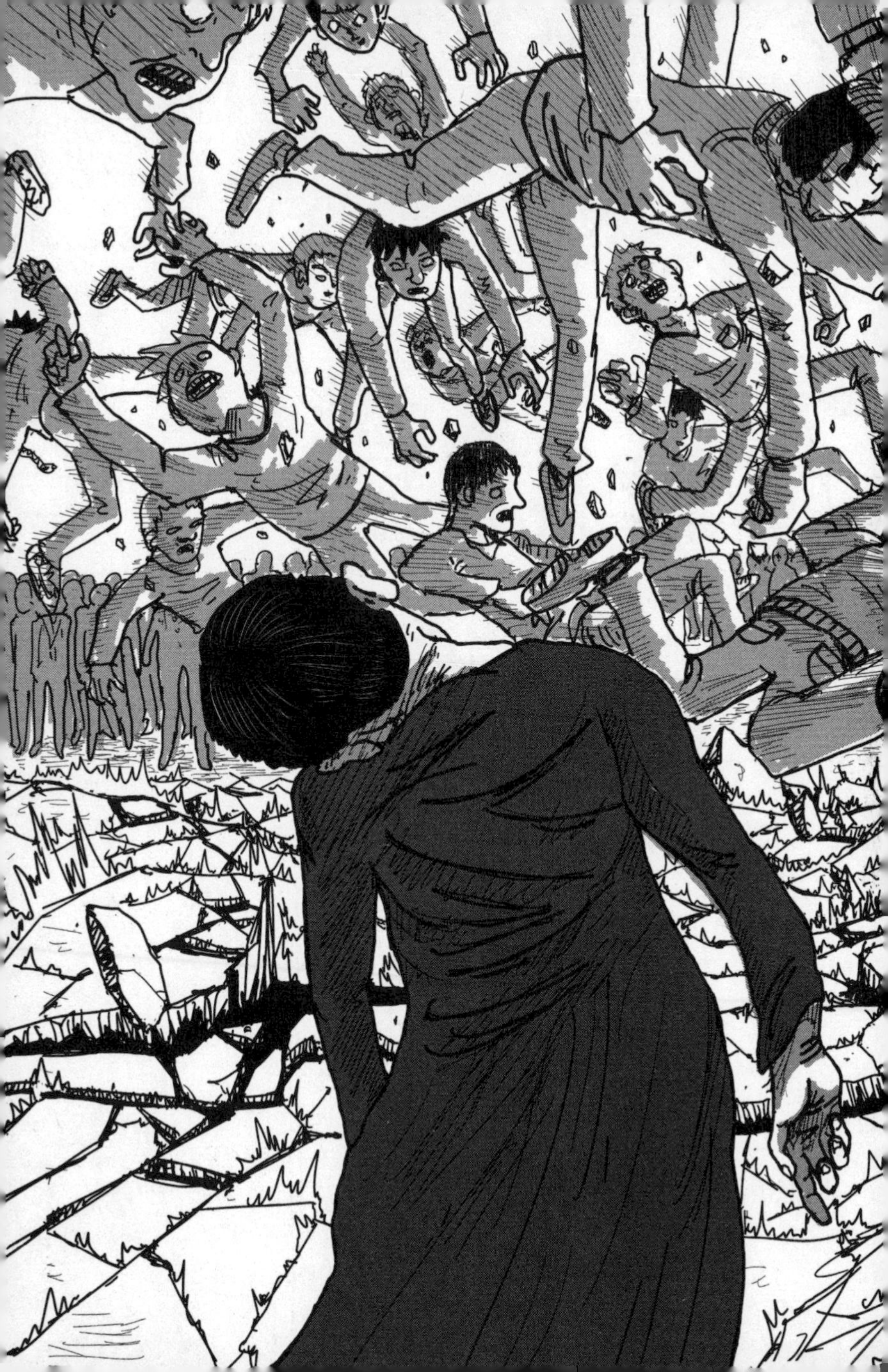

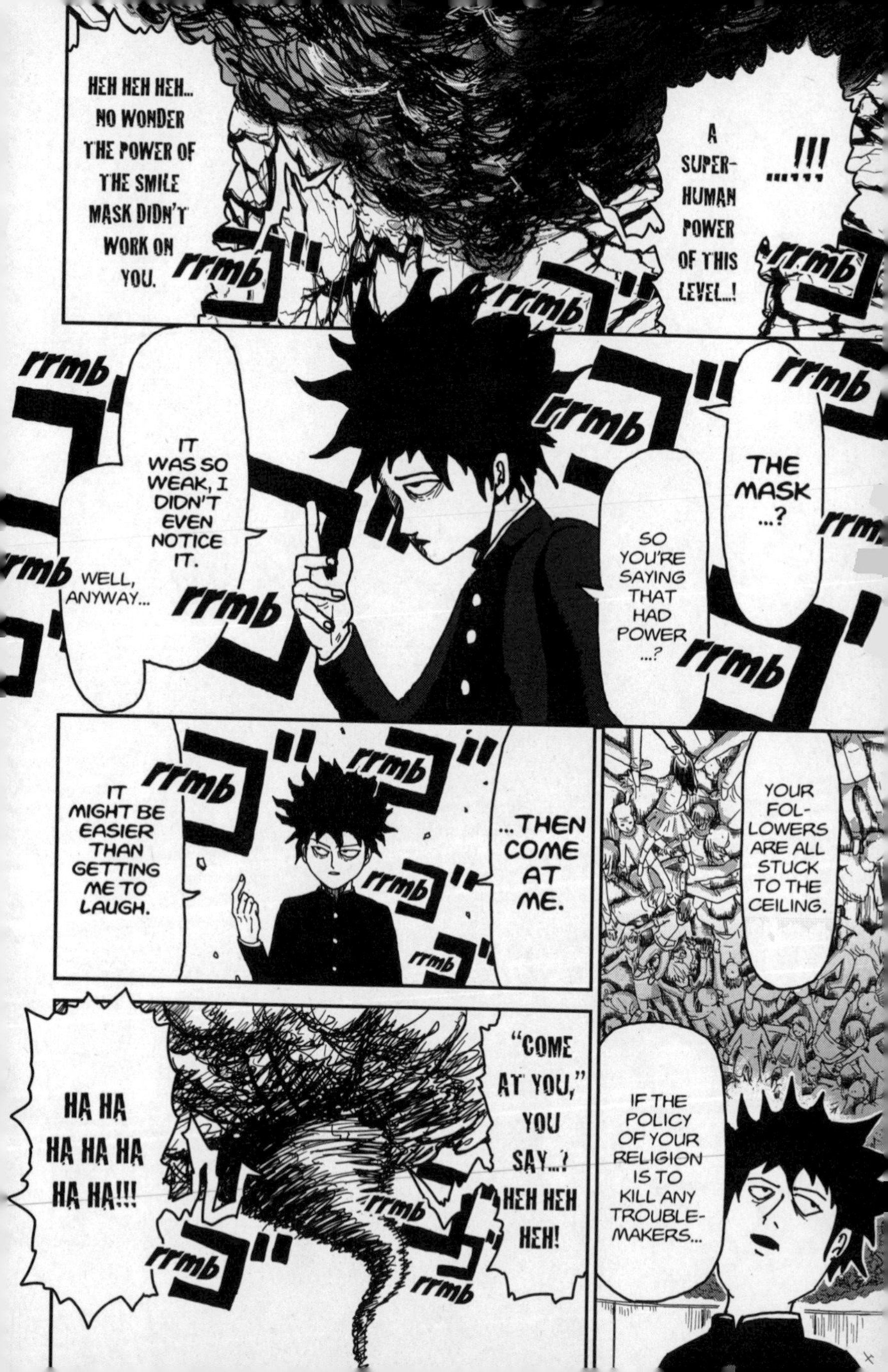
...!!!
A SUPER-HUMAN POWER OF THIS LEVEL...!
rrmb
rrmb
HEH HEH HEH... NO WONDER THE POWER OF THE SMILE MASK DIDN'T WORK ON YOU.
rrmb
rrmb
THE MASK ...?
rrmb
SO YOU'RE SAYING THAT HAD POWER ...?
rrmb
rrmb
IT WAS SO WEAK, I DIDN'T EVEN NOTICE IT.
rrmb
WELL, ANYWAY...
rrmb
rrmb
YOUR FOLLOWERS ARE ALL STUCK TO THE CEILING.
IF THE POLICY OF YOUR RELIGION IS TO KILL ANY TROUBLEMAKERS...
...THEN COME AT ME.
rrmb
rrmb
rrmb
rrmb
IT MIGHT BE EASIER THAN GETTING ME TO LAUGH.
"COME AT YOU," YOU SAY...? HEH HEH HEH!
rrmb
rrmb
rrmb
HA HA HA HA HA HA HA!!!

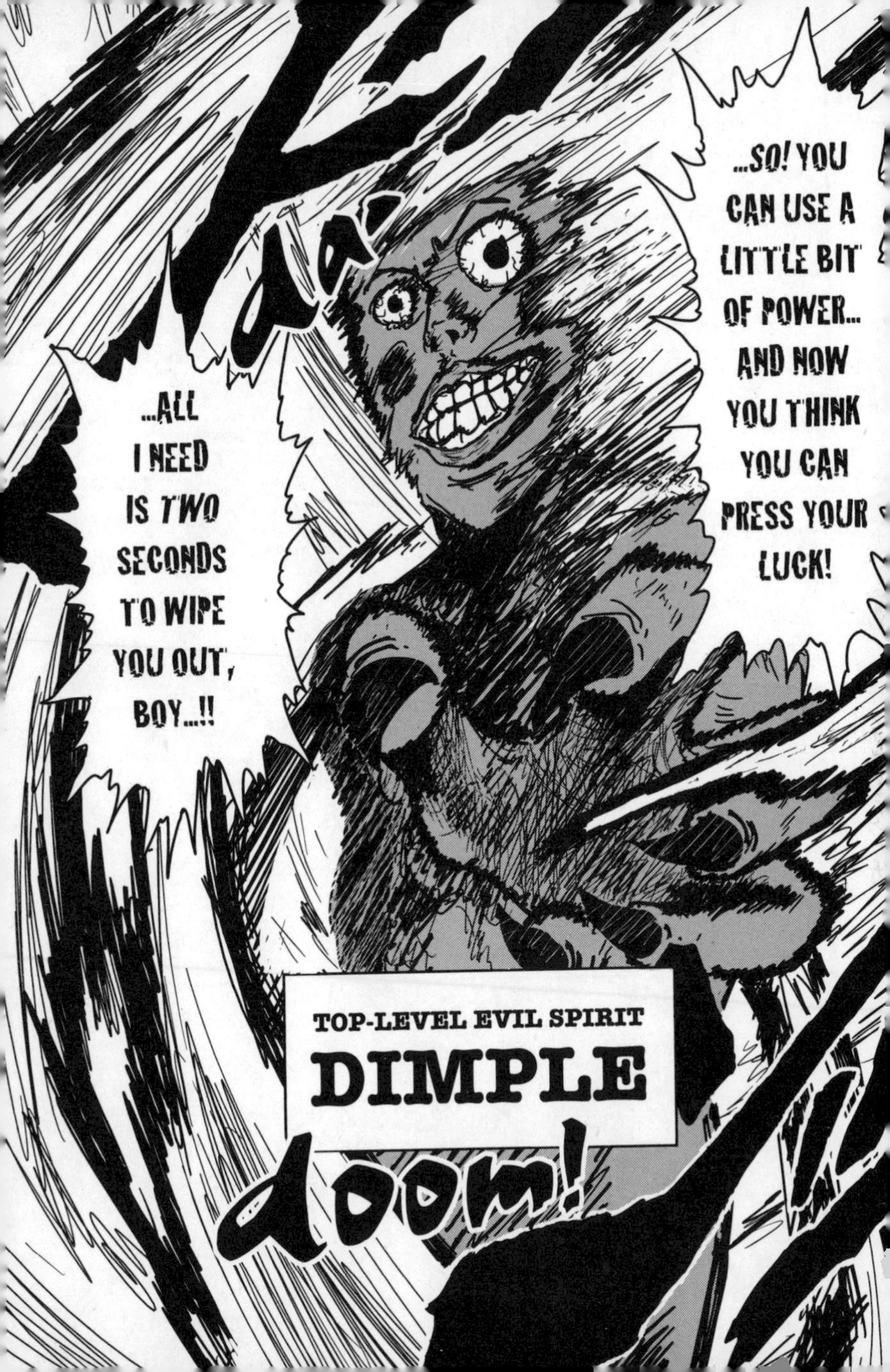
...SO! YOU CAN USE A LITTLE BIT OF POWER... AND NOW YOU THINK YOU CAN PRESS YOUR LUCK!
...ALL I NEED IS TWO SECONDS TO WIPE YOU OUT, BOY...!!
TOP-LEVEL EVIL SPIRIT
DIMPLE
doom!

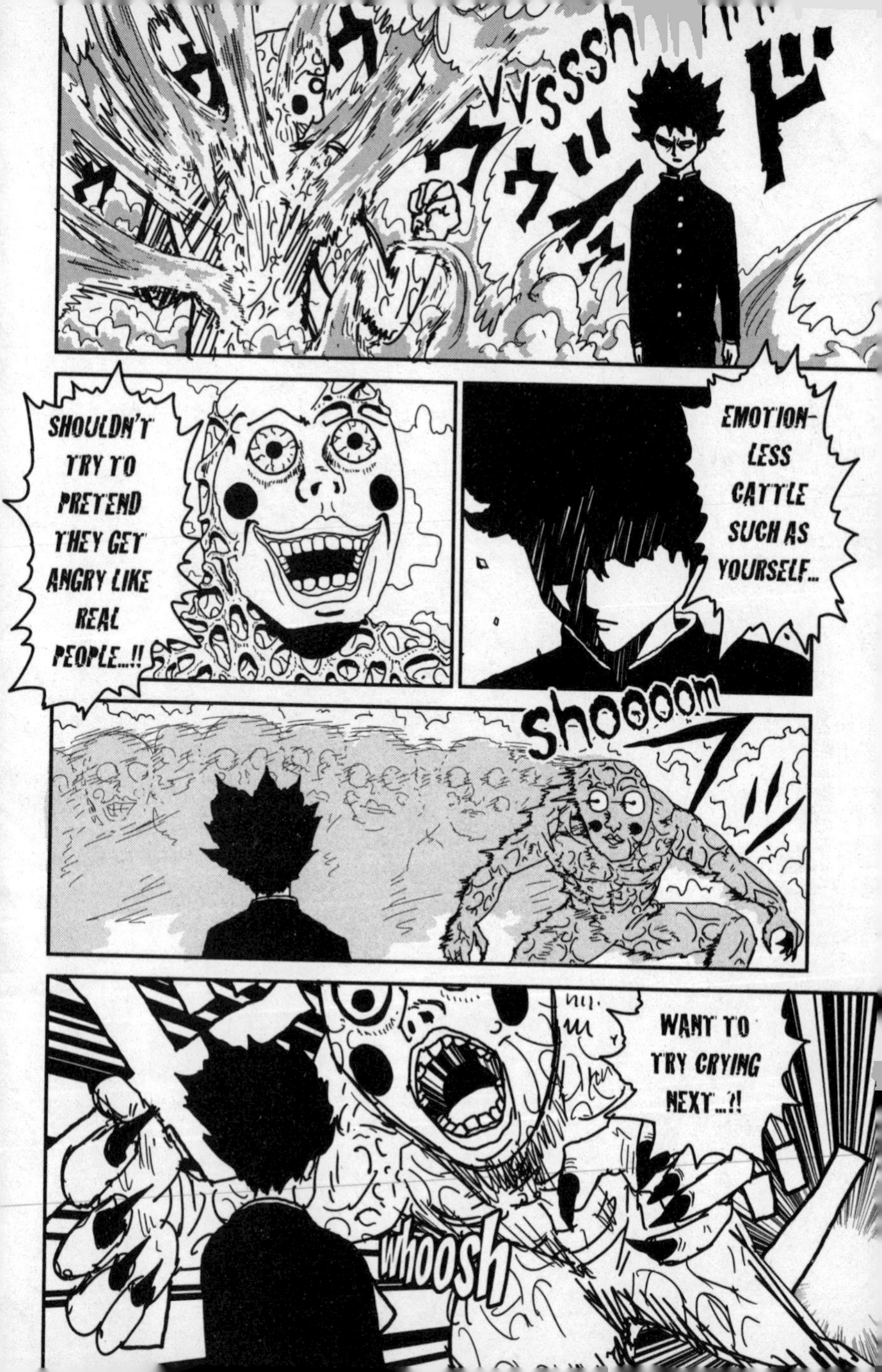
VVSSSH
EMOTION-LESS CATTLE SUCH AS YOURSELF...
SHOULDN'T TRY TO PRETEND THEY GET ANGRY LIKE REAL PEOPLE...!!
SHOOOOM
WANT TO TRY CRYING NEXT...?!
WHOOSH

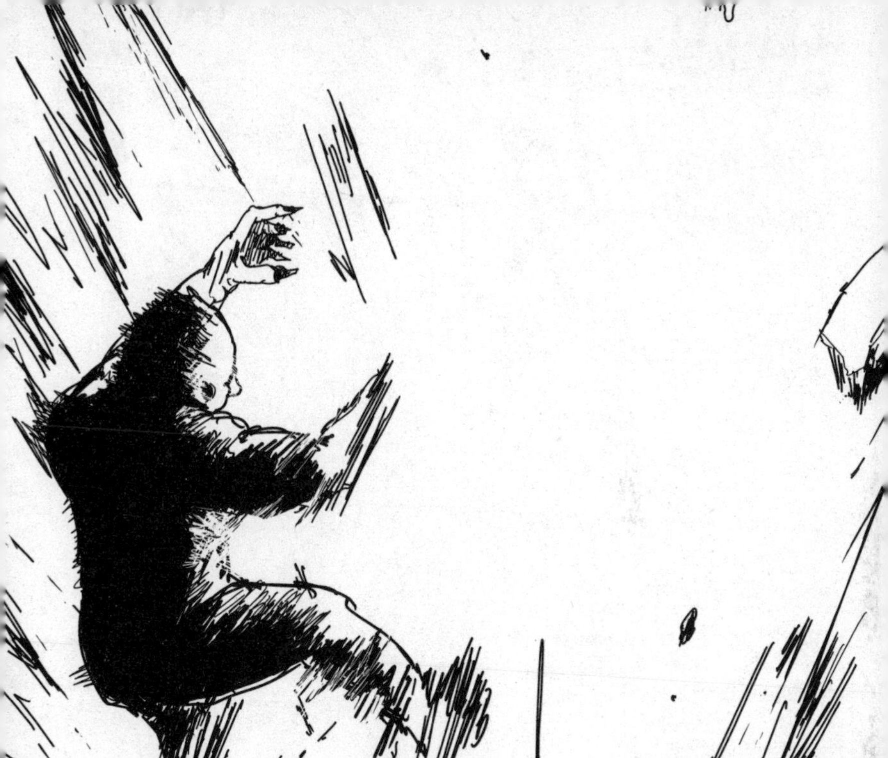
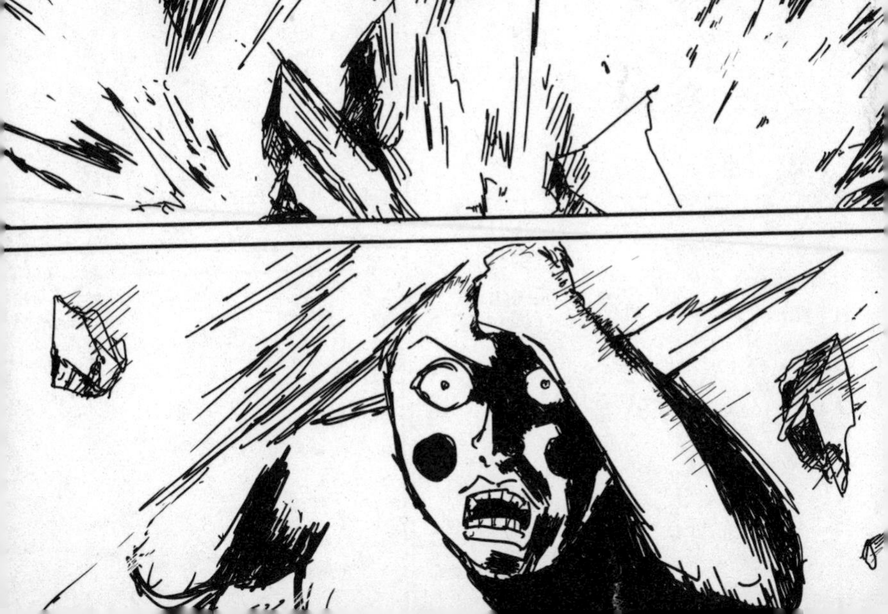

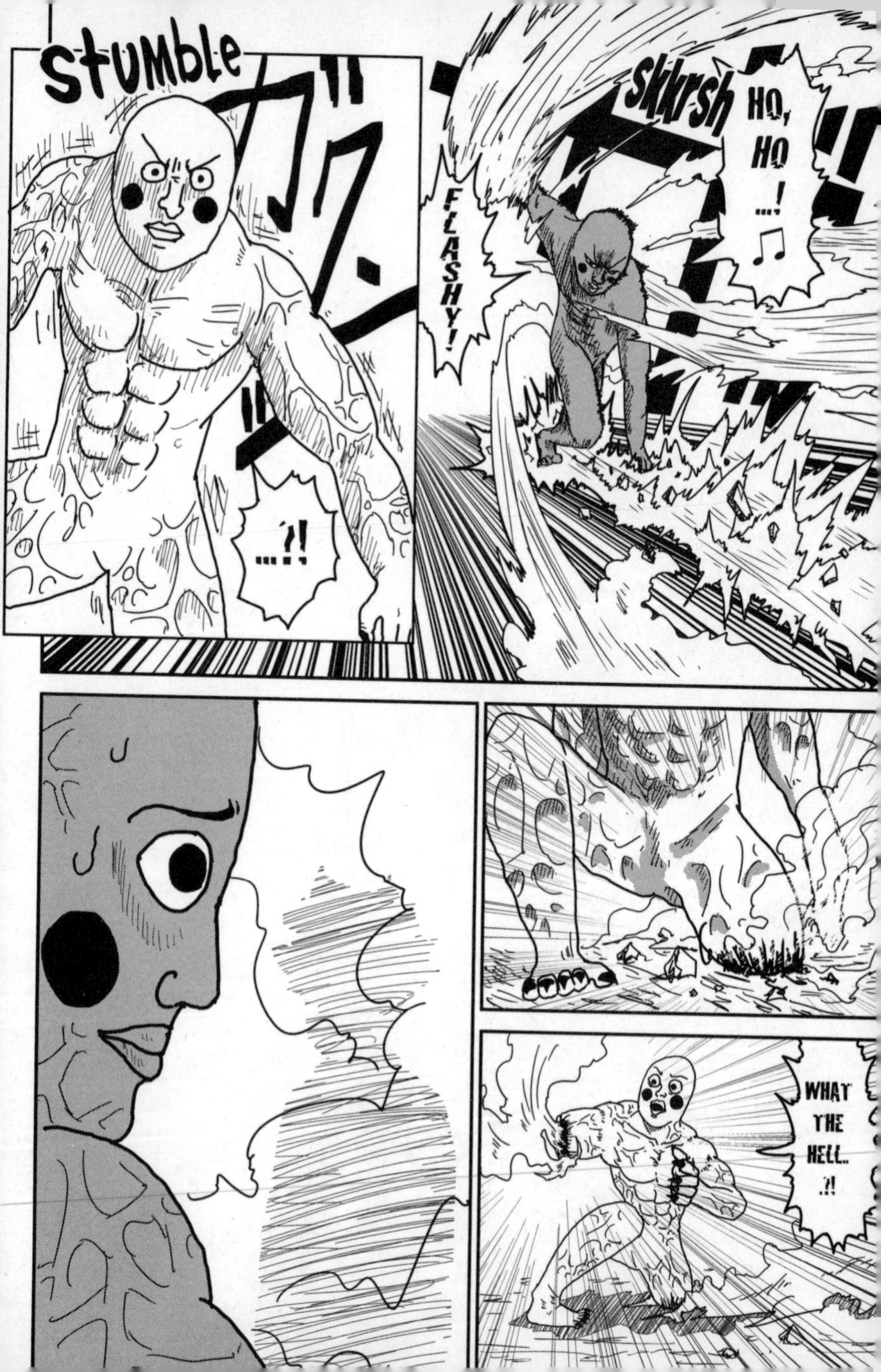
SKKRSH
HO, HO...! ♪
FLASHY!!
stumble
...?!
WHAT THE HELL..?!

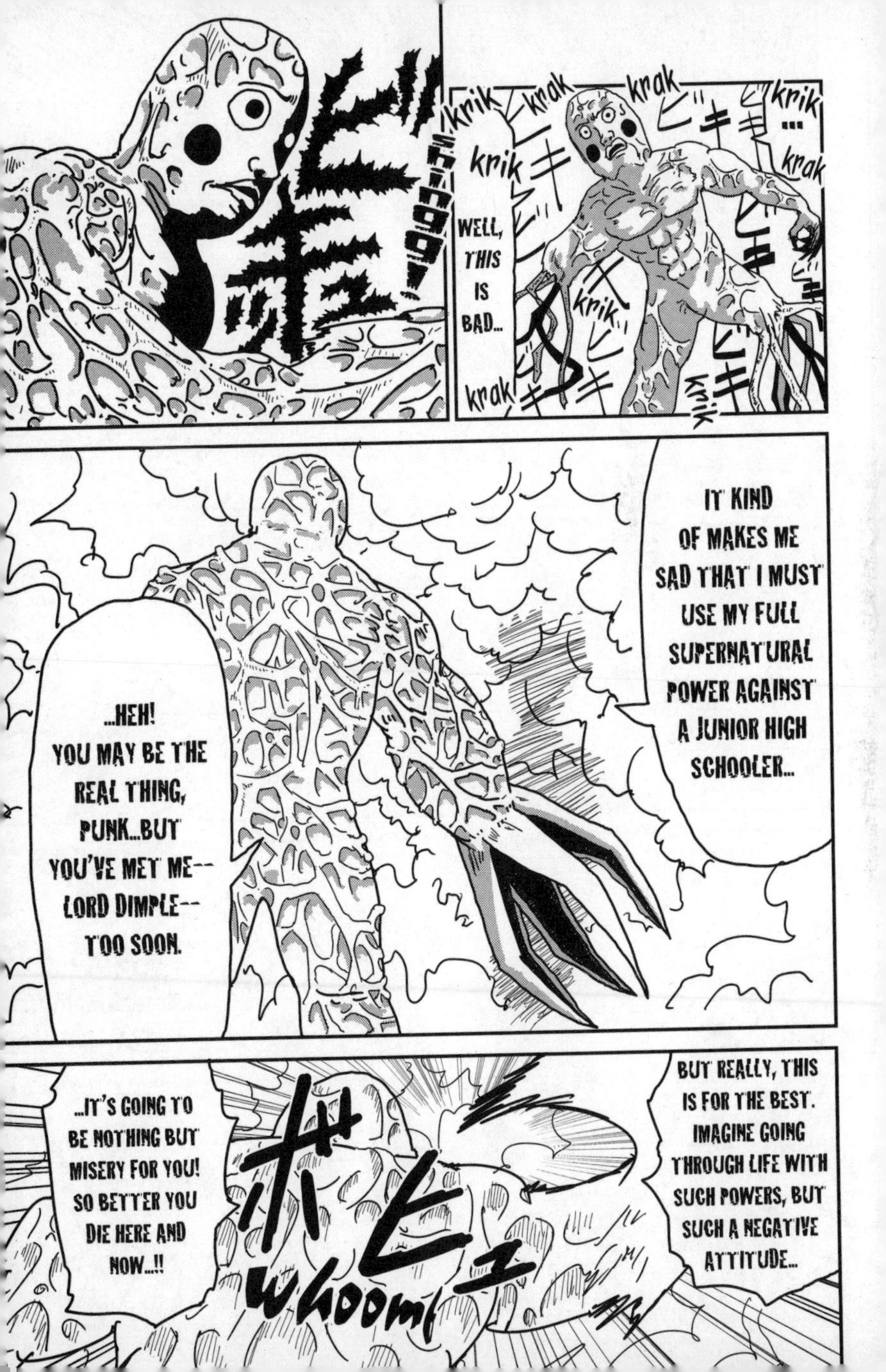
krik
krak
krak
krik
...
krak
krik
WELL, THIS IS BAD...
krik
krak
krik
shingg!
IT KIND OF MAKES ME SAD THAT I MUST USE MY FULL SUPERNATURAL POWER AGAINST A JUNIOR HIGH SCHOOLER...
...HEH! YOU MAY BE THE REAL THING, PUNK...BUT YOU'VE MET ME--LORD DIMPLE--TOO SOON.
BUT REALLY, THIS IS FOR THE BEST. IMAGINE GOING THROUGH LIFE WITH SUCH POWERS, BUT SUCH A NEGATIVE ATTITUDE...
whoom
...IT'S GOING TO BE NOTHING BUT MISERY FOR YOU! SO BETTER YOU DIE HERE AND NOW...!!

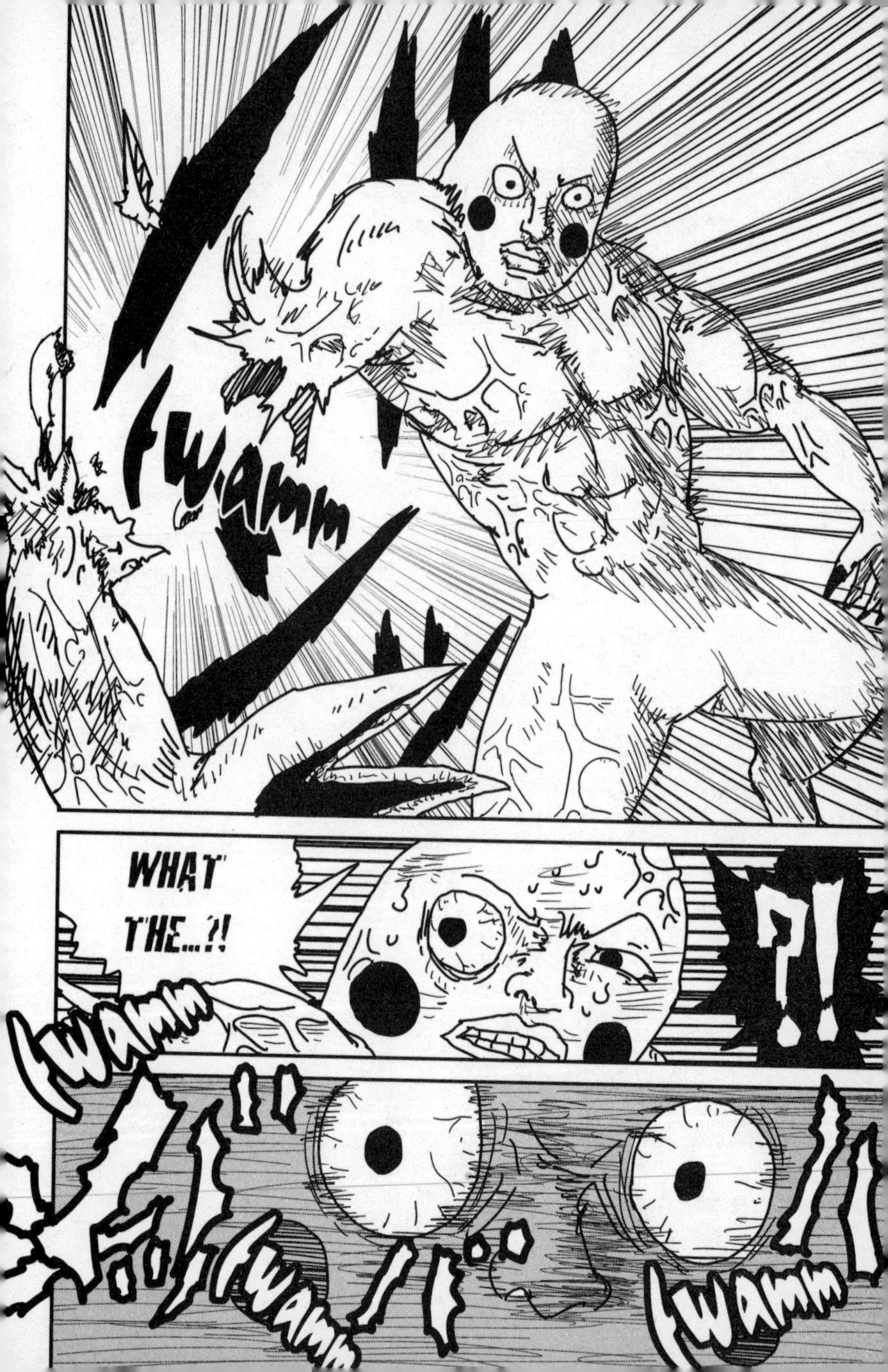
FWAMM
?!!
WHAT THE...?!
FWAMM
FWAMM
FWAMM

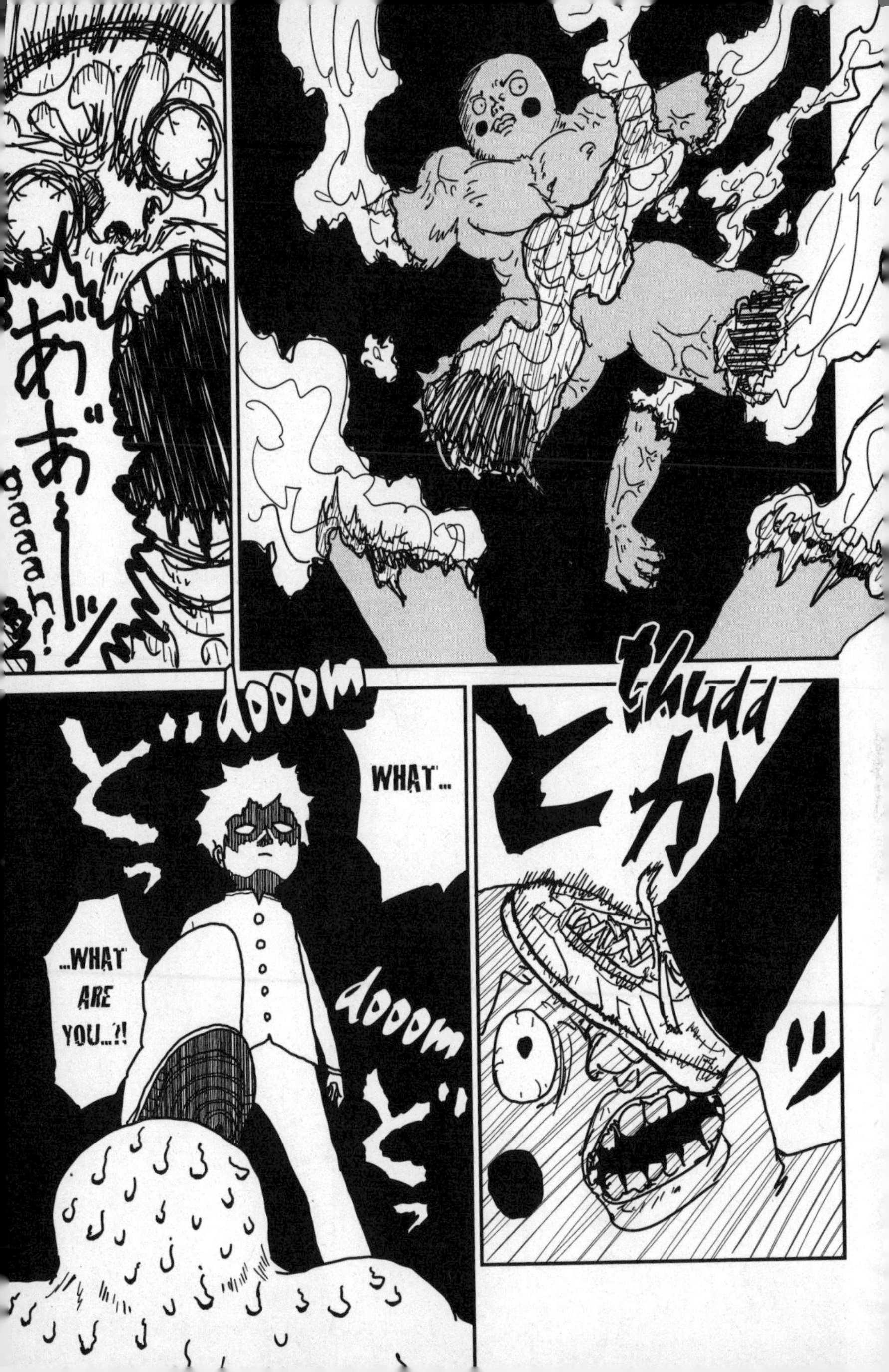
あ゛あ゛ーーッ
gaaaah?!
thuda
WHAT...
...WHAT ARE YOU...?!
dooom
dooom

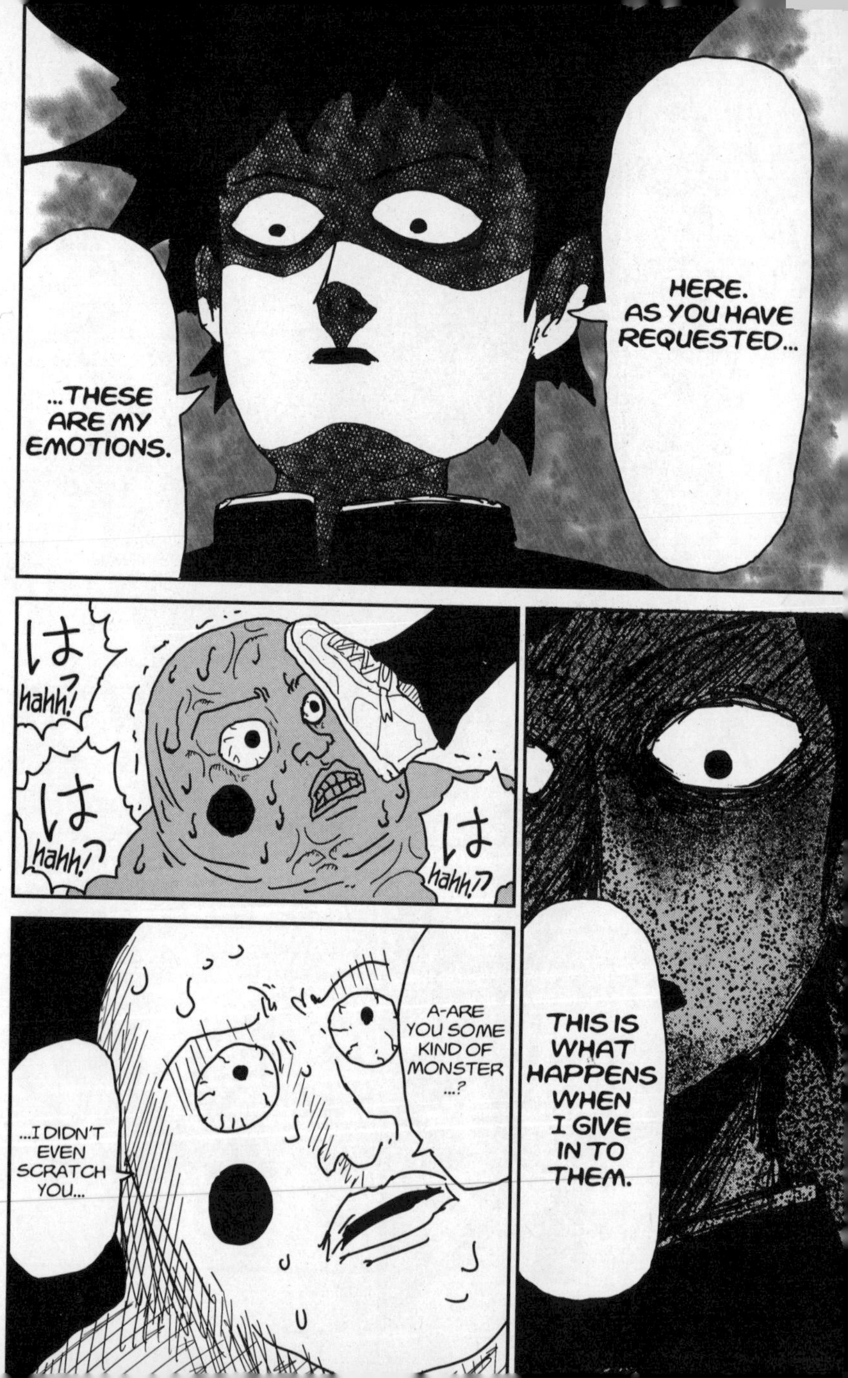
HERE. AS YOU HAVE REQUESTED...
...THESE ARE MY EMOTIONS.
THIS IS WHAT HAPPENS WHEN I GIVE IN TO THEM.
は hahh!?
は hahh!?
は hahh!?
A-ARE YOU SOME KIND OF MONSTER ...?
...I DIDN'T EVEN SCRATCH YOU...

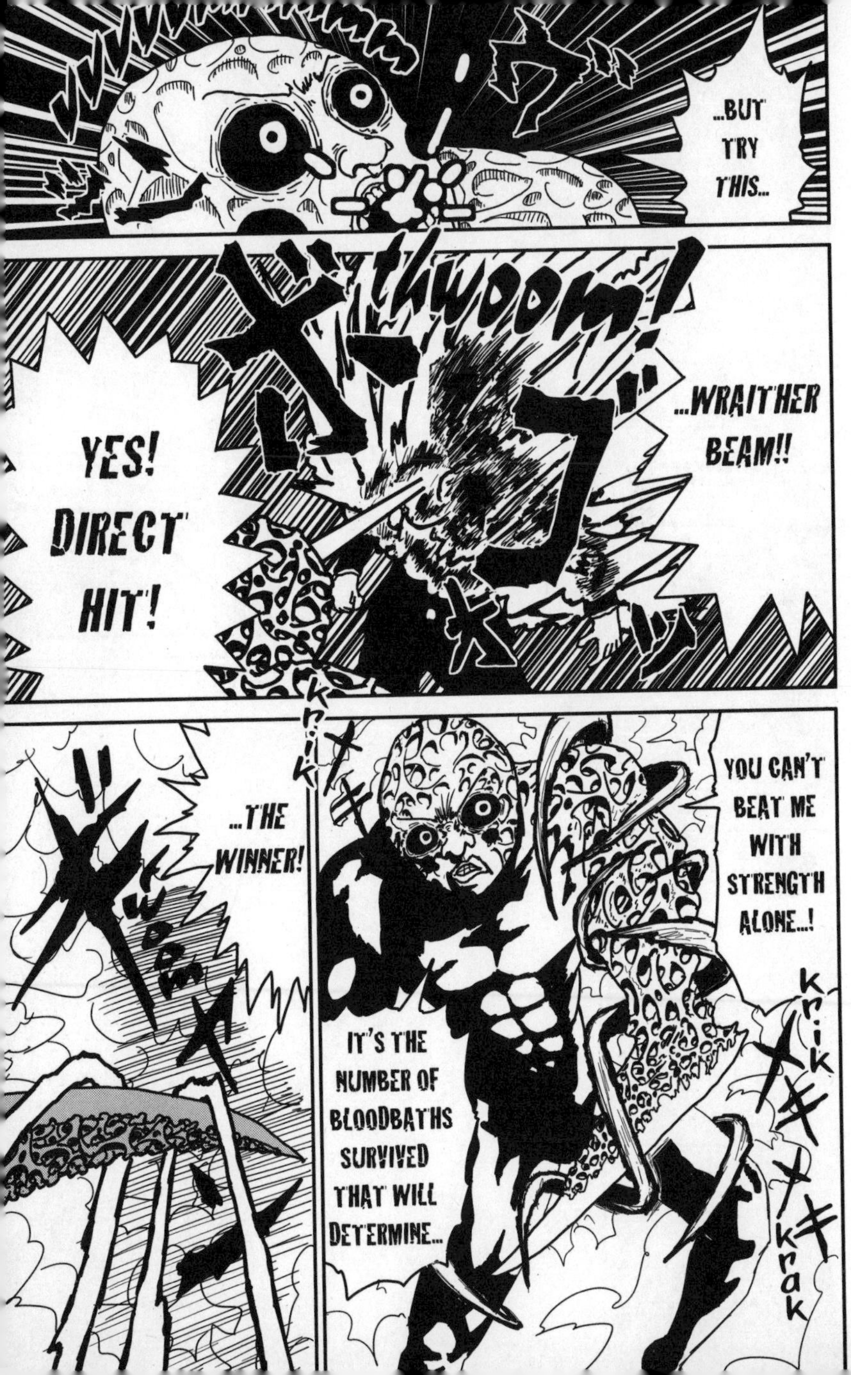
...BUT TRY THIS...
...WRAITHER BEAM!!
thwoom!
YES! DIRECT HIT!
krik
YOU CAN'T BEAT ME WITH STRENGTH ALONE...!
krik
krak
IT'S THE NUMBER OF BLOODBATHS SURVIVED THAT WILL DETERMINE...
...THE WINNER!

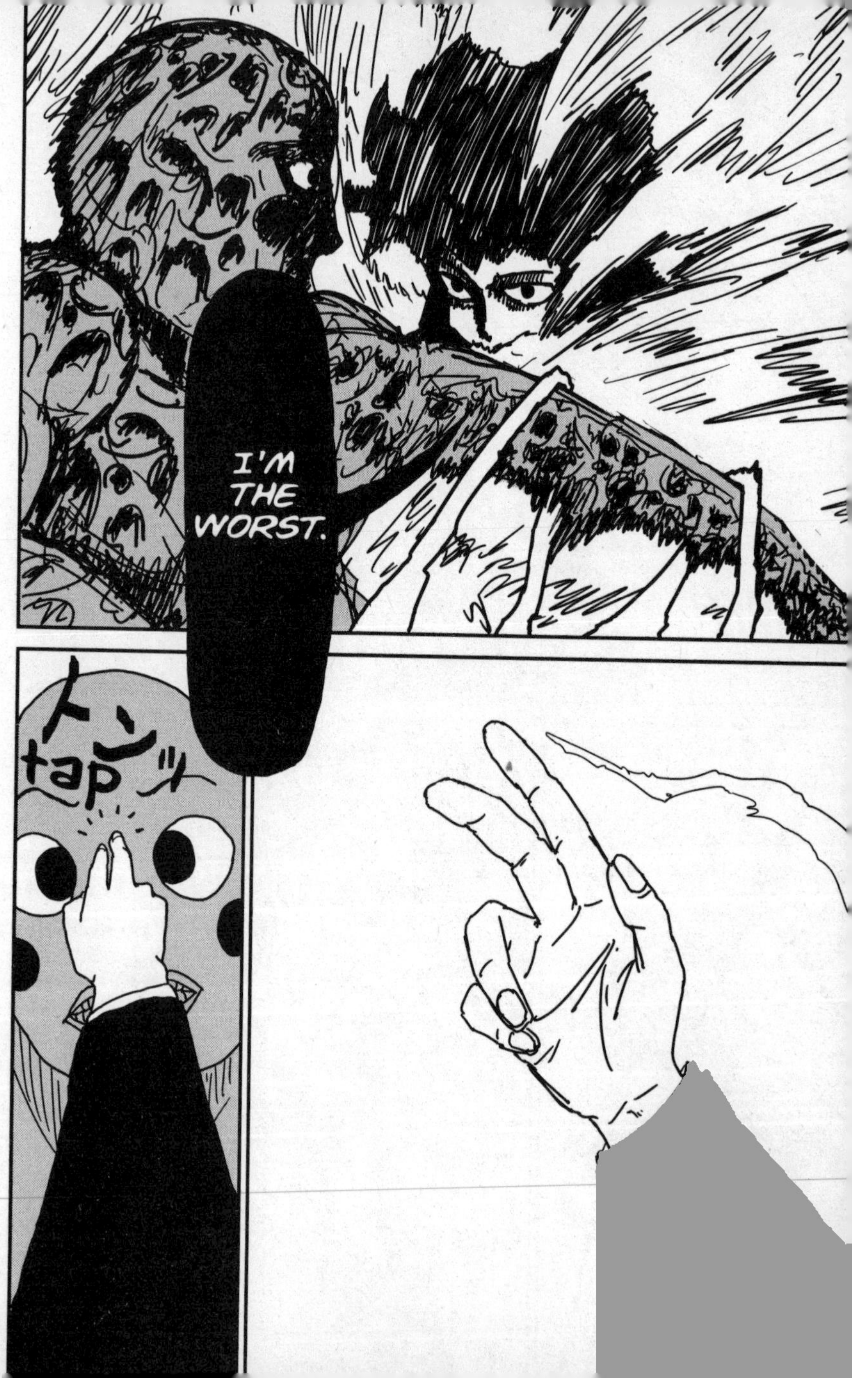
I'M THE WORST.
トンッ
tap

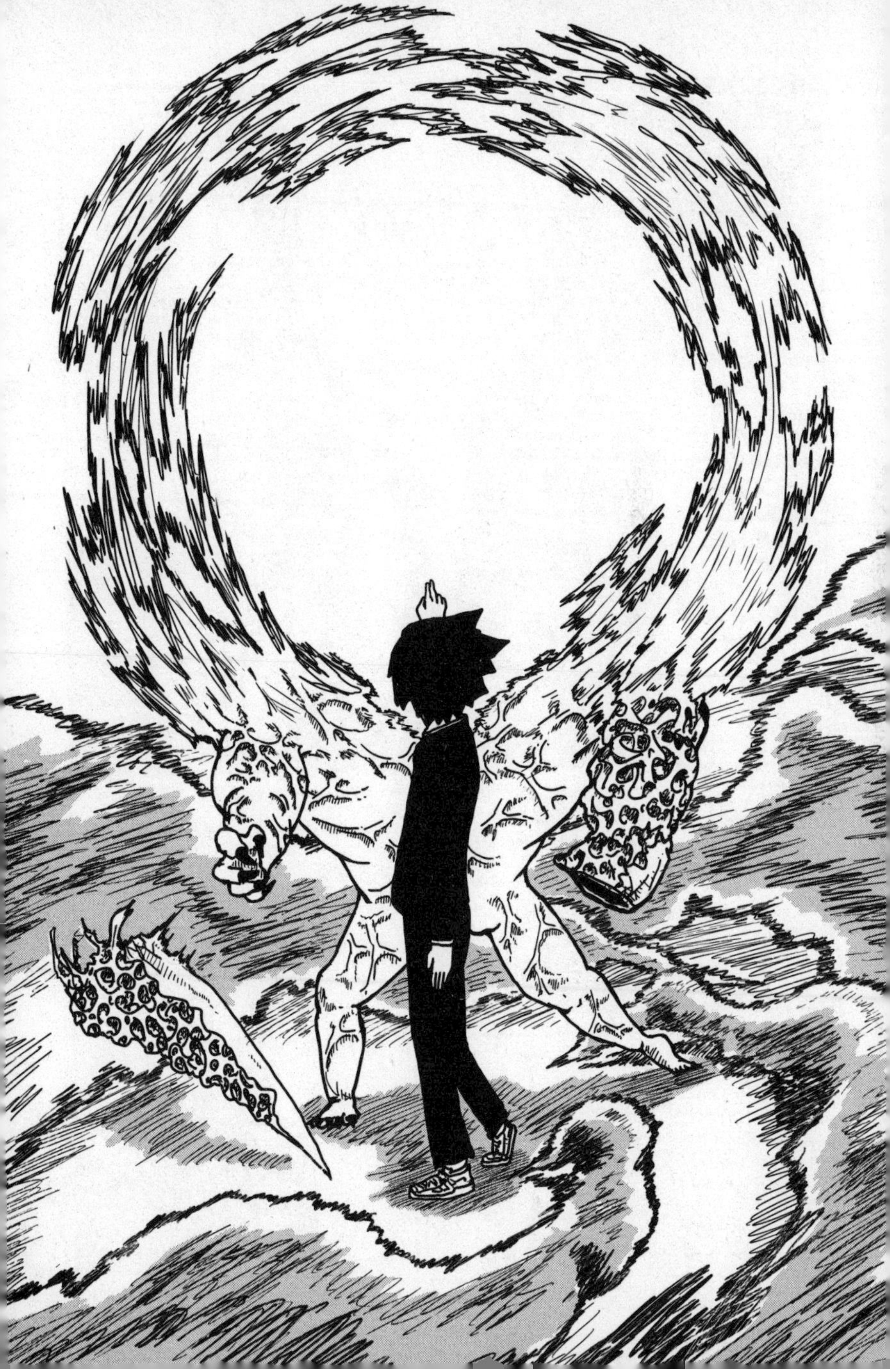

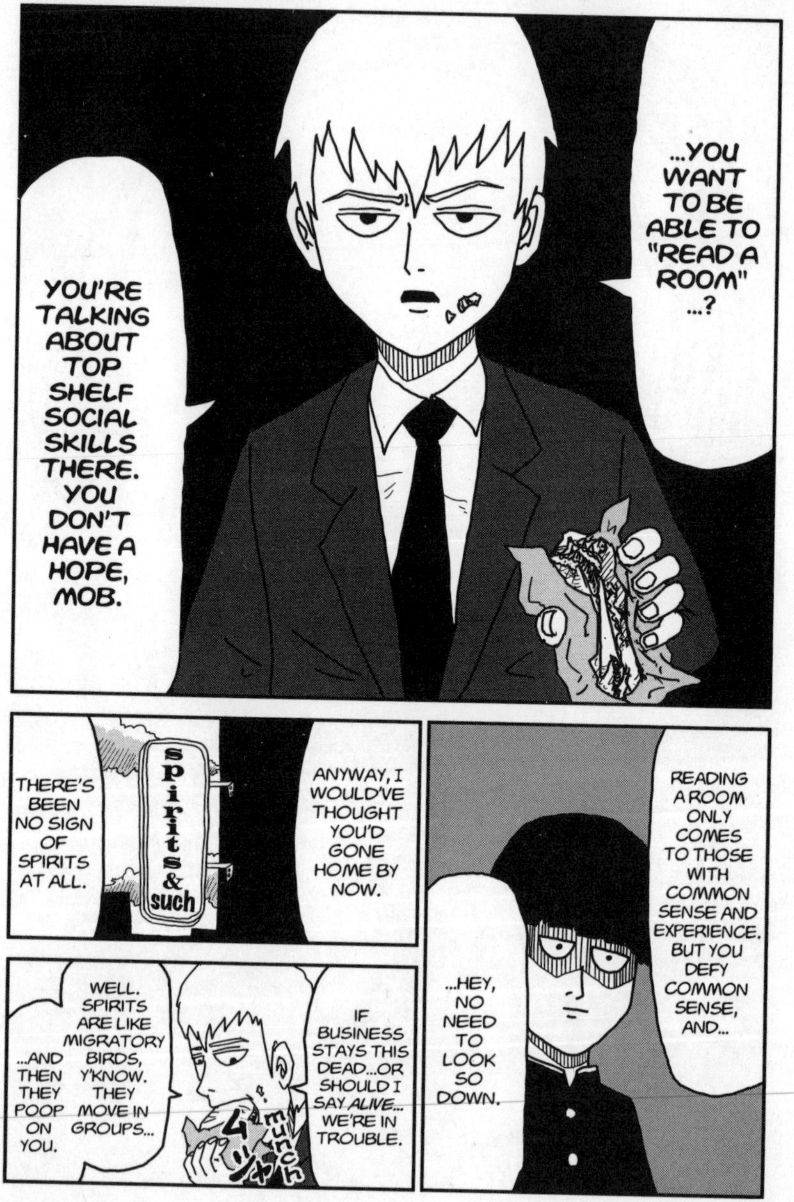
...YOU WANT TO BE ABLE TO "READ A ROOM" ...?
YOU'RE TALKING ABOUT TOP SHELF SOCIAL SKILLS THERE. YOU DON'T HAVE A HOPE, MOB.
READING A ROOM ONLY COMES TO THOSE WITH COMMON SENSE AND EXPERIENCE. BUT YOU DEFY COMMON SENSE, AND...
...HEY, NO NEED TO LOOK SO DOWN.
ANYWAY, I WOULD'VE THOUGHT YOU'D GONE HOME BY NOW.
spirits & such
THERE'S BEEN NO SIGN OF SPIRITS AT ALL.
IF BUSINESS STAYS THIS DEAD...OR SHOULD I SAY *ALIVE*... WE'RE IN TROUBLE.
WELL. SPIRITS ARE LIKE MIGRATORY BIRDS, Y'KNOW. THEY MOVE IN GROUPS...
...AND THEN THEY POOP ON YOU.
munch

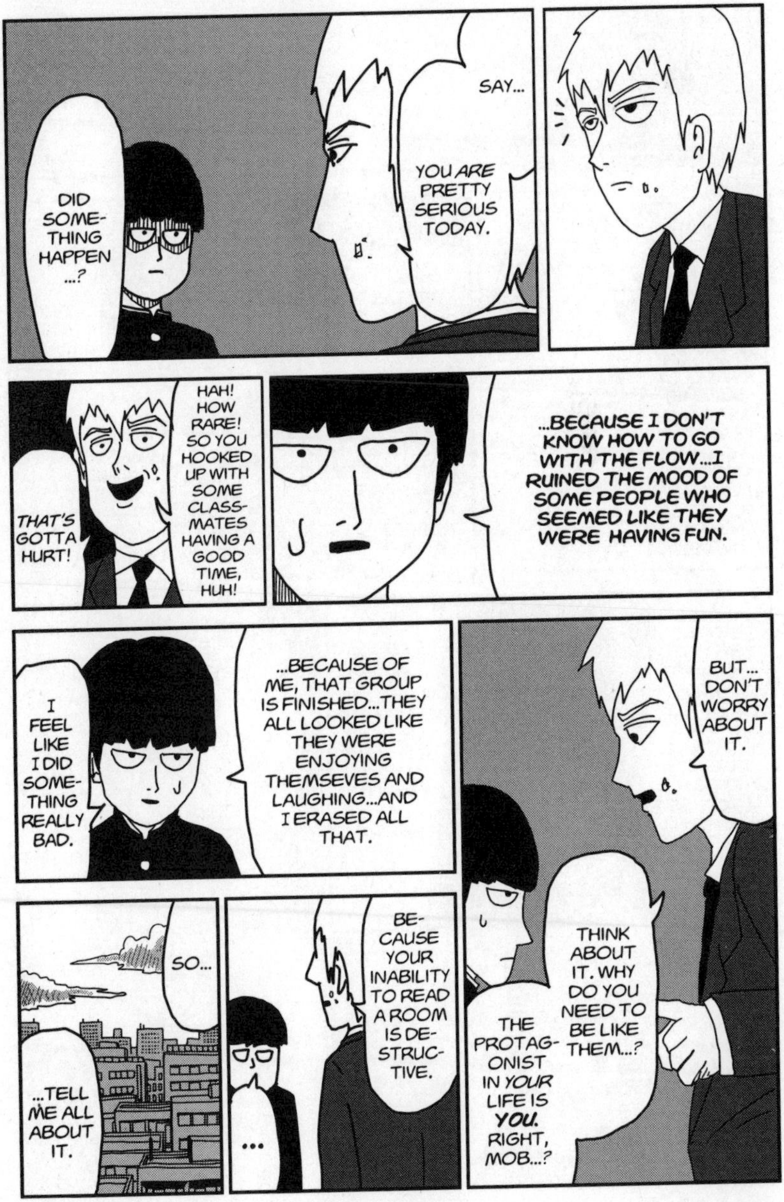
SAY...
YOU *ARE* PRETTY SERIOUS TODAY.
DID SOMETHING HAPPEN ...?
...BECAUSE I DON'T KNOW HOW TO GO WITH THE FLOW...I RUINED THE MOOD OF SOME PEOPLE WHO SEEMED LIKE THEY WERE HAVING FUN.
HAH! HOW RARE! SO YOU HOOKED UP WITH SOME CLASSMATES HAVING A GOOD TIME, HUH!
THAT'S GOTTA HURT!
BUT... DON'T WORRY ABOUT IT.
THINK ABOUT IT. WHY DO YOU NEED TO BE LIKE THEM...?
THE PROTAGONIST IN *YOUR* LIFE IS ***YOU.*** RIGHT, MOB...?
...BECAUSE OF ME, THAT GROUP IS FINISHED...THEY ALL LOOKED LIKE THEY WERE ENJOYING THEMSEVES AND LAUGHING...AND I ERASED ALL THAT.
I FEEL LIKE I DID SOMETHING REALLY BAD.
BECAUSE YOUR INABILITY TO READ A ROOM IS DESTRUCTIVE.
...
SO...
...TELL ME ALL ABOUT IT.

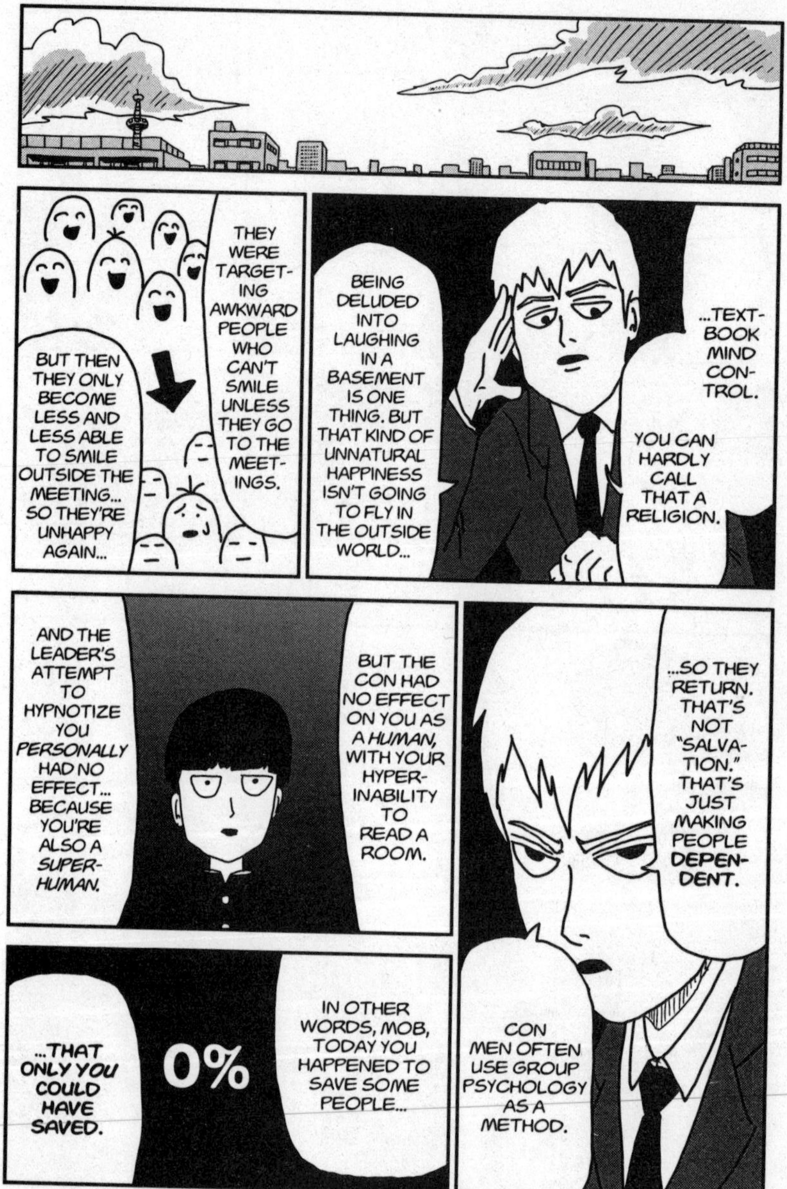
...TEXTBOOK MIND CONTROL.
YOU CAN HARDLY CALL THAT A RELIGION.
BEING DELUDED INTO LAUGHING IN A BASEMENT IS ONE THING. BUT THAT KIND OF UNNATURAL HAPPINESS ISN'T GOING TO FLY IN THE OUTSIDE WORLD...
THEY WERE TARGETING AWKWARD PEOPLE WHO CAN'T SMILE UNLESS THEY GO TO THE MEETINGS.
BUT THEN THEY ONLY BECOME LESS AND LESS ABLE TO SMILE OUTSIDE THE MEETING... SO THEY'RE UNHAPPY AGAIN...
...SO THEY RETURN. THAT'S NOT "SALVATION." THAT'S JUST MAKING PEOPLE **DEPENDENT**.
CON MEN OFTEN USE GROUP PSYCHOLOGY AS A METHOD.
BUT THE CON HAD NO EFFECT ON YOU AS A *HUMAN*, WITH YOUR HYPER-INABILITY TO READ A ROOM.
AND THE LEADER'S ATTEMPT TO HYPNOTIZE YOU *PERSONALLY* HAD NO EFFECT... BECAUSE YOU'RE ALSO A *SUPERHUMAN*.
IN OTHER WORDS, MOB, TODAY YOU HAPPENED TO SAVE SOME PEOPLE...
0%
...**THAT ONLY YOU COULD HAVE SAVED.**

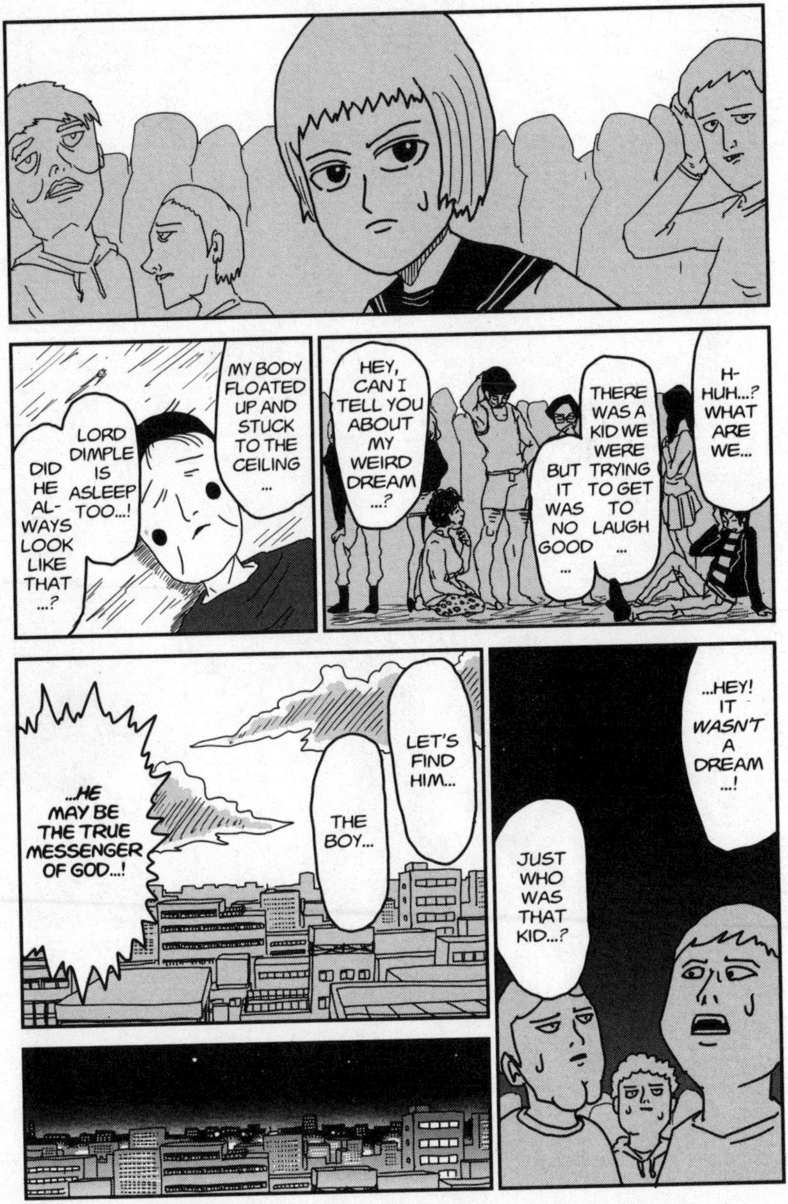
H-HUH...? WHAT ARE WE...
THERE WAS A KID WE WERE TRYING TO GET TO LAUGH...
BUT IT WAS NO GOOD...
HEY, CAN I TELL YOU ABOUT MY WEIRD DREAM...?
MY BODY FLOATED UP AND STUCK TO THE CEILING...
LORD DIMPLE IS ASLEEP TOO...!
DID HE AL-WAYS LOOK LIKE THAT...?
...HEY! IT WASN'T A DREAM...!
JUST WHO WAS THAT KID...?
LET'S FIND HIM...
THE BOY...
...HE MAY BE THE TRUE MESSENGER OF GOD...!

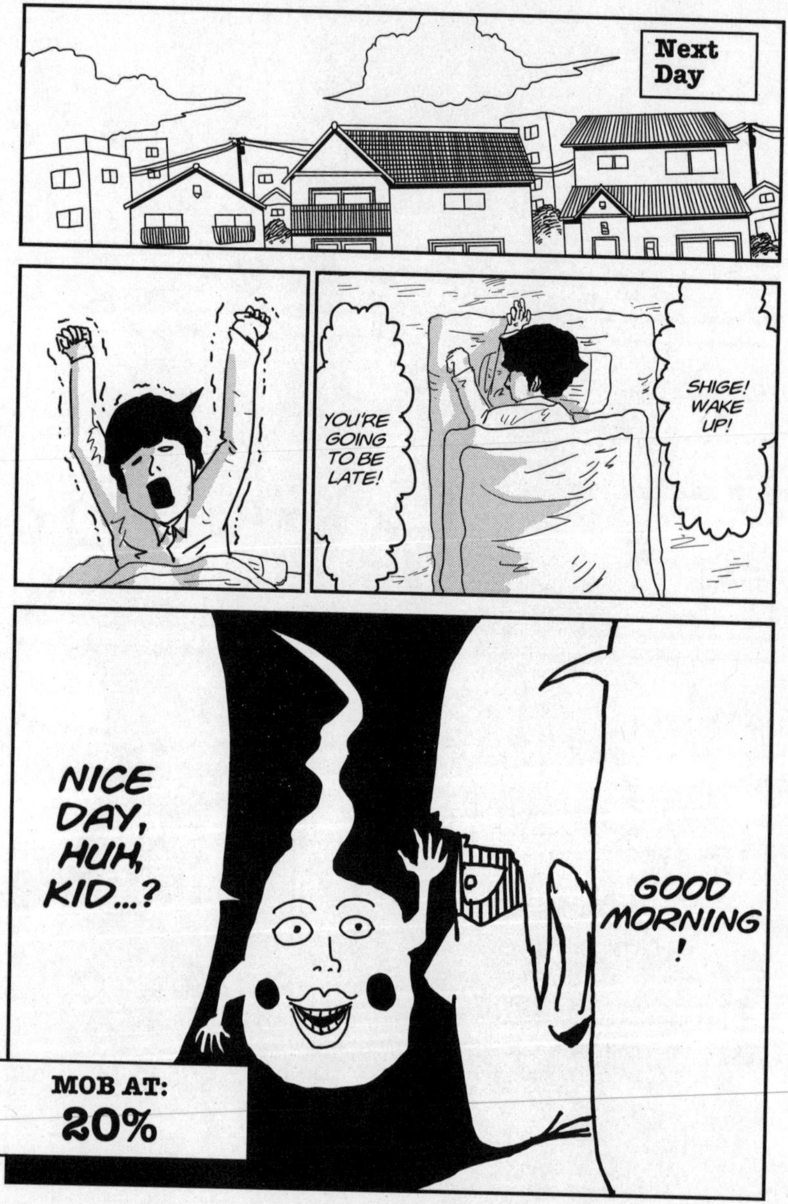
Next Day
SHIGE! WAKE UP!
YOU'RE GOING TO BE LATE!
GOOD MORNING!
NICE DAY, HUH, KID...?
MOB AT:
20%

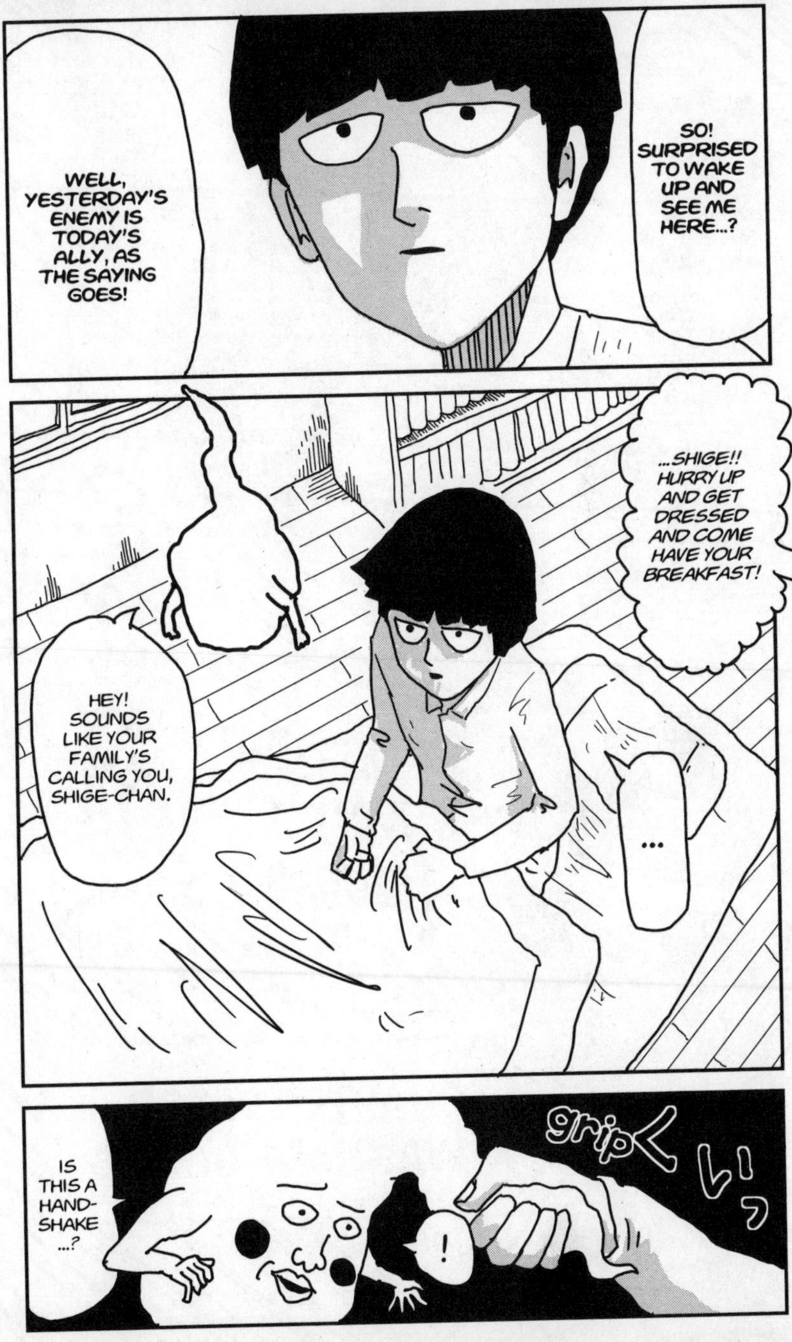
SO! SURPRISED TO WAKE UP AND SEE ME HERE...?
WELL, YESTERDAY'S ENEMY IS TODAY'S ALLY, AS THE SAYING GOES!
...SHIGE!! HURRY UP AND GET DRESSED AND COME HAVE YOUR BREAKFAST!
HEY! SOUNDS LIKE YOUR FAMILY'S CALLING YOU, SHIGE-CHAN.
...
grip
!
IS THIS A HAND-SHAKE ...?

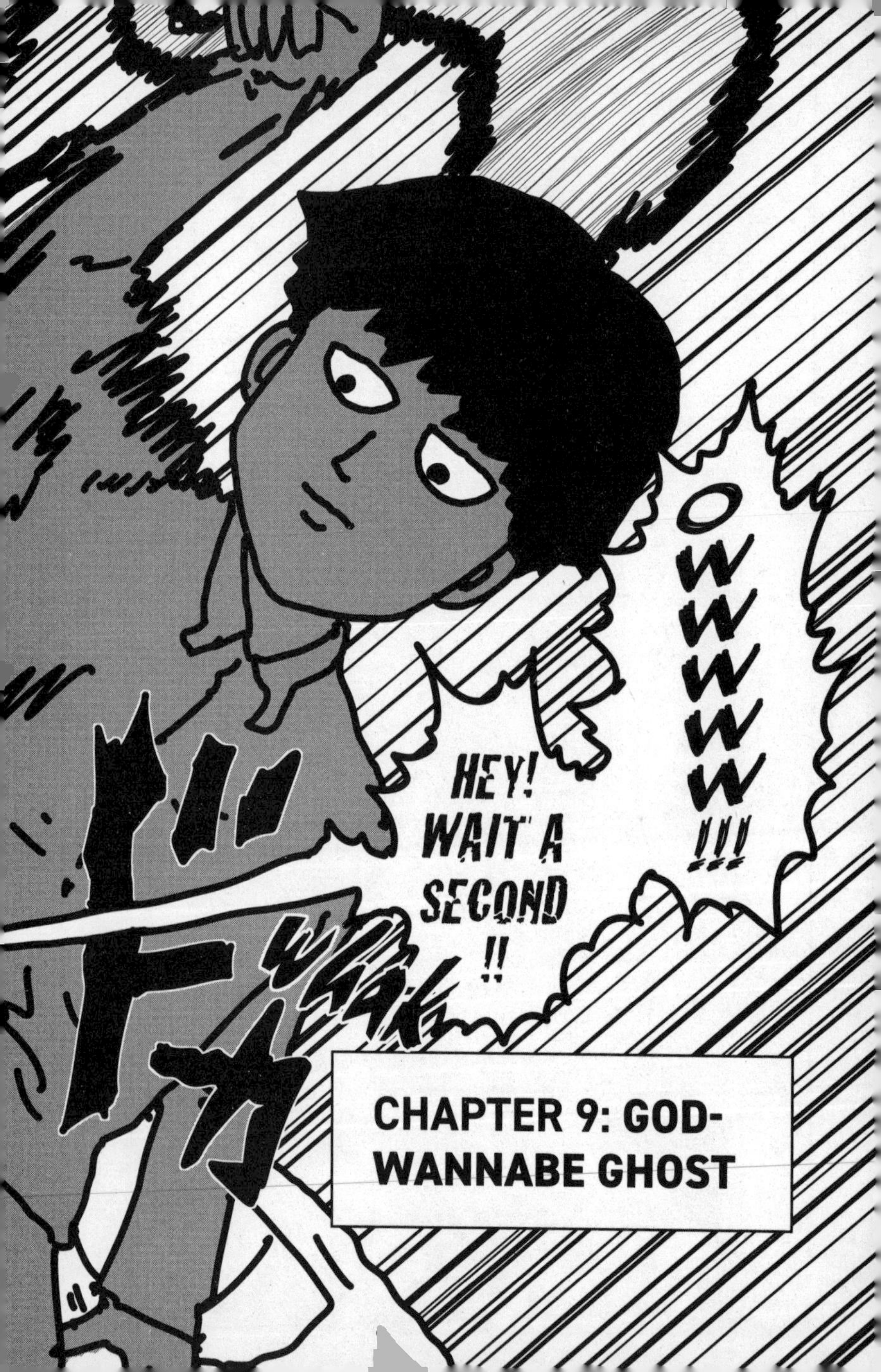
OWWWWWW!!!
HEY! WAIT A SECOND!!

CHAPTER 9: GOD-WANNABE GHOST

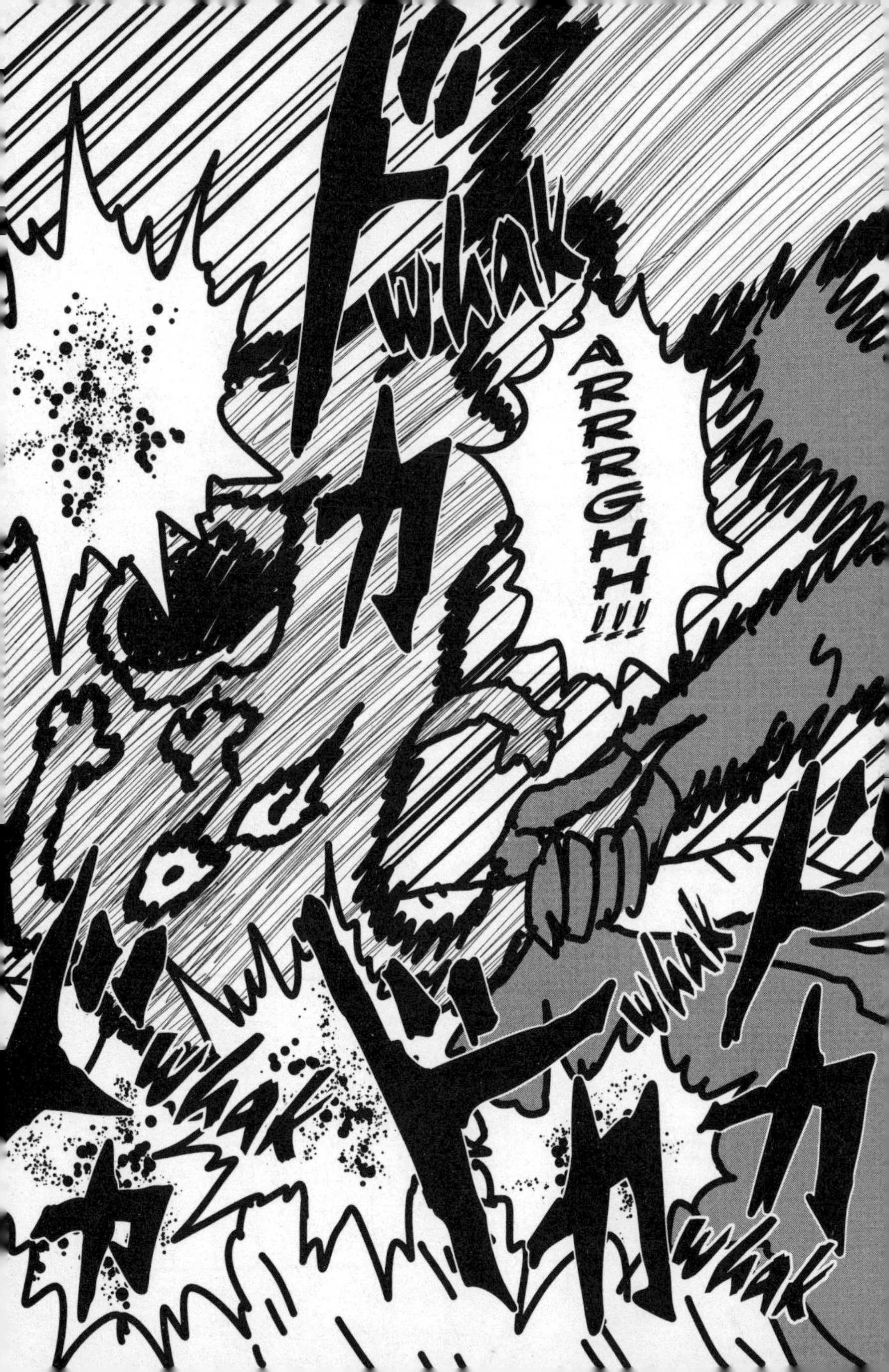
ARRRGHH!!!
ドカ
WHAK
ドカ
WHAK
ドカ
WHAK
ドカ
WHAK

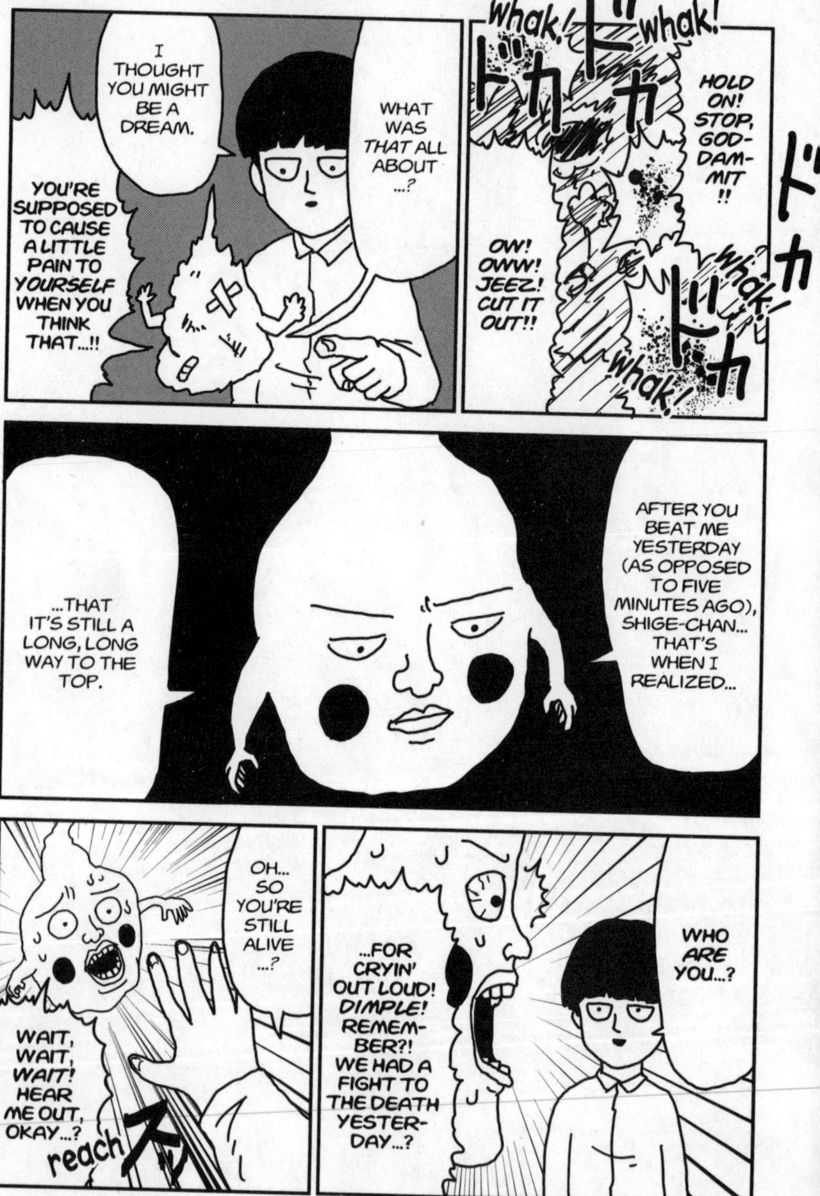
whak! whak!
HOLD ON! STOP, GOD-DAM-MIT!!
OW! OWW! JEEZ! CUT IT OUT!!
whak! whak!
WHAT WAS THAT ALL ABOUT ...?
I THOUGHT YOU MIGHT BE A DREAM.
YOU'RE SUPPOSED TO CAUSE A LITTLE PAIN TO YOURSELF WHEN YOU THINK THAT...!!
AFTER YOU BEAT ME YESTERDAY (AS OPPOSED TO FIVE MINUTES AGO), SHIGE-CHAN... THAT'S WHEN I REALIZED...
...THAT IT'S STILL A LONG, LONG WAY TO THE TOP.
WHO ARE YOU...?
...FOR CRYIN' OUT LOUD! DIMPLE! REMEM-BER?! WE HAD A FIGHT TO THE DEATH YESTER-DAY...?
OH... SO YOU'RE STILL ALIVE ...?
WAIT, WAIT, WAIT! HEAR ME OUT, OKAY...?
reach

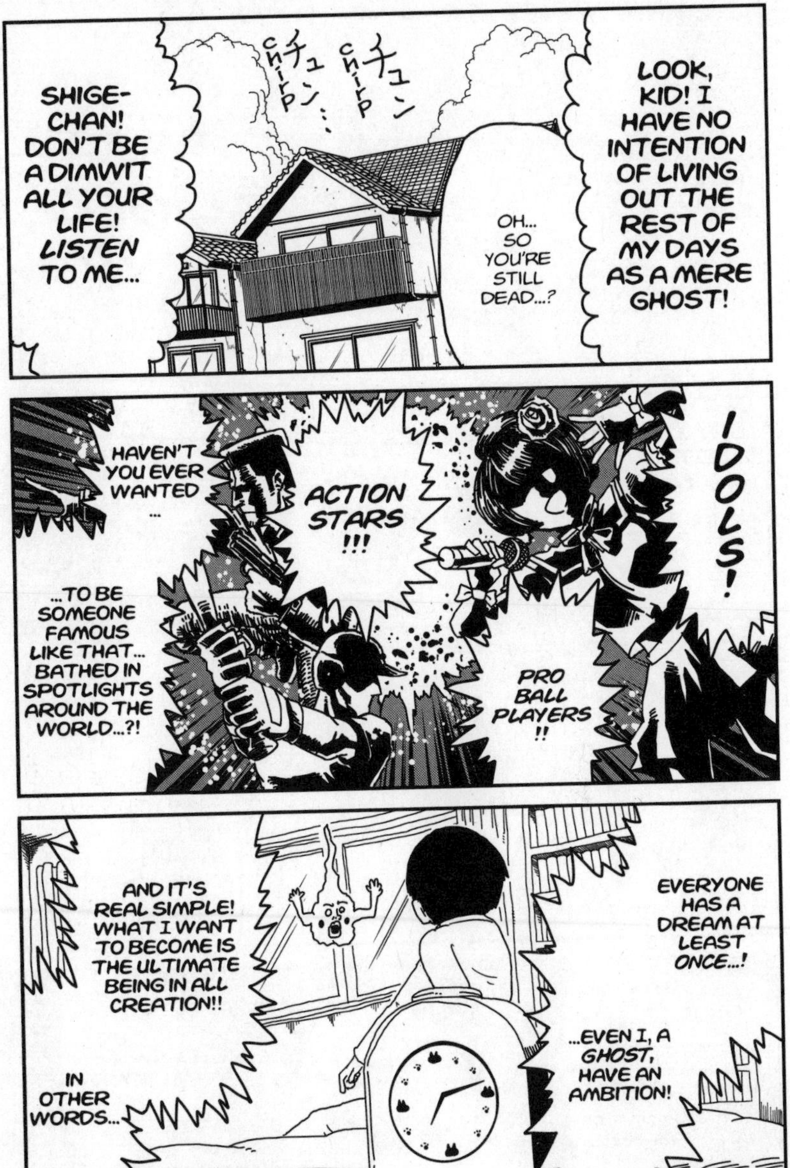
LOOK, KID! I HAVE NO INTENTION OF LIVING OUT THE REST OF MY DAYS AS A MERE GHOST!
OH... SO YOU'RE STILL DEAD...?
チュン chirp
チュン chirp...
SHIGE-CHAN! DON'T BE A DIMWIT ALL YOUR LIFE! LISTEN TO ME...
IDOLS!
PRO BALL PLAYERS!!
ACTION STARS!!!
HAVEN'T YOU EVER WANTED...
...TO BE SOMEONE FAMOUS LIKE THAT... BATHED IN SPOTLIGHTS AROUND THE WORLD...?!
EVERYONE HAS A DREAM AT LEAST ONCE...!
...EVEN I, A GHOST, HAVE AN AMBITION!
AND IT'S REAL SIMPLE! WHAT I WANT TO BECOME IS THE ULTIMATE BEING IN ALL CREATION!!
IN OTHER WORDS...

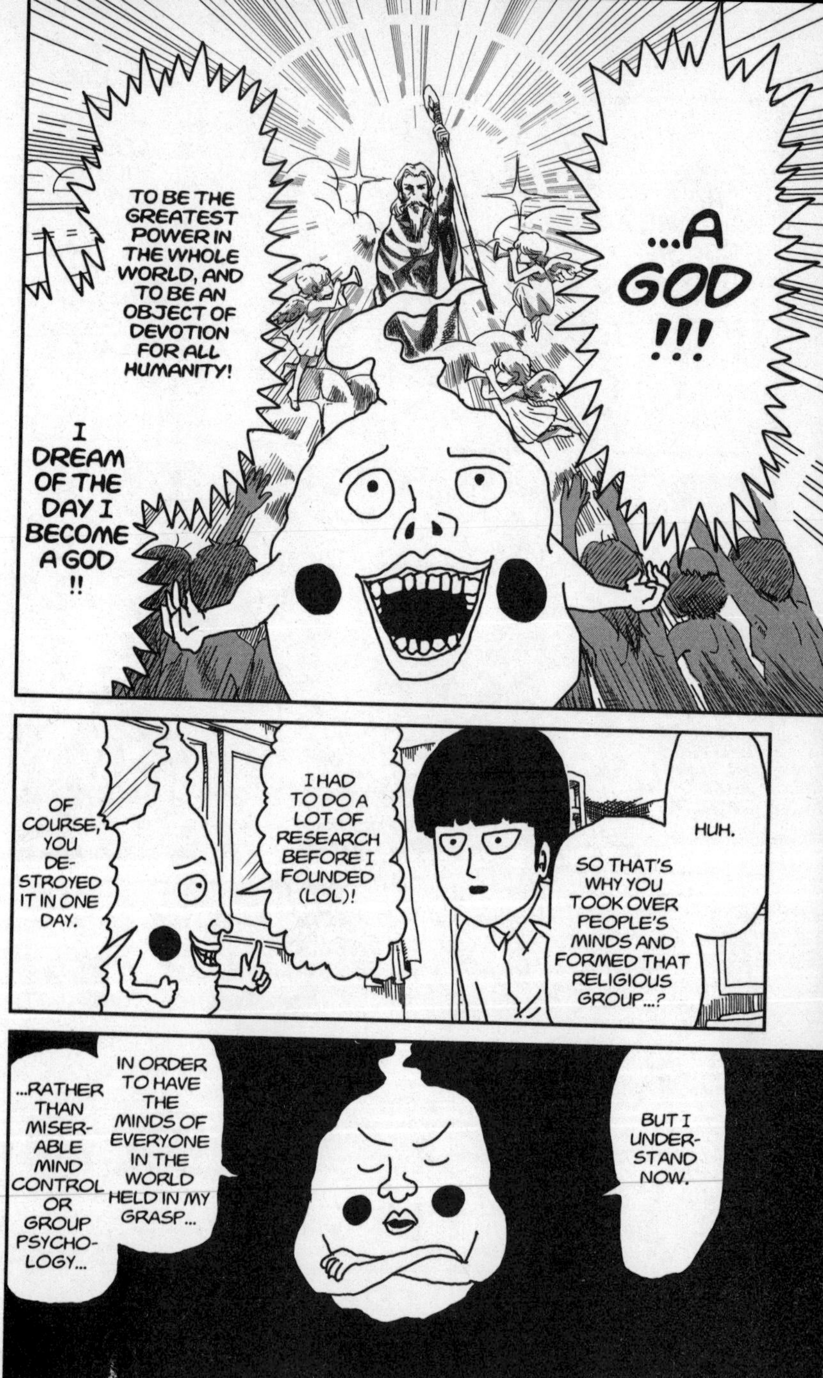
...A GOD!!!
TO BE THE GREATEST POWER IN THE WHOLE WORLD, AND TO BE AN OBJECT OF DEVOTION FOR ALL HUMANITY!
I DREAM OF THE DAY I BECOME A GOD!!
HUH.
SO THAT'S WHY YOU TOOK OVER PEOPLE'S MINDS AND FORMED THAT RELIGIOUS GROUP...?
I HAD TO DO A LOT OF RESEARCH BEFORE I FOUNDED (LOL)!
OF COURSE, YOU DE-STROYED IT IN ONE DAY.
BUT I UNDER-STAND NOW.
IN ORDER TO HAVE THE MINDS OF EVERYONE IN THE WORLD HELD IN MY GRASP...
...RATHER THAN MISER-ABLE MIND CONTROL OR GROUP PSYCHO-LOGY...

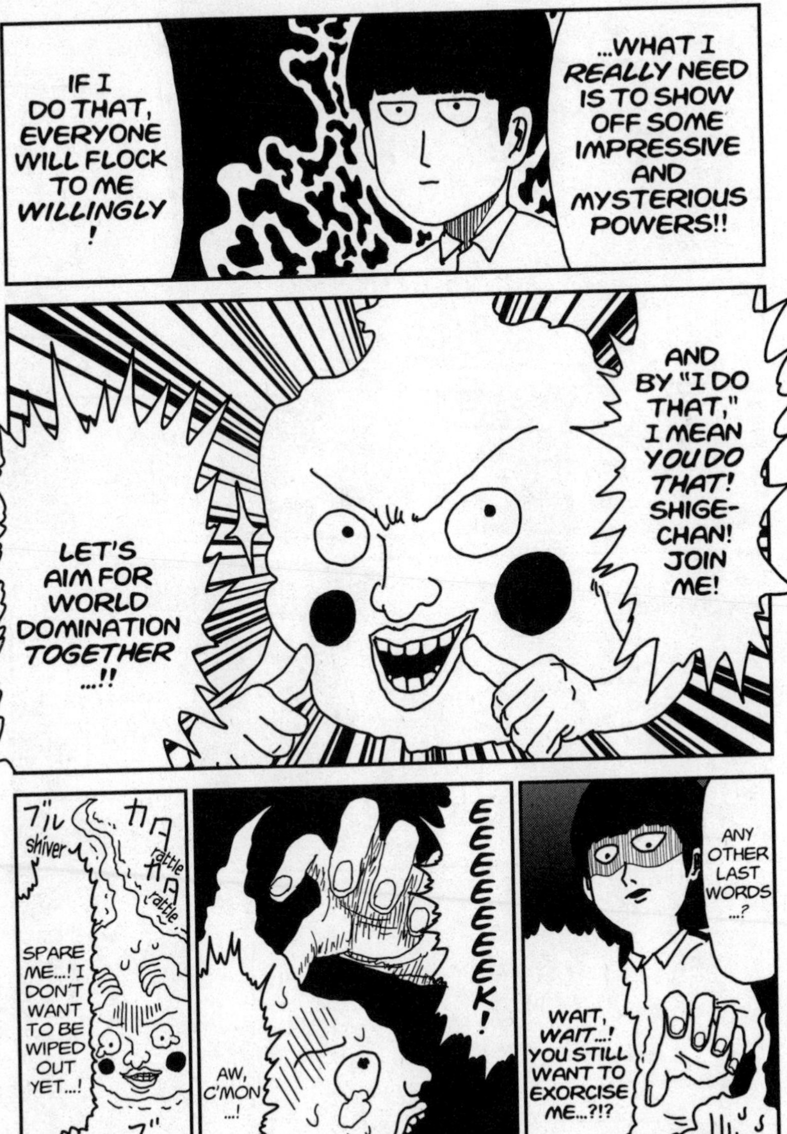
...WHAT I REALLY NEED IS TO SHOW OFF SOME IMPRESSIVE AND MYSTERIOUS POWERS!!
IF I DO THAT, EVERYONE WILL FLOCK TO ME WILLINGLY!
AND BY "I DO THAT," I MEAN YOU DO THAT! SHIGE-CHAN! JOIN ME!
LET'S AIM FOR WORLD DOMINATION TOGETHER...!!
ANY OTHER LAST WORDS...?
WAIT, WAIT...! YOU STILL WANT TO EXORCISE ME...?!?
EEEEEEEEK!
AW, C'MON...!
ブル shiver
カタ rattle
カタ rattle
SPARE ME...! I DON'T WANT TO BE WIPED OUT YET...!
ブル shiver ブル shiver ブル

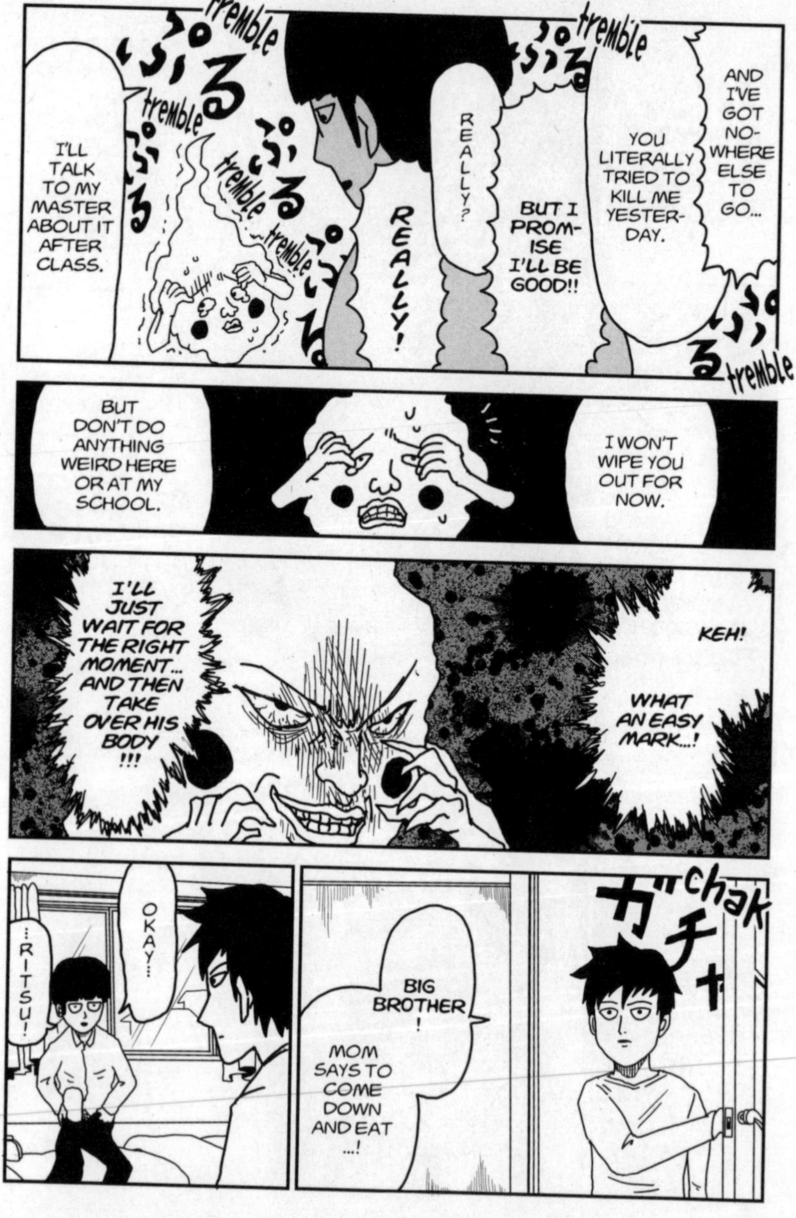
ぷる tremble
AND I'VE GOT NO-WHERE ELSE TO GO...
YOU LITERALLY TRIED TO KILL ME YESTER-DAY.
ぷる tremble
BUT I PROM-ISE I'LL BE GOOD!!
REALLY?
REALLY!
ぷる tremble
ぷる tremble
ぷる tremble
ぷる tremble
ぷる tremble
I'LL TALK TO MY MASTER ABOUT IT AFTER CLASS.
I WON'T WIPE YOU OUT FOR NOW.
BUT DON'T DO ANYTHING WEIRD HERE OR AT MY SCHOOL.
KEH!
WHAT AN EASY MARK...!
I'LL JUST WAIT FOR THE RIGHT MOMENT... AND THEN TAKE OVER HIS BODY!!!
ガチャ chak
BIG BROTHER!
MOM SAYS TO COME DOWN AND EAT...!
OKAY...
...RITSU!

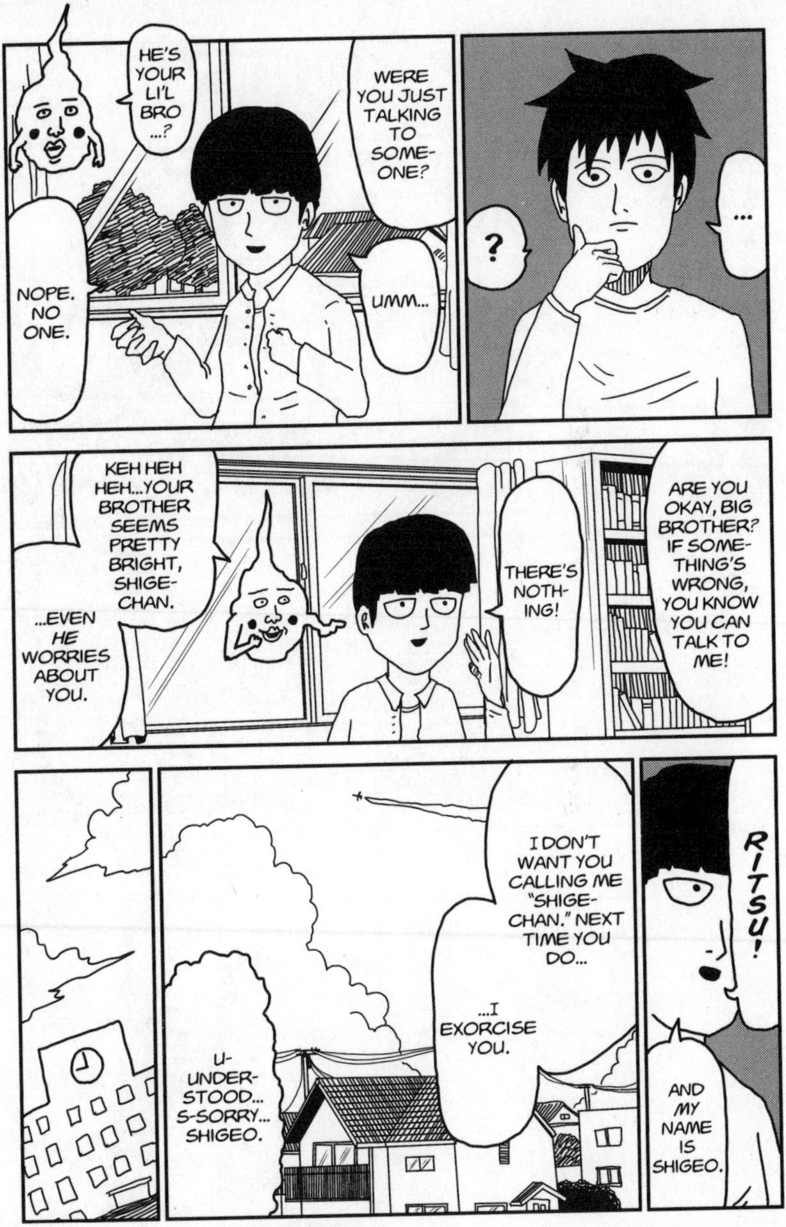
...
?
WERE YOU JUST TALKING TO SOME-ONE?
HE'S YOUR LI'L BRO ...?
UMM...
NOPE. NO ONE.
ARE YOU OKAY, BIG BROTHER? IF SOME-THING'S WRONG, YOU KNOW YOU CAN TALK TO ME!
THERE'S NOTH-ING!
KEH HEH HEH...YOUR BROTHER SEEMS PRETTY BRIGHT, SHIGE-CHAN.
...EVEN HE WORRIES ABOUT YOU.
RITSU!
AND MY NAME IS SHIGEO.
I DON'T WANT YOU CALLING ME "SHIGE-CHAN." NEXT TIME YOU DO...
...I EXORCISE YOU.
U-UNDER-STOOD... S-SORRY... SHIGEO.

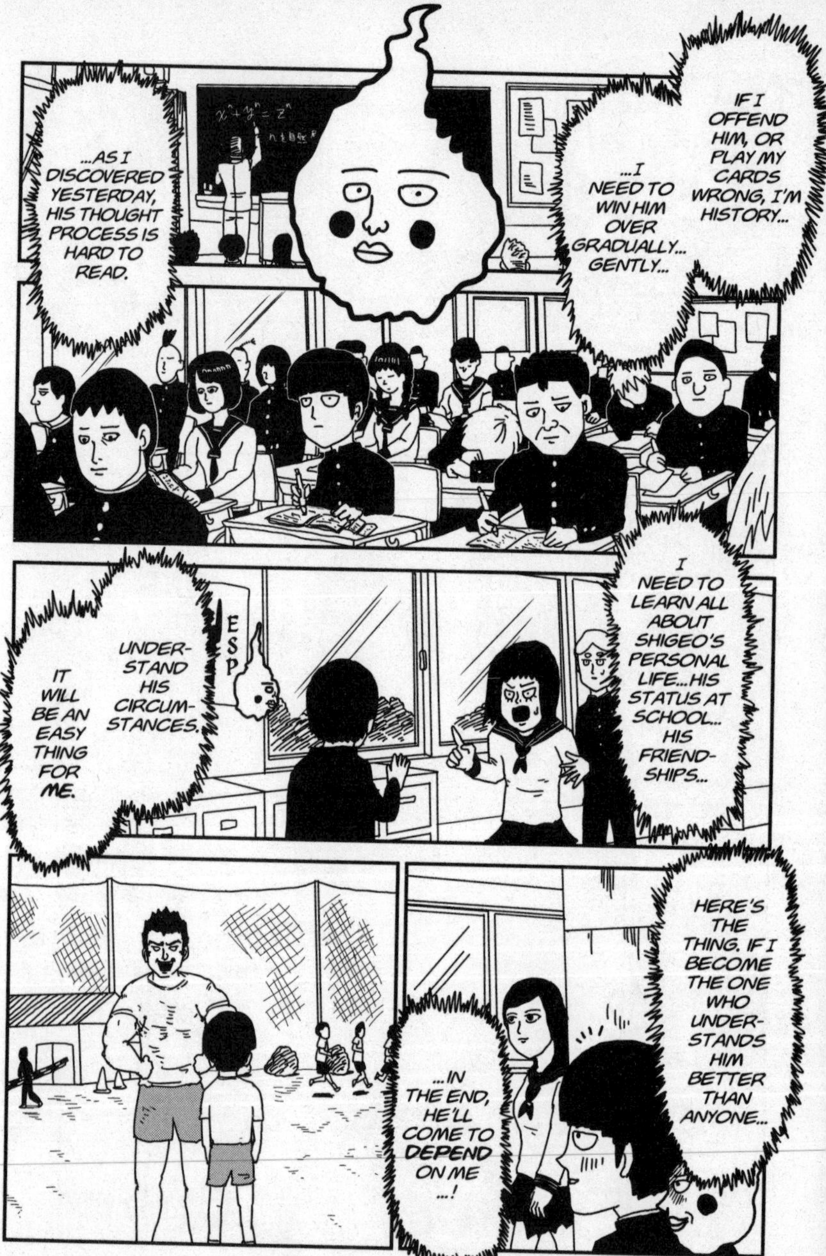
IF I OFFEND HIM, OR PLAY MY CARDS WRONG, I'M HISTORY...
...I NEED TO WIN HIM OVER GRADUALLY... GENTLY...
...AS I DISCOVERED YESTERDAY, HIS THOUGHT PROCESS IS HARD TO READ.
I NEED TO LEARN ALL ABOUT SHIGEO'S PERSONAL LIFE...HIS STATUS AT SCHOOL... HIS FRIENDSHIPS...
ESP
UNDERSTAND HIS CIRCUMSTANCES.
IT WILL BE AN EASY THING FOR ME.
HERE'S THE THING. IF I BECOME THE ONE WHO UNDERSTANDS HIM BETTER THAN ANYONE...
...IN THE END, HE'LL COME TO DEPEND ON ME ...!

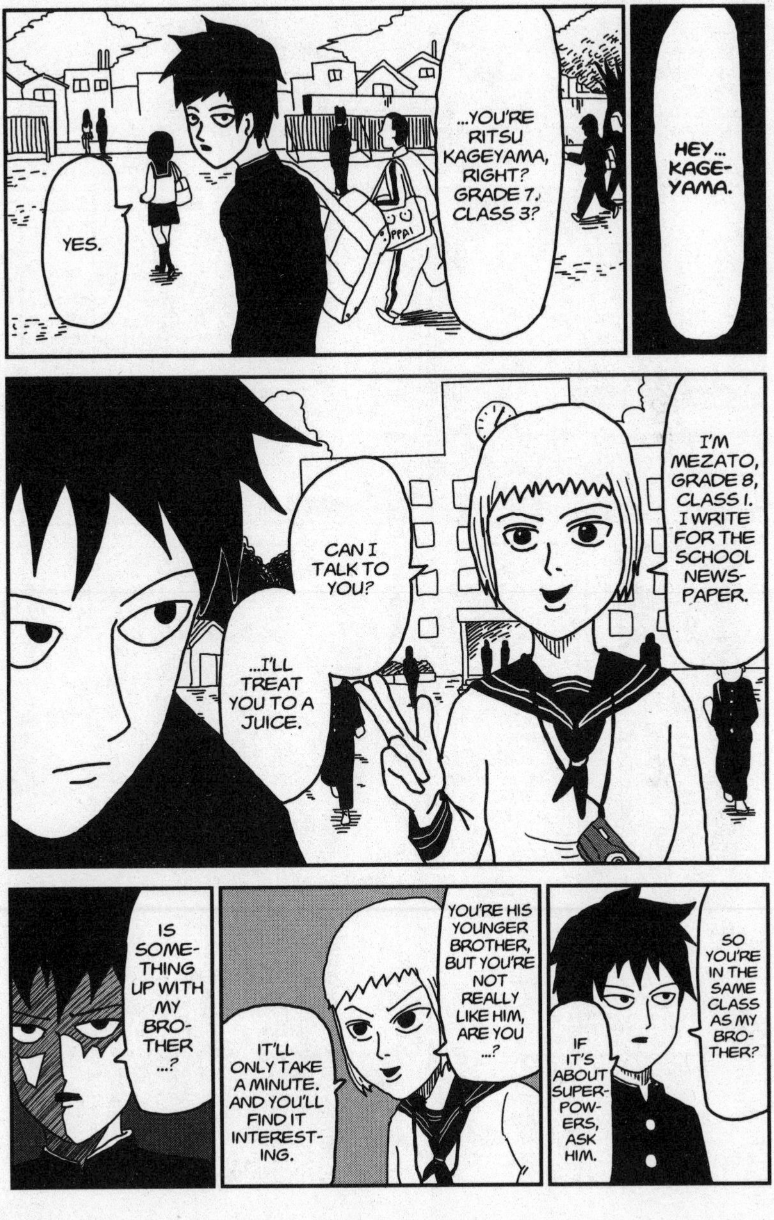
HEY... KAGE-YAMA.
...YOU'RE RITSU KAGEYAMA, RIGHT? GRADE 7, CLASS 3?
YES.
I'M MEZATO, GRADE 8, CLASS 1. I WRITE FOR THE SCHOOL NEWS-PAPER.
CAN I TALK TO YOU?
...I'LL TREAT YOU TO A JUICE.
SO YOU'RE IN THE SAME CLASS AS MY BRO-THER?
IF IT'S ABOUT SUPER-POW-ERS, ASK HIM.
YOU'RE HIS YOUNGER BROTHER, BUT YOU'RE NOT REALLY LIKE HIM, ARE YOU ...?
IT'LL ONLY TAKE A MINUTE. AND YOU'LL FIND IT INTEREST-ING.
IS SOME-THING UP WITH MY BRO-THER ...?

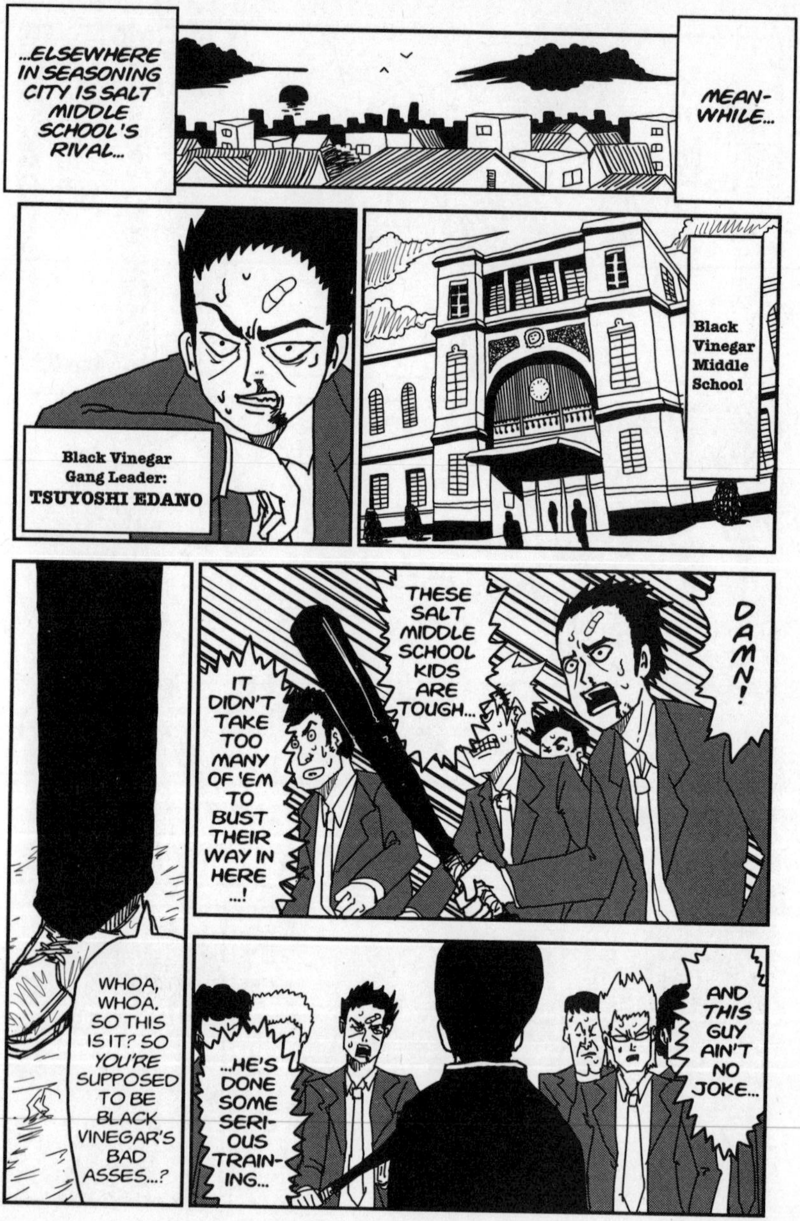
MEAN-WHILE...
...ELSEWHERE IN SEASONING CITY IS SALT MIDDLE SCHOOL'S RIVAL...
Black Vinegar Middle School
Black Vinegar Gang Leader: TSUYOSHI EDANO
DAMN!
THESE SALT MIDDLE SCHOOL KIDS ARE TOUGH...
IT DIDN'T TAKE TOO MANY OF 'EM TO BUST THEIR WAY IN HERE ...!
AND THIS GUY AIN'T NO JOKE...
...HE'S DONE SOME SERI-OUS TRAIN-ING...
WHOA, WHOA. SO THIS IS IT? SO YOU'RE SUPPOSED TO BE BLACK VINEGAR'S BAD ASSES...?

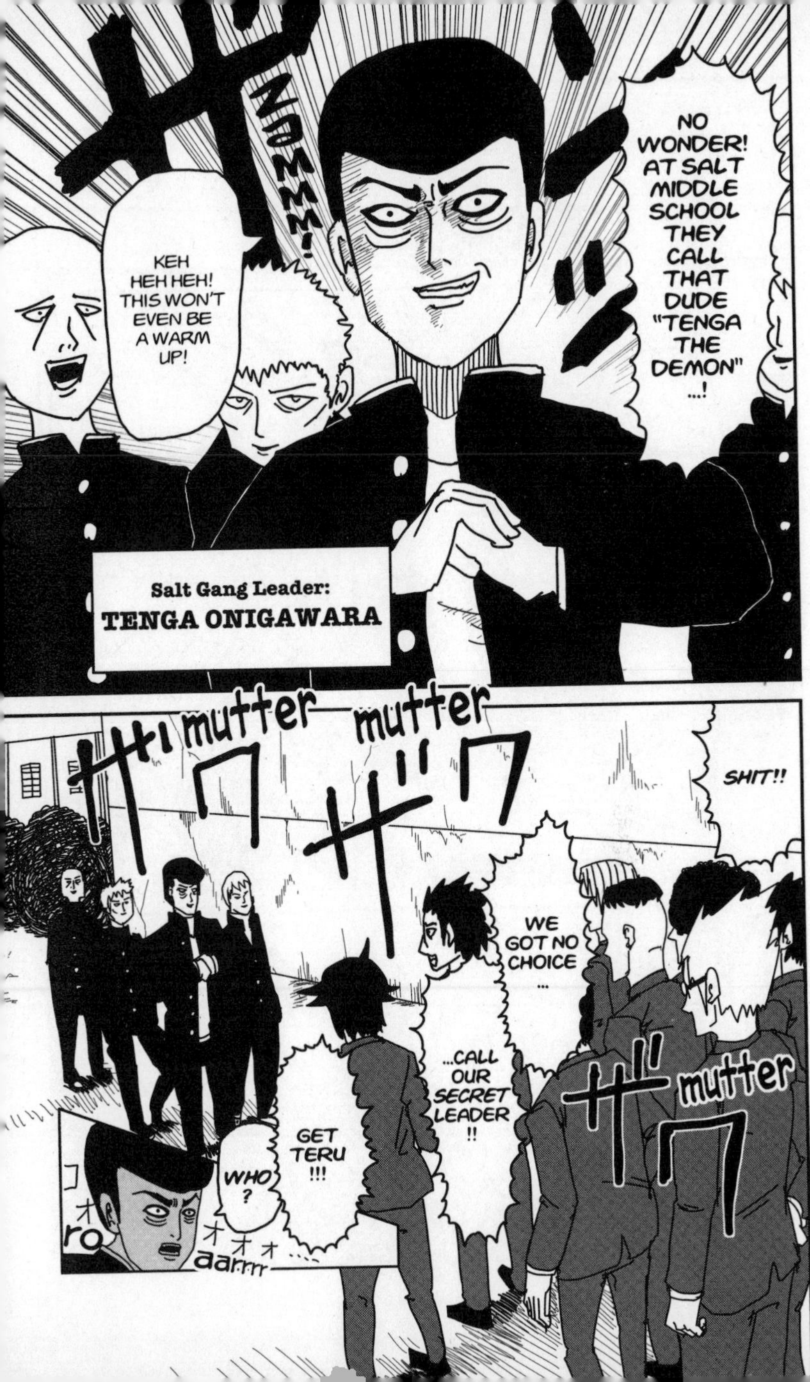
NO WONDER! AT SALT MIDDLE SCHOOL THEY CALL THAT DUDE "TENGA THE DEMON" ...!
ZAMMM!
KEH HEH HEH! THIS WON'T EVEN BE A WARM UP!
Salt Gang Leader:
TENGA ONIGAWARA
mutter mutter
SHIT!!
WE GOT NO CHOICE ...
...CALL OUR SECRET LEADER !!
mutter
GET TERU !!!
WHO ?
roaarrrr

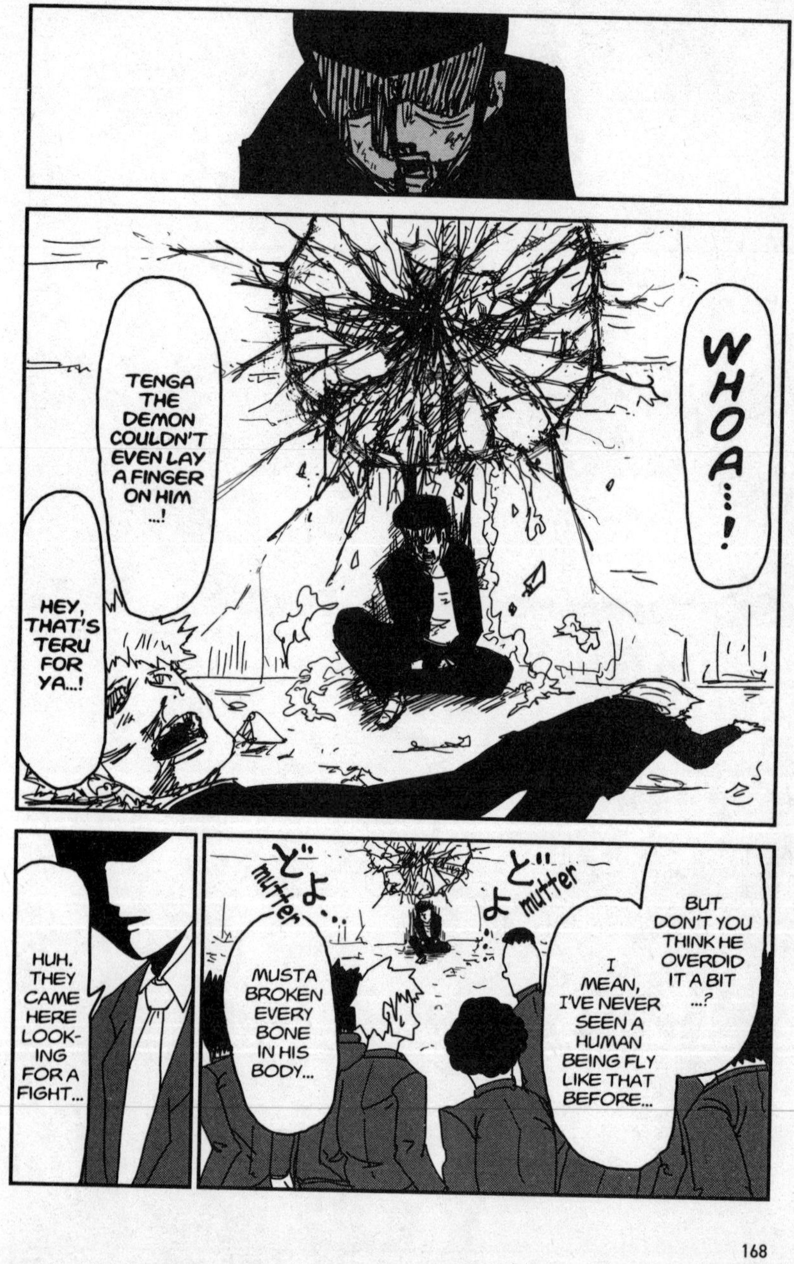
WHOA...!
TENGA THE DEMON COULDN'T EVEN LAY A FINGER ON HIM ...!
HEY, THAT'S TERU FOR YA...!
どよ mutter
どよ mutter
BUT DON'T YOU THINK HE OVERDID IT A BIT ...?
I MEAN, I'VE NEVER SEEN A HUMAN BEING FLY LIKE THAT BEFORE...
MUSTA BROKEN EVERY BONE IN HIS BODY...
HUH. THEY CAME HERE LOOKING FOR A FIGHT...

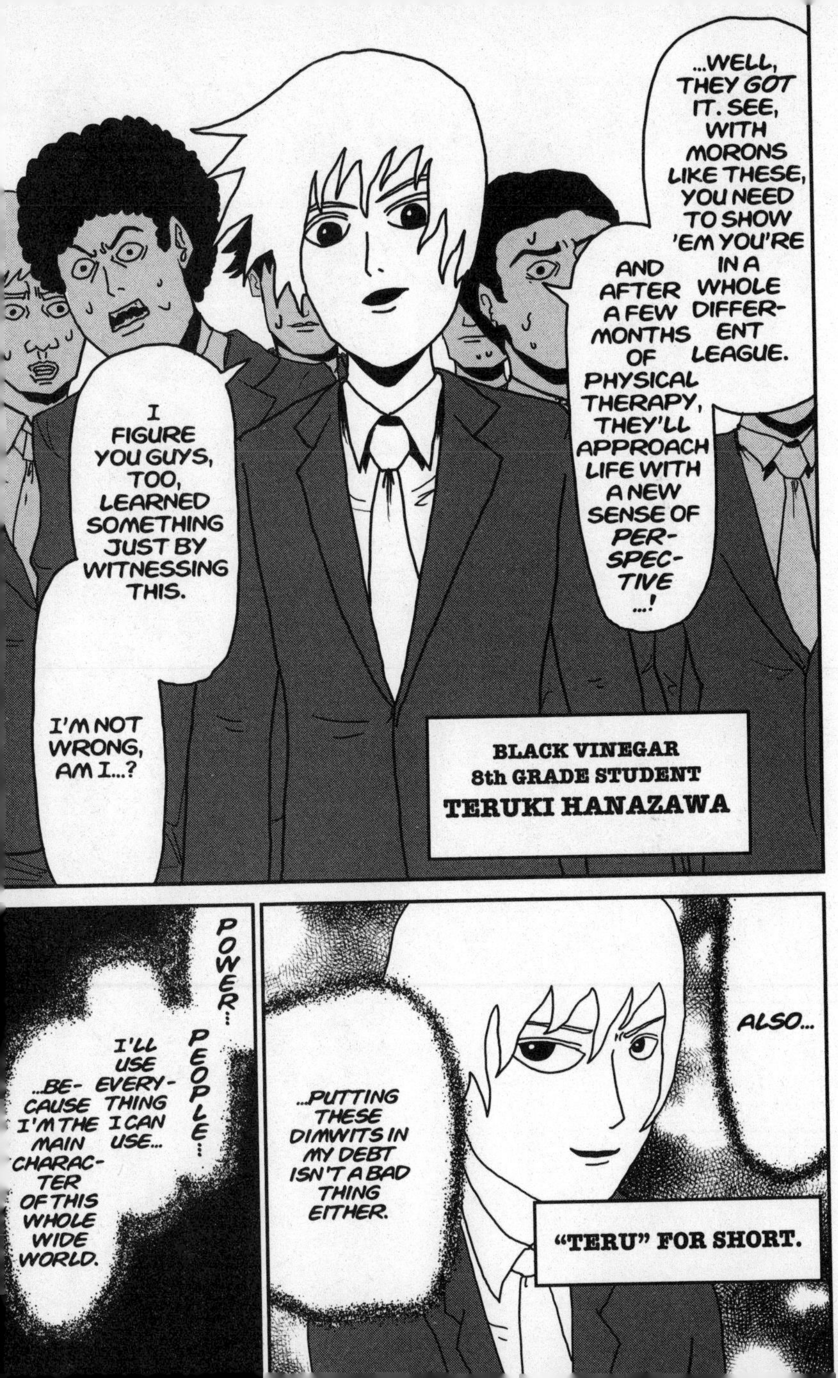
...WELL, THEY GOT IT. SEE, WITH MORONS LIKE THESE, YOU NEED TO SHOW 'EM YOU'RE IN A WHOLE DIFFERENT LEAGUE.
AND AFTER A FEW MONTHS OF PHYSICAL THERAPY, THEY'LL APPROACH LIFE WITH A NEW SENSE OF PERSPECTIVE...!
BLACK VINEGAR 8th GRADE STUDENT TERUKI HANAZAWA
I FIGURE YOU GUYS, TOO, LEARNED SOMETHING JUST BY WITNESSING THIS.
I'M NOT WRONG, AM I...?
ALSO...
...PUTTING THESE DIMWITS IN MY DEBT ISN'T A BAD THING EITHER.
“TERU” FOR SHORT.
POWER...
PEOPLE...
I'LL USE EVERYTHING I CAN USE...
...BECAUSE I'M THE MAIN CHARACTER OF THIS WHOLE WIDE WORLD.

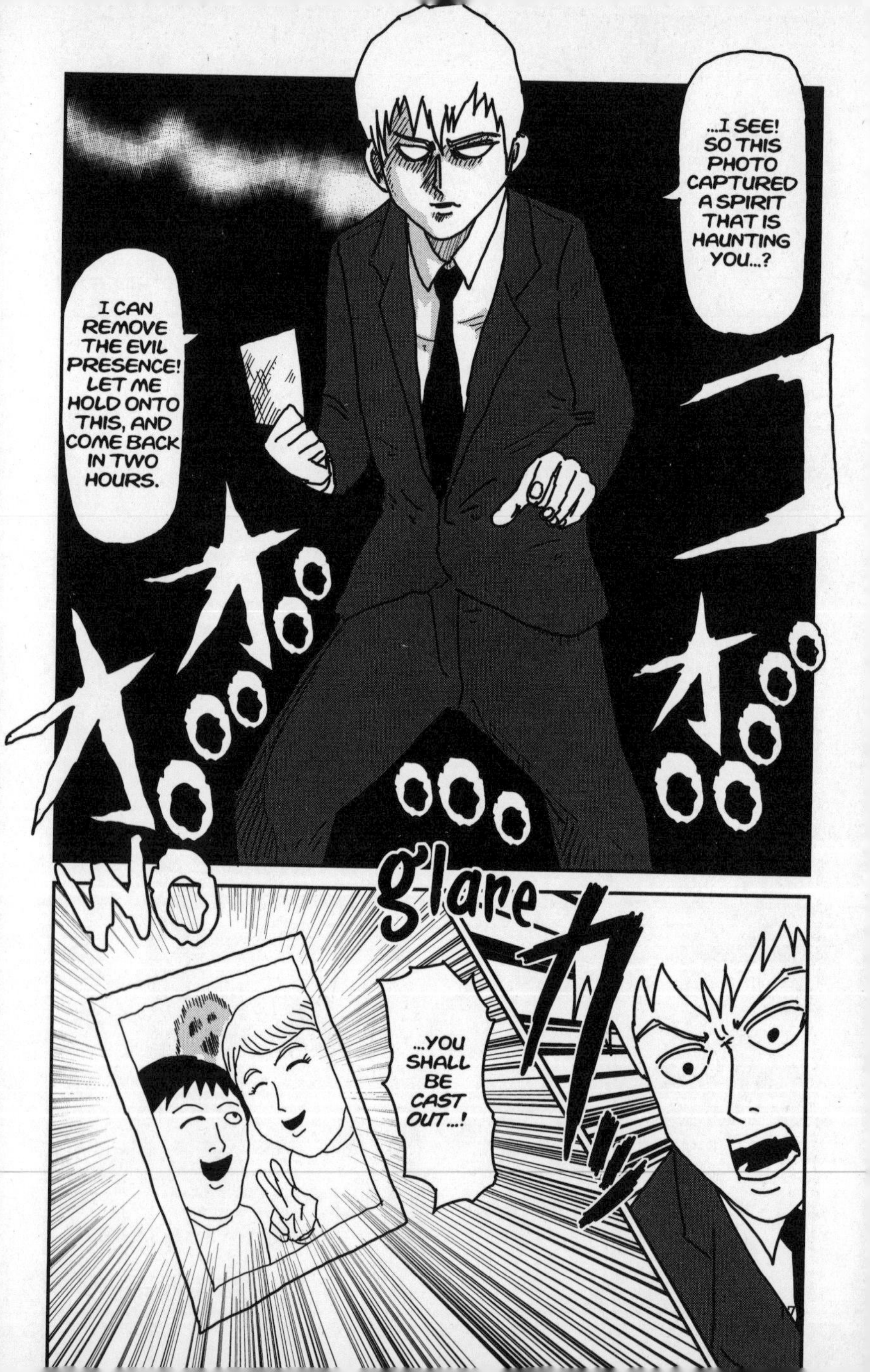
...I SEE! SO THIS PHOTO CAPTURED A SPIRIT THAT IS HAUNTING YOU...?
I CAN REMOVE THE EVIL PRESENCE! LET ME HOLD ONTO THIS, AND COME BACK IN TWO HOURS.
WO
glare
...YOU SHALL BE CAST OUT...!

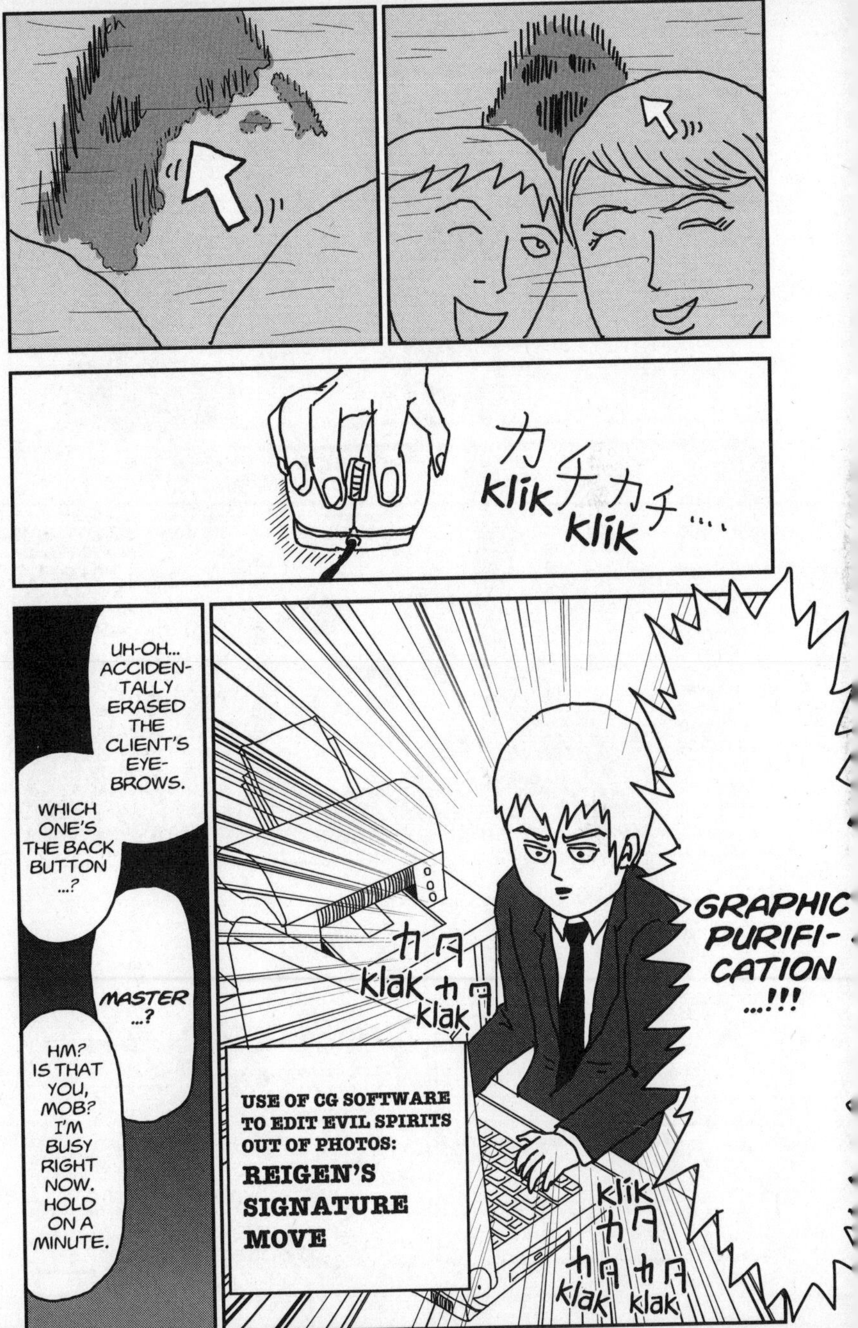
カチ klik
カチ klik....
GRAPHIC PURIFI-CATION ...!!!
カタ klak カタ klak
USE OF CG SOFTWARE TO EDIT EVIL SPIRITS OUT OF PHOTOS: REIGEN'S SIGNATURE MOVE
klik カタ カタ klak カタ klak
UH-OH... ACCIDEN-TALLY ERASED THE CLIENT'S EYE-BROWS.
WHICH ONE'S THE BACK BUTTON ...?
MASTER ...?
HM? IS THAT YOU, MOB? I'M BUSY RIGHT NOW. HOLD ON A MINUTE.

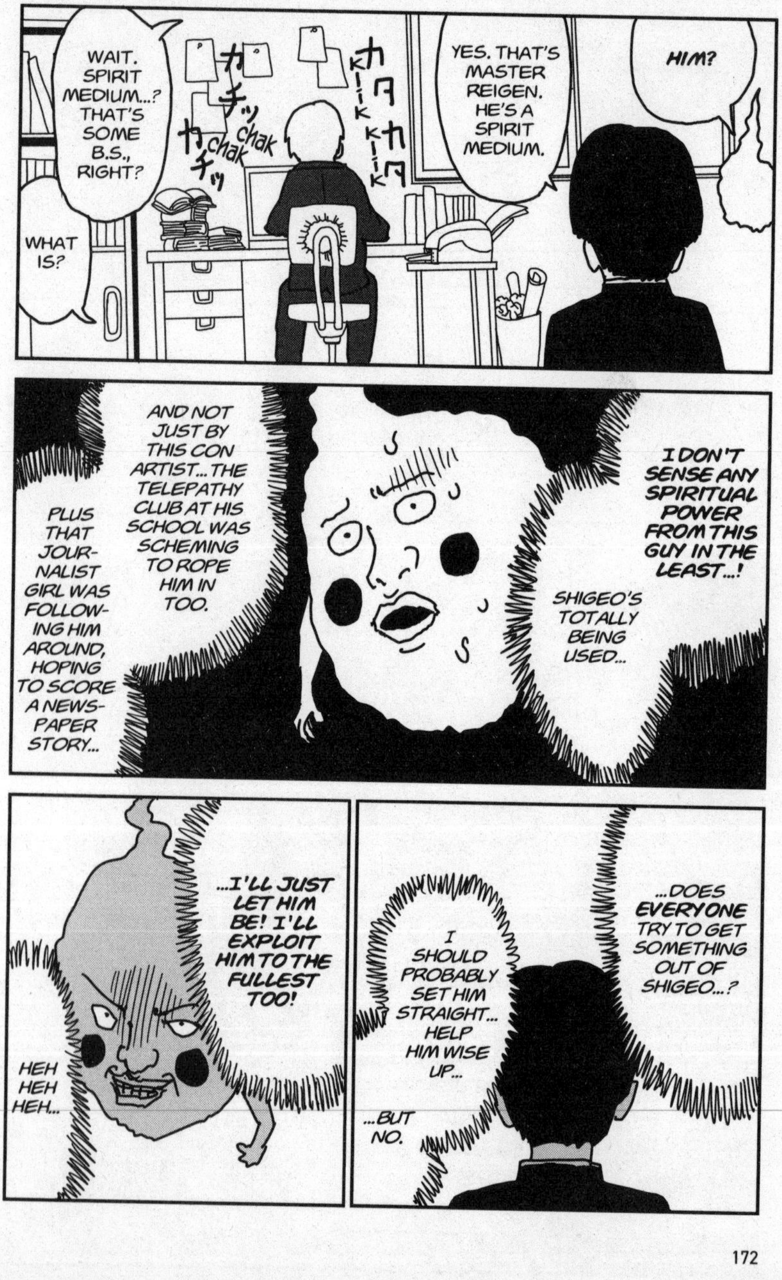
HIM?
YES. THAT'S MASTER REIGEN. HE'S A SPIRIT MEDIUM.
カタ klik
カタ klik
カチッ chak
カチッ chak
WAIT. SPIRIT MEDIUM...? THAT'S SOME B.S., RIGHT?
WHAT IS?
I DON'T SENSE ANY SPIRITUAL POWER FROM THIS GUY IN THE LEAST...!
SHIGEO'S TOTALLY BEING USED...
AND NOT JUST BY THIS CON ARTIST... THE TELEPATHY CLUB AT HIS SCHOOL WAS SCHEMING TO ROPE HIM IN TOO.
PLUS THAT JOUR-NALIST GIRL WAS FOLLOW-ING HIM AROUND, HOPING TO SCORE A NEWS-PAPER STORY...
...DOES EVERYONE TRY TO GET SOMETHING OUT OF SHIGEO...?
I SHOULD PROBABLY SET HIM STRAIGHT... HELP HIM WISE UP...
...BUT NO.
...I'LL JUST LET HIM BE! I'LL EXPLOIT HIM TO THE FULLEST TOO!
HEH HEH HEH...

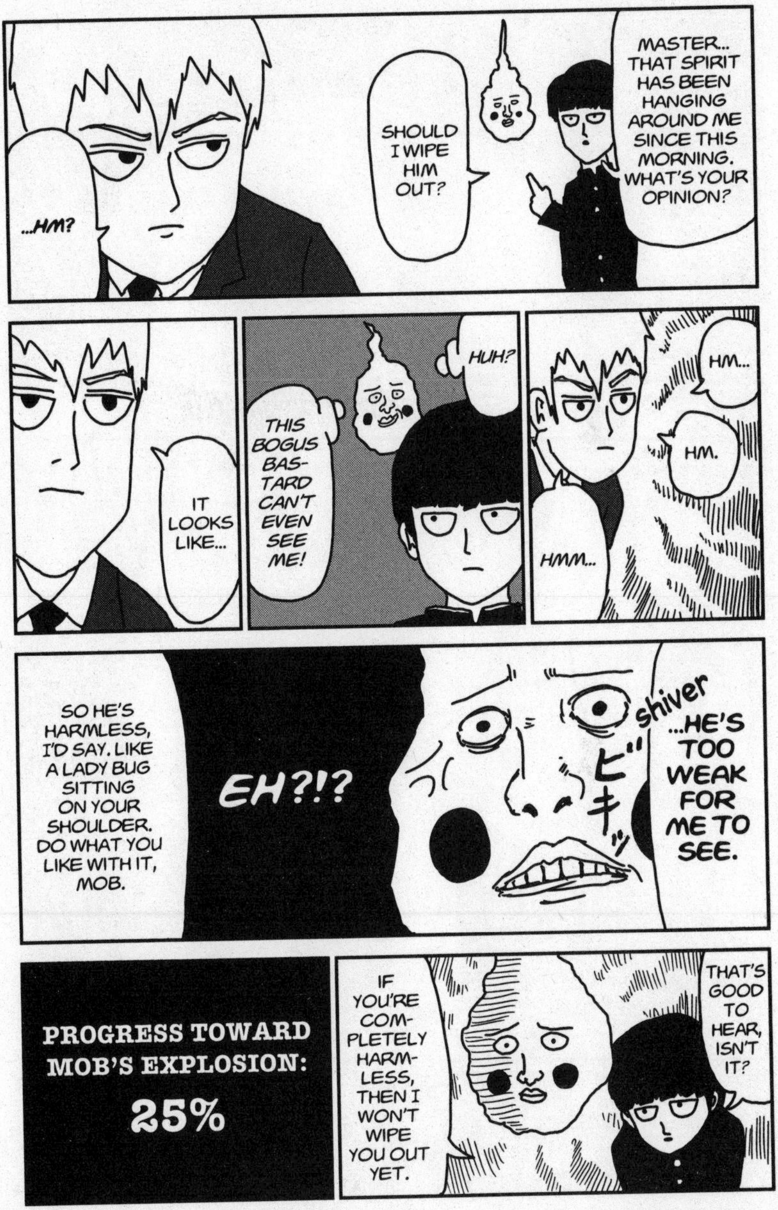
MASTER... THAT SPIRIT HAS BEEN HANGING AROUND ME SINCE THIS MORNING. WHAT'S YOUR OPINION?
SHOULD I WIPE HIM OUT?
...HM?
HM...
HM.
HMM...
HUH?
THIS BOGUS BAS-TARD CAN'T EVEN SEE ME!
IT LOOKS LIKE...
...HE'S TOO WEAK FOR ME TO SEE.
shiver
ビキッ
EH?!?
SO HE'S HARMLESS, I'D SAY. LIKE A LADY BUG SITTING ON YOUR SHOULDER. DO WHAT YOU LIKE WITH IT, MOB.
THAT'S GOOD TO HEAR, ISN'T IT?
IF YOU'RE COM-PLETELY HARM-LESS, THEN I WON'T WIPE YOU OUT YET.
PROGRESS TOWARD MOB'S EXPLOSION:
25%

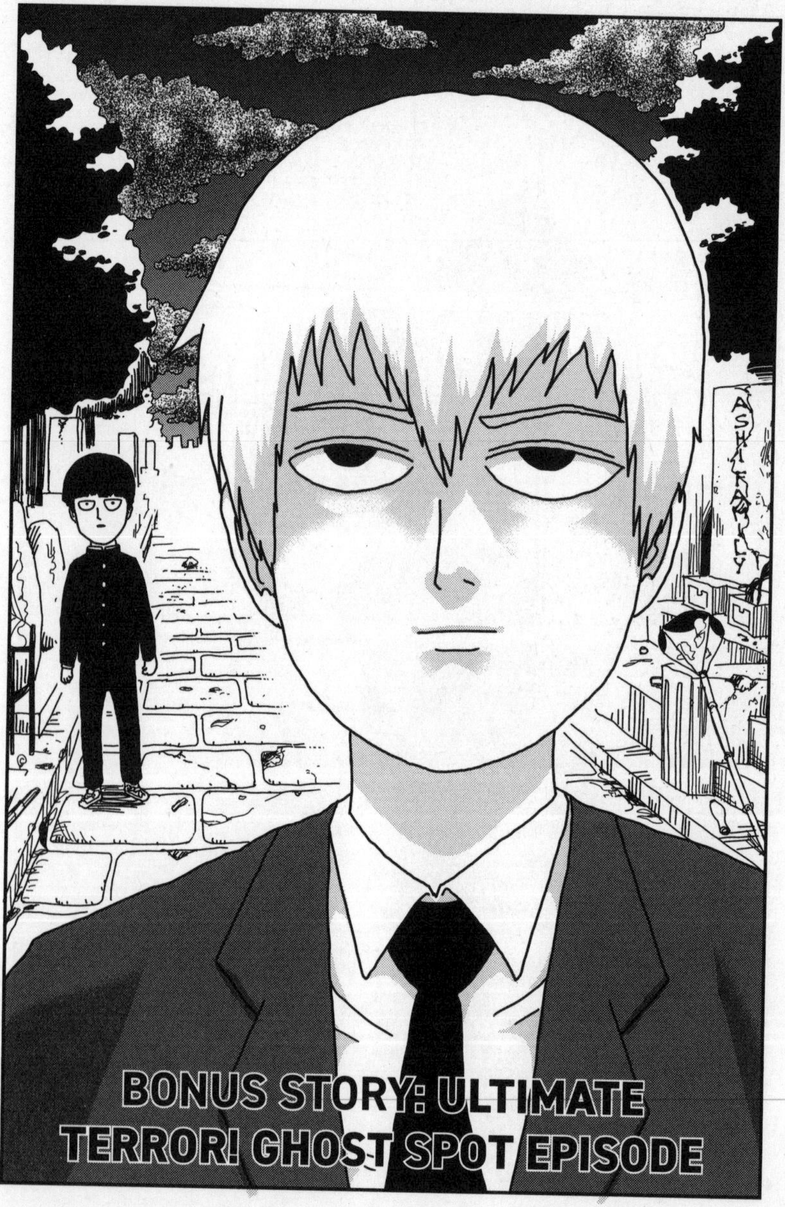
BONUS STORY: ULTIMATE
TERROR! GHOST SPOT EPISODE

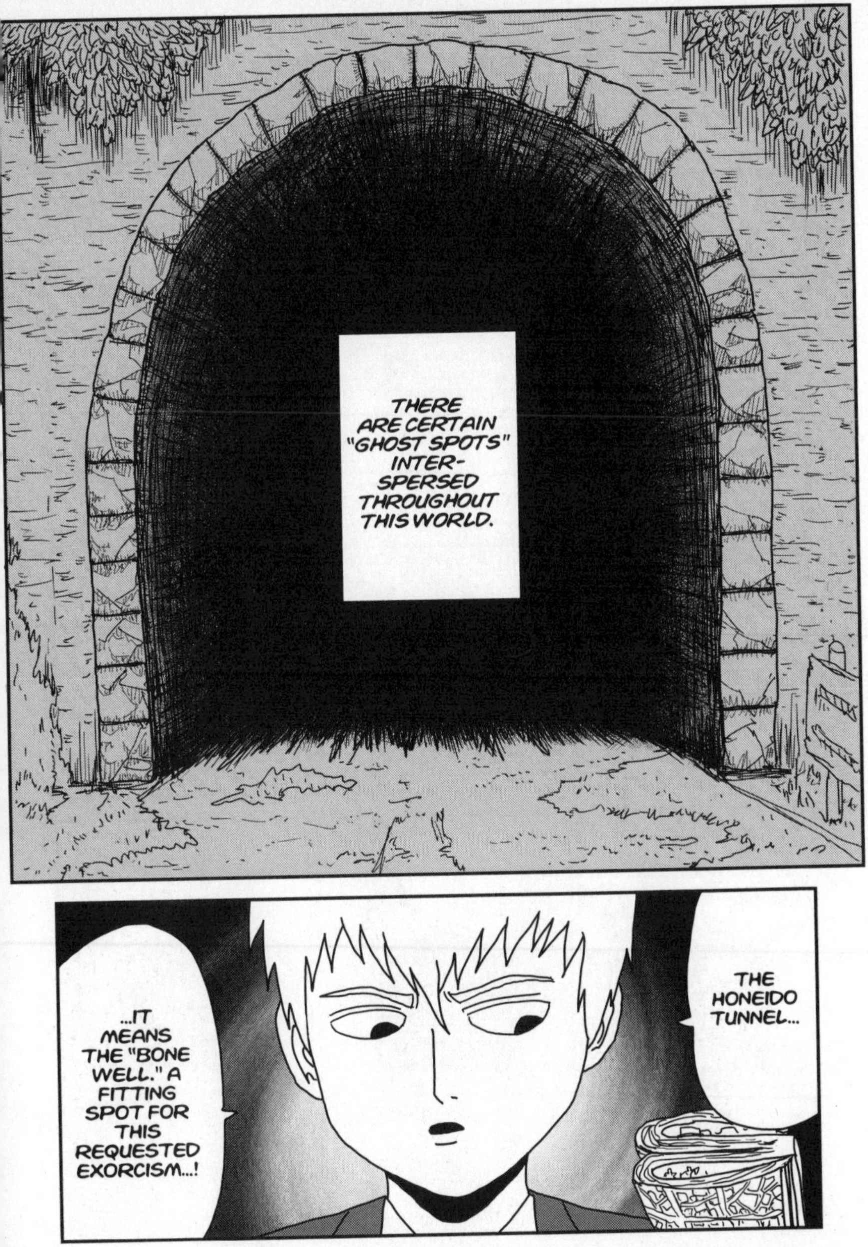
THERE ARE CERTAIN "GHOST SPOTS" INTER-SPERSED THROUGHOUT THIS WORLD.
THE HONEIDO TUNNEL...
...IT MEANS THE "BONE WELL." A FITTING SPOT FOR THIS REQUESTED EXORCISM...!

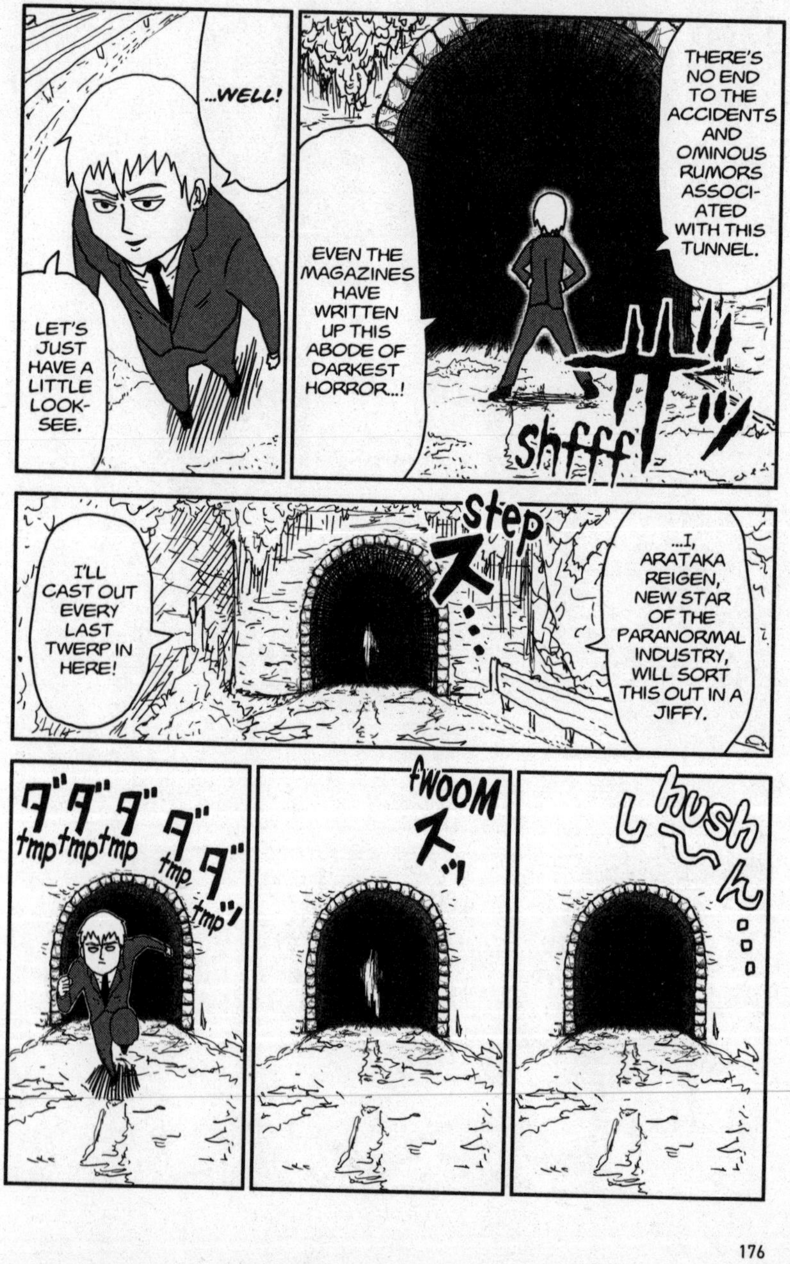
THERE'S NO END TO THE ACCIDENTS AND OMINOUS RUMORS ASSOCIATED WITH THIS TUNNEL.
EVEN THE MAGAZINES HAVE WRITTEN UP THIS ABODE OF DARKEST HORROR...!
ザッ
shfff
...WELL!
LET'S JUST HAVE A LITTLE LOOK-SEE.
...I, ARATAKA REIGEN, NEW STAR OF THE PARANORMAL INDUSTRY, WILL SORT THIS OUT IN A JIFFY.
ス...
step
I'LL CAST OUT EVERY LAST TWERP IN HERE!
し〜ん...
hush
スッ
fwoom
ダダダダダッ
tmp tmp tmp tmp tmp

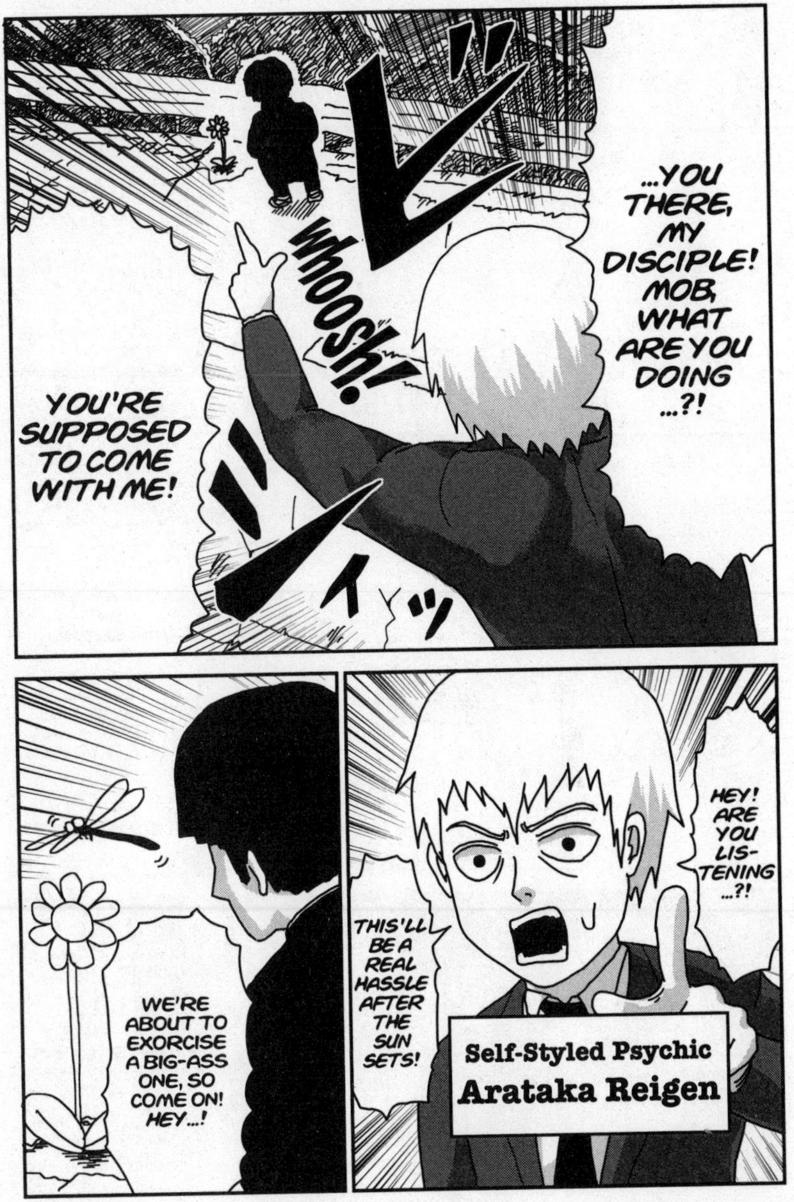
...YOU THERE, MY DISCIPLE! MOB, WHAT ARE YOU DOING ...?!
WHOOSH!
YOU'RE SUPPOSED TO COME WITH ME!
HEY! ARE YOU LIS-TENING ...?!
THIS'LL BE A REAL HASSLE AFTER THE SUN SETS!
Self-Styled Psychic
Arataka Reigen
WE'RE ABOUT TO EXORCISE A BIG-ASS ONE, SO COME ON! HEY...!

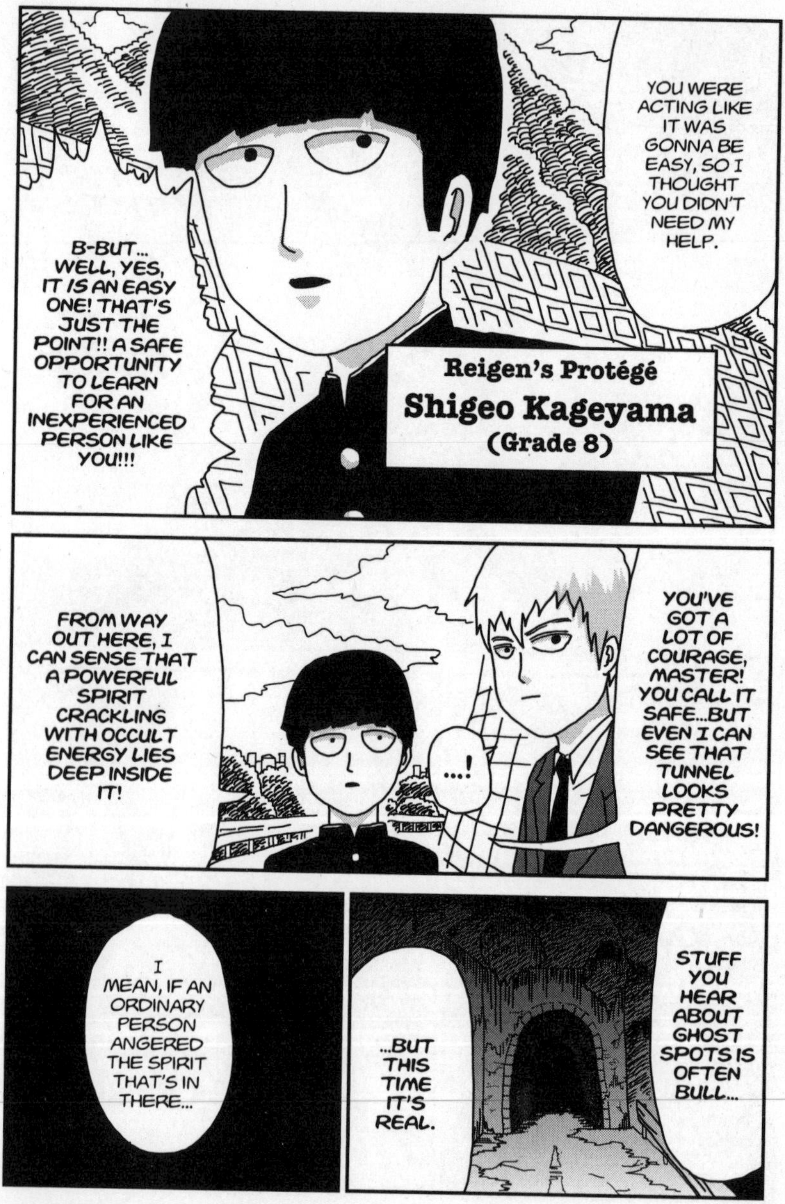
YOU WERE ACTING LIKE IT WAS GONNA BE EASY, SO I THOUGHT YOU DIDN'T NEED MY HELP.
B-BUT... WELL, YES, IT IS AN EASY ONE! THAT'S JUST THE POINT!! A SAFE OPPORTUNITY TO LEARN FOR AN INEXPERIENCED PERSON LIKE YOU!!!
Reigen's Protégé
Shigeo Kageyama
(Grade 8)
YOU'VE GOT A LOT OF COURAGE, MASTER! YOU CALL IT SAFE...BUT EVEN I CAN SEE THAT TUNNEL LOOKS PRETTY DANGEROUS!
...!
FROM WAY OUT HERE, I CAN SENSE THAT A POWERFUL SPIRIT CRACKLING WITH OCCULT ENERGY LIES DEEP INSIDE IT!
STUFF YOU HEAR ABOUT GHOST SPOTS IS OFTEN BULL...
...BUT THIS TIME IT'S REAL.
I MEAN, IF AN ORDINARY PERSON ANGERED THE SPIRIT THAT'S IN THERE...

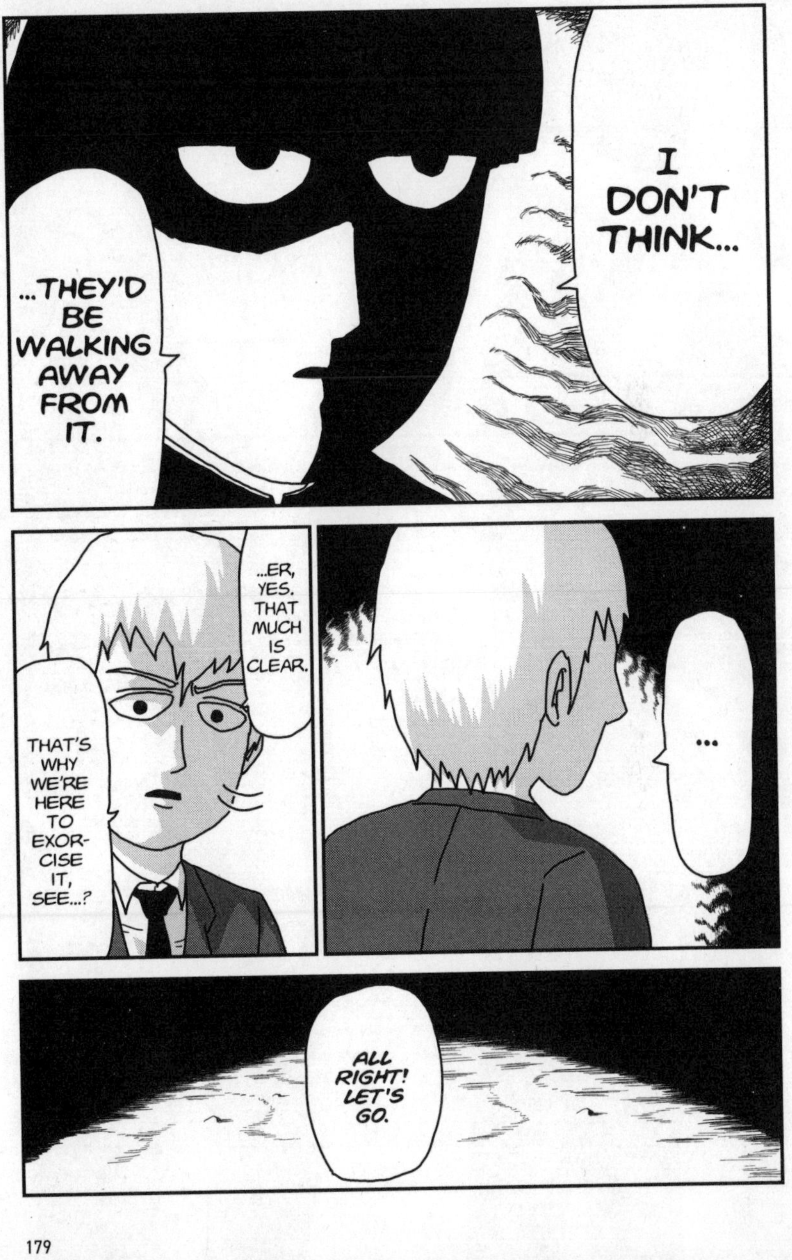

I DON'T THINK...
...THEY'D BE WALKING AWAY FROM IT.
...
...ER, YES. THAT MUCH IS CLEAR.
THAT'S WHY WE'RE HERE TO EXORCISE IT, SEE...?
ALL RIGHT! LET'S GO.

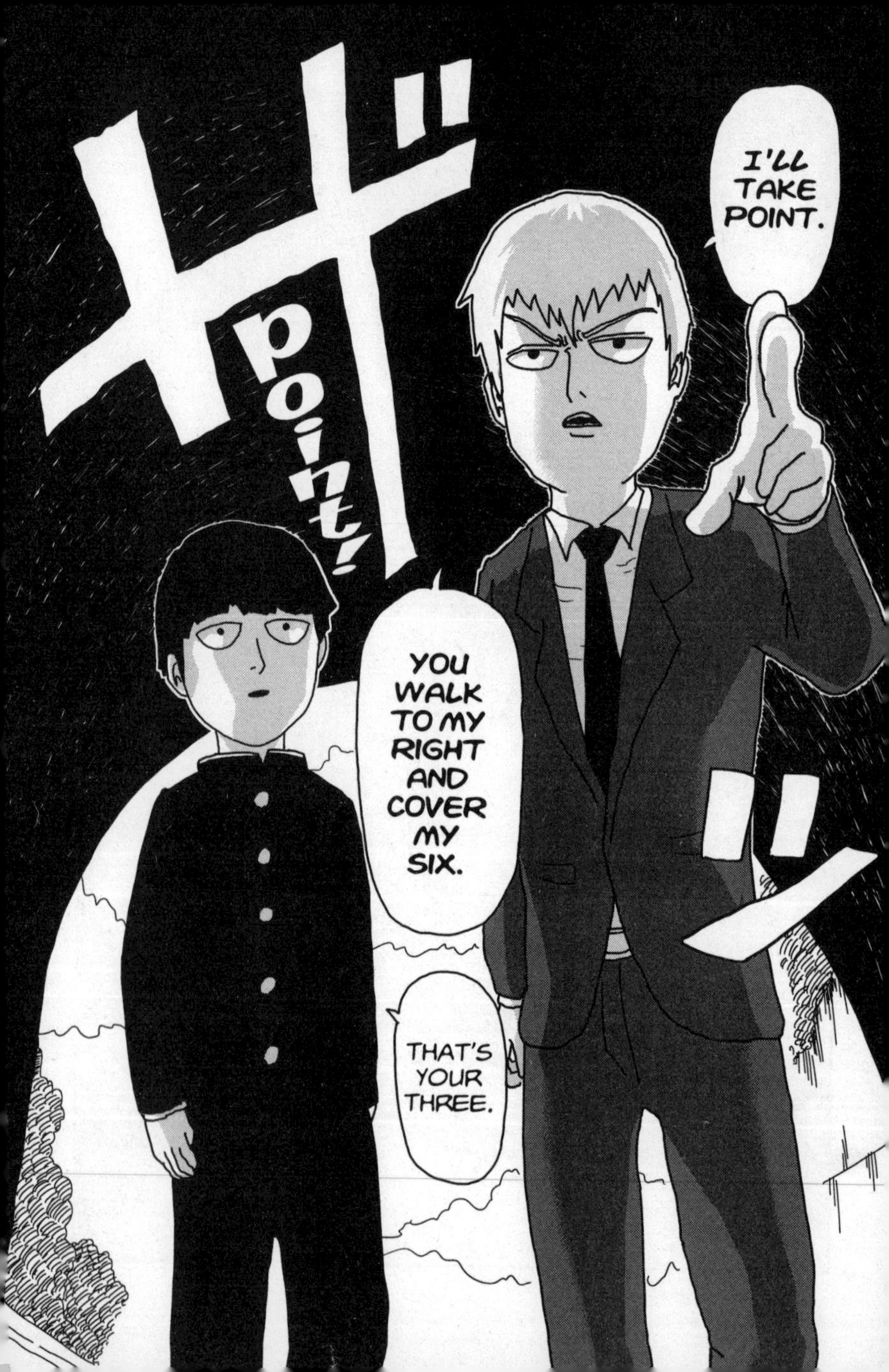
I'LL TAKE POINT.
point!
YOU WALK TO MY RIGHT AND COVER MY SIX.
THAT'S YOUR THREE.

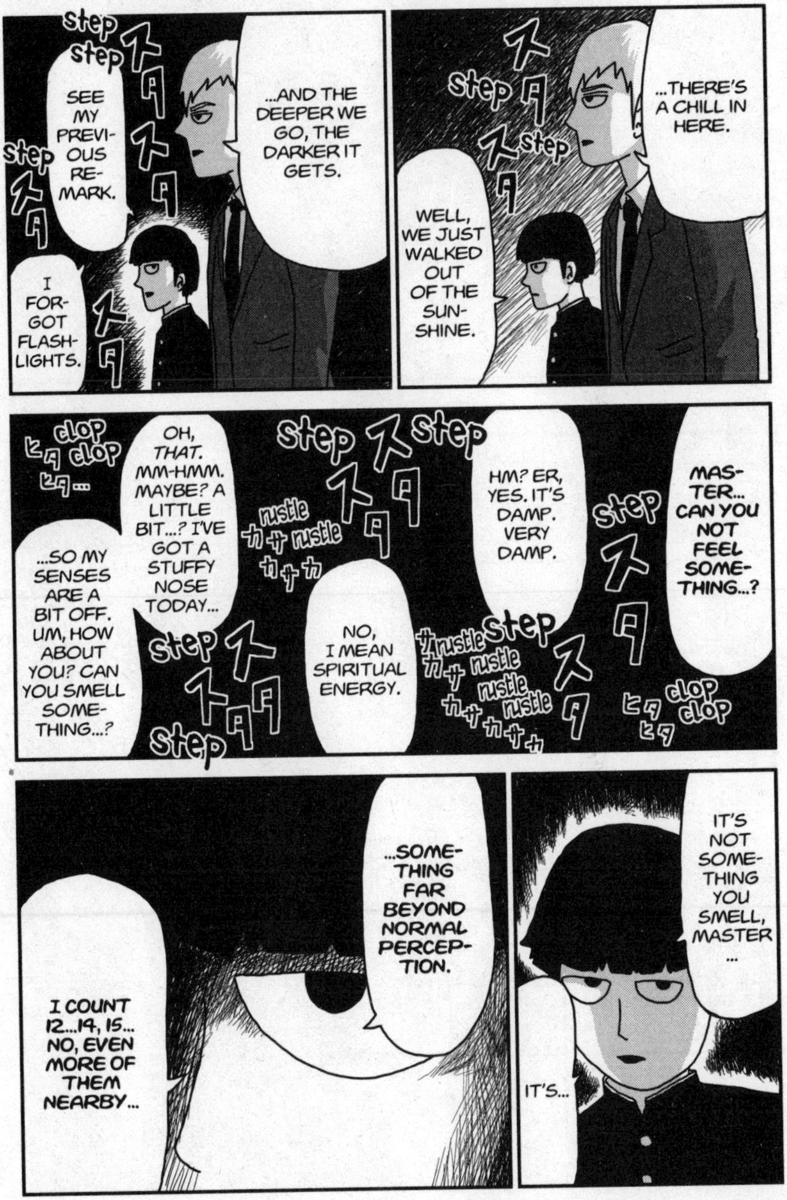
...THERE'S A CHILL IN HERE.
step スタ step スタ
WELL, WE JUST WALKED OUT OF THE SUNSHINE.
...AND THE DEEPER WE GO, THE DARKER IT GETS.
step step スタスタ
SEE MY PREVIOUS REMARK.
step スタ
I FORGOT FLASHLIGHTS.
スタ
MASTER... CAN YOU NOT FEEL SOMETHING...?
step スタ
clop clop ヒタヒタ
HM? ER, YES. IT'S DAMP. VERY DAMP.
step スタ step
step スタ
rustle rustle rustle rustle サカサ カサカサカ
NO, I MEAN SPIRITUAL ENERGY.
rustle カサ rustle カサカ
OH, THAT. MM-HMM. MAYBE? A LITTLE BIT...? I'VE GOT A STUFFY NOSE TODAY...
step スタスタ step
clop ヒタ clop ヒタ...
...SO MY SENSES ARE A BIT OFF. UM, HOW ABOUT YOU? CAN YOU SMELL SOMETHING...?
IT'S NOT SOMETHING YOU SMELL, MASTER...
IT'S...
...SOMETHING FAR BEYOND NORMAL PERCEPTION.
I COUNT 12...14, 15... NO, EVEN MORE OF THEM NEARBY...

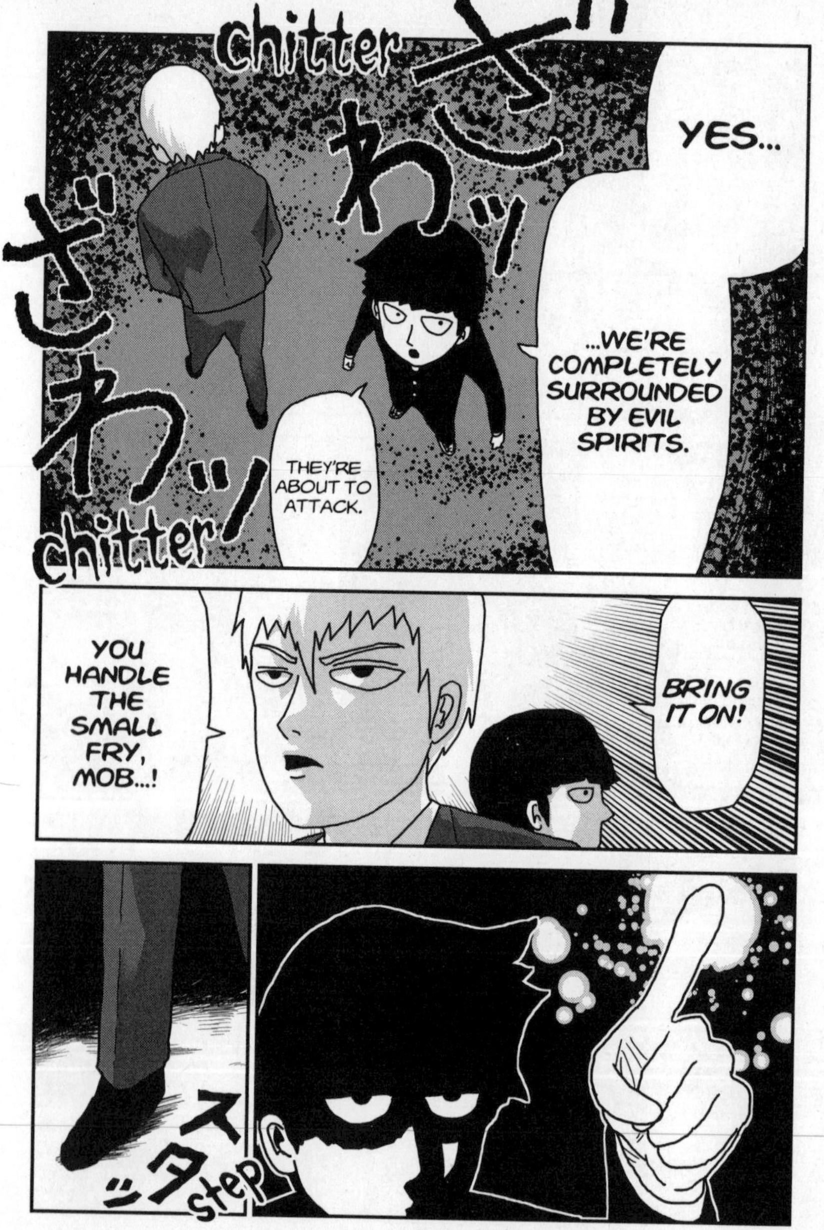
ざわ゛ッ
chitter
YES... ...WE'RE COMPLETELY SURROUNDED BY EVIL SPIRITS.
THEY'RE ABOUT TO ATTACK.
ざわ゛ッ
chitter
BRING IT ON!
YOU HANDLE THE SMALL FRY, MOB...!
スタッ
step

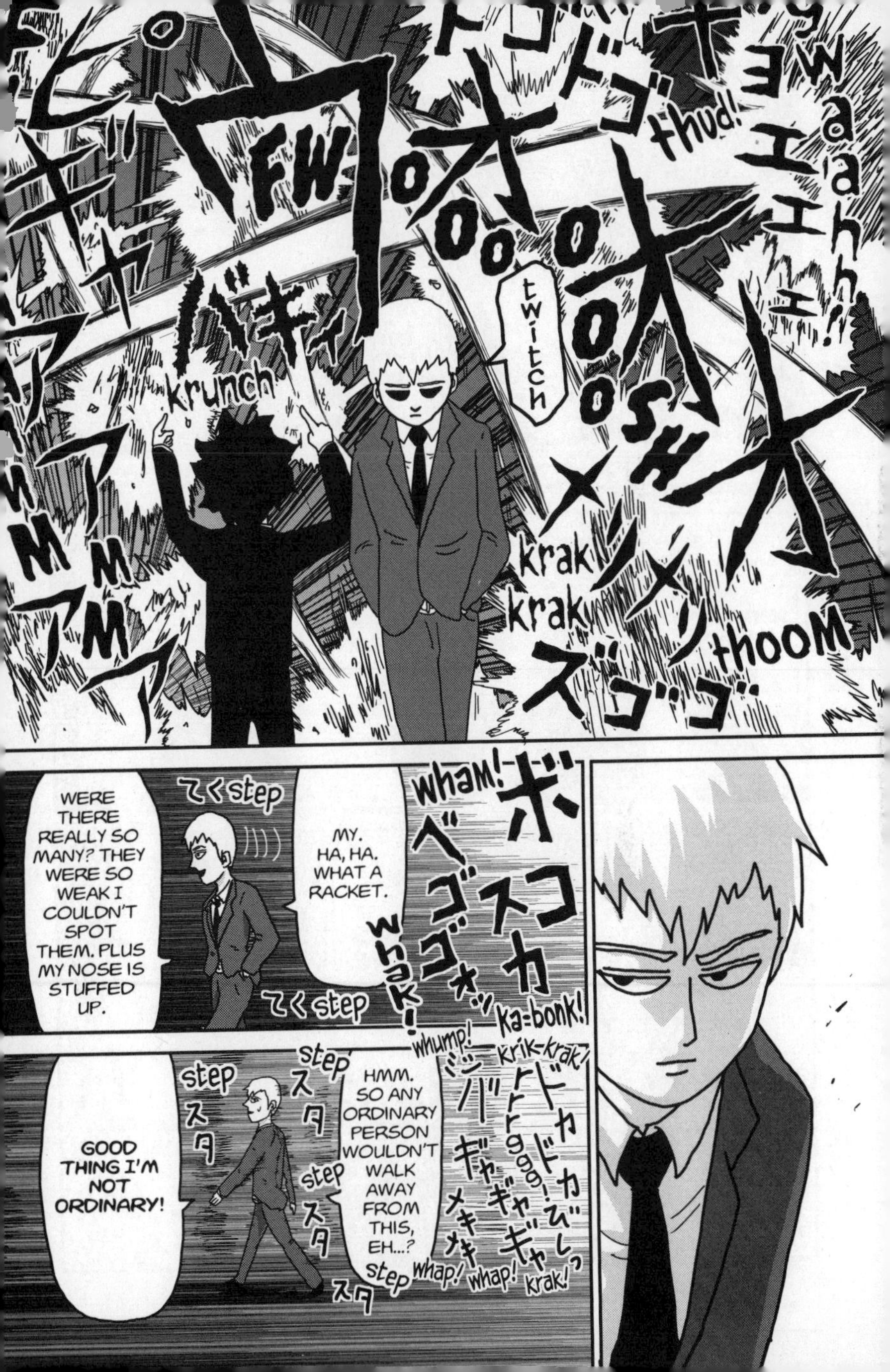
waahh!!
thud!
FWOOOOOOSH
twitch
バギィ
krunch
MMMM
krak krak
thoom
ズゴゴ
wham!
ボコスカ
whak!
ka-bonk!
krik-krak!
whump!
whap!
whap!
krak!
MY. HA, HA. WHAT A RACKET.
てく step
WERE THERE REALLY SO MANY? THEY WERE SO WEAK I COULDN'T SPOT THEM. PLUS MY NOSE IS STUFFED UP.
てく step
HMM. SO ANY ORDINARY PERSON WOULDN'T WALK AWAY FROM THIS, EH...?
step スタ
step スタ
step スタ
step スタ
GOOD THING I'M NOT ORDINARY!

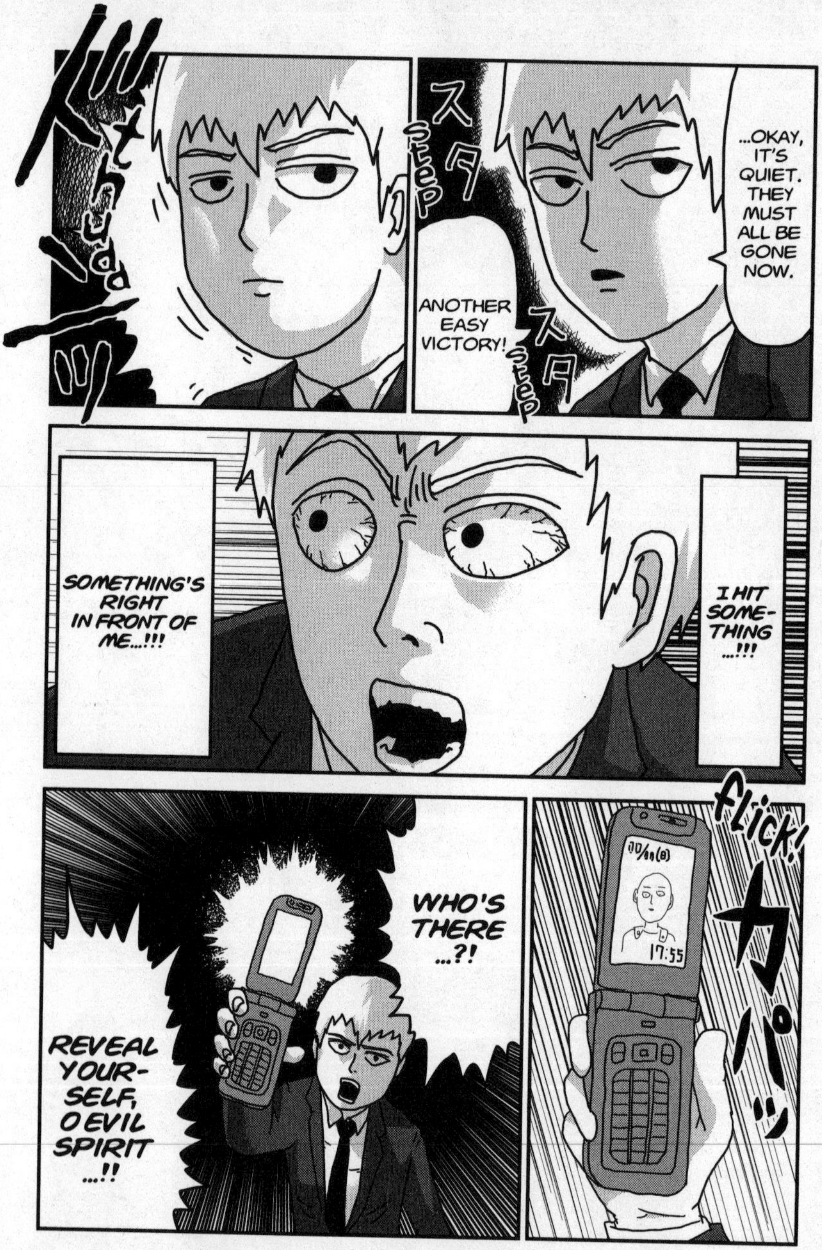
...OKAY, IT'S QUIET. THEY MUST ALL BE GONE NOW.
スタ step
スタ step
ANOTHER EASY VICTORY!
thump!
I HIT SOMETHING...!!!
SOMETHING'S RIGHT IN FRONT OF ME...!!!
flick!
カパッ
17:55
WHO'S THERE...?!
REVEAL YOURSELF, O EVIL SPIRIT...!!

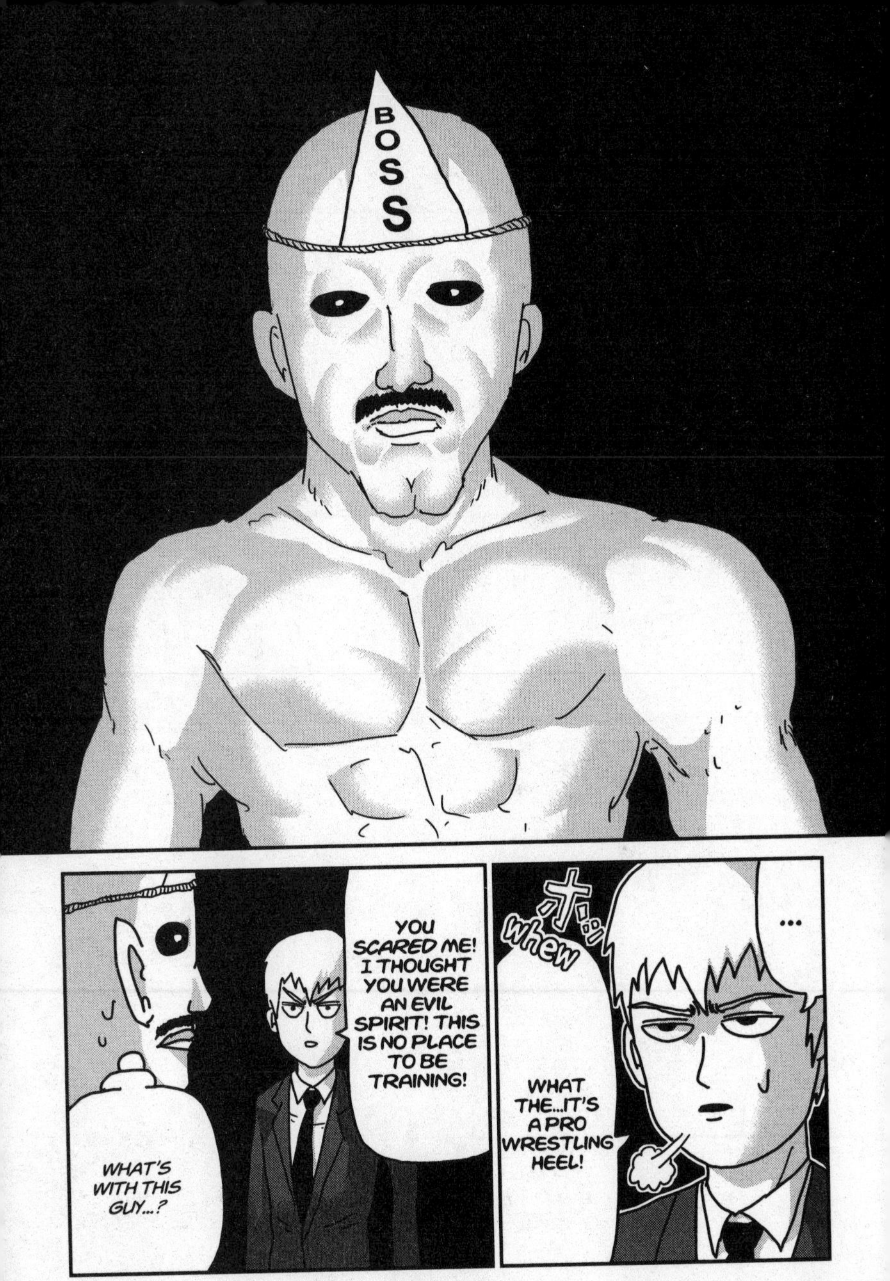
BOSS
...
whew
WHAT THE...IT'S A PRO WRESTLING HEEL!
YOU SCARED ME! I THOUGHT YOU WERE AN EVIL SPIRIT! THIS IS NO PLACE TO BE TRAINING!
WHAT'S WITH THIS GUY...?

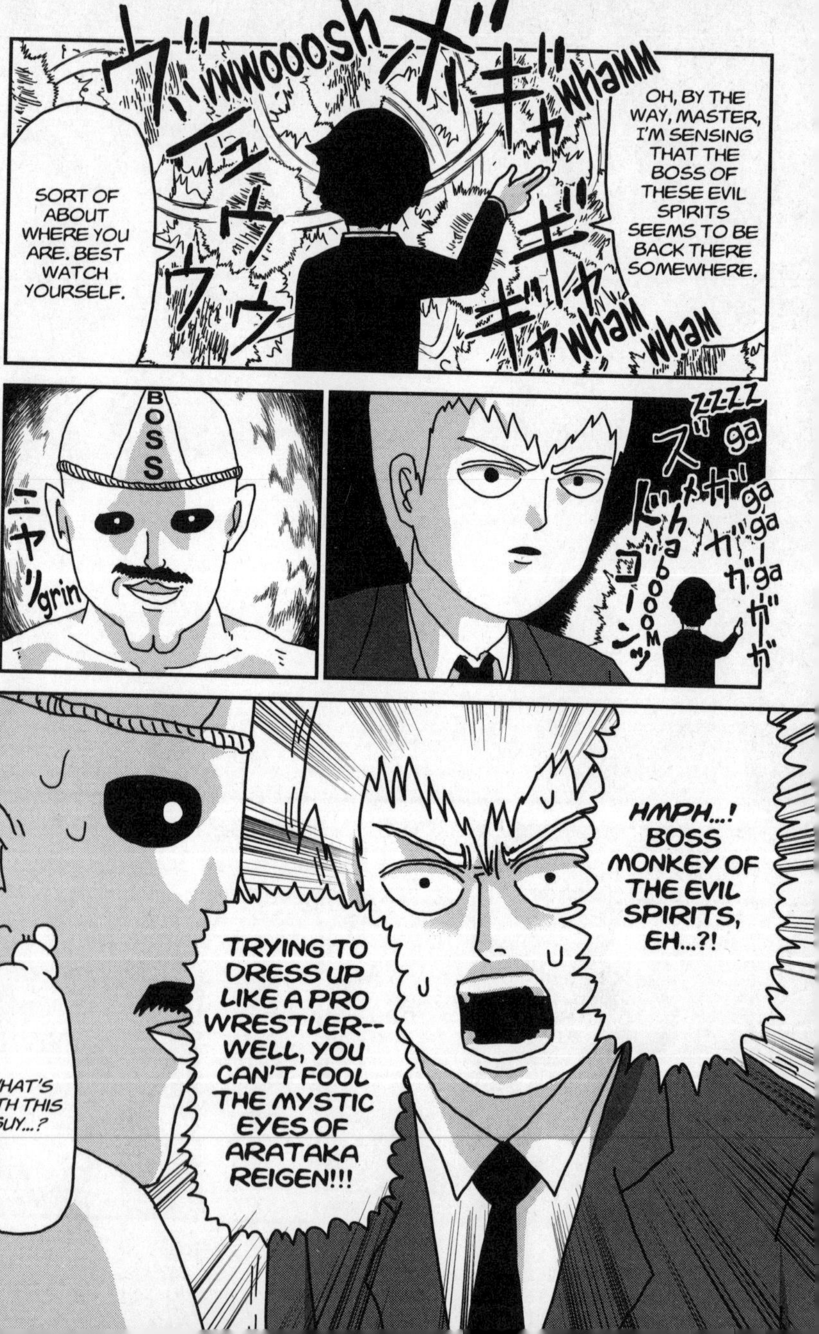
wwooosh
whamm
OH, BY THE WAY, MASTER, I'M SENSING THAT THE BOSS OF THESE EVIL SPIRITS SEEMS TO BE BACK THERE SOMEWHERE.
SORT OF ABOUT WHERE YOU ARE. BEST WATCH YOURSELF.
wham
wham
zzzzz
ga ga ga ga
kaboooom
BOSS
grin
HMPH...! BOSS MONKEY OF THE EVIL SPIRITS, EH...?!
TRYING TO DRESS UP LIKE A PRO WRESTLER--WELL, YOU CAN'T FOOL THE MYSTIC EYES OF ARATAKA REIGEN!!!
WHAT'S WITH THIS GUY...?

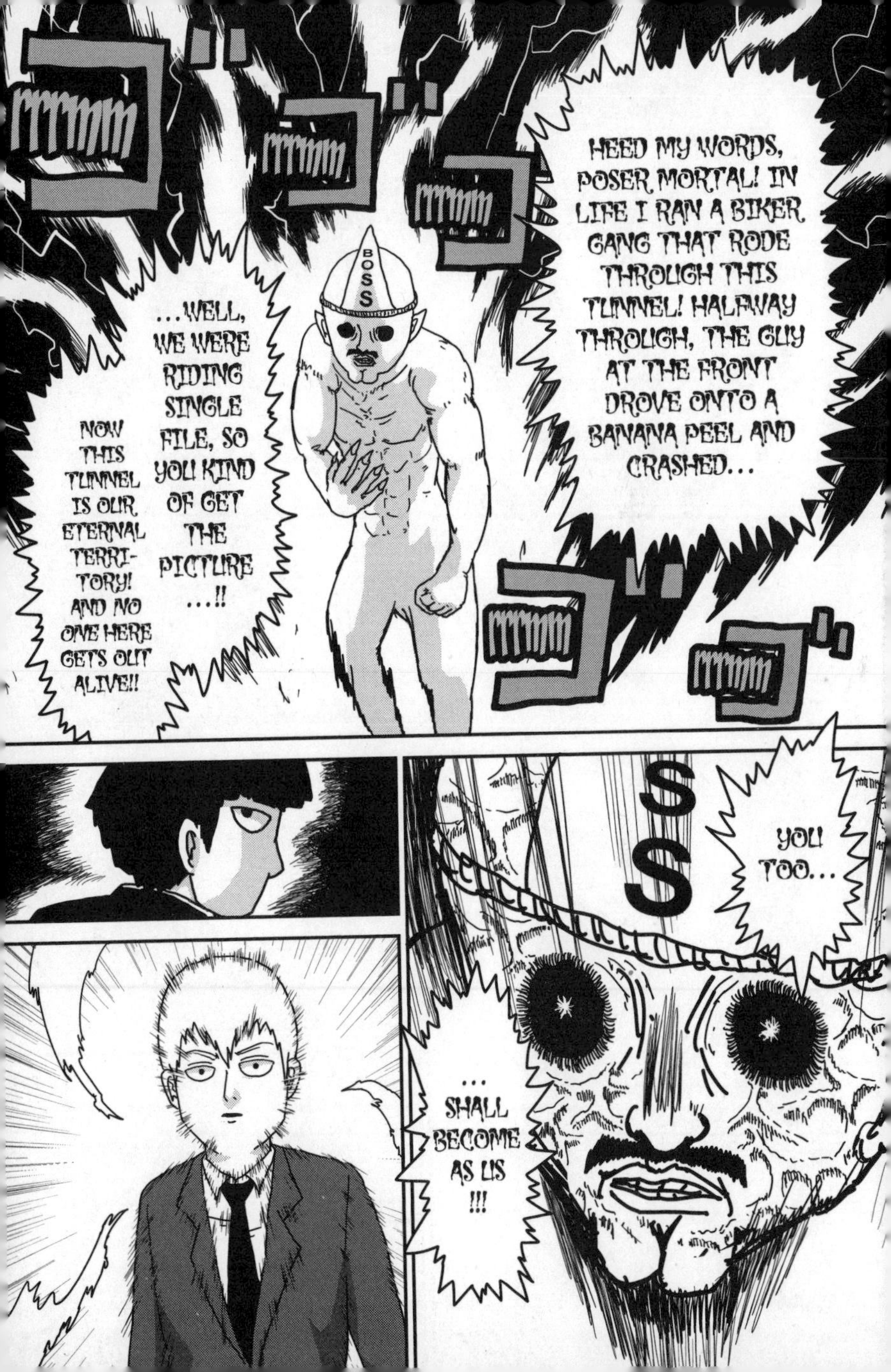
rrrmmm
rrrmmm
rrrmmm
HEED MY WORDS, POSER MORTAL! IN LIFE I RAN A BIKER GANG THAT RODE THROUGH THIS TUNNEL! HALFWAY THROUGH, THE GUY AT THE FRONT DROVE ONTO A BANANA PEEL AND CRASHED...
BOSS
...WELL, WE WERE RIDING SINGLE FILE, SO YOU KIND OF GET THE PICTURE ...!!
NOW THIS TUNNEL IS OUR ETERNAL TERRI-TORY! AND NO ONE HERE GETS OUT ALIVE!!
rrrmmm
rrrmmm
SS
YOU TOO...
...SHALL BECOME AS US !!!

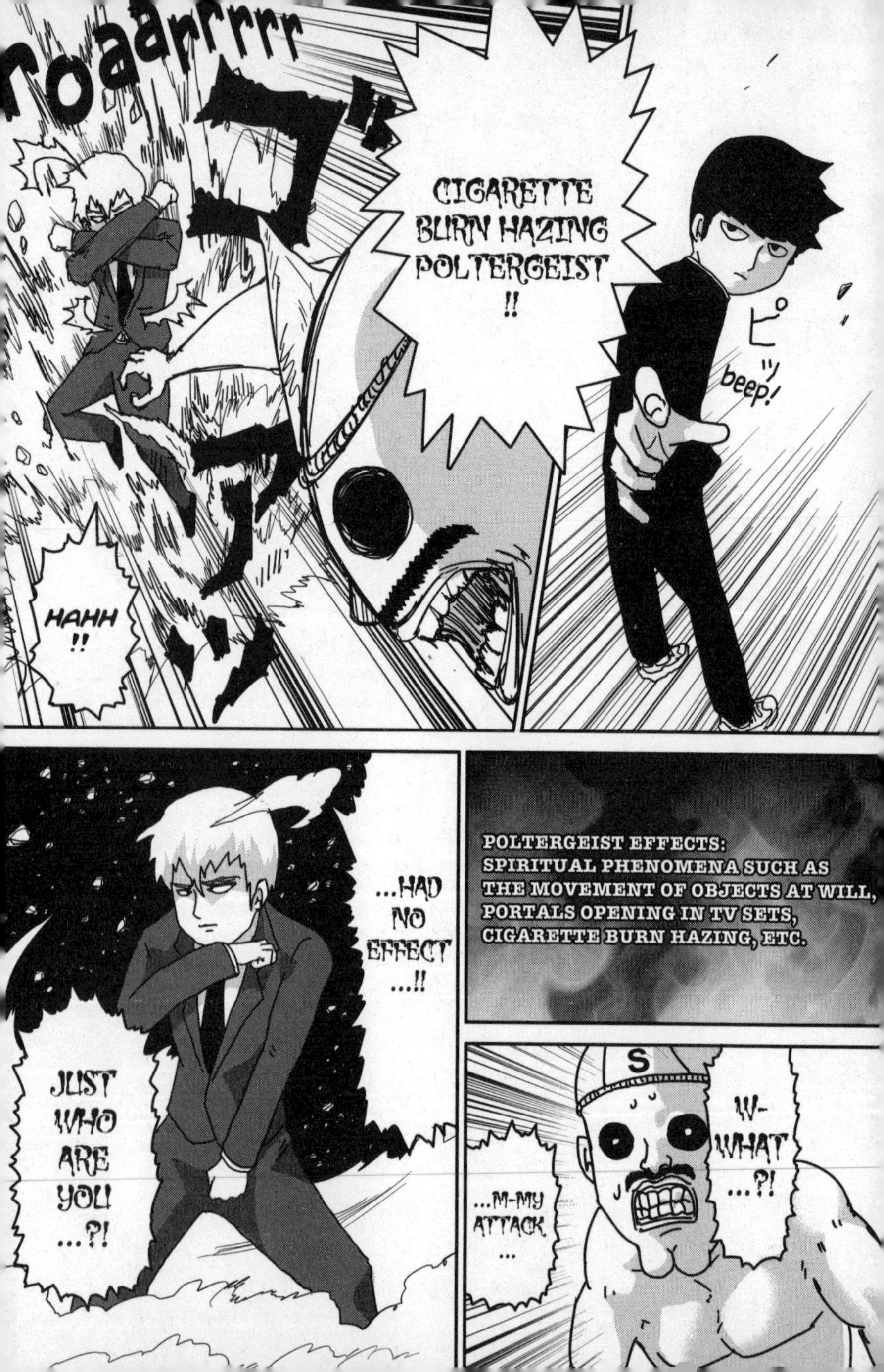
CIGARETTE BURN HAZING POLTERGEIST !!
ピッ
beep!
roaarrrr
ゴッ
HAHH !!
POLTERGEIST EFFECTS: SPIRITUAL PHENOMENA SUCH AS THE MOVEMENT OF OBJECTS AT WILL, PORTALS OPENING IN TV SETS, CIGARETTE BURN HAZING, ETC.
W-WHAT ...?!
...M-MY ATTACK ...
...HAD NO EFFECT ...!!
JUST WHO ARE YOU ...?!

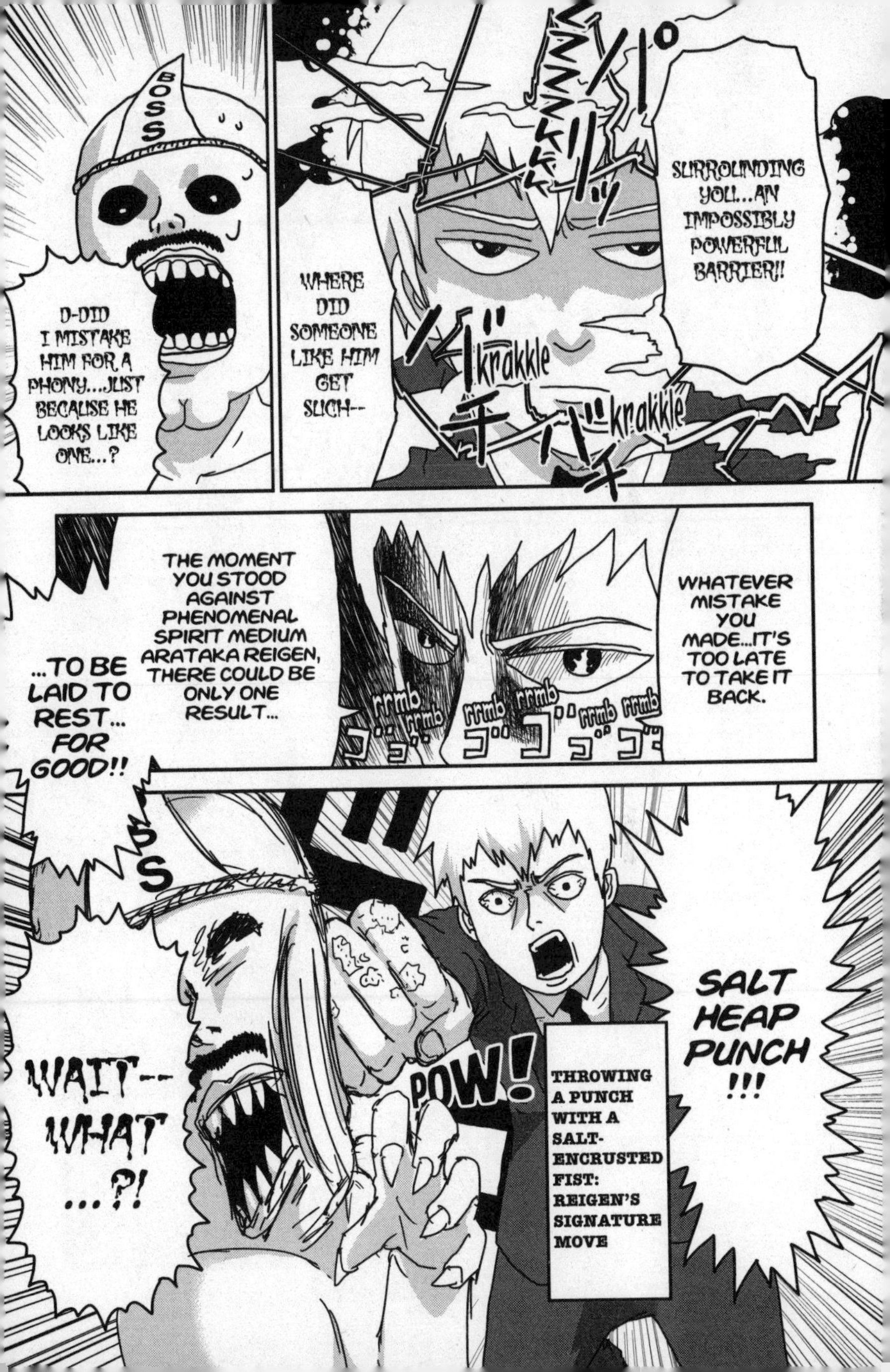
SURROUNDING YOU...AN IMPOSSIBLY POWERFUL BARRIER!!
WHERE DID SOMEONE LIKE HIM GET SUCH--
krakkle
krakkle
BOSS
D-DID I MISTAKE HIM FOR A PHONY...JUST BECAUSE HE LOOKS LIKE ONE...?
WHATEVER MISTAKE YOU MADE...IT'S TOO LATE TO TAKE IT BACK.
rrmb rrmb rrmb rrmb rrmb rrmb
THE MOMENT YOU STOOD AGAINST PHENOMENAL SPIRIT MEDIUM ARATAKA REIGEN, THERE COULD BE ONLY ONE RESULT...
...TO BE LAID TO REST... FOR GOOD!!
SALT HEAP PUNCH!!!
THROWING A PUNCH WITH A SALT-ENCRUSTED FIST: REIGEN'S SIGNATURE MOVE
POW!
WAIT-- WHAT ...?!

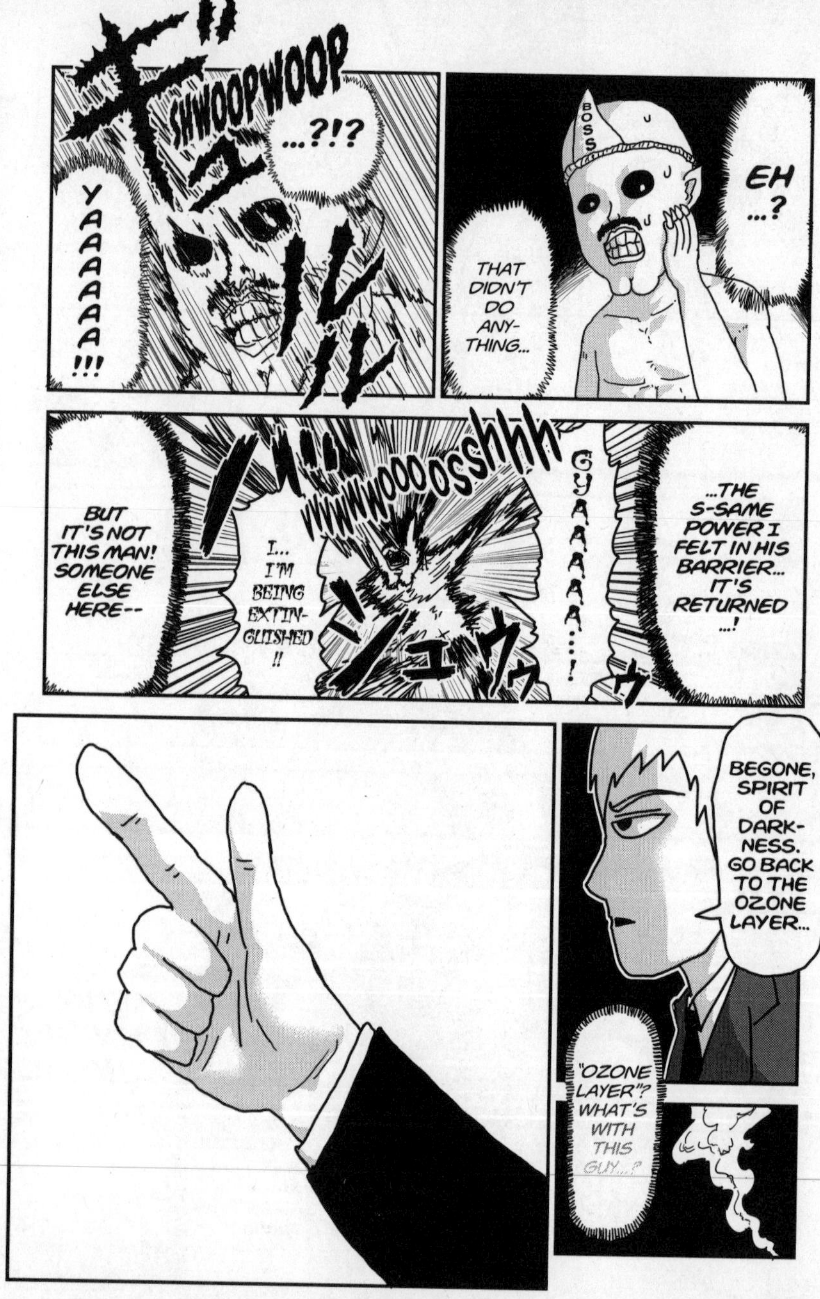
EH ...?
THAT DIDN'T DO ANYTHING...
SHWOOPWOOP
...?!?
YAAAAAAA!!!
...THE S-SAME POWER I FELT IN HIS BARRIER... IT'S RETURNED ...!
GYAAAAAA...!
VVVWWOOOOSSHHH
I... I'M BEING EXTIN-GUISHED !!
BUT IT'S NOT THIS MAN! SOMEONE ELSE HERE--
BEGONE, SPIRIT OF DARK-NESS. GO BACK TO THE OZONE LAYER...
"OZONE LAYER"? WHAT'S WITH THIS GUY...?

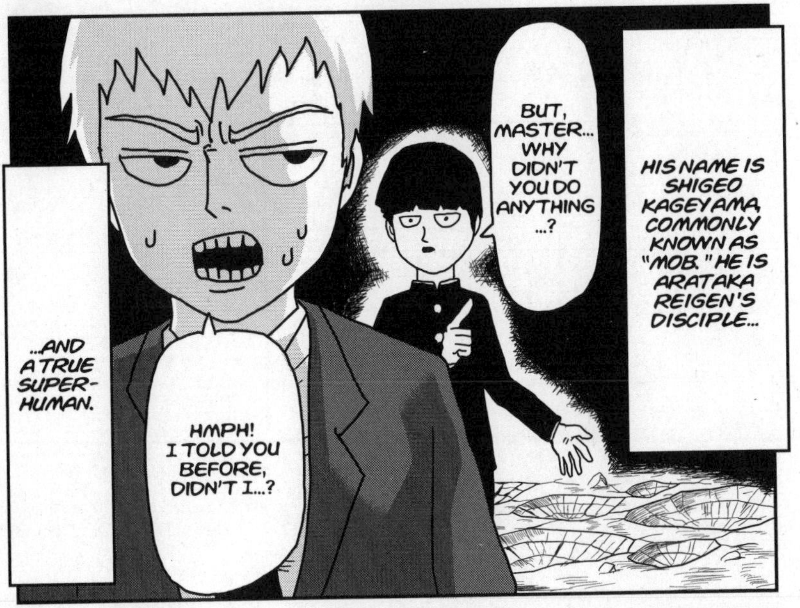
HIS NAME IS SHIGEO KAGEYAMA, COMMONLY KNOWN AS "MOB." HE IS ARATAKA REIGEN'S DISCIPLE...
BUT, MASTER... WHY DIDN'T YOU DO ANYTHING ...?
...AND A TRUE SUPER-HUMAN.
HMPH! I TOLD YOU BEFORE, DIDN'T I...?

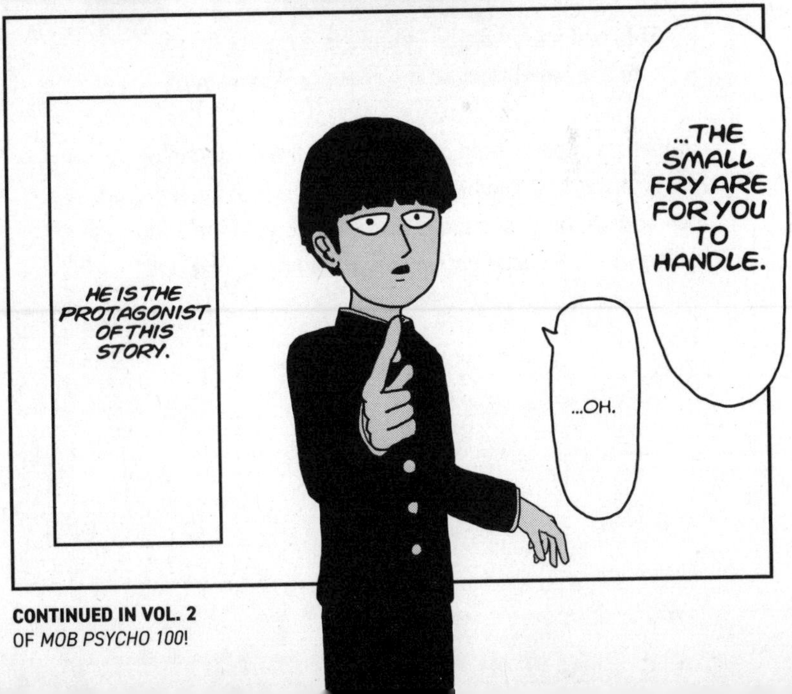
...THE SMALL FRY ARE FOR YOU TO HANDLE.
...OH.
HE IS THE PROTAGONIST OF THIS STORY.

CONTINUED IN VOL. 2
OF *MOB PSYCHO 100*!

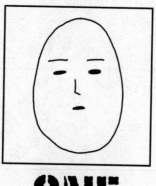

ONE

This collected edition volume is a reality thanks to the support of all my readers. Thank you!

Even a superhuman goes through the anxieties of adolescence, and maybe they deal with stress building up too—and so this manga was born. What will Mob's future bring . . . ? I hope you all keep reading to find out!

president and publisher
MIKE RICHARDSON

editor
CARL GUSTAV HORN

designer
SARAH TERRY

digital art technician
CHRIS HORN

English-language version produced by Dark Horse Comics

MOB PSYCHO 100

Published by Dark Horse Manga
A division of Dark Horse Comics LLC
10956 SE Main Street, Milwaukie, OR 97222

DarkHorse.com

To find a comics shop in your area, visit comicshoplocator.com.

First edition: October 2018 | ISBN 978-1-50670-987-1
Digital ISBN 978-1-50671-147-8

3 5 7 9 10 8 6 4 2

The battle for the Holy Grail begins!

The Fourth Holy Grail War has begun, and seven magi must summon heroes from history to battle to the death. Only one pair can claim the Grail, though—and it will grant them their wishes!

Check out the manga adaptation of Gen Urobuchi and Type-Moon's hit anime and novel series!

VOLUME 1 | 978-1-61655-919-9 | $11.99

VOLUME 2 | 978-1-61655-954-0 | $11.99

VOLUME 3 | 978-1-50670-021-2 | $11.99

VOLUME 4 | 978-1-50670-139-4 | $11.99

VOLUME 5 | 978-1-50670-175-2 | $11.99

VOLUME 6 | 978-1-50670-768-6 | $11.99

VOLUME 7 | 978-1-50670-769-3 | $11.99

REPENT, SINNERS! THEY'RE BACK!

Miss the anime?
Try the *Panty & Stocking with Garterbelt* manga! Nine ALL-NEW stories of your favorite filthy fallen angels, written and drawn by TAGRO, with a special afterword by *Kill La Kill* director Hiroyuki Imaishi!
978-1-61655-735-5 | $9.99

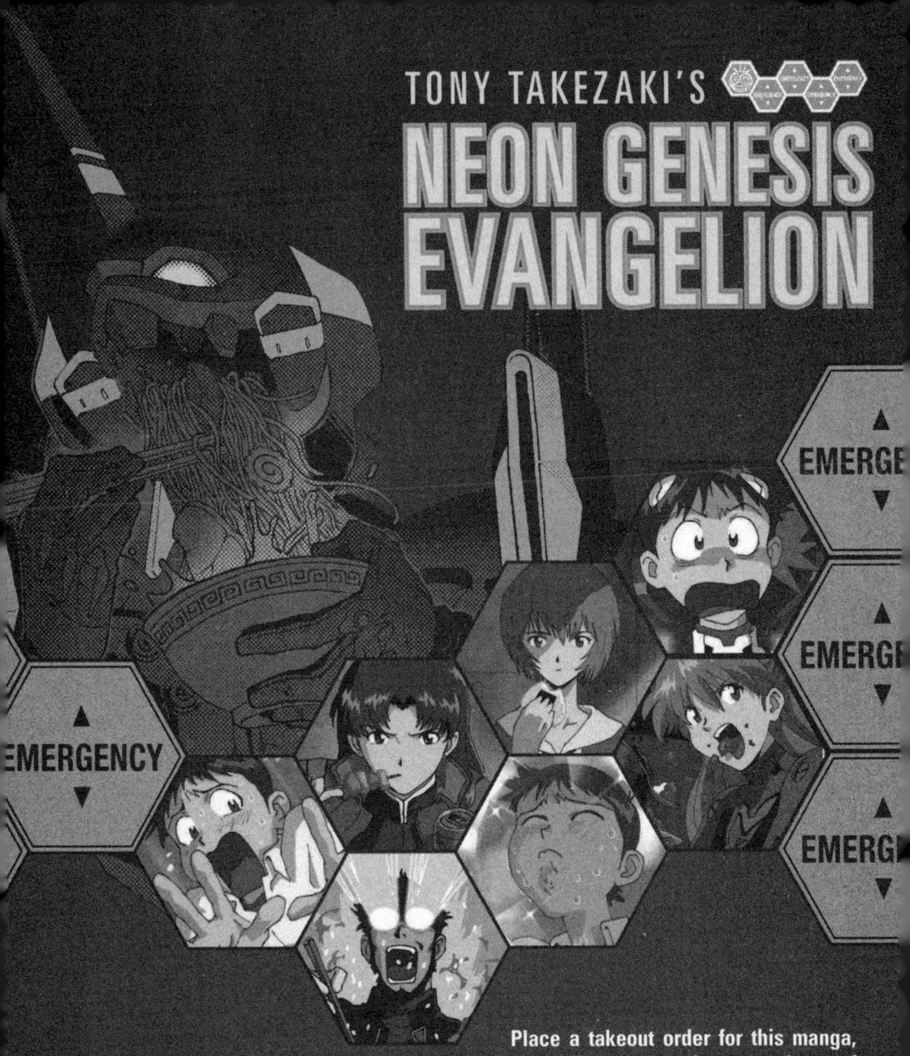
TONY TAKEZAKI'S
NEON GENESIS EVANGELION
EMERGENCY
EMERGE
EMERG
EMERG

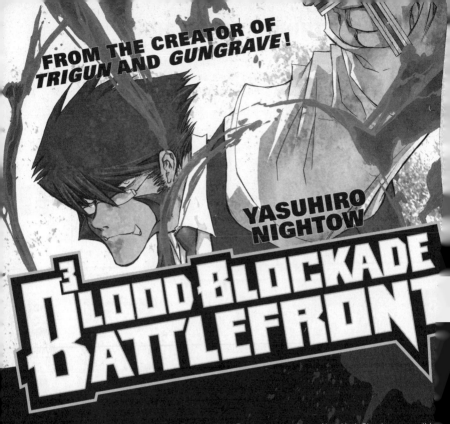

FROM THE CREATOR OF TRIGUN AND GUNGRAVE!

YASUHIRO NIGHTOW

³LOOD BLOCKADE BATTLEFRONT

Three years ago, a gateway between Earth and the Beyond opened over New York City. In one terrible night, New York was destroyed and rebuilt, trapping New Yorkers and extradimensional creatures alike in an impenetrable bubble. New York is now Jerusalem's Lot, a paranormal melting pot where magic and madness dwell alongside the mundane, where human vermin gather to exploit otherworldly assets for earthly profit. Now someone is threatening to breach the bubble and release New Jerusalem's horrors, but the mysterious superagents of Libra fight to prevent the unthinkable.

Trigun creator Yasuhiro Nightow returns with *Blood Blockade Battlefront*, an action-packed supernatural science-fiction steamroller as only Nightow can conjure.

VOLUME ONE
ISBN 978-1-59582-718-0 | $12.99

VOLUME TWO
ISBN 978-1-59582-912-2 | $10.99

VOLUME THREE
ISBN 978-1-59582-913-9 | $10.99

VOLUME FOUR
ISBN 978-1-61655-223-7 | $12.99

VOLUME FIVE
ISBN 978-1-61655-224-4 | $12.99

VOLUME SIX
ISBN 978-1-61655-557-3 | $12.99

VOLUME SEVEN
ISBN 978-1-61655-568-9 | $12.99

VOLUME EIGHT
ISBN 978-1-61655-583-2 | $12.99

VOLUME NINE
ISBN 978-1-50670-705-1 | $12.99

DARK HORSE MANGA

AVAILABLE AT YOUR LOCAL COMICS SHOP OR BOOKSTORE To find a comics shop in your area, visi comicshoplocator.com • For more information or to order direct: • On the web: DarkHorse.com E-mail: mailorder@darkhorse.com • Phone: 1-800-862-0052 Mon.–Fri. 9 AM to 5 PM Pacific Time.

Kekkai Sensen © Yasuhiro Nightow. All rights reserved. Original Japanese edition published by SHUEISHA, Inc. Tokyo. English translation rights in the United States and Canada arranged by SHUEISHA, Inc. /BL709

SOMETHING'S WRONG HERE . . .

You sense it, somehow. You suspect this story doesn't really go the way it should. You're suspicious! But a smooth talker like Reigen would know what to say at this point. *"Just flip the book around and start reading it the other way instead."* Aha! So this was really the last page of the book. You're saved! Thank you, Reigen-sensei! *"Now, about my fee . . . "*

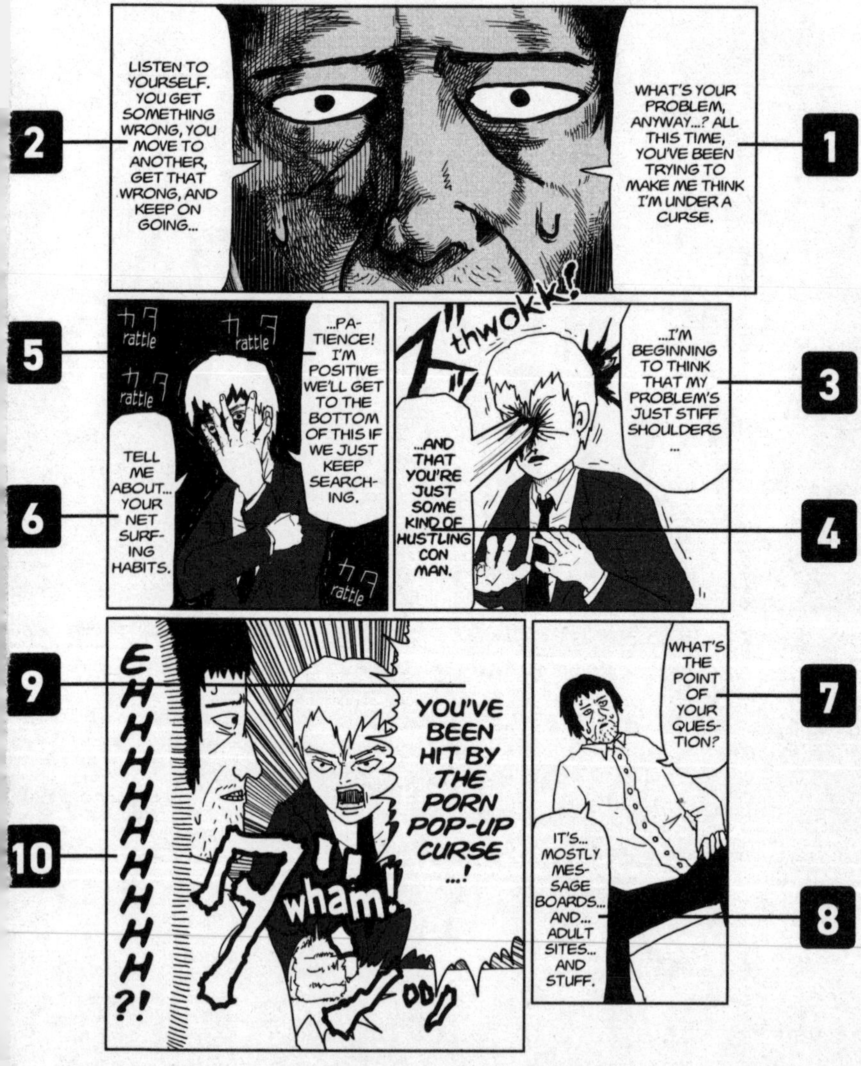
1
WHAT'S YOUR PROBLEM, ANYWAY...? ALL THIS TIME, YOU'VE BEEN TRYING TO MAKE ME THINK I'M UNDER A CURSE.
2
LISTEN TO YOURSELF. YOU GET SOMETHING WRONG, YOU MOVE TO ANOTHER, GET THAT WRONG, AND KEEP ON GOING...
thwokk!
3
...I'M BEGINNING TO THINK THAT MY PROBLEM'S JUST STIFF SHOULDERS...
4
...AND THAT YOU'RE JUST SOME KIND OF HUSTLING CON MAN.
カタ rattle
カタ rattle
カタ rattle
5
...PA-TIENCE! I'M POSITIVE WE'LL GET TO THE BOTTOM OF THIS IF WE JUST KEEP SEARCH-ING.
6
TELL ME ABOUT... YOUR NET SURF-ING HABITS.
カタ rattle
7
WHAT'S THE POINT OF YOUR QUES-TION?
8
IT'S... MOSTLY MES-SAGE BOARDS... AND... ADULT SITES... AND STUFF.
9
YOU'VE BEEN HIT BY THE PORN POP-UP CURSE...!
wham!
10
EHHHHHHHHHHHH?!